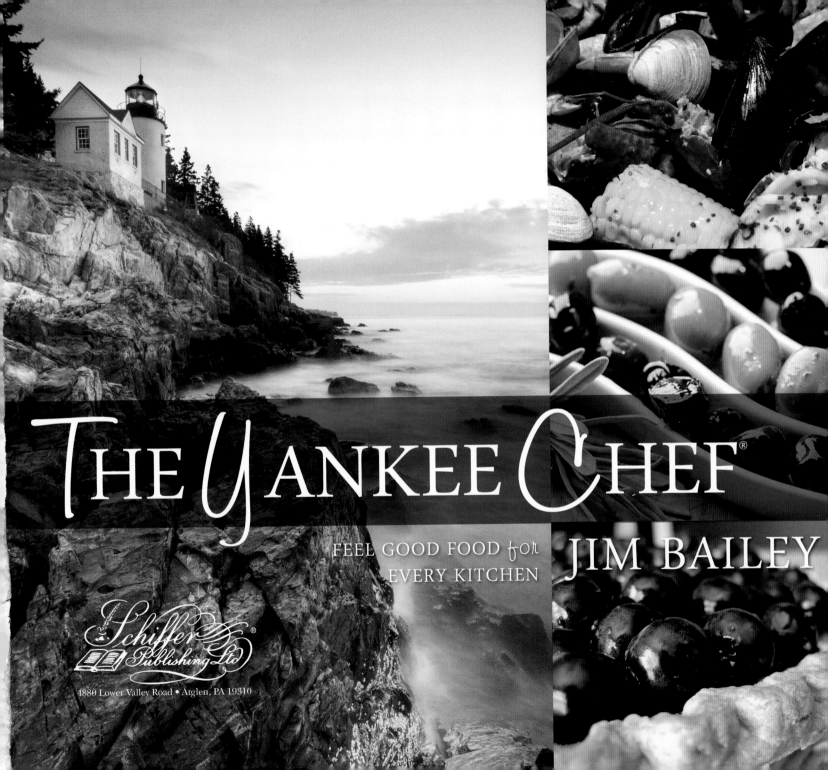

THE YANKEE CHEF®

FEEL GOOD FOOD *for* EVERY KITCHEN

JIM BAILEY

Schiffer ®
Publishing Ltd

4880 Lower Valley Road • Atglen, PA 19310

Other Schiffer Books on Related Subjects:
Cooking in Alaska, the Land of the Midnight Sun, 0-89865-628-1, $14.95
Off the Hook: Rudow's Recipes for Cooking Your Catch, 978-0-87033-574-7, $19.95

Designed by Justin Watkinson Cover by Danielle Farmer
Type set in Arabic Typesetting/Gill Sans Std /Minion Pro/CasablancaAntique

ISBN: 978-0-7643-4191-5
Printed in China

Published by Schiffer Publishing, Ltd.
4880 Lower Valley Road
Atglen, PA 19310
Phone: (610) 593-1777; Fax: (610) 593-2002
E-mail: Info@schifferbooks.com

For the largest selection of fine reference books on this and related subjects,
please visit our website at **www.schifferbooks.com.** You may also write for a free catalog.

This book may be purchased from the publisher.
Please try your bookstore first.

We are always looking for people to write books on new and related subjects.
If you have an idea for a book, please contact us at proposals@schifferbooks.com

Schiffer Books are available at special discounts for bulk purchases for sales promotions or premiums. Special editions, including personalized covers, corporate imprints, and excerpts can be created in large quantities for special needs. For more information contact the publisher.

In Europe, Schiffer books are distributed by
Bushwood Books
6 Marksbury Ave.
Kew Gardens
Surrey TW9 4JF England
Phone: 44 (0) 20 8392 8585; Fax: 44 (0) 20 8392 9876
E-mail: info@bushwoodbooks.co.uk
Website: www.bushwoodbooks.co.uk

To my Dad,
the second Yankee Chef,
and the consummate workaholic
who took more pride in his kitchens
than anyone I ever knew.

CONTENTS

Samuel B. Bailey

W elcome to my first cookbook, and certainly not my last. This cookbook was "written" by my father. Well not literally by him but many of his recipes are contained herein from a lifetime of cooking with, living in, and adoring our New England heritage. It is thrilling for me, my fathers' son, to not only carry on his cooking ability as a profession but to enlighten you on the comfort of New England cooking.

Let me back up a few years to 1902, Topsfield, Maine. Samuel Bailey was born to Frank and Alice Bailey. Frank was a laborer and tinkered with the fiddle and piano from time to time at Bailey Hall and other Grange halls within a few miles of their home in Topsfield, Maine. Grampy Sam learned to play the violin from a very early age and when high school was completed, he swiftly,

and with dignification seldom seen from very humble backgrounds, enrolled in the Boston Conservatory of Music. To help line his pockets with money he needed for the wild Charleston dance-a-thons so frequently held in dance halls of old, he picked up the spatula and entered any kitchen that would hire him. His mind was accustomed to acute details from the plentiful trills and double stopping he practiced as homework for the school. Authenticity was paramount in his music so as to capture the "heart" of a piece. These traits spilled over into everything he did, including cooking. He spent every year from 1920 until his death learning the true art of New England cooking, trying to answer such questions as: "Why do the words 'New England Cooking' bring the picture of warmth, togetherness, and family to your minds eye? Why is this dish so delicious with only three ingredients when the highest paid chefs in the world are spending hours with 20 plus ingredients and the taste is akin to spices, not the true 'heart' of the dish?" His answers, along with a lifetime of knowledge of Yankee cooking, is contained in this cookbook as well.

His son, Jack (my father), was born unto the whirling air of cooking and music. He, too, played the violin at an early age and Dad started his cooking career at the young age of 18, upon entering the United States Navy.

Upon being discharged from the Navy in 1960, he settled down and started his life as a Dad, his career as a chef, and his ambition as a violinist.

Jack D. Bailey

He entered the Bangor Conservatory of Music in 1974 until it closed its doors on all who attended. Dad spent two years there and was within one year of graduating when the diploma slipped from his fingers. He had worked so hard all of his life to replicate the life his father had, and then this! I believe he held that resentment with him the remainder of his life. Dad wanted to be just like his father, everything he did was either to please Grampy Sam or to be just like him.

He used to tell me of the hardships his father and he had growing up. You see, Grampy Sam was a drinker and at times found himself with his only child (Dad) without a bed to sleep or a roof over their head. They slept in the woods in Lincoln, Maine, during a portion of Dad's elementary school years. A tent, whatever game Grampy Sam shot, and the trusted violin were the only assets they declared. Grampy and Dad's mother, Grammy Doris, had separated before Dad was born, so Dad never really did have a mother throughout his life. Finally, my great-grandparents stepped in and offered to take care of "little Jackie." It was in this home that he finally was able to rely on a hot meal and a warm bed to foster not only his physical growth but his spiritual, emotional, and artistic growth, too. As the years went on, and high school was around the corner, Dad went to live with his Aunt Marion and Uncle Woody Bailey in Brewer, Maine.

In a nutshell, Dad entered the Navy in 1956 and returned occasionally on furloughs to visit his father, who by this time had marred his health with alcohol. Although Grampy Sam was imbibing freely, he still excelled musically by not only practicing religiously but by teaching the violin during his sober periods. Because his periods home were a type of celebration for him, Dad would join his father in sharing a bottle or two.

Now don't get me wrong, even though he was beginning to culture what would later become his downfall through drink, Dad was the commensurate pupil of the violin and culinary arts. Many stories abound of his talents in both arenas.

It was now 1967 and a year that secured the future for the entire Bailey family. Dad had been divorced and remarried and his fifth child was born. In August of that year, Grampy Sam quietly succumbed to an illness evolving from his persistent attraction to alcohol. Not being able to cope with his loss, Dad began overindulging; I believe to ease the pain of losing his idol, mentor, and teacher.

It was during this year that Dad gave me my first violin. I still remember how I felt when Dad stood there watching me strum the strings, proud that Dad was approving of me carrying on the musical tradition, in awe that he knew so much about the violin, and elated that I was going to be just like him when I grew up.

Throughout the years of my youth, Dad was very seldom able to pick up a baseball and toss it with my brothers and me. When a child is unable to spend sufficient time with a loved one, they find themselves coming up with all sorts of ideas on how to make the best of their time together. My idea was to excel in the things that made Dad happy, such as asking questions about his work (chef at a local restaurant), constantly practicing the violin, reading dictionaries and encyclopedias. Reading dictionaries and encyclopedias? You bet! Even though Dad was imbibing quite freely, he was always a student of education. Even though he treated everyone equally, Dad thought it was a sign of stupidity if one couldn't spell words correctly, carry on an intelligent conversation, understand their life's vocation from the inside out, or used one's free time idly. The term, "present-day Puritan," in many aspects, could be correctly attributed to him.

In order not to turn this cookbook into a biography, I will need to skip a few years to 1990-ish. It was yet another turning point in Dad's life that hastened his all-too-early departure from our lives.

I was by now drinking to excess. I had taken up the sport of boxing and relinquished it just as quickly, as Dad had done in the Navy. I was also on my way to becoming a chef, not by the quickest means possible, i.e. attending cooking schools, but by starting in the dish room of Dad's first restaurant. I was also a diligent "student of education," reading books on the history of food, New England cookery, our own genealogy, and still keeping up with the violin. A replica of my father, and proud of it!

It was during this time that Dad began having awful problems with his health. His esophagus began bleeding on a weekly basis, which needed to be cauterized just as often, and his liver had just about given out. There were many more complications from his drinking, just too many to list in this short forum. It came to the point of a transplant and an all-too-late reversal of his living habits. Although his body had begun to decline, even with his liver transplant, his wit and intellect were still as intact as ever. He continued strumming on the violin, cooking, and learning as much as he could about New England cookery. I, too, was immersed in the bibliographic world. I started accumulating as many books as I could on everything relating to our great heritage and English and Irish stock. If there were a week that went by without my father and me conversing about these topics in depth, I don't recall!

October 2000 was when he went into a local rehabilitation center for the care that we could not give him on a full-time basis. In a sense, I regret having to leave him there after each visit but I know now that it was the best decision to make without being selfish on my part or my family's part. I would bring my wife and children up to see him at least three times a week, regardless of how busy our lives had become. I knew we had a limited time with him and I wanted my children to know their grandfather as much as possible.

Dad was on a strict diet because of a host of complications. His diet was so limited, but then again, so was his time with us. Against all orders from his physicians and nurses, Dad would have us sneak in his favorite food, sweets and the like. And that is exactly what we did. And to this day, I sure am glad we did. Besides seeing his family, his passion for food and books was insatiable, and I am comforted knowing we made his last days so content and fulfilling.

Dad died on February 13, 2001, at Eastern Maine Medical Center after having been in intensive care for four days. I am also content to say that I spent those same four days in that ICU with him; he was my Dad.

ACKNOWLEDGMENTS

The picture of me, the group picture of my family on the back flap, as well as the landscape pictures in between the chapters were kindly offered to me by Patrick Downey. It is his generosity and expertise that gave this cookbook a colorful and comfortable feel, and for that, I thank him. Patrick Downey is a fine art landscape photographer from Ellsworth, Maine. His primary job as a land surveyor takes him all over the state of Maine and provides him with many photo opportunities of this great state. He has won awards for his landscape photos and has been published in various magazines. His entire collection of photos can be viewed and purchased through facebook.com/patrickdowneyphotography or by contacting him directly at patrickd71@aol.com or 207-460-4441.

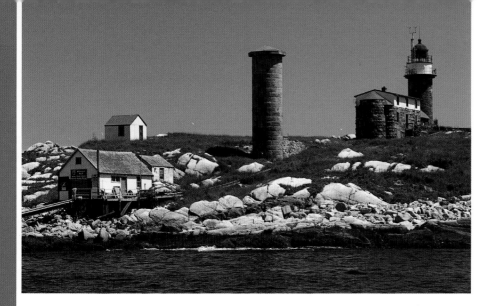

I have introduced you to my dad and now I would like to introduce you to this cookbook. When you sit around the breakfast, lunch, dinner, or supper table, everyone chats about the day's events, stories they may have heard in school, at work, or over the back fence, or maybe everyone's arguing about what's good for you and what's not. Many conversations take place at this laden table. This cookbook isn't just the food you are putting on that table. It is that age-old recipe that you remember as a child, that long forgotten dish that graced your family's table generations ago, and the food that made New England cuisine America's food.

It was not only inspired by my father, but "written" by him as well. Over the years, he wrote down his recipes, New England variations on the theme, and excerpts from the history of such foods as well as the accumulation of stories and history of our heritage. He wrote about the tales of the supernatural and adventures as told to him by his father and what he researched. As much as he tried to be non-romantic and a "man's man," he conveyed warmth and kindness in his own way, a way that would not hit you until some time after the fact, when you were alone and thinking about it. He was enamored with the dream of stepping back a century or two and marveling at the hard work our ancestors struggled with in their everyday lives. Yet the picture of comfort and hominess is somehow filtered through their daily, monotonous routines—imagine stepping back in time to catch the wisp of pork simmering in its own broth or to hear the slight cracklin' of a rasher of bacon as it tenders itself on a cast iron skillet. I could go on and on about how I think the past invades my senses but "use your own imagination" as my Dad would say. I won't tell you how to think or perceive the past, but I'll just help you along and pique your senses. I am doing the same with the following pages. As you peruse these recipes, go ahead and try them as they are written if you wish, but I implore you to add your own little touches, they will still be classically New England because of the recipes' roots

Many of the recipes contained herein are Yankee dishes. I have included as many New England favorites, both past and present, that I could think of. Along with our regional cuisine, I have also included many recipes that are indicative of our tastes today, from coast to coast, so that you can prepare meals often shown in the media. You may see a few recipes and ingredients that are foreign in title but that is because

New Englanders are a diverse group. You have the Swedish that settled in New Sweden, Maine; the Germans that settled in parts of Massachusetts; the French that inhabited (and still do) the northern parts of New England as well as myriad cultures that entered our cooking arena via the logging camps. Men from far away came to Maine and the surrounding states in order to better themselves. Not finding work suited for them, or just simply not having an avocation, they sauntered into the woods hoping to be a "cookee" or cook. River drivers, axe-men, and lumberers alike brought their homeland ideas to the cooking stoves of old, along with their ballads, stories, and temperaments.

There is a story of my great, great, great uncle, Gus Bailey, who was a river driver. For one reason or another, the camp cook had disappeared, most likely running to another camp for better wages. The cookee ("gopher" to be more accurate) was quite under-qualified to take over the stove for that evening's meal, so Uncle Gus took the position. He began with mixing a big batch of bread from the starter dough on the table next to the stove, no problem. Next came the baking of the beans in the ground, still no problem considering anyone could whip up this pure New England dish. Next came the frying of the pork, again pretty mundane in his eyes. Now for the dessert, the hard working woodsman would rattle his bones if there was not some type of sweet to top off their greasy, gassy meal. So Uncle Gus decided on lemon meringue pie. Not many woodsmen would attempt such a delicate pie but Uncle Gus saw a barrel full of what looked like prepared lemon filling stored up on a crate to keep the mice out of it. He rolled out a biscuit dough (he couldn't remember a pie dough recipe) just as thin as possible and lined a couple of large square pans and commenced to brown the crust. Having heaped each pan with the filling, he placed it outside in the cool September air to chill and hopefully thicken a mite. After dinner had been consumed, he proudly began cutting into his creation, of course without the meringue, for eggs were seldom if at all kept at lumber camps.

As soon as the first batch of teamsters sat down to enjoy this treat, that same group of men began spitting, coughing and swearing up a storm. "What to hell's wrong with you fellars?" Uncle shouted. "You gave us grease, you damned fool!" retorted one particularly large fellow woodsman. He went to check on what was left in the barrel and indeed he had used lard, thinking it to be pie filling. Well, needless to say, the crew ridiculed him the remainder of the fall and winter and he stuck to river driving as his forté.

There is hardly more of a legacy that is handed down than the preparation of food. Sure there were herbal remedies for a variety of illnesses, family lore, and land titles, but the one true legacy was the way one's grandparents created dishes from their childhood. I can still remember my grandmother's blueberry cake coming from the oven when I was a child. Having the blueberry field next to her house afforded us many different blueberry treats as well as the beginning of tasting the difference between store-bought pies compared to what could be grown and baked at home. Boy, Grammy Esther Clark is still fondly remembered not only for her charm, kindness, and warmth, but for those fresh pies she would cook every time we ate at her country home.

This book deals primarily with authentic New England recipes that were handed down to me and my father, as well as dishes that reflect general traditions of New England families—from the popular clam chowder to the traditional baked beans. From the comparatively "new" fried clams to the archaically brewed Sack-Posset, my father enlisted every reference book available to him in order to acclimate himself with the joy of cooking that initiates a feeling of home. As hard work is synonymous with New England culture, so is comfort food so closely associated with Yankee cookery. From Finnan Haddie, macaroni and cheese, and freshly baked breads to apple pies, Boston Cream Pie, and old fashioned gingerbread, the recipes included in this cookbook will fill the air with comforting, wafting aromas. I have added modern day touches to some basic recipes, that I believe truly show the fact that we are not stubborn Yankees as most think. We do add a little, take away a little, and tweak on a custom from time to time.

And finally, throughout this book if the recipes don't transport you back in time, I hope the New England trivia, little known facts, and very old recipes (such as Pigeon Pie and Cape Cod

Turkey) will get you thinking about your ancestors and their lives.

Brillat-Savarin, the famous chef and the Einstein of the kitchen, lived during the eighteenth century and once journeyed to Massachusetts for a hunting trip. After having a successful hunt and an even more successful banquet following, he proclaimed, "Tell me what you eat and I will tell you what you are." What a fitting and associative summary of our New England ancestors.

I designed this book to correspond with the New England weather in mind. Dishes that can be baked in the winter and food that can be made in the summer are included here. You will also find recipes that will help you take care of the leftovers that we, as Yankees, are so adept at anyway. I truly hope that you prepare some of these dishes for your family and loved ones. Not only will everyone delight in the presentation and tastes of these dishes, but many memories are sure to come to the forefront, thusly forcing you to remember those members of your family that used to make these old dishes. Just imagine your mother or father, or even grandparents, sitting down and enjoying a piece of Baptist cake and exclaiming, "I haven't had this since I was a child!" That remembrance alone is cause enough to enjoy the times, the life, and the heritage of your family.

So, as you sit over the meal that was prepared with love, gaze at an empty spot, if there is one at the table, peer into the living room across the way, and listen intently at the fleeting stillness that may pop up. You can see and hear those loved ones that were once here, smiling at the love that is shared and laughing with you all during the glee that is celebrated. They truly are the inspiration behind this cookbook and my endeavor to become The Yankee Chef.

CHAPTER 1

Gone are the mornings of yesteryear, when the beef nestled with the vegetables, the biscuits "sided" up next to a pitcher of molasses, and the pie cuddled with the flapjacks. That's right, all this for breakfast and, in many instances, much more. Although New Englanders ate heartily wherever you went, they did not eat the same fare. Along the coast you can bet that the large Yankee families ate well of fresh or salted fish, while in the hinterland, game was the centerpiece.

Henry David Thoreau, while in Cape Cod, woke up to fried eels, buttermilk cake, bread, green beans, doughnuts and applesauce, all cooked before an open fireplace. I remember my father

telling me of his father's breakfast even up until the early 1920s, which consisted of eggs, fried pork, steaks, pie, tea, rolls, cake, and so on. During the early colonization of America to about the mid-1800s, alcoholic cider was shared by the tankard between adults and children alike, before and during breakfast.

S.S. Pierce and Company of Boston, Massachusetts, published a book called *The Epicure* in the mid-1800s. This "receipt" book called for stewed pigeons with mushrooms, deviled gizzards, liver pudding, hashed poultry, pork cheese, game birds, venison pasty, minced veal, hash balls, fish cakes, sausages, rice cakes, and broiled tomatoes to adorn the Yankee breakfast table during the fall and winter months.

Codfish cakes were a staple of New England weekend breakfasts for many generations. Even until the mid-1900s, near Jonesport, Maine, I have spoken to many natives who have related to me that lobster stew, oatmeal, and custard pie were the norm for their first meal of the day.

While we probably shouldn't eat the way our ancestors did, you will find many tempting and filling ideas ahead to start your day off right. Find time every so often to surprise family and friends with a hearty breakfast. Not only will you find enjoyable aromas filling the air as a worthy remembrance of your ancestors, but a pleased palate will follow you throughout the day.

As you may notice in the following recipes, I could very well give you a universal muffin recipe, whereas you would simply add the assortment of fruits and nuts and seasonings that you desire. I have not done this. The reason? Some fruited muffins require more, or less, liquid while others require more, or less, seasonings. I find that more nutmeg is needed for peach muffins than strawberry muffins, whereas apple muffins require more cinnamon than other fruited muffins. Each muffin should be distinct in its flavor as well as characteristics.

Crunchy Corn Muffins

Talk about naturally sweet, crispy topped muffins, these gems are great for grilling with a slather of butter.

 1 c. yellow coarse ground
    corn meal (polenta)
 1 c. flour
 4 T. sugar
 2 t. baking powder
 1/2 t. baking soda
 Pinch salt
 1 c. buttermilk
 1/4 c. margarine, melted
 1 egg
 Extra 1/4 c. polenta mixed
    with 1 T. sugar

Preheat oven to 350°F. Grease a 12-cup muffin tin. Combine all dry ingredients (except 1/4 c. polenta) in large mixing bowl. Add buttermilk, margarine, and egg and stir until just combined. Spoon batter into muffin tins until level with top and sprinkle extra polenta/sugar mixture over tops of each muffin. Bake for 20 to 25 minutes or until toothpick inserted into middle comes out clean.

Although the word polenta may be southern, corn meal was as essential to our New England forebears as the clothes on their backs. Corn was utilized in any imaginable fashion, from food for human and fowl to padding their beds with the silk.

Good Ol' Bran Muffins

Normally, bran muffins are quite flavorless, but these have all the taste you desire while still being good for you. As an alternative technique, try soaking 1 1/2 c. of an all-bran cereal in 1 c. milk. Add it to the following recipe while deleting the cereal listed and use 1/2 c. less milk than this recipe calls for.

 1 1/2 c. bran cereal
 1/2 c. brown sugar
 2 t. baking powder
 1/2 t. baking soda
 1 1/2 c. flour
 1 c. milk
 1 egg
 1/4 c. vegetable oil

Preheat oven to 350°F. Grease a 12-cup muffin tin. Combine all dry ingredients in large mixing bowl. Add remaining wet ingredients and stir just until combined; it's fine if it's still lumpy. Scoop muffin batter into cups until almost level with top and bake for 20 to 25 minutes or until either a toothpick inserted into middle comes out clean or the muffin springs back when pressing the top it.

Strawberry Muffins

Ahhh, to have strawberries for breakfast! In any form, strawberries have always been a perennial favorite for centuries. But something about the smell, texture, and taste of strawberries in any form has a distinct, welcome setting on the breakfast table.

2 c. flour
1 c. sugar
1 1/2 t. baking powder
1/2 t. baking soda
1/4 t. nutmeg
Pinch salt
1 c. milk
2 eggs
3 T. margarine, melted
2 c. chopped strawberries

Preheat oven to 350°F. Grease a 12-cup muffin tin. Combine all dry ingredients well in large mixing bowl. Add all wet ingredients, except strawberries, and combine well. Fold in chopped strawberries and evenly distribute. Scoop into muffin tin and bake for 20 to 25 minutes or until pick inserted in center comes out clean.

Apple Cider Muffins

Sure you can buy apple muffins anywhere, but by using apple cider, you can taste autumn in New England in every bite.

1 1/4 c. whole wheat flour
3/4 c. all-purpose flour
1/2 c. brown sugar
1/2 t. baking soda
1 1/2 t. baking powder
Pinch salt
1/2 t. cinnamon
1 c. apple cider
1 egg
1/4 c. vegetable oil

Preheat oven to 350°F. Follow muffin tin preparations for strawberry muffins. In large bowl combine whole wheat flour, all-purpose flour, brown sugar, baking soda, baking powder, and salt until well combined. Add remaining ingredients until batter is still lumpy. Bake 20 to 25 minutes or until a toothpick inserted in the middle comes out clean.

Apple Streusel Muffin

There's just something about having streusel crumbs falling after every bite that makes you eat more. These muffins have fresh apple in the topping for that extra apple flavor.

One recipe for Apple Cider Muffins
1 c. chopped apples

Streusel Topping
1 c. flour
4 t. cinnamon
1/2 c. brown sugar
1/2 c. minced apple
1/2 c. margarine, melted

Add chopped apples to "Apple Cider Muffins" mix. In separate bowl combine all streusel ingredients and sprinkle on top of muffins. Bake 20 to 25 minutes or until toothpick inserted in the middle comes out clean.

According to Robert A. Ronzio, PhD., C.N.S., in his *Encyclopedia of Nutrition and Good Health*, the pectin found in apples, berries, vegetables, and beans lowers blood pressure and cholesterol, helps maintain blood sugar, and helps reduce the risk of colon cancer.

For many generations, muffins were known as "gems." Shortly after the introduction of baking powder, gem pans, connected metal custard cups, gained popularity because of their design. Even today in certain parts of the country, muffins are still referred to as gems.

Maple Streusel Muffins

The combination of streusel topping and maple syrup is, I believe, the perfect marriage. This muffin is the superb accompaniment to a cup of coffee or a glass of juice. Either way, taste the gift of nature in these gems.

2 c. flour
6 T. sugar
3 t. baking powder
Pinch salt
1/2 c. milk
1 egg
1/2 c. maple syrup
Streusel topping from "Apple
    Streusel Muffin" recipe

Preheat oven to 350°F. Oil a 12-cup muffin tin. In large mixing bowl, combine all dry ingredients. Add wet ingredients and combine until still a little lumpy. Scoop into muffin cups and top with streusel topping. Bake for 20 to 25 minutes or until a toothpick inserted into middle comes out clean.

Orange Graham Muffins

"Sunshine in your hand!" That's what my daughter said the first time she tried these, and I must admit, she's not too far off.

1 c. flour
1 1/2 c. crushed graham crackers
1/4 c. sugar
1 1/2 t. baking powder
1/2 t. baking soda
Pinch salt
1/2 c. orange juice
1/2 c. milk
1 egg
1/4 c. vegetable oil
1 T. orange zest

Preheat oven to 350°F. Grease a 12-cup muffin tin. In large mixing bowl, combine all dry ingredients well. Add all wet ingredients, except orange zest, and combine well. Add orange zest and fold in until evenly distributed. Scoop evenly into muffin cups and bake for 20 to 25 minutes or until toothpick inserted into center comes out clean.

Cinnamon Peach Muffins

This recipe comes from a lady who addressed herself as "Mrs. Jane Ellsmore...Lafayette National Park, Maine." Well, who among you readers knows where Lafayette National Park is (or was)? A hint...the recipe was dated 1919. Still nothing? Well, no wonder, it was only incorporated for about 10 years until the State of Maine renamed it Acadia National Park. Gotcha!

2 c. flour
1/4 c. brown sugar
1/4 c. granular sugar
3 t. baking powder
1/2 t. salt
1 1/2 t. cinnamon
1 c. milk
1 egg
1/4 c. margarine, melted
1 t. almond extract
1 c. chopped, fresh peaches

Preheat oven to 350°F. Grease a 12-cup muffin tin. In large bowl, combine all dry ingredients. Add all wet ingredients, except peaches. After incorporating wet and dry, add peaches and scoop until almost level with tops. Bake for 20 to 25 minutes or until toothpick inserted in center comes out clean.

Cranberry Orange Muffins

When you taste tang with sweet, a single syllable word utters past your lips, "Mmmmm!"

2 c. flour
1/2 c. sugar
1 1/2 t. baking powder
1/4 t. baking soda
Pinch salt
3/4 c. orange juice
1 egg
3 T. margarine, melted
1 T. grated orange zest
1 c. cooked cranberries, drained

Preheat oven to 350°F and prepare muffin tin as directed in previous muffin recipes. Combine all dry ingredients in medium-sized bowl and mix well. Add remaining dry ingredients, with the exception of the cranberries; combine well but leave batter lumpy. Add cranberries and gently fold in until they are even throughout the batter. Scoop into muffin cups, filling 3/4 of the way full, and bake 20 to 25 minutes or until done.

Blueberry Muffins

Follow exactly the recipe for "Strawberry Muffins" but substitute 2 c. fresh blueberries for the strawberries.

Banana Muffins

I know many of you don't want to bother with browned, soft bananas, but the flavor is doubled when you use those bananas you forgot about on your sideboard, behind that loaf of bread, remember? You know, it's where all the fruit flies are gathering right about now.

2 c. flour
1/3 c. sugar
2 t. baking powder
1 1/2 t. cinnamon
1/2 t. salt
1 c. milk
1 c. mashed, ripe bananas
1 egg
1/4 c. margarine, melted
1/2 c. chopped walnuts

Preheat oven to 350°F. In a bowl, combine all dry ingredients until well blended. Add remaining ingredients and stir until just incorporated but still lumpy. Prepare muffin tins as directed in Strawberry Muffin recipe and fill 3/4 full of batter. Bake 30 to 35 minutes or until toothpick inserted in middle comes out clean.

Cheddar Cheese Muffins

The aroma, color, and taste of these muffins pair especially well with a hearty New England breakfast such as flapjacks and sausage or bacon and eggs. And people, don't forget to slice them right down the middle, add a little butter, and take to the grill.

2 eggs
1/4 c. vegetable oil
1 c. milk
1 t. celery salt
1/8 t. black pepper
1 c. whole wheat flour
2 1/2 t. baking powder
1/4 c. minced onion
1 1/2 c. extra-sharp Cheddar
   cheese, grated

Preheat oven to 350°F; grease a 12-cup muffin tin. In a mixing bowl beat eggs, oil, and milk. Combine dry ingredients in a separate bowl and fold gently into egg mixture and stir in cheese and onion, mixing only until combined. Batter will be lumpy but that's okay. Spoon into muffin tins and bake for 20 to 25 minutes or until the muffin springs back when pressing the top of it.

To Make Muffins: Mix two pounds of flour with two eggs, two ounces of butter melted in a pint of milk, and four or five spoonfuls of yeast. Beat it thoroughly and set it to rise two or three hours. Bake on a hot hearth in flat cakes. When done on one side, turn them.

–*A New System of Domestic Cookery*, 1807

8-Hour Sticky Buns

Although not your typical "driving to work" breakfast, these sticky buns will force you to eat with one hand, hold a napkin with the second hand and wash it down with coffee with your third... whoops. Well, you get the picture. They are called "8-Hour" because you need to make them the night before, and as you rise in the morning these buns will have risen as well, ready to pop in the oven while coffee is brewing.

Dough:
1 pkg. dry yeast
1/4 c. plus 1 t. sugar
4 c. flour
1 t. salt
3/4 c. milk
4 T. butter or margarine, softened
3 egg yolks

Filling:
1/2 c. brown sugar
4 T. butter or margarine
1 T. cinnamon
1/4 c. raisins

Topping:
2/3 c. brown sugar
3 T. butter or margarine
3 T. light corn syrup
3 T. honey
1 1/2 c. pecans, chopped

To prepare dough: in a cup, combine yeast, 1 t. sugar, and 1/4 c. warm water and let stand 5 minutes. In a large bowl combine 2 1/2 c. flour, milk, margarine, salt, egg yolks, remaining 1/4 c. sugar, and yeast water. Using an electric mixer beat on low speed until well blended. Remove mixer and with wooden spoon stir in remaining 1 1/2 c. flour. Turn out onto lightly floured surface and knead until smooth and elastic, about 10 minutes. Add more flour if necessary. Shape into a ball and place in a greased bowl. Spray the top with non-stick cooking spray and cover. Let rise in a warm spot for about an hour and a half, or until doubled in bulk.

Prepare filling by combining brown sugar, raisins, and cinnamon in a small bowl. Set aside the melted margarine.

Now prepare the topping by heating brown sugar, margarine, corn syrup, and honey in a 1-quart saucepan over low heat, stirring occasionally until all is melted. Grease a 12 × 9-inch metal baking pan; pour melted brown-sugar mixture into the pan and sprinkle evenly with the chopped pecans and set aside.

Punch down the dough; turn onto a lightly floured work surface again. Let rest for 15 minutes then roll dough into an 18 × 12-inch rectangle. Brush dough with melted margarine that has been set aside. Sprinkle the filling evenly over the butter. Now starting on the long side of the rectangle, roll either toward you or away from you in a tight jelly roll fashion, ending with the seam side down. Cut dough into about 20 slices and place onto baking pan, cut side down, so that there is even space between each roll. Sprinkle topping over each, cover with plastic wrap and place in fridge overnight.

In the morning, preheat the oven to 375°F. Remove plastic wrap and bake about 30 minutes or until well browned. Remove from oven and immediately place another baking pan or serving platter (as large as or larger than the hot pan out of the oven) over the rolls. Carefully invert so that the buns are topside down on serving platter. Let rest 5 minutes and enjoy their stickiness!

Chef Jacks New England Cake Donuts

Tested and eaten by thousands of patrons at my father's restaurant, I can assure you that these donuts are worth the effort.

3 1/4 c. flour
2 t. baking powder
1/2 t. cinnamon
1/2 t. salt
1/2 t. nutmeg
2 eggs, beaten
2/3 c. sugar
1 t. vanilla
2/3 c. buttermilk
1/4 c. shortening, melted
Vegetable oil for frying

In a large bowl, combine all ingredients and beat with electric mixer on low speed until well blended, scraping sides of bowl as needed. Refrigerate dough for 30 minutes.

On well-floured surface roll out dough to about 1/2 to 3/4 inch thick with rolling pin, do not knead! With a floured 3 1/2-inch doughnut cutter, cut dough into rings and press the centers out. Place all trimmings together and continue rolling and cutting until all dough is used.

In the meantime, heat 4 inches of vegetable oil in a 3- to 4-qt. saucepan over medium heat until it reaches a temperature of between 360°F and 375°F. Fry doughnuts, a few at a time, 2 to 3 minutes per side, or until golden brown. When they rise in the oil, carefully turn to cook on the other side. Remove from oil, and let drain for a minute or two before eating or dusting with powdered sugar.

Chocolate Doughnuts: Combine 3 T. cocoa with 2 T. vegetable oil and add to doughnut mixture before mixing. Don't forget to drizzle some glaze (1/2 c. powdered sugar mixed with 2 T. milk) over the top.

Coconut Doughnuts ("Shaggy's" as we once called them): Combine 1 c. confectioners' sugar with 3 T. water and whisk until icing is smooth. Dip each doughnut into icing, covering it entirely and place 2 c. flaked coconut into a large bag. Insert wet, glazed doughnut, seal top and shake.

A Captain Hanson Gregory of Rockport, Maine, in 1847 was said to have been the first to invent the doughnut (or donut). His wife had just finished making him a certain pastry on board and noticed that the middle of these were still soggy and uncooked. So Captain Gregory tore out the middle and continued eating them, telling his wife about it later. His wife, from that time on, punched out a hole in the center of each pastry and cooked them thusly. As for the naming of "doughnut"? Pretty simple if you think about the shape.

New England Popovers

Long forgotten are these puffed delights. Generally found served with prime rib to sop up the juices, popovers were originally cooked from the juices of meat that had been roasting in a fire, on a spit. The juices would be caught in a drip pan, added to this recipe and served for breakfast.

5 eggs
1 2/3 c. half and half
1 2/3 c. flour
1 t. salt
Melted butter or jam
1 1/2 c. muffin pan

Preheat oven to 450°F. Place eggs and half and half in a large bowl, beat with a whisk until blended. Add flour and salt and mix well. Mixture should resemble pancake batter—small lumps are okay. Even if you have a non-stick muffin pan, use a light coat of cooking spray. Fill each cup 3/4 full. Place on middle rack of oven. Make sure that the top rack is placed high enough so that the popovers do not come in contact with it as they rise. Close the door and do not peek for 30 minutes. Serve with melted butter or jam.

Little AMERICANS Do your bit
Eat Oatmeal-Corn meal mush-Hominy-other corn cereals-and Rice with milk. Save the wheat for our soldiers. Leave nothing on your plate

UNITED STATES FOOD ADMINISTRATION

Fall Pumpkin Maple Oatmeal

1/2 c. uncooked quick or old-fashioned oats
2 T. pure pumpkin puree
1 T. maple syrup

Cook oatmeal according to package directions. Place in bowl. Top with pumpkin and syrup.

Hearty Sausage Mini Quiches

The children will love these filling morsels right before school on a cold New England day. Packed with "stick to your ribs" fillings, make sure you put away a few for yourself.

1 lb. bulk sausage, cooked, crumbled, and drained
8 eggs, lightly beaten
1/4 c. milk or water
1/2 to 1 c. shredded Cheddar, mozzarella, or provolone cheese
1 t. salt
1/4 t. black pepper
1 t. olive oil, butter, or margarine
1/2 c. thinly sliced green onion
1/2 c. diced sweet red pepper (optional)
1 c. thinly sliced mushrooms or yellow squash (optional)
1 c. frozen Southern-style hash brown potatoes or diced, pre-baked red potatoes (optional)
1/4 c. Parmesan cheese (optional)

Preheat oven to 350°F. In large mixing bowl combine eggs, milk (or water), cheese, salt, and pepper; set aside. Heat olive oil or butter in large skillet; sauté onions and any optional vegetables desired until vegetables are tender. Add vegetables and sausage to egg mixture; stir well. Place 12 foil baking cups into cupcake pan. Distribute sausage and egg mixture evenly into baking cups. Bake 22 minutes or until eggs are set. Remove from oven. Sprinkle with Parmesan if desired.

Old-Fashioned Buttermilk Biscuits With Sausage and Black Pepper Gravy

Now this breakfast is something that has been enjoyed for generations by woodsman and "city-folk" alike. Skip the poultry seasoning all too often found in sausage gravy recipes, it simply does not belong in this dish, period! When you do see it "muckin" up this delicious dish, ask, "Where's the poultry?"

Sausage Gravy:
1 lb. ground pork
   (either hot or mild)
3/4 c. flour
4 1/2 c. milk
1 T. hot sauce
1/2 T. freshly cracked black pepper
Salt to taste
2 T. butter or margarine
Buttermilk biscuits,
   found in this cookbook

Preheat oven to 450°F. In large mixing bowl combine flour, sugar, baking powder, baking soda, salt and cayenne pepper. Cut in shortening with a pastry blender or two forks until crumbly. Gradually add buttermilk, stirring just until dry ingredients are moistened. Dough should be sticky. Do not overwork dough.

On a lightly floured surface, roll dough to 1/2-inch thickness with floured rolling pin. Cut 12 biscuits with a 2 1/2-inch round biscuit cutter. Place biscuits in cast iron skillet or hoecake pan that has been sprayed with non-stick spray, and brush tops with half of melted butter. Bake for 12 to 14 minutes, or until lightly browned. Brush with remaining melted butter before serving.

While biscuits are baking, start gravy. In large sauté pan or cast iron skillet, cook sausage over medium-high heat until browned and crumbly. Reduce heat to medium and add flour to sausage; mix thoroughly. Cook until flour browns, about 4 minutes, stirring constantly.

Add milk slowly and increase heat to medium-high. Continue to stir. Add hot sauce, pepper, and salt. As the gravy comes to a boil, it will thicken. If too thick, add additional milk. After boiling, reduce heat to a simmer and add butter.

To serve, place two buttermilk biscuits on each plate and top with sausage gravy and garnish with freshly cracked pepper.

Buttermilk Pancakes

Hardwood ashes were used in place of any leavening by the poorer communities generations ago. Families simply poured boiling water over sifted ashes in a cup, let the ashes settle and used the liquid as we use leavening today. There are references to snow being used as a leavening agent in nineteenth-century New England as well. Apparently, whatever ammonia existed in newly fallen snow was "enough to leaven a batch of biscuits," so says one account written by a lumber camp cook.

1 1/4 c. flour
3 T. sugar
2 t. baking powder
1/2 t. salt
1 1/3 c. buttermilk
2 eggs
3 T. butter or margarine, melted

In large bowl combine flour, sugar, baking powder, and salt. Add buttermilk, egg, and melted butter; stir until flour is just moistened. The pancake batter will be lumpy but that's okay. If you would like thicker pancakes, simply lower your flour to one cup.

Heat griddle or skillet over medium heat until water dropped on the surface fizzles and disappears. Spray or oil liberally and pour batter to the size wanted. Cook until bubbles of air start popping up around the edges and toward the center. Carefully flip cake and cook for about the same amount of time.

Blueberry Pancakes: Add 3/4 c. fresh blueberries, or 1 1/4 c. frozen blueberries, make batter with 1 cup of flour.

Buckwheat Pancakes: Substitute 1 1/2 c. buckwheat in place of flour.

Yankee Punkin' Pancakes: Substitute buttermilk with evaporated milk, add 1 t. allspice, 2 t. cinnamon, and 1 c. solid pack pumpkin.

Maine Rye Cakes

The texture of these are a little different than your run-of-the-mill pancakes because of the lack of fat, but that's what separates these Yankee cakes from all others. Enjoy these all-too-hearty pancakes when you find yourself being lured to your thermostat.

1 c. flour
1 c. rye flour
1 t. baking powder
2 eggs
1/2 c. molasses
1 c. milk*

In large bowl, mix all ingredients together. Heat 3 inches of vegetable oil in large, deep saucepan to between 340 to 365°F. Drop batter by the teaspoonful into the hot oil, a few at a time, until floating and nicely browned. Serve hot with maple syrup.

Original recipe calls for soured milk. This can be made by adding 1/2 t. vinegar or lemon juice to 1 c. milk and letting it sit for 10 minutes before using.

Apple Brancakes

When I was researching bran to add some info about it here, I was absolutely amazed at the benefits of including bran in your diet. Simply put, it improves joint wellness, bone growth, glucose tolerance and LDL levels (even in diabetics), stabilizes blood fat and cholesterol, and minimizes the risk of heart disease, irritable bowel, colon cancer, and the diseases of civilization (constipation, cancer, diverticulosis, and hemorrhoids). The list keeps getting larger as medical science looks into it. I have only just begun to list the virtues of this natural wonder.

3/4 c. milk
3/4 c. applesauce
2 eggs
3/4 c. 100% bran
3/4 c. flour
2 t. sugar
1 T. baking powder
2 T. butter or margarine, melted
Sliced apples and walnuts
    for topping

Combine milk, apple sauce, eggs, and bran; mix well. In separate bowl combine flour, sugar, and baking powder; mix well. Stir in the melted butter. Mix all together until just incorporated but still lumpy. Follow directions for cooking under "Buttermilk Pancakes." Top with walnuts and sliced apples and don't forget the syrup.

Sunshine Orange Pancakes

No need for syrup on these pancakes, maybe some whipped cream, but even then, I think you will find the orange sauce more than satisfying. There isn't a more fitting name for these vibrantly laced pancakes.

Pancakes:
2 1/4 c. flour
1/2 c. sugar
3 T. baking powder
2 eggs
4 T. butter, melted
1/2 c. orange juice concentrate,
    thawed
3/4 c. milk

Old Fashioned Griddle Cakes

Old fashioned is right! This recipe was made by the first Yankee Chef at the Bangor House Hotel in Bangor, Maine, during the 1920s. A currant berry is so versatile and tasty, it's a shame they are not utilized more often, but because of a disease outbreak in the early part of the twentieth century, the federal government banned the planting of currants here in the U.S. Although this ban was lifted in the 60s, they never did make a comeback.

2 c. flour
2 t. baking powder
3/4 c. sugar
1/4 t. cinnamon
1/4 t. nutmeg
1/4 t. ginger
1/4 T. butter, melted
2 eggs, beaten
2 T. milk
1/2 c. currants

Blend dry ingredients in large bowl, add all other ingredients and stir until soft but not sticky. If you have sticky dough, add 2 T. additional flour at a time until dough is right. Lightly coat work surface with flour and roll out dough to 1/4 inch thick. Cut out with cookie cutter to preferred size. Heat large skillet on medium heat with either 2 T. vegetable oil or nonstick cooking spray. Grill each cake until browned, about 3 to 4 minutes per side. Enjoy with syrup, preserves, or margarine.

Try this Cider Syrup, from many years ago, with any of your pancakes, waffles, or French toast. Mix together 1 quart of apple cider with 1/2 cup sugar in large saucepan. Simmer over medium-low heat, stirring frequently, until only 2 cups of liquid remain and it is syrupy.

Orange Sauce:
1/4 c. sugar
1 T. cornstarch
1 1/4 c. orange juice
2 t. butter or margarine
One 8-ounce can pineapple chunks, drained
1 banana, sliced

For sauce: In a small saucepan combine 1/4 c. sugar and cornstarch. Stir in orange juice and cook over medium heat until thickened and bubbly. Cook an additional 3 minutes, remove from heat and add 2 t. margarine and pineapple; stir till incorporated. Add banana and gently stir.

For pancakes: In a medium bowl stir together flour, 1/2 c. sugar, baking powder, eggs, melted margarine, and thawed concentrate. Stir until well combined but still a little lumpy. Cook according to "Buttermilk Pancake" recipe. Top with orange sauce.

Cheddar-Orange Breakfast Toast

This is my spin on stuffed French toast, and you will find no equal. The sweetness and sourness of the marmalade with the saltiness of the Canadian bacon covers every taste bud you need to trudge into work early in the morning.

8 thick slices French or Italian bread
1/2 c. orange marmalade
4 slices Canadian bacon
2 c. shredded Cheddar cheese
4 eggs
1/2 c. orange juice
2 t. brown sugar
1/4 c. butter or margarine
Confectioners' sugar

Spread 4 slices of bread evenly with marmalade. Top each with 1 slice Canadian bacon and some shredded cheese. Top with remaining bread slices, pressing lightly. Beat eggs in a pie plate; stir in orange juice and brown sugar, mixing well.

Dip breakfast sandwiches to coat into egg mixture. Let stand 15 to 20 seconds on each side to absorb liquid. Melt butter in large skillet over medium heat and place each sandwich into pan to cook. Fry until golden brown on each side and cheese is melted. Remove and sprinkle with confectioners' sugar.

To preserve cheese against mites, take one red pepper and put it into a piece of fine linen, moisten it with fresh butter, and rub your cheese with it frequently; it is so pungent that no fly will touch the cheese and it gives it a very fine color.

–The Yankee Chef Archives, 1810

Croissant French Toast with Blueberries and Almonds

You'll feel like you're at a cross between a roadside diner and a first-class restaurant. Decadence and simplicity do go hand-in-hand in this appealing, scrumptious breakfast.

4 eggs
4 c. half and half
1 T. vanilla
1 T. cinnamon
1 T. almond extract
2 T. sugar
8 to 10 croissants, chilled
Fresh blueberries
Almond slivers
2 T. butter or margarine
Powdered sugar as needed
Whipped cream as needed

Slice croissants horizontally, into three layers. In large bowl combine all above ingredients except blueberries, almonds, and croissants, and whisk very well. Place croissants in batter and soak for 10 minutes. Heat nonstick skillet over medium-high. Add 2 T. butter or margarine, when melted grill croissant French toast until golden brown on both sides, about 3 to 4 minutes per side. Repeat until done. Top with blueberries, almonds; sprinkle with powdered sugar and a dollop of whipped cream.

Pecan-Orange French Toast

Pecans are one of America's favorite nuts. The name comes from the Algonquin Indian word *paccan* or *pakan*, meaning "a nut so hard it had to be cracked with a stone." Certain Native American tribes of Texas used the nuts as their sole sustenance for 2 to 4 months out of the year. The heartiness of the pecan tree is why they are so popular. They can grow to be over 100 feet tall and live to 1,000 years. Native to the Mississippi basin, it takes ten years to produce a profitable crop. One tree can yield 400 pounds a year. Cholesterol and sodium free, these nuts provide a significant source of fiber. They also contain over nineteen vitamins and minerals like E and magnesium and boast a variety of phytochemicals. A handful of these nuts provides about 25 percent more oleic acid than a tablespoon of olive oil.

4 eggs
1/2 c. milk mixed with
  1/2 c. orange juice
1/4 c. sugar
1/4 t. cinnamon
1/4 t. nutmeg
1/2 t. vanilla
Melted butter or margarine,
  as needed
1 loaf French bread, sliced
3/4 c. pecans
2 T. butter or margarine, melted
1 t. grated orange rind

Place eggs, milk mixture, sugar, nutmeg, cinnamon, and vanilla in a medium bowl and whisk to combine. Brush the bottom of a 12 × 8-inch casserole with melted butter or margarine. Place the bread sliced in a single layer in the pan and pour the egg mixture over the bread, covering it evenly. Turn the bread once after a few minutes. Cover the pan with plastic wrap and place in the refrigerator for one hour, or overnight if you would like.

Preheat oven to 425°F. Remove French toast and remove plastic wrap. Sprinkle the top with pecans and grated orange rind. Drizzle with melted butter or margarine. Bake for 20 to 25 minutes, or until bread slices puff up and pecans are deep brown but not burned. Serve warm with maple syrup.

Overnight Banana French Toast

Make this the night before so you can spend a little more time with the kids the next morning. Not only will they love you for it but maybe they'll give you a sticky kiss after.

1 loaf French bread, cubed
1 (8 oz.) pkg. cream cheese,
  cut into pieces
3 bananas, sliced
6 eggs
4 c. milk
3/4 c. sugar
1/4 c. butter or margarine, melted
1/2 c. maple syrup
3/4 t. cinnamon

Arrange half of bread cubes in a lightly greased 13 x 9-inch pan. Sprinkle evenly with cream cheese and bananas; top with remaining bread cubes. Whisk together eggs, 4 cups milk, sugar, butter, and maple syrup; pour over bread mixture, pressing bread cubes to absorb egg mixture. Cover and chill 8 hours, or overnight. Sprinkle with cinnamon and bake, covered, at 350°F for 30 minutes. Uncover and bake 30 more minutes or until lightly browned and set. Let stand 5 minutes before serving.

June butter was the term used for the butter made during the spring, when it would have the deepest yellow color, due to the abundance of chlorophyll absorbed by the cow feeding on the lush green pasture. Artificial color for butter was not in use in those days. As towns grew to the stage where there was no longer a cow in every barn, the nearby farm family with the facilities to keep a few more cows than home use required, found a ready sale for any dairy products. The old fashioned churn with up and down paddle made long, slow work, and was followed by hand working of the butter, kneading out the traces of butter milk and mixing in, evenly, the proper amount of salt. In later years, better churns came into use, along with wooden rollers to work the butter more easily. Nowadays, however, dairy butter is a rare product in New England. It is only occasionally made and sold, and then only in localities where a few old-timers still prefer the homemade article.

French Toast Strata

A great start to the day. You can make this dish the night before as well and cook it the next morning while you're in the shower.

1/2 lb. ground sausage
2 apples, peeled, cored,
   and thinly sliced
5 eggs
2 c. milk
1/2 c. maple syrup
1/2 t. nutmeg
1/2 loaf French or Italian bread,
   cut into 1/2-inch slices

Butter or oil a 10-inch pie pan; set aside. In a large skillet, over medium high heat, thoroughly cook sausage, crumbling with the back of a spoon while cooking. When done, strain and add apple slices. Reduce heat to medium and cook for 3 minutes, covered.

In medium bowl beat eggs, add milk, maple syrup, and nutmeg; mix well. Arrange 3/4 of the bread slices in the prepared pan. Top with sausage, apples, and remaining bread slices.

Pour milk mixture evenly over top and cover. Refrigerate at least one hour or overnight if you wish. Preheat oven to 350°F. Bake, uncovered, for 55 to 60 minutes or until set and golden brown. Serve immediately with additional maple syrup.

Remember the days when your parents didn't want you to eat too much sugar because it would keep you awake and bouncing off the walls? Now we know that not to be true, but there are some effects of too much sugar intake. With the excessive intake of sugar comes an excess of calories, which in turn amount to an excess of fat. It should be noted, however, that starches and sugars are not in themselves inherently fattening unless they present excess calories. Simple sugar and sucrose over-abundance may also lead to fluctuation of blood sugars. In contrast, starches in vegetables and legumes are slowly digested, whereby the glucose is absorbed more slowly. This permits a more balanced control of blood sugar. Another reason to avoid excessive sugar in your diet of course are those nasty cavities.

Northern Potato Omelet

A hearty omelet combining the usual side-dish you have with an omelet anyway. You will love the subtle addition of cinnamon.

1/4 c. butter or margarine
3 medium potatoes, peeled and
   thinly sliced
Salt and pepper to taste
1 medium onion, chopped
Juice of 1 lemon
2 medium tomatoes, sliced
6 eggs
1/2 t. cinnamon
1/4 t. salt

Add half the potatoes; cook until lightly browned on both sides and nearly tender. Remove from skillet; season with salt and pepper. Repeat with remaining butter or margarine and potatoes. Set aside. Add onion to skillet; cook until tender. Remove onion from skillet with slotted spoon; place in small bowl and sprinkle with lemon juice.

Return potatoes to skillet; add tomatoes and onions. Cover and cook over low heat 10 minutes or until potatoes are tender.

Beat eggs, cinnamon and 1/4 t. salt in small bowl; pour over onions. Cover and cook until eggs are completely set. Cut into wedges and serve immediately.

Yankee Toast, often called a "Country Breakfast Dish" by chroniclers of old, was prepared thusly, according to the first Yankee Chef: "Slice lengthwise, but do not peel, about twice the number of apples you think your family should eat for breakfast and fry them in butter with 3 T water and 1/2 c. sugar for ever 5 apples. Serve on French toast with broiled bacon."

Chef Jack's Baked Eggs

From The Oak Pond Restaurant in Maine, this is a great winter's breakfast.

1/4 c. sliced onions
1/4 c. sliced mushrooms
3 T. butter or margarine
1 c. fresh spinach
2 T. heavy cream
2 eggs
Salt & pepper to taste
3 T. grated Parmesan cheese

Preheat oven to 500°F. In a small, oven-safe, fry pan, sauté onions and mushrooms in butter, over medium-high heat, until onions and mushrooms are soft. Add spinach, heavy cream, and salt and pepper to taste. Stir until spinach is just wilted. Crack eggs on top. Cook in the oven until done (up to 8 minutes). Sprinkle with Parmesan cheese.

Potato Eggs Benedict

I think you'll agree that the addition of the hash browns makes a mountain of a dish—eat them on the side if you like. Either way, eat up. I hope you're hungry.

2 T. butter or margarine
2 T. flour
2 c. milk
1/2 t. salt
Pinch white pepper
3 egg yolks
1/4 c. sour cream
2 T. lemon juice
6 formed hash brown potatoes
Vegetable oil as needed
6 slices Canadian bacon
6 eggs, poached to your liking
3 English muffins, split and toasted

Melt butter or margarine in medium-sized saucepan on medium heat. Add flour and blend. While still on heat, add milk slowly, stirring constantly, until mixture thickens, about 6 to 7 minutes. Season with salt and pepper. Beat egg yolks in separate bowl until creamy. Stir in small amount of the hot mixture, whisking until smooth, this is called tempering. Add this back into the saucepan and whisk, cooking an additional 2 minutes. Remove from heat. Add sour cream and lemon juice; mix well.

Preheat slices of Canadian bacon either in frying pan for just a few seconds on each side or microwave for 15 seconds on high. Remove and set aside.

Assemble Potato Eggs Benedict to order. Lay half an English muffin on a plate. Cook hash brown on oiled griddle or skillet until browned; sprinkle with salt and pepper to taste. Top with cooked Canadian bacon and remove to the top of the English muffin. Add the poached egg and ladle the sauce over this "mountain" and serve immediately.

An Egg Pie: Shred the yolks of twenty hard eggs with the same quantity of marrow and beef suet; season it with sweet spice, citron, orange and lemon: fill and close the pie.
- The New England Cookery, 1808

Blender Hollandaise Sauce

Although there may be a mystique and aura of complication to making Hollandaise Sauce, this is entirely untrue. See for yourself with the following recipe.

1 c. (2 sticks) butter, cubed	1 T. lemon juice
2 egg yolks	Salt and black pepper to taste

Melt butter in a small saucepan over medium heat; remove from heat. Put egg yolks and lemon juice in blender; cover and blend until combined. Working quickly and with blender running, remove small circular insert on top and slowly pour hot butter into blender in a thin stream, discarding the whey at the bottom of the saucepan. Blend until creamy. Season to taste with salt and pepper, and more lemon juice if desired. Serve immediately.

You can also, if whisking quickly and if you have a flat-bottomed bowl on a damp towel, use a whisk and whip this yourself. Just remember to slowly pour in the melted butter.

Here are some variations on the classic Eggs Benedict:

Eggs Blackstone substitutes streaky bacon for the ham and adds a tomato slice.

Eggs Florentine substitutes spinach for the ham. Older versions of Eggs Florentine add spinach to poached or shirred Eggs Mornay, which are eggs covered in Mornay sauce.

Eggs Montreal or Eggs Royale substitutes salmon for the ham. This is a common variation found in Australia and New Zealand.

Eggs Hussarde substitutes Holland rusks for the English muffin and adds Marchand de Vin sauce.

Eggs Sardou substitutes artichoke bottoms and anchovy fillets for the English muffin and ham, and then tops the hollandaise sauce with chopped ham and a truffle slice. The dish was created at Antoine's Restaurant in New Orleans in honor of the French playwright Victorien Sardou. A more widespread version of the dish starts with a base of creamed spinach, substitutes artichoke bottoms for the English muffin, and eliminates the ham.

Artichoke Benedict replaces the English muffin with a hollowed artichoke.

Country Benedict, sometimes known as Eggs Beauregard, replaces the English muffin, ham, and Hollandaise sauce with an American biscuit, sausage patties, and country gravy. The poached eggs are replaced with eggs fried to choice.

Irish Benedict replaces the ham with corned beef. Although unknown in Ireland itself, corned beef and cabbage is the iconic Irish-American dish, with more than half of the 50 million pounds of corned beef sold annually in the United States sold in the two weeks prior to Saint Patrick's Day.

Spin-offs of Hollandaise Sauce

Being a mother sauce, Hollandaise sauce is the foundation for many derivatives created by adding or changing ingredients. The following is a exhaustive listing of such sauces.

The most common derivative is Sauce Béarnaise. It can be produced by replacing the acidifying agent (vinegar reduction or lemon juice) in a preparation with a strained reduction of vinegar, shallots, fresh chervil, fresh tarragon, and (if to taste) crushed peppercorns. Alternatively, the flavorings may be added to a standard Hollandaise. Béarnaise, and its "children," are often used on steak or other "assertive" grilled meats and fish.

Sauce Choron is a variation of béarnaise without tarragon or chervil, plus added tomato purée.

Sauce Foyot (aka Valois) is béarnaise with meat glaze (Glace de Viande) added.

Sauce Colbert is Sauce Foyot with the addition of reduced white wine.

Sauce Café de Paris is béarnaise with curry powder added.

Sauce Paloise is a version of béarnaise with mint substituted for tarragon.

Sauce au Vin Blanc (for fish) is produced by adding a reduction of white wine and fish stock to Hollandaise

Sauce Bavaroise is Hollandaise with added cream, horseradish, and thyme.

Sauce Crème Fleurette is Hollandaise with crème fraîche added.

Sauce Dijon, also known as Sauce Moutarde or Sauce Girondine, is Hollandaise with Dijon mustard.

Sauce Maltaise is Hollandaise to which blanched orange zest and the juice of blood orange is added.

Sauce Mousseline, also known as Sauce Chantilly, is produced by folding whipped cream into Hollandaise. If reduced sherry is first folded into the whipped cream, the result is Sauce Divine.

Sauce Noisette is a Hollandaise variation made with browned butter (beurre noisette).

CHAPTER 2

Medieval bakery in England

Master Recipe for Rising & Baking Yeast Bread

Place your dough in a greased bowl, the pinched or sealed side down. Spray top of dough with cooking spray or brush lightly with oil, cover with wet cloth and set aside in warmest part of the kitchen until risen to double in bulk, about 2 to 4 hours. Punch down and lightly flour work surface.

Empty dough onto work surface and knead for 2 to 3 minutes until dough is not sticky anymore. Work into a loaf shape and place in greased bread loaf pan. Again brush or spray with oil, cover with wet cloth, and let rise once again until double in bulk. Bake in preheated 350°F oven for 40 to 45 minutes, or until quite browned on top. Remove from oven, let rest for 10 minutes and remove to wire rack to cool before slicing. Now the top will be crusty. If you desire a softer top to your bread, spray or butter the tops with butter or butter-flavored spray when still warm.

Anadama Bread

Add 2 c. frozen blueberries after the addition of the molasses to "gussy" up this old Yankee favorite. Best served directly from the oven. Makes 1 loaf

1 1/2 c. cold water	1 t. salt	1/2 t. baking soda	3 c. flour
1/3 c. molasses	1 package dry yeast	1 1/2 c. whole wheat flour	Flour for working
2 T. vegetable shortening	1/4 c. warm water	3/4 c. cornmeal	

In small saucepan heat cold water, molasses, shortening, and salt on medium heat until shortening has melted; remove from heat immediately. Let cool until tepid. In separate small bowl, sprinkle yeast over 1/4 c. warm water and let sit 5 minutes until absorbed. In a large mixing bowl, mix together all other dry ingredients well. Add yeast/water and molasses mixture; blending with your hands or in electric mixer until well combined. Refer to "Master Recipe for Rising and Baking Yeast Bread" at the beginning of this chapter for dough preparation and baking.

Old Maine Black Bread

There's a nice tangy bite to this earthy black bread that you just can't taste in any other bread. I dare say you can't find a more flavorful rye bread anywhere. Makes 1 loaf

1 package dry yeast	1 1/2 c. flour
1 3/4 c. warm water, divided	1 t. sugar
2 T. cider vinegar	1 t. salt
1/4 c. molasses	1 c. bran cereal
1 square (1 oz.)	1 T. caraway seeds
unsweetened chocolate	1 t. instant coffee
2 T. butter or shortening	1 t. onion powder
2 c. rye flour	

Dissolve yeast in the 1/2 c. warm water; set aside. In saucepan heat vinegar, the remainder of the water, molasses, chocolate, and butter or shortening, Do not boil! Combine dry ingredients and gradually add to liquid mixture, beating well after each addition until dough is soft. Refer to "Master Recipe for Rising and Baking Yeast Bread" at the beginning of this chapter for dough preparation and baking.

Basic White Yeast Bread

A nice, white bread with a crust that doesn't "peel" off. This fragrant classic will have you baking more often. Makes 2 loaves

1 package dry yeast
1/4 c. warm water
2 T. honey
1/4 c. shortening
1 T. salt
1 c. milk, scalded
1 c. cold water
5 to 6 c. flour

Dissolve yeast in the warm water, set aside. In large bowl mix together honey, shortening, salt, and scalded milk. Add the cup of cold water and allow mixture to cool to lukewarm. Add dissolved yeast. Gradually add flour until dough is stiff. Place dough on lightly floured work surface and knead until dough is smooth and elastic. Refer to "Master Recipe for Rising and Baking Yeast Bread" at the beginning of this chapter for dough preparation and baking.

This recipe makes perfect yeast rolls as well. Just pinch off a 1/4-cup ball of dough, roll it out with your hands until seams and cracks are hidden and place on baking sheet about an inch apart. Bake for 10 to 12 minutes, or until nicely browned on top.

Honey Oatmeal Bread

This slightly sweet bread topped with oatmeal is made even healthier by adding 1 cup of wheat germ with the dry ingredients. Hey, if my father can eat wheat germ and milk for breakfast, you can add a little to bread. Makes 2 loaves

2 packages dry yeast
1/2 c. warm water
2 1/4 c. milk, scalded
1/2 c. honey
1/3 c. plus 1 T. butter or margarine
2 t. salt
6 to 7 c. flour
2 c. old fashioned oats

Dissolve yeast in warm water; set aside. In large mixing bowl combine scalded milk, honey, butter, salt and stir until smooth. When mixture has cooled to lukewarm, add dissolved yeast. Gradually add flour and oats, mixing thoroughly until dough is stiff. Knead on floured surface for 8 to 10 minutes until smooth and elastic. Refer to "Master Recipe for Rising and Baking Yeast Bread" at the beginning of this chapter for dough preparation and baking.

Whole Wheat Bread

This bread is proof that great flavor and "good for you" work well together. Want to add a touch more flavor? Add 1/2 c. maple syrup while adding the melted butter and cut back to 1/4 c. on the warm water. Makes 2 loaves

2 packages of dry yeast
1/2 c. warm water
1 c. boiling water
1/2 c. honey
5 to 6 c. whole wheat flour
3/4 c. lukewarm water
2 1/2 t. salt
3 T. butter or margarine, melted

Dissolve yeast in the 1/2 c. warm water; set aside. Pour the cup of boiling water into a large mixing bowl and stir in honey. Cool to lukewarm, and then add dissolved yeast. Blend in 2 c. of the wheat flour, cover bowl, place over hot water and allow mixture to double in size. When doubled, punch down and beat in the 3/4 c. lukewarm water, salt, melted butter, and remaining flour. Dough will be stiff. Knead on a floured surface until very smooth. Place dough in a greased bowl. Refer to "Master Recipe for Rising and Baking Yeast Bread" at the beginning of this chapter for dough preparation and baking.

When wheat malt was mixed with oat malt in colonial times and earlier, a beverage named Mumm was enjoyed.

Pumpernickel Bread

You can find three basic types of pumpernickel bread at the supermarkets: medium dark, dark, and extra dark. The darker the bread, the more sour tasting it is and the more chewy it will be. Makes 2 round loaves

2 packages dry yeast
1/2 c. warm water
1 c. cold water
1/2 c. molasses
1 t. salt
2 3/4 c. rye flour
2 T. caraway seeds
2 T. shortening
3 c. plus flour

Dissolve yeast in warm water and set aside. In small saucepan combine cold water, shortening, molasses and salt; melt on low heat, set aside until tepid. In large mixing bowl combine rye flour, yeast, caraway seeds, and shortening mixtures until smooth. Slowly add flour until dough becomes stiff. Turn out on floured work surface and knead 8 to 10 minutes until smooth and elastic. Refer to "Master Recipe for Rising and Baking Yeast Bread" at the beginning of this chapter for dough preparation and baking.

Oatmeal Molasses Bread

Although this bread is a favorite of many New Englanders, I must admit, adding 1 T. anise seed with the dry ingredients gives this Yankee Chef a licorice kick in the pants. Love it! Makes 2 loaves

2 packages dry yeast
1/2 c. warm water
1/2 c. molasses
4 T. butter
4 T. brown sugar
5 to 6 c. flour
1 c. whole wheat flour
1 c. old-fashioned oats
3 t. salt
1 t. ginger
2 c. milk, scalded

Dissolve yeast in warm water. To scalded milk, add molasses, butter, and brown sugar until blended and butter melted. Allow mixture to cool to lukewarm then add dissolved yeast. In large bowl mix dry ingredients and gradually add milk mixture, stirring until dough is well mixed. Turn dough onto floured surface and knead about 5 minutes. Refer to "Master Recipe for Rising and Baking Yeast Bread" at the beginning of this chapter for dough preparation and baking.

Here is a recipe used in the early nineteenth century for making starch: "Steep wheat in cold water until it becomes soft and yields a milky juice by pleasure; then put it in to a linen cloth and press it in a vessel of cold water as long as any milky juice exudes a white poseer subsides, which is starch."

Aroostook Potato Bread

Once you have tried potato bread, either homemade or store bought, you will find it very difficult to return to white bread. The texture is firm yet moist and the taste is unsurpassed. If this is what the County Kids (a Maine term for children from the northern county of Aroostook) ate growing up, boy, I sure missed the potato wagon! Makes 2 loaves

2 medium potatoes
2 1/2 c. water
1 package dry yeast
2 T. butter
3 T. sugar
1 T. salt
6 c. flour

Cook potatoes until tender in the 2 1/2 c. water. Remove 1/4 c. of the potato water and let cool. Mash the potatoes in the remaining liquid. Dissolve yeast in the reserved 1/4 c. potato water. (Be sure water is cooled). In large mixing bowl combine mashed potato liquid, butter, sugar, and salt. Blend until smooth. Stir in dissolved yeast.

Gradually add flour, beating well. Turn dough onto floured surface and knead 8 to 10 minutes until smooth and elastic. Refer to "Master Recipe for Rising and Baking Yeast Bread" at the beginning of this chapter for dough preparation and baking.

Iced Raisin-Cinnamon Bread

The icing gives a delightful sweetness to this raisin bread—it won't uncurl on you when you want it the most because it is not rolled as most other raisin breads are. Makes 2 loaves

1 package dry yeast	4 t. cinnamon
1/4 c. warm water	2 t. salt
2 c. milk, scalded	5 to 6 c. flour
1/3 c. butter	2 c. raisins, parboiled in 1/4 c. water for 5 minutes
1/3 c. sugar	Icing, *recipe below*

Dissolve yeast in the warm water, set aside. Pour the scalded milk over butter and stir to melt. Add sugar, cinnamon, and salt; let cool. Add yeast. Stir in about 3 c. of flour, beat well. Cover and let rise about 45 minutes. Dough will be light and bubbly. Gradually add remaining flour alternately with raisins. Dough should be smooth and satiny. Turn onto floured surface and knead 8 to 10 minutes. Refer to "Master Recipe for Rising and Baking Yeast Bread" at the beginning of this chapter for dough preparation and baking. After pulling out bread from oven and letting cool until warm, frost with icing.

Icing:
2 T. butter or margarine	1/2 t. vanilla
1 c. powdered sugar	1 1/2 T. milk

Blend all ingredients together well.

Hot Cross Buns:
A New England Tradition

Any of these yeast breads are easy to make rolls from. Simply pinch off the size you want and roll them. Bake them on a cookie sheet at the same temperature but a shorter cooking time. If you enjoy crusty rolls, space them apart. If you enjoy fluffy and soft-sided rolls, nestle them together before baking.

1 package dry yeast
1/4 c. warm water
1/2 c. sugar
1/2 t. salt
3 T. butter or margarine, melted
1 c. milk, scalded
2 eggs, beaten\
3 c. flour
3/4 t. cinnamon
1/2 c. raisins

Icing:
1 c. powdered sugar
4 T. water or milk

Preheat oven to 350°F. Grease baking pan. Sprinkle yeast into 1/4 c. warm water, let sit for 5 minutes. Combine the sugar, salt, butter, and milk. When lukewarm, add the yeast water and eggs and mix well. In larger bowl combine flour and cinnamon together and stir in the yeast mixture. Add raisins and mix thoroughly. Cover and let rise until double in bulk. Shape dough into large rounds and place on baking pan. Let rise again. In the meantime, beat one egg and brush top of each roll. With a sharp knife make a cross on the top of each roll and bake 20 to 25 minutes or until golden brown. Remove from oven and let stand 10 minutes before serving.

Make icing by whisking both ingredients until very smooth. Carefully pour thin lines of icing into each cross to form a white cross on each roll. Let cool before serving.

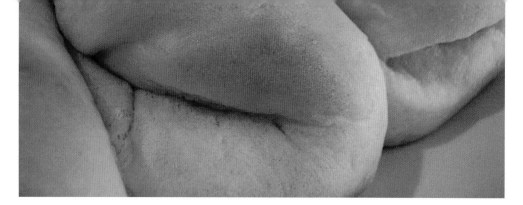

Parker House Rolls

The Omni Parker House is a luxury hotel in Boston. Built in 1858, the hotel offers more than 500 guest rooms and is within walking distance of Beacon Hill, Faneuil Hall, and Quincy Market. This hotel has had unexplained activities on the third floor. One such ghost is Charlotte Cushman, a nineteenth-century stage actress who died in her room in 1876. In addition, a business man also died on the same floor. Guests have reported smelling whiskey and hearing boisterous laughter. Stories abound of an elevator that travels to the third floor without it being requested. The hotel's founder, Harvey Parker, who died in 1884, is said to unexpectedly inquire about a guest's stay.

6 T. plus 1 t. sugar
2 pkg. (1/4-oz. each) dry yeast
1 c. warm water (110 to 115°F), divided
1 c. warm milk (110 to 115°F)
2 t. salt
1 egg
2 T. plus 2 t. vegetable oil
3 c. wheat flour mixed with 3 c. white flour
3 T. butter or margarine, melted

In a large bowl dissolve yeast and 1 t. sugar in 1/2 c. warm water; let stand 5 minutes. Add milk, salt, egg, oil, and remaining sugar, water, and 2 c. flour. Beat until smooth. Stir in enough remaining flour to make soft dough. Turn onto a floured work surface; knead until smooth and elastic, about 6 to 8 minutes. Place in a greased bowl, turning once to grease top. Cover and let rise in a warm place until doubled, about 45 minutes. Punch dough down and turn onto a lightly floured surface; divide in half. Roll out each piece to about 1/2-inch thickness. Cut with a floured 2 1/2-inch biscuit cutter.

Using the dull edge of a table knife, make an off-center crease in each roll. Fold along crease so the large half is on top; press along folded edge. Place 2 inches apart on greased baking sheets. Cover and let rise until doubled again, about 30 minutes if in a warm place. Bake in 375°F oven for 12 to 15 minutes or until golden brown. Remove from pans to wire racks to cool. Makes about 2 1/2 dozen

Quick Breads and Sweet Breads

Johnny Bread (Yankee Corn Bread)

The age-old argument on the name Johnny bread is even older than the argument over red or white chowder. Is it Johnny, Jonny, or Journey? Was it named after Johnny Trumbull or not? I dare not venture a guess, although I have my thoughts. Let's just say...I ain't gonna go there! Let's just enjoy.

3/4 c. flour
2 1/2 t. baking powder
1/4 c. sugar
3/4 t. salt
1 1/4 c. yellow corn meal
2 eggs, beaten
3 T. butter or margarine, melted
1 c. milk

Preheat oven to 400°F. If you have a cast iron frying pan, it would be ideal for this bread, if not, spray a 9 × 9-inch pan with nonstick cooking spray oil or use vegetable oil. Place in oven to get very hot while mixing batter. Mix together flour, baking powder, sugar, salt, and cornmeal. Add eggs, butter, and milk to dry ingredients and combine with just a few rapid strokes until combined but still lumpy. Remove pan from oven; pour batter evenly into pan and bake 25 to 30 minutes or until toothpick inserted in middle comes out clean.

To Make Johnny Cake or Hoe Cake: Scald one pint of milk and put to three pints of Indian meal and half pint of flour. Bake before the fire. Scald with milk two thirds of the Indian meal or wet two thirds with boiling water, add salt, molasses and shortening. Work up with cold water pretty stiff and bake as above.

– *The New England Cookery*, 1808

Baked Boston Brown Bread

I bake instead of steam here for several reasons. Many people don't have the desire, time, energy, or patience to use a mold and steam brown bread anymore, which is a shame. At least you can take comfort in knowing that this version is as sweet and tasty as the steamed version, without the care needed. I don't need to tell you that this bread is an ideal match for baked beans, now do I?

Here's a little dittie for the ingredients that I picked up at my father's restaurant. My uncle, also a chef, told me he first heard it when he was a child.

Three cups corn meal,
One of rye flour;
Three cups of sweet milk,
One cup of sour;
A cup of molasses
To render it sweet,
Two teaspoons of soda
Will make it complete.

Or use today's recipe:

2 c. graham flour
I c. flour
3 T. sugar
I t. salt
I t. baking soda
I c. buttermilk
I c. molasses
I c. raisins (optional)

Preheat oven to 350°F. Grease 2 loaf pans. In large bowl mix dry ingredients until well incorporated. Add remainder of ingredients and mix until combined. Evenly distribute between both pans and bake 45 to 50 minutes or until toothpick inserted in middle comes out clean.

To have marmalade on toast! We loved that as children and apparently, our ancestors did as well. Here is an old recipe for Yankee Apple Marmalade:

2 1/2 lb. sugar, 1 1/4 c. water, 2 1/2 c. tart apples, peeled, 1 orange and 1 lemon. Heat the sugar and water until the sugar is dissolved. Slice and core the apples; add the juice of the orange and lemon and the peel sliced very thin. Simmer until mixture is thickened, about 1 1/2 hours. Turn into glasses and, when cold, cover with paraffin.

Pumpkin Bread

This bread actually tastes better either at room temperature or cold. Add some apple butter to it and you won't go back to toast for breakfast.

4 1/2 c. flour
3 c. sugar
1 1/2 t. baking soda
1 t. cinnamon
1 t. nutmeg
1/2 c. vegetable oil
1/2 c. applesauce
2 c. pumpkin pie filling
4 eggs, beaten
2/3 c. milk

Preheat oven to 350°F. Grease 2 loaf pans. In large mixing bowl, combine all dry ingredients until well blended. Add remainder of ingredients until well incorporated. Divide, evenly, between both loaf pans and bake 45 to 50 minutes, or until toothpick inserted in middle comes out clean.

Pumpkins, or *pompions*, as the Pilgrims called them, were used in various ways on colonial tables. John Joselyn, author of *New England Rarities* in the early 1600s, called pumpkin stewed with a little butter, spice, and vinegar the "Ancient New England stand in-dish," and Edward Johnson said in 1651, "Let no man make a jest of pumpkin, for with this fruit the Lord was pleased to feed his people till corn and cattle were increased."

Banana Bread

Want to give the kids (or yourself) a treat? Add some chocolate chips, chopped cherries (well drained), and pineapple and you've got yourself a Banana Split Bread.

2 c. flour
1/4 t. baking soda
2 t. baking powder
1/2 c. sugar
2 eggs, beaten
1/4 c. butter or margarine, melted
2 c. mashed bananas
1 t. banana extract (optional)
1/2 t. salt

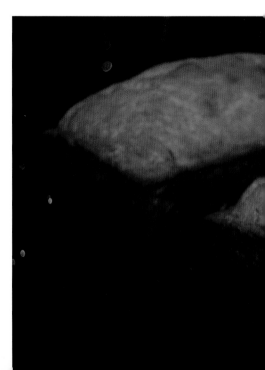

Preheat oven to 350°F. Grease 1 loaf pan. In large bowl, combine all dry ingredients until well mixed. Add remainder of ingredients until well blended and pour into prepared pan. You may sprinkle top with sugar if desired. Bake 45 to 50 minutes or until toothpick inserted in middle comes out clean.

To make Indian Slapjacks: [combine] one quart of milk, one pint of Indian meal, four spoons flour, little fat, beat together and bake on griddles or fry in dry pan, or bake in a pan which has been rubbed with suet, lard or butter.

–*American Cookery*, 1796

Apple Cheese Bread

2 3/4 c. flour
I T. baking powder
1/2 t. salt
1/2 t. nutmeg
1/2 t. cinnamon
1/2 c. sugar
1/4 c. butter or margarine, melted
2 eggs, beaten
I to I 1/2 c. milk
I 3/4 c. Cheddar cheese, grated
2 c. peeled, cored, and grated apple
    tossed with 3 T. sugar
I c. apple jelly

Preheat oven to 350 °F. Grease a 9 × 5-inch loaf pan or equivalent. In large mixing bowl, combine flour, baking powder, salt, nutmeg, cinnamon, and sugar. In separate bowl, mix together melted butter, beaten eggs, and milk; set aside. Mix cheese and apple into dry ingredients. Add milk mixture and stir only until batter is evenly moistened, it will be lumpy. Pour into loaf pan and bake for 45 to 50 minutes or until toothpick inserted in center comes out clean.

Meanwhile, melt apple jelly either on stove top or in microwave. When bread is done and while still hot, pour apple jelly over top and let cool in pan until jelly resets. Remove to wire rack and cool completely.

Cranberry Bread

I intentionally didn't add any nut to this recipe because I, personally, don't like them in my Cranberry Bread. I want to taste just that sweet, tart cranberry popping out when I enjoy this recipe. But by all means, add 1 c. chopped pecans, walnuts, or almonds.

2/3 c. sugar
1/3 c. butter or margarine
2 eggs, beaten
I c. boiling water
1/4 c. orange juice
I c. frozen cranberries,
    thawed and chopped
I t. baking powder
1/2 t. salt
1/2 t. baking soda
2 c. flour

Preheat oven to 350°F. Grease loaf pan or 9 × 9-inch square baking pan. Cream sugar and butter together until well incorporated. Blend in eggs. Stir in water and orange juice until combined. Add cranberries (and nuts). In separate bowl, mix together the dry ingredients and blend into wet mixture only until blended throughout. Pour into loaf pan and bake 45 to 50 minutes or until toothpick inserted in middle comes out clean.

Cherry Nut Bread

This bread slices into rich and moist pieces with a crispy, golden crust. What more could you ask for as a midday snack?

1 c. sugar
1/2 c. butter or margarine
2 eggs
2 c. flour
1 t. baking powder
1/2 t. salt
1 jar (10 oz.) maraschino cherries, drained (reserve liquid)
1 t. vanilla
3/4 c. walnuts, chopped

Preheat oven to 350°F. Grease a 9 × 5-inch loaf pan or equivalent. In a large bowl cream sugar and butter until well blended. Add eggs, one at a time, beating well after each addition. Stir together flour, baking powder, and salt. Measure cherry juice, adding water if necessary, to equal 1/2 cup. Add dry ingredients alternately with cherry juice and vanilla to creamed mixture; blend well. Cut cherries in half and stir into the batter. Stir in nuts. Pour batter into the prepared pan. Bake for 50 to 55 minutes or until toothpick inserted in middle comes out clean.

Zucchini Bread

The addition of the honey and applesauce lends some New England orchard flavor to this age-old recipe.

1/4 c. vegetable oil
1/2 c. applesauce
1 1/2 c. honey
1/4 t. baking powder
2 t. cinnamon
1 t. baking soda
3 eggs, beaten until frothy
2 t. vanilla
2 c. zucchini, peeled and
1 c. walnuts, chopped grated

Preheat oven to 350°F. Grease 2 loaf pans. Combine oil, applesauce and honey. Combine dry ingredients and blend in egg and vanilla. Stir in zucchini. Fold in nuts. Evenly distribute between the two prepared loaf pans and bake for 45 to 50 minutes or until toothpick inserted in middle comes out clean.

Orange Yogurt Bread

With the combination of sweet and tang, how can you not like this? Use some imagination with the yogurt. Lemon yogurt could only add to the taste.

1 1/2 c. sugar
1/2 c. butter or margarine
2 eggs
1 1/2 c. flour
1 1/2 t baking powder
1/2 t. salt
1/2 c. orange juice
1 T. grated orange peel
1 c. plain yogurt
Orange Icing, *recipe below*

Preheat oven to 350°F. Grease and flour a 9 × 5-inch loaf pan. In a large mixing bowl cream butter and sugar until fluffy. Add eggs; beat well. In a separate bowl, stir together flour, baking powder, and salt. In a small bowl combine orange juice, orange peel, and yogurt. Add dry ingredients to creamed mixture alternately with yogurt mixture. Pour batter into prepared pan. Bake for 50 to 55 minutes or until toothpick inserted in middle comes out clean. Cool in pan 10 minutes. Remove bread from pan and cool on a rack. Frost with Orange Icing while bread is still warm.

Orange Icing:
3/4 c. powdered sugar
4 T. orange juice
1 T. orange liqueur or
    Triple Sec (optional)

In a small bowl combine all ingredients and beat until mixture is smooth.

> To Keep Oranges and Lemons; Take small sand and make it very dry; after it is cold, put a quantity of it into a clean vessel; then take your oranges and set a laying of them in the sand so they do not touch, and strew in some of the sand to cover them two inches deep. Then set your vessel in a cold place, and you will find your fruit high preserved in several months.
>
> –*The Family Receipt Book*, 1819

Sweet Butters

These butters are delicious on muffins, sweet breads, French toast, pancakes, waffles... or try them on your morning toast as well.

1/2 c. sweet butter, softened to room temperature

With the back of a wooden spoon, cream the butter until it is light and fluffy. Gradually blend in any of the following flavorings:

To make **Cinnamon Butter:** add 1/2 c. dark brown sugar and 1 t. ground cinnamon

To make **Honey Butter:** add 1/2 c. honey

To make **Honey Nut Butter:** add 1/2 c. honey and 1/4 c. finely chopped walnuts or pecans

To make **Raspberry Butter:** add 3/4 c. sweetened, frozen raspberries

To make **Strawberry Butter:** add 1/2 c. mashed fresh strawberries and 1/2 c. powdered sugar

To make **Maple Butter:** add 2 T. real maple syrup. The darker the grade, the more intense the flavor

Bakewell Cream Biscuits

If I had to choose a biscuit for my last supper, it would be these. Maybe I am biased because this is all my father ever made at his restaurants but to be quite honest, they are the bomb. I know, I have to learn today's lingo but I am too old for that. Better than saying groovy isn't it?

4 c. flour
4 t. Bakewell Cream
2 t. baking soda
1 t. salt
1/2 c. vegetable shortening
1 1/2 to 2 c. milk

Preheat oven to 475°F. Mix and sift the dry ingredients. Add the shortening and mix with a pastry blender. Add milk at once and stir quickly with a large, sturdy spoon, or use your hands, to make a nice, soft dough. Turn out onto a floured board and knead 5 or 6 times. Roll or pat to 1/2- to 3/4-inch thickness. Cut with a biscuit cutter and place on ungreased cookie sheet. Bake for 5 minutes. Turn off heat and leave in the oven for 8 to 10 minutes, or until golden brown.

Baking Powder Biscuits

The old stand-by. Why I don't see many people making these fluffy, creamy white biscuits anymore is beyond me. I can't eat barbecued chicken without Baking Powder Biscuits.

2 c. flour
1 T. baking powder
1 t. salt
1/4 c. vegetable shortening
3/4 c. milk

Preheat oven to 350°F. Into a large bowl, stir flour, baking powder, and salt; stir until combined. With your hands or pastry blender, cut shortening into mixture until it resembles coarse crumbs. Stir in milk; quickly mix just until mixture forms a soft dough that leaves side of bowl. Turn dough onto lightly floured surface; knead only until it holds together. With floured rolling pin, roll out dough 1/2 inch for high fluffy biscuits or 1/4 inch for thin, crusty ones.

With floured biscuit cutter, cut out biscuits. Remove to ungreased baking pan so that they are barely touching each other for soft biscuits and separated by a 1/2 inch for crusty biscuits all-around. Press trimmings together and repeat process until dough is completely used. You may brush tops with either milk or beaten egg to form a golden crusted top if desired. Bake 18 to 20 minutes or until golden brown and toothpick inserted in middle comes out clean.

For **Drop Biscuits:** Use 1 c. milk and simply drop the dough (without kneading) onto baking sheet and cook as previously directed.

For **Flavored Biscuits:**

Add 1/2 c. cooked, crumbled bacon to dough before kneading.

Add 1/2 c. Cheddar cheese, shredded, before kneading.

Add 1/2 c. chopped ham before kneading.

Add 3 T. fresh chopped chives before kneading.

Add imagination.

Drop Biscuits

Beat eight eggs very light, add to them twelve ounces of flour and one pound of sugar. When perfectly light, drop them on tin sheets and bake them in a quick oven.

-*The Virginia Housewife*, 1825

Buttermilk Biscuits

Let's try cake flour for a light and very fluffy biscuit. I think you'll find buttermilk makes all the difference.

3 c. cake flour
2 1/4 t. baking powder
3/4 t. baking soda
3/4 t. salt
1/2 c. vegetable shortening
1 c. buttermilk

Preheat oven to 350°F. In large bowl combine cake flour, baking powder, baking soda, and salt. With pastry blender or hands, cut in shortening until evenly distributed and about the size of a half a pea. Add buttermilk to flour mixture; mix together with hand just until dough forms. On lightly floured surface, pat dough into a square about 7 inches by 7 inches. Cut dough into 4 strips, and then cut each strip crosswise into 4 pieces to make 16 square biscuits. Place biscuits on ungreased large cookie sheet and bake until lightly golden, about 18 to 20 minutes.

To make **Sour Cream Biscuits:** Substitute 1 c. sour cream for the buttermilk.

To make **Maple Sugar Biscuits:** Brush tops of biscuits with melted butter or margarine and sprinkle grated maple sugar over the top.

Pumpkin Biscuits

Go ahead and get the spiced pumpkin filling if you have to, but go for the plain pumpkin puree first, only because the pumpkin flavor will be more pronounced.

2 1/2 c. flour
2 t. baking powder
1/2 t. salt
1/4 c. sugar
1/4 t. mace
1/2 c. shortening
1/2 can (1 cup) pumpkin filling
1 c. milk

Preheat oven to 350°F. Combine all dry ingredients in large bowl; blend well. With your hands or beater, mix in the shortening until it forms nuggets the size of peas. Add remainder of ingredients and mix until just blended. Turn out on lightly floured work surface and knead only until it holds together, about 1 minute. Roll out 1/2 inch thick with floured rolling pin. Use biscuit cutter or cut out in squares by hand, and place biscuits on ungreased baking sheet just barely touching each other.

Repeat the process with dough scraps until it is all used. Brush tops with milk or beaten egg and bake 18 to 20 minutes or until golden brown. Insert toothpick in middle. If it comes out clean, the biscuits are done.

Biscuits, as well as any other bread or pie, were always served to the visiting parson, maybe washed down with a little rum as well. The parson's cupboard was a little space in the chimney above the mantel that didn't get too hot and was great for anything that needed to be hidden. Here was kept the bottle of Yankee rum, from which it was the custom for the good householder to treat the parson when he called. Some speculation arose, at times, as to how many calls it was wise for the parson to make in one afternoon. One minister had his grown daughter driving him in the chaise. He made several calls while his daughter attended to the horse. Late in the afternoon, she noted that the good father walked a bit unsteady and cautioned him about the amount of good cheer he should take on the last call. But the host was so persuasive that on approaching the chaise, the minister looked at his daughter and said, "Who is that girl sitting beside you?"

Stuffings

Sausage and Cornbread Stuffing

As you can see, I have taken the liberty of making this recipe a quick and easy one. I don't normally use prepackaged stuffing mixes but if I don't use one here, you would be left to prepare cornbread from scratch, bake it, cool it, and crumble it. This recipe is truly delicious as it is, without losing its New England flavor or distinction.

1 lb. sausage meat
3 stalks celery, chopped
4 T. butter or margarine
1 onion, chopped
1 red bell pepper, chopped
1 can (14 to 16 oz.) chicken broth
3/4 c. water
1/2 t. black pepper
1 pkg. (14 to 16 oz.) cornbread stuffing mix
1 c. pecans, toasted in oven at 350°F for 5 minutes, then chopped

Heat skillet over medium-high heat. Add sausage meat and cook, breaking sausage up with side of large spoon, until well browned; drain all liquid, reserving 2 tablespoons. Place back on burner and add reserved drippings, celery, margarine, onion, and red pepper; cook, stirring occasionally, until vegetables are browned. Stir in broth, water, and black pepper; heat to boiling, stirring to loosen and lift the browned bits from the bottom of the skillet. Add vegetable mixture, cornbread stuffing mix, and pecans to sausage; stir to mix well. Use to stuff poultry or spoon into baking dish and bake, uncovered, at 325°F until browned and crisp on top and heated through.

Corn Meal Bread

Rub a piece of butter the size of an egg into a pint of corn meal. Make it a batter with two eggs and some new milk. Add a spoonful of yeast. Set it by the fire an hour to rise. Butter little pans and bake it.

—The Virginia Housewife, 1825

Wild Rice Stuffing

Although this recipe has the same basic ingredients as regular stuffing, the texture is what distinguishes this colorful and aromatic dressing.

4 c. chicken broth
1 1/2 c. water
3/4 c. wild rice
1 t. salt
1/2 t. dried thyme
4 medium carrots, peeled and sliced
2 stalks celery, sliced
1 medium onion, chopped
10 oz. mushrooms,
   cleaned and sliced
1 1/2 c. long grain rice
3 T. vegetable oil

In 4-quart saucepan, heat broth, water, wild rice, salt and thyme to boiling over high heat. Reduce heat to low; cover and simmer 35 minutes.

Meanwhile, in nonstick skillet, heat 1 T. oil over medium-high heat. Add carrots, celery, and onion and cook until tender-crisp, stirring occasionally. Transfer carrot mixture to bowl. In same skillet, heat remaining oil over medium-high heat and add mushrooms; cook, stirring occasionally, until golden brown and liquid has evaporated.

Stir long-grain rice, carrot mixture, and mushrooms into wild rice; heat to boiling over high heat. Reduce heat to low; cover and simmer until liquid has been absorbed, about 20 minutes longer. Use to stuff poultry or bake in oven until crisp on top.

Some Tips When Using Rice

Uncooked rice to cooked rice is always about a 1 to 3 ratio or 1 c. rice to 3 c. water.

We are so used to having fluffy and separated rice that we have forgotten that rice is meant to be sticky and starchy when eaten. Think about this, how else are people supposed to pick up the rice with chopsticks, a grain at a time?

A teaspoon or two of lemon juice in cooking rice will help to keep it white.

Apple Chestnut Stuffing

You can find chestnuts year-round in health food stores. If you wait until the holidays, the major supermarkets carry them as well. Try this recipe for the taste your ancestors enjoyed.

2 lbs. chestnuts in the shell
6 T. butter or margarine
2 stalks celery, sliced
1 medium onion, chopped
4 apples, peeled, cored, chopped
2 t. poultry seasoning
2 c. chicken broth
1 c. water
1 t. salt
1 loaf day-old French bread, sliced
   and cut in 1/2 -inch cubes

In 3-quart saucepan, place chestnuts and enough water to cover. Heat to boiling over high heat. Reduce heat to medium; cover and cook 10 minutes. Remove saucepan from heat and with slotted spoon, transfer 3 or 4 chestnuts at

a time from water to cutting board. Cut each chestnut in half. With spoon or tip of small knife, scrape out chestnut meat from its shell. Chop any large pieces of chestnut meat; place chestnuts in large bowl. Discard cooking water and toss bread cubes with chestnuts.

In same saucepan, melt margarine over medium heat. Add celery and onion and cook, stirring occasionally, until vegetables are golden brown and tender, about 10 minutes. Add apples and poultry seasoning; cook, stirring occasionally, 2 minutes longer. Stir in broth, water and salt, and heat to boiling over high heat. Pour apple mixture into chestnut mixture; toss with the bread cubes to mix well. Use to stuff poultry or bake in oven, uncovered, until crisp and heated through.

Herbed Mushroom Stuffing

This stuffing is great for poultry and pork alike. Slice pork chops horizontally all the way to the bone. Place a tablespoon of cooked stuffing inside and bake until chops are done. The fragrance of the sage lends itself to this stuffing in a way few other spices are able to.

1 lb. fresh mushrooms, sliced
4 lg. stalks celery, sliced
1 onion, chopped
1/2 c. butter or margarine
3/4 c. chicken broth
1 day-old loaf of bread, cubed
1 (8-oz.) can water chestnuts, drained and chopped
2 t. poultry seasoning
3/4 t. rubbed sage
1/2 . t. black pepper

In large skillet, cook mushrooms, celery, and onion in margarine until tender. Add chicken broth, remove from heat. In large bowl combine remaining ingredients; add broth mixture and mix well. Use to stuff poultry or bake in oven, uncovered, until crisp and heated through.

Seasoned Bread Stuffing

Now I know it's much easier to buy packaged stuffing, but take the time (and it doesn't take much) to give everyone a gift of this side dish. Perfect and reminiscent of the glory days of home cooking.

1 small onion, chopped
1/2 c. finely chopped celery
1/4 c. butter or margarine
10 c. day-old bread cubes
1 t. poultry seasoning
1 t. ground sage
1/2 t. black pepper
2 c. chicken broth
4 eggs, beaten

Cook onion and celery in butter over medium-high heat 5 minutes, or until soft. Combine with all other ingredients and toss until well incorporated. Use to stuff poultry or grease oven-proof baking pan and bake at 350°F for 40 to 45 minutes, uncovered, until browned on top and set in the middle.

On Sage

Sage staies [sic] abortion, causeth fruitfullness, is singular good for the brain, helps stitches and pains in the sides.

–Nicholas Culpepper, author of *English Herbals*, first published in 1653

Fruited Stuffing

Rolled in a loin of pork, this stuffing is sick! (There I go again, isn't that what the young people call something cool, neat, awesome…) However you describe this, it's a great blend of fruit and nuts.

10 c. day-old bread, cubed
3 medium oranges, peeled, sectioned, and chopped
2 apples, peeled, cored, and chopped
3/4 c. raisins
1/2 c. pecans, toasted in 300°F oven for 10 min., then chopped
2 c. chicken broth
3 eggs, beaten
1 t. nutmeg

In large mixing bowl combine all ingredients until well blended. Use as stuffing for poultry or bake in 300°F oven, uncovered, 45 to 50 minutes or until well browned on top and set in the middle.

Seafood Stuffing

This stuffing is great with stuffed fish, jumbo shrimp, or put it in the bottom of a greased baking pan and topped with any seafood or fish you desire. Bake in 400°F oven, uncovered, until any topping is cooked through. Remove from oven and dish out immediately.

1/2 c. chopped onion
1/2 c. chopped celery
4 oz. sea scallops
1 lb. butter, divided
2 1/4 lb. saltine crackers
1 t. dried thyme
3 eggs, beaten
1 t. black pepper
1 can (7 oz.) cooked shrimp
1 can (7 oz.) crabmeat

In medium sized saucepan, cook onion, celery, and scallops in 4 T. butter on medium-high heat until scallops are cooked through, about 7 to 8 minutes, turning often. Remove from heat and with butter knife and fork, cut scallops penny size. In large bowl crush crackers into crumbs and add the thyme. Add the cooked shrimp and crabmeat along with any cooking liquid, eggs, pepper, and 3/4 c. melted butter. Toss until well moistened throughout. If needed, melt more butter and add until stuffing is moist.

Fall in New England

CHAPTER 3

Beverages

Old World Sack Posset

This beverage has been enjoyed for many centuries, both in the Mother country (England) and in New England since the time of colonization. Posset is derived from *pos* ("cold in the head") and *waet* ("drink"), in other words a drink good for a cold in the head. That is why this drink was and is mainly consumed in the colder months in New England. Sack is a synonym for a strong, light colored wine originally coming from Spain and the Canary Islands.

1/2 c. sugar
1 qt. dry sherry*
3 t. nutmeg
1 t. cinnamon
18 eggs, well beaten
2 qt. milk, or half and half

Combine sugar, sherry, and spices in a nonstick saucepan. Heat thoroughly but do not bring to a boil! Keep stirring frequently until sugar is dissolved; remove from heat and cool to tepid.

Beat eggs until well mixed and frothy; pour into saucepan with the milk and return to low heat. You may also use a double boiler if unable to tend to it constantly. Cook, stirring quite frequently, until thick enough to coat the back of a spoon.

Serve hot or cold, dusted with spices.

You may substitute sherry with your choice of a dry, light-colored wine.

A health to the King and Queene here.
Nexte crown the Bowle full
With gentle lamb's woll;
Add sugar, nutmeg and ginger,
With store of ale-too;
And this ye must do
to make a wassail a swinger.

—Robert Herrick, 1591–1674

Sack Posset

Take ten eggs, beat the yolks and whites together and strain them into a quart of cream. Season it with nutmeg, cinnamon and sugar, put to them a pint of canary, stir them well together, put them in your basin, then set it over a chaffing dish of coals, and stir it till it be indifferently thick, then scrape on sugar and serve it.

– *The Family Dictionary,* 1705

Wassail

Since medieval times, this spiced ale has been favored; its name coming from the Anglo-Saxon *was hal*, meaning "be Hale." This drink was passed around the table and everyone drank from this communal mug. Those poorer celebrants would carry an empty wooden bowl through the streets of Old England while singing hymnals and carols, hoping someone would share their warmed brew.

1 qt. of choice ale*
3 or 4 sticks of cinnamon
1 1/2 t. dried ginger
1 orange, sliced thin
1 lemon, sliced thin
Sugar, to taste
3 apples, baked until almost soft
A couple toast slices (optional)

Heat your favorite ale in an enameled saucepan until almost boiling. Stir in the ginger, cinnamon sticks, and sugar. Stir until sugar dissolves; reduce heat to low and simmer for at least 30 minutes, uncovered. Keep checking to make sure it does not boil. Float the baked apples on top with the toast and serve.

During the 1700s, beer was added instead of ale and brown sugar had begun to be added.

Apple juice or cider may be substituted for the ale, thereby making this a Cider Wassail. You may also substitute dark rum for what is called an English Farmers Wassail or experiment with your favorite unflavored liquor for your own pleasure and name it yourself.

Swedish Glogg

True Swedish Glogg is flamed using sugar cubes that have been soaked in rum for a few minutes and then lit while being held over the punch with a strainer of some type. Here is an Americanized version of this Swedish Christmas punch that began in the Scandinavian countries and was brought over to New England by the Swedes. It is still enjoyed by settlements scattered throughout the Yankee states.

2 qts. apple juice or cider
4 sticks of cinnamon
3 T. whole cloves
10 whole cardamom, shelled and
   crushed
1/2 t. nutmeg
1 lb. raisins
2 unpeeled oranges
32 oz. of your favorite brandy
1 liter dark rum

Combine apple juice or cider, cinnamon, cloves, cardamom, and nutmeg in large enameled saucepan; simmer, covered, for 30 minutes. Pour in the raisins and replace cover. Remove to refrigerator and let set overnight.

One hour before serving bring mixture to a boil, reduce heat to low and simmer for 30 minutes. Quarter unpeeled orange and add to saucepan along with brandy and rum; remove from heat. Let stand 30 minutes and serve warm.

Today we know that city councils and state ordinances everywhere do not allow taverns and bars from locating themselves anywhere near schools and churches. But during the early years of the colonization of America, and many generations afterwards, the newly formed laws of this land stated that taverns, "ordinaries" as they were referred to then, were to be built in close proximity to schools, churches, town halls, and anywhere a public gathering could be held. "For the convenience of its citizens" was the only reason this was allowed!

Orange-Cranberry Tea

Cut the chill on a cold winter morning with a mug of this fruited tea drink.

1 c. orange juice
1 c. cranberry juice cocktail
2 T. sugar
4, 2-inch long cinnamon sticks
2 c. water
4 tea bags
Whole cranberries
Sliced oranges

In a medium saucepan stir together orange juice, cranberry juice cocktail, sugar, cinnamon, and 2 c. water. Bring to boil; reduce heat to low and simmer with cover 15 minutes. Remove from heat and add tea bags. Cover and let stand for 10 minutes; discard tea bags. To serve, pour into 4 mugs, each mug to get 1 cinnamon stick. Garnish with whole cranberries and orange slices if desired.

Tea drinking has been around since 2700 B.C. The word tea was pronounced *tay* until the mid 1700s, when it was generally pronounced *tea*. The colonists first boiled the tea leaves for a long time, drank the tea without milk or sugar, and then sprinkled seasonings on these used tea leaves and ate them. Being a thrifty Yankee compelled these settlers to use them as sustenance, especially with tea selling at the rate of $30–$50 dollars a pound. If it wasn't for the Boston Tea Party, Americans would be a nation of tea drinkers. But because of this incident, coffee came into vogue.

Orange Cider

Cider is to New England as water is to a sailor. You will never be able to separate the two. One reason Yankees are so associated with cider is that water during the early colonization of New England was dreadfully ill tasting at times. Cider was drunk morning, noon, and night by all members of the family, including children. Now you're probably saying that's no so bad! The cider of generations gone by was alcoholic cider, quite tame, proof-wise, but spirituous nonetheless. Enjoy this beverage without the alcoholic content.

3 c. orange juice
1 c. apple cider or apple juice
1 cinnamon stick
1/4 t. whole cloves

In a saucepan combine all ingredients and bring to a boil; reduce heat to low and simmer, covered, for 15 minutes. Remove from heat, sieve to remove cloves and cinnamon stick, and pour into mugs to enjoy. Dust with powdered cinnamon if desired.

Cider from 1823

Cider should be made from ripe apples only, and for this reason and to prevent fermentation, it is better to make it late in the season. Use only the best-flavored grafted fruit, rejecting all that are decayed or wormy. The best mills crush, not grind, the apples. The utmost neatness is necessary throughout the process. Press and strain juice as it comes from the press through a woolen cloth into a perfectly clean barrel; let stand two or three days if cool, if warm, not more than a day; rack once a week for four weeks, put in bottles and cork tightly. This will make perfect unfermented cider. Do not put anything in it to preserve it, as all so-called preservatives are humbugs. Lay the bottles away on the sides in sawdust.

–The Yankee Chef Archives

Cranberry Hot Toddy

Originally, this was called Bailey Hill Toddy. My great, great, great uncle's name was Gus Bailey. He and two other family members owned a tavern in Topsfield during the mid-1800s. He is said to have served only one kind of toddy at this ramshackle tavern, and this was it. He would boil down maple sap to syrup consistency at home and then bring this sweet syrup to the tavern. Here he would let the fermentation begin until complete. He then would add an equal amount of creek water from Bailey Stream on top of Bailey Hill and some molasses. When a woodsman came in from the cold and wanted some toddy, he would ladle it out into a pot hanging over the open fire and bring it to the guest scalding. Pouring this mixture into a mug, it certainly warmed the innards of a cold soul once a jigger or two of rum was added.

4 tangerines
40 whole cloves
3 qts. cranberry juice, not cocktail
1 c. sugar, or more to taste
3 c. favorite rum

Cut the tangerines in half and remove as many seeds as possible. Squeeze juice into separate container. Stud each tangerine with 10 cloves each. In large saucepan simmer cranberry juice, tangerines, and reserved tangerine juice, and sugar to taste for 15 minutes with cover on. Remove from heat and add rum. Either serve in large punch bowl or divide into mugs insuring no seed or whole cloves escape the tangerines.

Here are some every-day items that hold odd traditional names:

Halleluiah was a dish made of salt pork, onions and potatoes.

A *Piggin* was a Yankee pail with an upright stave for its handle.

A *Skeel* was a shallow trencher to hold milk while it separated.

A *Losset* was a wooden container to hold fresh milk for the family.

A *Noggin* was a small mug with a carved handle on its side.

Hot Buttered Rum

A simple and purely authentic New England drink.

1 piece cinnamon stick
1 t. sugar, granular or powdered
1 slice lemon
2 jiggers rum (3 oz. each)
Boiling water
Butter or margarine

In a hot, old fashioned mug, combine cinnamon stick, sugar, lemon, and rum and stir until sugar is dissolved. Float a butter pat on top.

Deluxe Hot Chocolate

Deluxe? That doesn't even begin to describe the smooth, ultra-chocolaty, richness.

2 bars (1 oz. each) unsweetened baking chocolate, broken into pieces
1 can (14 oz.) sweetened condensed milk
4 c. boiling water
1 t. vanilla extract
Whipped cream
Ground cinnamon

Melt chocolate in large heavy saucepan over low heat. When thoroughly melted, add sweetened condensed milk. Slowly add boiling water until well blended. Stir in vanilla and garnish with whipped cream sprinkled with cinnamon.

Coffee Milk

Boil a dessert spoonful of ground coffee, in nearly a pint of milk, a quarter of an hour; then put into it a shaving or two of isinglass and clear it. Let it boil a few minutes and set it on the side of the fire to grow fine.

—A New System of Domestic Cookery, 1807

Peppermint Mocha Coffee

An ideal Christmas morning brew that sparks the festive occasion quite well, or simply a soothing, warm beverage that may help you forget about that nasty cold you picked up in the wintry outdoors of New England.

6 c. freshly brewed coffee
4 squares semi-sweet
   baking chocolate
1 1/2 c. hot milk
1 t. peppermint extract
Peppermint sticks

Pour coffee into large saucepan. Add chocolate; cook on low heat for 5 minutes or until chocolate is melted, stirring frequently. Add milk and extract; stir until well blended and garnish each serving with a peppermint stick to stir with.

From a tavern in Hartford, Connecticut, comes the following bill, dated 1784, for three ministers visiting the city for 2 days. This bill was presented to the Second Congregational Church to be paid when the ministers had left. Today, the English pound (£) is worth about a buck and a half, the English shilling (sh) is worth about $0.25 and the English pence (d) is but a little over a penny.

> May 4th: to Keeping Ministers, etc.
>   2 mugs toddy 2 sh 4 d
>   1 pt wine 5 sh 10 d
>
> May 5th
>   15 bowles punch 1 £ 10 sh
>   11 bottles wine 6 sh
>   5 mugs flip 5 sh 10 d
>   3 boles punch 6 sh
>   3 boles toddy 3 sh 6 d

I must say that three ministers drank quite a sum for under $20, remembering that prices naturally were much different than today. But I also wonder what the temperance-minded Puritans must have thought about this. Their "punch" was not the punch our children drink today!

Wines

A good wine makes the meal, toasts the occasion, and caps the celebration. But which wine is best for which event? At your neighborhood store, you will find hundreds of premium selections from celebrated vineyards the world over. Rich, ripe, sweet, or dry, you may be a little confused at which type of wine to serve or enjoy with your loved one. Here are a few hints to help you decide.

Cabernet

This wine is often called the "king" of red grapes. Cabernet Sauvignon, along with Merlot, is the Bordeaux regions' favorite. California, Washington, Italy, Australia, and other countries also make superb Cabernets. It is considered dry to medium and full-bodied. Pair this wine with a cheese tray or appetizers containing meat.

Chardonnay

One of the most popular white grape varieties in America and throughout the new world, as well as the white grape of the Burgundy region of France. Very easy to enjoy thanks to its full, round body and buttery, apple flavor laced with toastiness. This toastiness is from the aged oak barrels used in making this favorite of wines. Chardonnay goes extremely well with many dishes, while not pairing very well with meat dishes, pasta, or desserts. Pouilly-fume, Chablis, Sauvignon Blanc, Puilly Fuisse, and Gewürztraminer are other light-bodied white wines that favor the same pairings.

Merlot

This is the most widely planted grape in Bordeaux, the red Merlot grape is also grown in most of the same places as Cabernet Sauvignon. In fact, the two are often blended together. Mocha and boysenberry are two flavors Merlot is associated with.
Full-bodied and fruity, enjoy this wine with cheese, beef, veal, pork, pasta, and poultry dishes.

Pinot Grigio

Like Pinot Blanc and Riesling, Pinot Grigio is grown best in cold climates. The best Pinot comes from northern Italy, particularly those regions that border the Alps, as well as Alsace (where it is called Pinot Gris). Light almond, lemon, and vanilla flavors are predominant. With its crisp taste, almost anything goes well with this wine, saving beef and lamb for another wine.

Zinfandel

The classic red grape of California, zinfandel is rarely found anywhere else. It is believed to have originally come to America with Central European emigrants. Zinfandel has a berry like flavor that is sometimes described as being thick and sweet. White Zinfandel is made without the deep purple skins when the grapes are fermented. This would be the perfect accompaniment with meats and lamb. Shiraz, Beaujolais, Chianti, and Pinot Noir are other wines favored with like pairings.

Champagne

Champagne refers to a particular method of wine producing in the Champagne region of France. Elsewhere, it is referred to as sparkling wine due to the bubbles produced during the unusual double fermentation process. Sparkling wine is not a variety itself but most often a combination of the varieties Chardonnay, Pinot Noir, and Pinot Meunier. There is also Blanc de Blancs, which is an ideal aperitif. Extra dry, brut, and rose are dry and are considered great dinner drinks. Sec Champagne is slightly sweet but not so much as Doux, which is very sweet.

Temperature can have a significant influence on the quality of your wine. White and blush should be served at 55 to 60°F, red at 62 to 67°F, and Champagne at a crisp 45°F. If tasting more than one type of wine, remember to drink light before heavy, white before red, and simple before more complex.

Wine Tasting Terminology:

Acid: sour or tart taste in wine

Aroma: the fruity scent in a young wine

Body: the concentration or substance of a wine in the mouth (light, medium, or full-bodied)

Bouquet: the complex scent of older wines

Crisp: the sharp taste of wine

Dry: wine containing little sugar

Fermentation: the process by which grape juice is made into wine

Finish: the impression a wine leaves on your tongue

Soft: smooth rather than crisp, not sweet

Vintage: the year the grapes are harvested

Dandelion Wine

Why is this recipe here? Because more often than not, someone in your family made this if you are a Yankee. My father hid it from us kids growing up. He kept it in the cellar and we all knew to stay out of Dad's stash, and we did!

2 qt. whole dandelion flowers
4 qt. water
3 T. lime juice
I c. orange juice
3 T. lemon juice
1/2 t. dried ginger
8 whole cloves
3 T. coarsely chopped orange zest;
    avoid any white pith
I T. coarsely chopped lemon zest;
    avoid any white pith
6 c. sugar
I package dried brewing yeast
1/4 c. warm water

Wash and clean the blossoms well. Place the blossoms in the four quarts of water, along with the lime, orange, and lemon juices. Stir in the ginger, cloves, orange peels, lemon peels, and sugar. Bring the mix to a boil for an hour.

Soak flowers for two days. Strain the dandelion liquid. Strain through coffee filters. Let the liquid cool down for a while. Stir the yeast into the 1/4 cup warm water and then add into this wine-to-be while still warm, but below 100 °F. Cover it and leave it alone, let it stand overnight.

Pour it into bottles, poke a few holes in some balloons and place over the tops of the bottles to create an airlock that keeps out unwanted wild yeasts. Store them in a dark place for at least three weeks so that it can ferment. At this point, you now have wine. Rack the wine several times, optional. Racking means waiting until the wine clears, then siphoning or pouring the liquid into another container, leaving the lees (sediment) at the bottom of the first container. Cork and store the bottles in a cool place. Allow the wine a while to age. Most recipes recommend waiting at least six months, preferably a year.

Blueberry Shrub

Shrubs have also been part of our Yankee fare since colonial times. The following is a new version of this ole' summertime drink. Look familiar? It should, it eerily resembles smoothies of today.

I 1/2 c. skim milk
I 1/2 c. plain yogurt
I 1/2 c. fresh blueberries
3 T. honey
I t. vanilla or almond extract

Puree all ingredients until smooth, refrigerate, and enjoy topped with whipped cream and a straw.

The Classic Milkshake: In a blender combine 3 scoops of chocolate ice cream with 1 c. whole milk and 2 T. chocolate fudge sauce; blend until smooth. Drizzle chocolate syrup into a chilled glass and pour the shake into it. Top with shaved chocolate and whipped cream. Before pouring into glasses, blend in some chocolate vodka, orange liqueur, coffee vodka, or a fruit-infused tequila for something a little different.

Blueberry-Watermelon Frosty: In a blender combine 6 oz. frozen limeade or lemonade concentrate, 2 c. fresh blueberries, and 2 c. seedless watermelon cubes. Puree until smooth and add 1 c. ice cubes. Blend until slushy and add sugar if needed

The Elvis Shake (OK, so maybe the kids have never heard of Elvis, but they will enjoy this beverage nonetheless): In a blender combine 1 c. crushed ice, 1 1/4 c. milk, 3 T. peanut butter, and a banana that has been peeled and sliced. Pulse until it is smooth. Add 1 1/2 c. vanilla ice cream that has been softened a bit and continue whirling in the blender until it is smooth. Serve.

Pomegranate Cosmos: Fill a pitcher with ice and add 3/4 c. vodka, 1/3 c. triple sec, 1/3 c. sweetened lime juice, and 1/3 c. pomegranate juice; stir. Dip rims of 4 glasses in water and then in some coarse sugar. Strain drink into the glasses and prop some slices of lime on the rims for garnish.

Egg Nog (An 1836 recipe): "Beat well the Yolks of 3 dozen Eggs, slowly beat in 2 and a half Pounds of sugar. Add Slowly, Drop by drop, one Pint of Brandy. Let stand while you Beat the whites very light with Half Pound of Sugar. Add to the Yolks two Quarts of Milk, two Quarts of cream and one Gallon of Brandy. Add the Whites and grate in Nutmeg." From The Yankee Chef Archives.

Chocolate Mint Frosty: Pour 2 c. milk and 6 ice cubes into a blender with 1 c. frozen, whipped topping; 1 package (4-serving size) instant chocolate pudding mix; and 6 mint patties. Puree until smooth.

Fruity Float: Mix 1 T. grape-flavored drink powder (sugar-added) to 1/2 c. ginger ale in a tall glass. Add 1 scoop vanilla ice cream and top with a dollop of thawed, whipped topping and a cherry. Try this using any flavored drink powder, as long as it is pre-sweetened.

The Shandy: This beverage is for adults only. A British drink now very popular in the Caribbean, it is traditionally equal parts beer and ginger beer or ginger ale, but you can make this a Pink Shandy by using equal parts thawed pink lemonade concentrate with beer. Mix well and serve very cold. The types of beer best for this beverage are bock, lager, pilsner, or Mexican.

Rocky Road Freeze: In small bowl, stir 1 can (14 oz.) sweetened condensed milk with 1/2 c. chocolate-flavored syrup until blended; set aside. In large bowl, with mixer at medium speed, beat 2 c. heavy cream until stiff peaks form. With rubber spatula, fold chocolate mixture, 1 c. mini-marshmallows, 6 oz. chopped chocolate pieces, and 1/2 c. your favorite peanuts into whipped cream until blended. Cover bowl with plastic wrap; freeze until firm, about 4 hours. Scoop out when ready to serve.

Homemade Lemonade

Dr. Zerobabel Endecott, of Salem, Massachusetts, left a manuscript listing medical recipes during the seventeenth century: "For Extreme Thirst & Vomiting in a Malignant Feuer [fever], Take salt of wormwood and a spoonfull of the juce of Lemonds, mix them in a spoon & giue it the patient."

2/3 c. water
6 T. sugar
1 t. grated lemon zest
1/2 c. lemon juice
Sparkling water
6 ice cubes

Put the water, sugar, and lemon zest into a small pan and bring to a boil, constantly stirring. Continue to boil for 5 minutes; remove from heat and let cool to room temperature. Stir in the lemon juice, transfer to a pitcher, cover with film wrap, and refrigerate for at least 2 hours. When done, take two glasses with ice cubes and pour your drink over cubes along with sparkling water. The ratio should be one part lemonade to three parts sparkling water.

New Fashioned Pineapple Soda

Pineapple has a substance called bromelaine, a powerful tenderizer. Still called *pinas*, meaning "cone," in Latin America, it takes between 18 to 21 months to produce a single pineapple. They are a symbol of hospitality and at one time were so rare they were referred to as "the fruit of the Kings."

3/4 c. pineapple juice
1/3 c. coconut milk
7 oz. vanilla ice cream
5 oz. pineapple chunks
3/4 c. sparkling water

Pour the pineapple juice and coconut milk into a food processor and add the ice cream; process till smooth. Add the pineapple chunks and process well. Pour the mixture into tall glasses, until two-thirds full, top with sparkling water.

A popular drink for us Yankees during the 1800s was the Cherry Bounce, made as follows:

High falutin' people called this cherry cordial. Fill a gallon jar with wild cherries and pour in enough rum to cover. Let stand for 3 weeks then pour off the clear liquor and set aside. Mash the cherries, breaking the stones, and drain in a bag. Add this to the first pouring off. For every 2 quarts of liquor from the cherries, take a pound of white sugar dissolved in a gill of water, bring to boil and mix with the liquor. Bottle and stand for several weeks.

–Recipe from the author's collection

Strawberry Orange Smoothie

The ultimate smoothie. A thick blend of your favorite fruit and juice.

1/2 c. plain yogurt
3/4 c. strawberry yogurt
1/2 c. orange juice
3/4 c. frozen strawberries
1 banana, sliced and frozen

Pour the plain and strawberry yogurts into a food processor and process until mixed. Add the orange juice and process until well combined. Add the strawberries and banana and process until smooth.

Orange-Carrot Smoothie

Vitamin A is known to prevent "night blindness," and carrots are loaded with Vitamin A. One carrot provides more than 200% of recommended daily intake of Vitamin A.

3/4 c. carrot juice
3/4 c. orange juice
6 oz. vanilla ice cream
6 ice cubes

Pour the carrot and orange juices into a food processor and process gently until well combined. Add the ice cream and process until blended. Add the ice cubes and process till smooth.

Peach-Pineapple Smoothie

A tropical delight that eases your sweet tooth and makes you feel like spending the day outside.

1/2 c. pineapple juice
Juice of 1 lemon
1/2 c. water
3 T. brown sugar
3/4 c. plain yogurt
1 peach, chunked and frozen
4 oz. pineapple chunks, frozen

Pour the pineapple and lemon juices, along with the water, into a food processor. Add the sugar and yogurt and process until blended. Add the peach and pineapple chunks and process until smooth.

Hawaiian Shake

The word coconut comes from the Spanish *coco*, meaning "a grimacing face," which describes the three dark spots at the bottom of a coconut that resemble a human or monkey face.

1 c. milk
1/4 c. coconut milk
6 oz. vanilla ice cream
2 bananas, sliced and frozen
7 oz. pineapple chunks, drained
1 papaya, seeded and diced

Pour the milks into a food processor and process gently until combined. Add half of the ice cream and process gently, and then add the remaining ice cream and process until smooth. Add the bananas and process well, and then add the pineapple chunks and papaya and process until smooth.

CHAPTER 4
Soups, Stews, and Chowders

Throughout history, soup has been no more than broth flavored with no more than the item cooking in it. Mutton, wild game, poultry, or vegetables were the norm. One of the earliest mentions of soup is found in the Bible where, in the Book of Genesis, Esau sold his birthright for a pottage of lentils (or a red lentil soup that was probably much thicker than what we associate with soup).

What a difference just a generation or two makes. From the West Coast to the East, from the shores of the Great Lakes to the panhandle of Florida, the meals through the day have decreased in size and flavor. Take, for example, Roy Webster's 1985 book, *Under a Buttermilk Moon: A Country Memoir.*

Just an ordinary day started out with breakfast, not an ounce box of cereal, but a real meal. I'm talking about home-cured bacon, more than a couple of slices too, eggs, at least two, a glass or two of Maude's milk that tested five or six percent butterfat, biscuits usually, but sometimes a few slices of homemade light bread loaded with pure home-churned butter and toasted in the hot oven of a wood-burning range, then smeared with a quarter of an inch of homemade strawberry preserves. When you got up from the table you were fortified—not for all day—just 'til noon.

Then there's dinner, not lunch. In the spring and early summer, it would be a big kettle of navy beans that had been soaked overnight, then cooked all morning with a big ham hock the size of your two fists.... There was a big bowl of wild greens that...had been picked the day before, washed, blanched, seasoned with bacon rinds, then simmered on the back of the stove 'til dinnertime. A batch of stone-ground corn bread baked in too large a pan so it would be thin and crusty. About 20 or 30 minutes of this and you were fortified again—'til chore time.

For supper, not dinner, it would be a kettle of black-eyed peas seasoned with bacon fryings, and corn on the cob with melted butter running down between the kernels, and a slice or two of country-cured ham. For dessert, a cobbler with a golden brown crust, dished out into an oatmeal bowl and covered with thick folds of hand-skimmed cream....

Did we overeat? Lands no. Following a team of quick stepping horses between the two handles of a walking plow solved the calorie problem... you did well to last a half day.

Dutch Vegetable Soup

This is called Dutch because of the use of Dutch ovens for cooking soups and stews from the earliest times to the, more recent, early twentieth century. A Dutch oven is a deep, heavy pot with a tight fitting lid that many a Yankee kept as a family heirloom for many generations.

1/2 lb. bacon, diced small
2 lg. carrots, thinly sliced
2 lg. leeks, thinly sliced
1 medium onion, diced

2 lg. potatoes, diced
1 med. cauliflower, cut into small florets
6 c. chicken broth
French Bread

Sauté bacon in large nonstick saucepan until crisp. Remove bacon, leaving bacon drippings in pan. Add sliced carrots and sauté over low-medium heat, covered, for 15 minutes. Add leeks and onion and sauté an additional 5 minutes without the lid. Add diced potatoes, cauliflower, potatoes, and chicken broth. Bring to a boil, reduce heat and simmer, covered, for 1 hour.

In the meantime, butter sliced French bread with your favorite herbed butter or plain butter and broil until tanned. When serving soup, float French bread slices on top of soup.

To Make Vegetable Soup

Pare and slice five or six cucumbers, the inside of as many cos lettuces [Romaine]; a sprig or two of mint; two or three onions, some pepper and salt, a pint and a half of young peas, and a little parsley. Put these with a half a pound of fresh butter, into a sauce pan to stew in their own liquor near a gentle fire half and hour; then pour two quarts of boiling water to the vegetables, and steam them two hours. Rub down a little flour into a teacup of water; boil it with the rest fifteen or twenty minutes and serve it.

–A New System of Domestic Cookery, 1807

Creamy Broccoli Cheese Soup

Simply follow "Cream of Broccoli Soup" directions but add 2 cups of your favorite cheese at the very end. Stir until melted and serve. My suggestion is shredded colby, Monterey Jack cheese, mild Cheddar, or simply, American.

Cream of Broccoli Soup

Classic cream of broccoli soup is made with the stalks of the broccoli plant. After they are boiled for about an hour and a half, they are put into a food processor and pureed as smooth as possible. Although this is a great way of using the "waste" of the plant, below you will find a suitable replacement for the stems. The soup will be a brighter green color and the taste will be nearly indistinguishable.

3 c. broccoli florets
1 can (7 oz.) chicken broth
1 qt. whole milk
Salt and pepper to taste
8 T. margarine
8 T. flour

In medium nonstick saucepan cover broccoli with 2 inches of water. On high heat, boil until broccoli is very soft, about 15 to 20 minutes. Pour half the water with all the broccoli into a blender or food processor and puree until all lumps have disappeared. Discard the remaining water in pot and return pureed broccoli and water to saucepan. Add chicken broth and milk and bring to scalding on medium heat, DO NOT BOIL! In the meantime, melt butter and whisk with flour until well blended. When broccoli mixture is scalding, add butter/flour paste into soup and whisk until completely absorbed. Stirring constantly, leave on medium heat for 5 minutes and then remove.

Lard and Cracklin's (c. 1830)

Fat is cut from the hams, shoulders, middlin, entrails, etc. Leave out all night in pot so it will become solidified and be easier to cut up. The next morning, cut the fat into pieces the size of a small hen's egg and put in a pot with just a small amount of water to keep it from sticking to the bottom and sides while cooking. The pot is placed over the fire, and allowed to cook slowly. Stir it often. By nightfall, the grease will have boiled out, the water evaporated, and the hard residue called 'cracklins' will have fallen to the bottom. The grease is poured into buckets or any other container, allowed to harden, and is used all winter for cooking. The cracklins are saved for bread. Add soda if you don't want many cracklin's. The soda also keeps it from smelling while cooking and from tasting strong.

–The Yankee Chef Archives

The Best Cheddar Cheese Soup...Period!

The infusion of carrots, potatoes, and beef stock (instead of chicken stock) in this soup gives it a pronounced flavor you can't find with any seasoning.

6 large potatoes, peeled and diced
3 large carrots, peeled and sliced
2 large onions, peeled and diced
6 c. beef broth
2 c. heavy cream
1 lb. sharp, orange Cheddar cheese
Salt and pepper to taste
1/2 c. sour cream

In a large saucepan place potatoes, carrots, onion, and water to cover over medium-high heat and cook until all vegetables are done. Strain and puree vegetables in food processor or blender in stages until all are pureed. Return to pot and add beef broth and heavy cream over medium heat to almost scalding stage, stirring often. Add Cheddar cheese and stir until cheese has melted. Remove from heat and add sour cream and seasoning to taste.

Cream of Potato Soup

Being from Maine and having the Aroostook potatoes at hand whenever needed, I am humbled to say that the use of potato flakes in this recipe makes a nice shortcut without diminishing the taste of this recipe one bit. Enjoy this soup with crushed bacon bits, snipped chives, or Parmesan cheese sprinkled over the top.

1 qt. hot milk
1 pt. chicken broth
6 oz. (weight) dehydrated potato
    flakes
1 t. salt
2 t. onion powder
1/2 t. ground black pepper
1/4 t. celery salt
1/2 t. dried parsley
2 t. butter or margarine

Bring milk and broth to a light boil; stir in remaining ingredients. Return mixture to a boil; reduce heat and simmer, uncovered, 15 minutes. Stir frequently to prevent scorching. Do not boil!

Potato Folklore
• A potato crop should be planted at night during a new moon so that the plants will thrive.
• If planted on Good Friday, the crop will be poor.
• Once pulled from the ground, potato storage stability will be insured if the family that grew them ate the first ones harvested.
• Carry potatoes in your pocket to ward off sciatica and rheumatism.
• In Holland, only a stolen potato can ward off sciatica and rheumatism.
• The Irish used to rub boiled potato water on their aching joints and broken bones for pain relief.

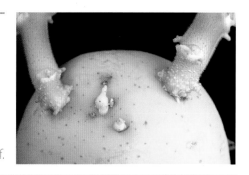

Pumpkin and Mussel Soup

These familiar mollusks are as delicious to the French as any seafood they prepare. Mussels have been overlooked for many years by us New Englanders. Why? I don't know, but remember that at one point in America's colonization, lobsters were so plentiful along the beaches of New England that we overlooked their entrance into our cuisine also. We thought ourselves to be above eating these shellfish. When the meat of the mussel is cooked, it is bright orange and complements the color of this recipe.

They are easy to find and are quite abundant along any rock-strewn portion of our Yankee coast. At low tide, hunt for them where the rock is exposed to the open, pounding surf along our coast; they will have attached themselves to the rocks with tough, brown, hair-like byssus or "whiskers." Pry them off the rocks with a crowbar or a sturdy screwdriver. Do not take any mussels that have opened in the least bit, they are dead. Put them in a bucket and cover them with seaweed to transport.

2 lbs. mussels
1 sm. onion, minced
2 garlic cloves, peeled and minced
1/4 c. dry white wine
2 c. fish broth or 1 c. clam broth
   with 1 c. water or 2 c. chicken broth

2 T. tapioca (that's right, tapioca!)
2 cans (8 oz.) pureed pumpkin
Salt and pepper to taste
Seasoned croutons
Parsley for garnish

Clean mussels thoroughly, scouring off the "beards." In a large saucepan, over medium-high heat, combine onion, garlic and wine and bring to a boil. Add mussels; cover and boil 5 to 6 minutes or until mussel shells open. Remove from heat.

In a separate pot bring broth to a boil over medium-high heat and add tapioca and pumpkin. Reduce heat to medium-low, cover, and simmer 6 to 7 minutes. Reduce heat to low and strain the mussel mixture liquid into the pumpkin mixture; stir thoroughly. You can either pick out the mussels and remove the meat to add to the soup or add the mussels, shells and all, to the soup. Remove from heat and garnish with parsley and croutons to serve.

Colorful Cauliflower and Cheese Soup

Served with a salad and crispy bread, this is a perfect lunch that just doesn't weigh you down for the rest of the day.

1/2 c. onion, minced
1/4 c. plus 2 T. butter or margarine
1/2 c. flour
4 c. chicken broth
1/2 c. carrot, minced
1/2 c. celery, minced
2 c. cauliflower florets, cooked
4 c. milk
8 oz. Cheddar or American cheese, diced
Salt and pepper to taste

In large saucepan cook onion in 2 T. butter over medium-low heat until tender. Meanwhile, melt 1/4 c. butter and blend in flour until paste is formed; set aside. Add chicken broth, carrot, celery, and cauliflower to pot with the cooked onions. Cover and cook until cauliflower is tender (about 10 to 12 minutes). Add butter/flour mixture and blend until smooth and thickened. Add milk and cheese and, while constantly stirring, cook until cheese has melted. Season to taste and serve.

It takes about 10 pints of whole milk to make a pound of cheese, which retains most of the original fat. This saturated fat accounts for 65–75 % of the calories of most cheeses. So two slices of cheese contain as much fat as 3.5 pats of butter, and is higher in fat than the same weight in sirloin steak! A slice of Cheddar provides 204 mg or 20% of your RDA of calcium. Between 200–400 mg of sodium per slice of cheese makes cheese a high sodium food as well. Cream cheese, however, beats all cheeses in fat content with 90% of the calories coming from fat.

Soupe a l'Oignon Gratinee (Onion Soup Gratinee)

I titled this recipe in French because this soup is worthy of its French nomenclature. Served with a bottle of red wine, green salad, and fresh fruit, this French classic is a hearty main course. Always use French bread in this recipe. A chewy type of bread does not disintegrate as Italian or other types would, and that's what we are looking for.

3 T. butter or margarine	1 bay leaf
5 to 6 med. onions, thinly sliced	1/2 t. sage
1 t. salt	1 c. heavy cream
1 t. sugar	1 loaf of French bread
3 T. flour	1/4 c. melted butter or margarine
2 cans beef broth plus 3 c. water	8 slices of Swiss cheese
1 c. red wine	Parmesan cheese

Melt butter in large saucepan; add sliced onions and cover. Over low heat, cook for 15 to 20 minutes, stirring occasionally until onions are soft. Uncover, raise heat to medium-high and add salt and sugar. This will caramelize the onions and turn them brown. Stir for 15 to 20 minutes until onions are browned. Reduce heat to medium and stir in flour, blending well; cook an additional 2 minutes. Pour in beef broth, water, and wine, bay leaf, sage, and heavy cream. Heat to scalding and remove from heat.

Cut bread into 1-inch-thick slices, paint with melted butter, and bake in preheated 375°F oven for 15 minutes, or until bread starts to toast. These are called *croûtes*. Pour hot soup into individual crock or serving dishes that are ovenproof. Top each serving container with slice of baked French bread, top each with slice of Swiss cheese, and finally top with grated Parmesan cheese. Return to oven to melt cheese or place under broiler at least 4 inches from heat source and carefully brown the Swiss and Parmesan cheeses. Keeping a constant eye on it, remove crocks of soup and serve immediately with any remaining French bread.

Split Pea Soup

Dry peas well over 5,000 years old have been found in the remains of the Swiss "lake dwellers." They have also been found in many ancient Egyptian tombs. However, field peas are relatively new and have only been cultivated and eaten since about the sixth or seventh century B.C. in the near east. The early Greek and Roman street vendors sold pea soup to the public. It was not until the Middle Ages that field peas were consumed by the masses. During this time, they were cooked in their pods and shelled afterwards to eat.

2 c. dried green split peas
8 c. water
1 carrot, peeled and diced
1 onion, peeled and minced
1 c. chopped ham
1 c. chicken broth
1 c. light cream
6 T. dry sherry (optional)
Salt and pepper to taste

Wash split peas and place them in a large saucepan with 8 c. water, carrots, onions, and ham. Bring to a boil over medium-high heat; reduce heat to low, cover, and simmer for at least 1 1/2 hours, stirring occasionally, until peas are no longer visible but have transformed into a thick porridge. Remove from heat, add chicken broth, light cream, dry sherry, and salt and pepper to taste.

Canadian Split Pea Soup

The same as above but use yellow split peas instead of green.

Dad's Bean Swagan

Originally called Bean Swagger, Swagan is probably the oldest soup in America. I wish I could give this recipe a whole page by itself because this is a great soup. No one, I mean no one, could make this soup better than my Dad, Chef Jack, the second Yankee Chef. I have never been able to duplicate it because of an ingredient he used that he wouldn't even tell me, but this is a close second.

Use the same recipe as "Split Pea Soup" but substitute great northern beans or other dried beans to suit your taste. Omit the cream and add 1/2 c. tomato ketchup instead. Some people prefer cooked bacon in their Bean Swagan in place of ham (as I do). If desired, cook bacon separately and add at the end of the recipe when soup is finished.

Honey and Spice Butternut Squash Soup

This may seem like a large lot of soup but the yield is only twelve, 1-cup servings, and believe me you will need every drop for seconds and probably thirds.

5 onions, chopped
1/4 c. butter or margarine
6 cloves garlic, peeled
6 lbs. butternut squash, peeled and cubed
2 qts. chicken broth
1 T. ground cumin

2 t. salt
1/4 t. cayenne pepper
2 c. heavy cream
1 1/2 c. honey
1 c. sour cream
1 T. dried cilantro (optional)

Sauté onion in butter until soft, about 10 minutes. Stir in garlic, squash, chicken broth, cumin, salt, and cayenne pepper. Simmer over medium-low heat until squash is very soft. Puree in small lots with food processor or blender and return to saucepan. Stir in cream, honey, and heat thoroughly. Serve with dollop of sour cream and cilantro on top.

If you use skim milk in place of heavy cream and low fat margarine in this recipe, the saturated fat will be reduced 75%. Try these stats on fat by the teaspoonful!

An all-beef hot dog........2 1/2 t. fat	1 strip bacon.................1 1/4 t.	1 slice bologna.................2 t.
Big Mac.................7 to 9 t.	3 oz. lean beef.................2 t.	Chicken breast, no skin..........1 t.
10 potato chips.................2 t.	10 Ritz crackers.................2 t.	1 c. peanut butter...........1 3/4 t.
1 oz. American cheese..........2 t.	1 c. low-fat milk.................1 t.	1 c. whole milk.................2 t.

Savory Chicken and Noodle Soup

This is probably the best chicken noodle soup you will ever have. This recipe comes from an elderly lady whose family had served this many generations ago when they were Shakers. Very few memories of this small community exist today, so I am proud to keep this recipe alive and well.

12 c. chicken broth, divided
1/4 c. dry vermouth (optional)
1/4 c. butter or margarine
1 c. heavy cream
1 pkg. (12 oz.) dry egg noodles
1/2 c. butter or margarine, melted
6 T. all-purpose flour
3 c. diced, cooked chicken
1 c. frozen peas
Salt and pepper to taste

Combine 1 c. broth, vermouth, and butter in small saucepan. Bring to a boil on medium-high heat and cook until liquid is reduced to 1/4 cup and is quite syrupy. Stir in the cream and set aside.
Bring remaining broth to a boil in another large saucepan. Add noodles and cook until just tender. In separate container combine melted butter and flour; mix until smooth paste forms. Stir into broth mixture and cook over medium heat until thickened, stirring constantly. Stir in the cream mixture, chicken, and peas. Season to taste with salt and pepper.

Yankee Seafood Bisque

Artichokes give this menagerie of flavors an earthy tone that truly lends this bisque a comforting flavor.

2 T. olive oil
1 onion, minced
16 oz.-can cooked
   artichokes with its liquid
2 c. chicken broth
1 lb. mixed seafood (shrimp, crab,
   scallops) shelled and cooked
1 c. heavy cream
Parsley
1 T. salt
1/2 t. white pepper
3/4 t. dried nutmeg

Heat oil in large saucepan over medium-high heat; add onion and cook for 6 to 7 minutes until done. Add artichokes and chicken broth; cook for 6 to 7 minutes longer. Remove from heat and puree in food processor or blender until smooth. Return to saucepan and add shellfish, cream, parsley, salt, pepper, and nutmeg. Reduce heat and simmer on low for 5 to 6 minutes, uncovered. Do not bring to a boil! Serve immediately.

Scallop Bisque

Bay or sea? Yankees are more familiar with bay scallops, which live along the New England and Gulf coasts. I prefer bay scallops because they are smaller (therefore easier to handle and cook with) and they have a taste superior to sea scallops, which live along the north and middle parts of the Atlantic coast—their shells do not have the ridges as the bay scallops do. Some of the old-time New Englanders eat raw scallops and, yes, clams.

1 lb. scallops, fresh or frozen
1 can (4 oz.) mushroom stems and
   pieces, drained
1/4 c. melted butter or margarine
1 t. Dijon-style mustard
Salt and pepper to taste
1/4 c. all-purpose flour
4 c. milk
Paprika (optional)

Thaw frozen scallops. Eyeball the scallops and remove any errant shell particles; rinse. In medium-sized saucepan, combine scallops and mushrooms, butter, mustard, salt and pepper and cook over medium-high heat until scallops are all white and done, about 6 to 8 minutes. Blend in flour and whisk until creamy. Add milk and blend thoroughly. Remove to food processor or blender and puree until smooth. There may be very small pieces of scallops still visible, but that will only add texture. Remove to saucepan once again and continue cooking over medium heat, stirring almost constantly, until mixture thickens, about 8 to 10 minutes longer. Let sit for 2 to 3 minutes and serve hot.

When Benjamin Franklin warned, in *Poor Richard's Almanac*, that both fish and visitors smelled in three days, he was touching on a major problem confronting early settlers; food preservation. Keeping fish and shellfish from spoiling before its use in the winter was a puzzle that faced all colonists, and there were many ways of "keeping" fish stable, including this solution from *The Family Receipt Book* (1819): "To Cure Tainted Shellfish and Fish: Tainted fish may be much restored to its proper flavor by mixing a quantity of vinegar and salt in the water in which the fish is to be boilede [sic]."

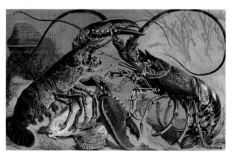

When you order a boiled lobster in a restaurant and the tail is curled up under, you know you got a fresh lobster. If the tail is straight out, the lobster was dead when it was cooked.

In the midwinter season, it takes about 4 1/2 pounds of live lobsters to equal 1 pound of lobster meat. During the molting season, that number rises to about 9 live lobsters to equal 1 pound of lobster meat.

Lobsters should be less expensive between August and November, when most lobsters are harvested.

You can always tell if a lobster is done cooking when an antenna pulls out easily.

Lobster meat contains omega-3, unsaturated fatty acids, the substance that reduces hardening of the arteries and decreases the risk of heart disease.

Yes, lobsters do have their teeth in their stomachs.

Shrimp Bisque

1 lb. cooked shrimp
3 T. chopped onion
3 T. chopped celery
1/4 c. butter or margarine, melted
2 T. all-purpose flour
1 t. salt
1/4 t. paprika
Dash white pepper
4 c. milk

In food processor or blender, chop shrimp very fine, leave in blender or food processor. Cook onion and celery in butter over medium-high heat until done, about 7 to 9 minutes. Lower heat to medium and add flour and seasonings; blend well. Add milk and continue cooking until milk has thickened. Pour into blender or food processor, in portions if need be, and blend until pureed. Return to saucepan and bring up to temperature. Serve when desired heat is attained.

Savory Lobster Bisque

1 lb. cooked lobster meat, finely chopped
1/4 c. butter or margarine
1/2 c. flour
1/2 t. dried thyme
Salt and pepper to taste
Chopped parsley
4 c. half and half

Sauté lobster in butter over medium heat for 8 to 9 minutes. Add flour, thyme, salt and pepper, and parsley. Stir well until flour is dissolved completely. Add an additional 3 to 4 T. melted butter or margarine if needed to provide a smooth base. Add sherry and half and half. With whisk, beat until margarine/flour mixture is no longer visible. Remove from heat and puree in blender or food processor until completely smooth. Return to heat and heat over medium-low heat until thoroughly heated and thickened, about 15 to 20 minutes. Serve.

Chicken Stew and Dumplings

I have scoured cookbook upon cookbook and I am unable to find a chicken stew with dumplings recipe anywhere. What a shame! This is a hearty main dish that deserves more recognition and mass appeal than I can tell you. Although there is a way to prepare this recipe all in one pot, I have found it to be much easier and foolproof to make the stew in one pot and the dumplings in another, combining them before serving. As you are able to become more accomplished at this dish, you can cook the dumplings on top of the stew without fear of undercooking the dumplings. One note, however, do not ever let your dumplings boil; simmering allows these floured delights to expand and become light as a feather rather than tough and compact.

4 carrots, peeled and sliced
1 lg. onion, finely chopped
2 ribs celery, sliced
8 c. chicken broth
2 potatoes, peeled and diced
1 1/2 c. frozen peas
1/4 c. butter or margarine, melted
4 T. all-purpose flour
3 c. cooked chicken or turkey, cubed

Dumplings:
2 c. all-purpose flour
4 t. baking powder
1 t. salt
1 c. milk
4 T. vegetable oil

Stew:

Combine in a large saucepan carrots, onion, celery, and chicken broth and bring to a boil over medium-high heat for 15 to 20 minutes or until vegetables are crisp tender. Add potatoes and peas. Cook for an additional 10 to 12 minutes until potatoes are tender. In a bowl, blend melted butter and flour until smooth paste is formed and add to stew. Stir into stew thoroughly until well incorporated and reduce heat to low. Add the cooked chicken and continue simmering while dumplings are being made, stirring frequently.

Dumplings:

In another large pot, half fill with hot water and bring to a simmer over medium-low heat. Combine flour, baking powder, and salt; blend well. In separate bowl mix oil with milk and add to dry ingredients. Stir until just combined and holding together. Drop by the spoonful into simmering water, enough spoonfuls to almost entirely cover water. Place a tight-fitting lid on top and simmer 15 to 17 minutes. Remove cover and test as you would a cake, by inserting a toothpick into a dumpling. If it comes out without wet dumpling mix clinging to it, scoop out with slotted spoon directly into chicken stew. Repeat the process with remaining dumpling mix. Remove chicken stew from heat and place a tight-fitting cover on it until serving time.

The Chinese were the first to make dumplings. Called Chu-pao-pa, they were eaten in soups much the same way we do today. The English and Scandinavian kitchens utilized these "drop biscuits" more so than other civilizations. In Italy, dumplings are ravioli while in Germany they are called *kloesee*, *knodel*, or *spaetzle*. In Lithuania, they are referred to as *kolodny*, and in the old Czech Republic, *knedlik*. Dumplings are called *blintzes* in Slavic countries and *tamales* or *empanadas* in Spanish-speaking countries.

Boiled, steamed, or baked dumplings are the three main categories. Boiled dumplings are simmered in broth that will be served as its accompaniment.

Steamed dumplings are made from biscuit dough. It is usually shaped around a bit of fruit and then cooked over steam either in custard cups or in a perforated pan. It is then served with cream or a sauce.

Baked dumplings are plain pastries or sweet biscuit dough and wrapped around a bit of fruit served with thin, sweet syrup of some sort.

Fall Vegetable Beef Stew

Can one think of any other region in the United States where turnips are eaten more often than in New England? Some people will turn up their nose to this bulbous vegetable, but the mild taste is unworthy of its reputation. The turnip has been around for many centuries, although its roots (no pun intended) have not been specified to one particular region of the world. We know that the Greeks and Romans devoured them with fervor. Pliny writes that in Northern Italy, it was unsurpassed as a vegetable.

1 1/2 lbs. cubed stew beef
6 T. flour, divided
Salt and pepper to taste
4 T. vegetable oil
2 c. beef broth
2 bay leaves
1 lb. turnips, peeled and cubed
1 yellow onion, cut into wedges cubed
3 carrots, peeled and sliced
1/2 c. cold water

Toss beef cubes with 2 T. flour, salt, and pepper until beef is coated. Heat oil in a large nonstick pot over medium-high heat. Add meat and brown on all sides. Add broth and bay leaves, cover, reduce heat to low and simmer for 1 1/2 to 2 hours. Carefully remove lid and check for meat to be fairly tender. Add all the vegetables; salt and pepper to taste and return cover to pot. Continue simmering for 30 minutes. Dissolve remaining flour in water and stir into the stew until thickened.

Classic Yankee Beef Stew*

Joe Booker is a beef stew that was made famous near Boothbay Harbor, Maine. It was generally enjoyed by those lumberers and men who cut ice from the rivers in the winter. No one knows for whom it was named, but the legacy it has left is indelible. Many recipes called for thickening it with oats, but the original Joe Booker was a hearty but not thickened beef, salt pork, and vegetable stew. This recipe is at least 125 years old and comes from a family in Sherman Mills, Maine. The family's name has been lost but we will keep this recipe around.

5 T. shortening
2 lb. stew beef
1/2 c. flour
Salt and pepper to taste
2 med. potatoes, diced
4 lg. carrots, diced
2 med. onions, diced
1/2 sm. turnip, diced
1 sm. cabbage, chopped
1 lg. can diced tomatoes in juice
2 stalks celery, diced

Add shortening to large nonstick pot over medium-high heat. Toss beef with the salt and pepper-seasoned flour and add to pot. Brown on all sides. Cover, reduce heat, and simmer for 45 minutes. Add remaining ingredients, cover with water to about 2 inches above contents. Bring to a boil over high heat, reduce to low, replace lid and simmer for 30 to 40 minutes, or until vegetables are tender.

This recipe does not call for beef broth or beef extract of any kind. I recommend you replace the water with 2 to 3 cans of prepared beef broth for a more pronounced beef flavor.

Oyster Stew

This rich, fragrant stew is made in a matter of minutes. Go ahead and add some finely diced bacon while you are cooking the onion. Just be sure to drain well before adding the rest of the ingredients.

1/2 c. onion, minced
2 T. butter or margarine
1 pint shucked oysters
1/2 t. salt
Dash black pepper
Dash ground red pepper
2 c. half and half
1 c. milk

In large saucepan cook onion in butter until tender over medium high heat. Stir in oysters with its liquid, salt, black pepper, red pepper, and simmer until edges of oysters curl. Stir in half and half and milk; heat through while stirring almost constantly. Serve hot.

Lobster Stew

Here is the Holy Grail of Maine coastal cooking. You think it's good eaten directly after you make it? Try it the next day!

1 lb. cooked lobster meat
1/4 c. butter or margarine
1 t. salt
1/4 t. paprika
Dash white pepper
Dash of nutmeg
1 pint of milk
1 pt. half and half

Cut lobster into bite-sized pieces and place in medium sized saucepan. Add butter and seasonings and sauté for 8 to 10 minutes over medium heat. Add milk and half and half and heat, stirring frequently, until stew is heated through. Serve.

Dutch Corn Chowder

Unlike "Dutch Vegetable Soup," this is not named after the Dutch oven but for the Gouda cheese used in the recipe. Gouda was first made in the thirteenth century in Holland and is a semi-soft, mild cheese that intensifies with age. The Dutch brought this cheese with them to New York and incorporated it with an old Native American favorite... corn. Although not a Yankee dish, and including tomatoes in any dish called chowder is not a very New England thing to do, we nonetheless thank the Dutch emigrants for this recipe. (See, we are not as stubborn as people make us out to be!)

1/2 c. olive oil
1/2 head celery, diced
1 red bell pepper, diced
2 leeks, diced
2 c. frozen corn, thawed
2 lg. onions, diced
1 c. diced, fresh tomatoes
3 lg. potatoes, peeled and diced

1 clove garlic, peeled and minced
1 T. dried thyme
Salt and pepper to taste
4 c. heavy cream
1 1/2 T. cornstarch, dissolved in 1/2 c. milk
1/4 c. butter or margarine
Tabasco® sauce as needed
8 oz. grated Gouda cheese

In large nonstick pot add olive oil and all the vegetables, except potatoes. Sauté on high for 4 minutes, stirring frequently. Add potatoes, garlic, thyme, salt, and pepper. Mix well and add heavy cream. Bring to a boil.

Immediately reduce heat to low, stirring constantly, and simmer, uncovered, for 20 minutes. Stir frequently. Add cornstarch mixture slowly while stirring, until thickened. Add Tabasco, grated cheese, and butter; serve.

Years ago, I am talking many generations now, Yankee bread was eaten with oyster stew and all types of soups. Here is a recipe that dates to the middle years of the 1700s:

Take 2 measures of Indian and 1 of rye meal, mix with milk or water, to the consistency of stiff hasty pudding and add yeast. Bake in iron pans or iron kettles 4 or 5 hours. Eat with fresh butter and soup. And if while warm the better. Yankee bread is very good or very bad, according the manner in which it is made. We commend it to dyspeptics. The Indian meal should be either bolted or sifted.

And the following recipe may have helped the breadmaker of the family:

To drive the flies away while making the bread take 1/2 t. well pounded pepper, 1 t. brown sugar, 1 t. cream and mix. Put it on a platter in a room where the flies are troublesome and they will soon disappear.

What would chowder be without the potatoes? Pretty thin, I must say. My mother's ancestor, John Pease of Martha's Vineyard, is supposedly the first to put potatoes in chowder. I have come across a couple of written, family references regarding this. Upon further research, there is no other source claiming this "title" but much circumstantial evidence entitling John Pease, Inventor of today's *Chowdah*!

Corn Chowder with Bacon

For us Yankees, there is just something about creamy corn chowder. Whether it is the ease of preparation or the simple taste of corn and potatoes, it fills our stomachs with warm satisfaction and our minds with a pleasing afterthought. This classic, if eaten in moderation before a meal, will certainly prepare your soul for a gut busting Thanksgiving dinner or a palate pleasing dinner of any origin. Substitute ham for the bacon if you like.

1/2 med. onion, minced
6 strips bacon, chopped
   (or use 1 c. finely diced ham)
3 c. chicken stock
3 med. potatoes, peeled and diced
2 c. cream style corn
1 c. whole kernel corn
1 1/2 c. light cream
1 1/2 T. brown sugar (optional)
Salt and pepper to taste

In large saucepan over medium-high heat, sauté onion and bacon together until bacon is done but not crisp. Add chicken stock and potatoes; bring to a boil over medium-high heat and then reduce to low. Simmer with lid on for 15 to 20 minutes or until potatoes are tender. Add creamed corn, whole kernel corn, light cream, and brown sugar. Season to taste.

Watch Out for those Stalks!
   My father used to relate to me (albeit tongue-in-cheek) that his grandfather used to boil ears of corn by bringing a pot of water to a boil on the stove. He then took it off the stove and ran, as fast as he could, with it to his corn stalks growing out back. He would then set it down, husk the ear of corn while still attached to the stalk and bend it over into the pot. It was only then that he would cut the ear off. Once it was submersed in the very hot water, he would then run like the dickens back to the house to further cook it. The reason for this dangerous race was that he didn't want the sugar in the corn to turn to starch, which by the way happens almost immediately when picked.

Roast Turkey Chowder

Whether you use leftover roast turkey from the holidays or buy roasted turkey from the deli, this chowder could be served as a main dish in itself.

1/4 lb. bacon diced
1 carrot, diced
2 lg. onions, chopped
3 ribs celery, chopped
2 t. salt
1/4 c. flour
2 qts. chicken or turkey stock
1 lb. red potatoes, diced
3 c. diced, cooked turkey
2 c. heavy cream
1 1/2 t. dried thyme
1/2 t. black pepper
1 t. salt
2 bay leaves

In a large soup pot, brown bacon. Remove and leave fat in pan; reserving bacon. In this fat, sauté carrots over medium-high heat for 5 to 7 minutes. Add onion and celery and continue sautéing until they are tender. Lower heat to medium and cook 5 minutes. Add flour; blending well. Add stock, potatoes, turkey, and bacon; lower heat to low and simmer for an additional 30 minutes with lid on. Uncover and add cream and spices, stirring and simmering for 5 minutes or until heated through. Remove bay leaf when ready to serve.

Here are some old-time terms that you may (or may not have) heard of:

Cape Cod Turkey: another name for a codfish
Bombay Duck: strong flavored fish
Colonial Goose: mutton with herbs
Mexican Rabbit: green peppers, onions, cheese, eggs and tomatoes
Fannie Daddies: Cape Cod for fried clams
Scotch Woodcock: scrambled eggs with anchovies
Deacon Porter's Hat: suet rice pudding
Golden Buck: poached eggs, Welsh rabbit (or rarebit), and anchovies

New England Fish Chowder

Fish chowder is probably the earliest chowder made in New England. As mentioned, it is said that John Pease of Martha's Vineyard was the first colonist to add potatoes in chowder during the seventeenth century. It is quite probable that other vegetables were added to the fish and water boiling in a large kettle over the fire, because of the abundant vegetables grown in each family's garden. Most stews during the early colonization of America were filled with whatever was reaped from each family's garden, plus whatever meat, game, or fowl was readily available and killed. If I were to be true to the first fish chowder made, you would think it more of a potpourri than a chowder, not identifying the taste of fish but of the abundant other tastes cooking together.

1/2 lb. bacon
1 lg. onion diced
5 med. sized potatoes, peeled and diced
1 1/2 lb. haddock, diced
1 qt. milk
Salt and pepper to taste
A sprig of thyme

In a large pot, sauté bacon until almost crisp. Add onion and sauté over medium-high heat until tender; drain. Add potatoes and cover with 2 inches of water. Boil for 15 minutes or until potatoes are tender. Add haddock that has been diced and cook for 10 to 12 minutes longer. Lower heat to low and add milk and seasoning. Stir once and bring up to serving temperature. Remove from heat and add pats of butter or margarine and thyme if desired.

The word bacon comes from the Middle High German word *backe*, meaning the "rear" or the "back" end. In old England, it changed to *bacoun*.

A rasher (4 slices) of bacon comes from *rashe*, or "to cut." The words razor and raze have the same root meaning as well. In twelfth-century England, a side of bacon was given to any man who could enter the church and swear on a Bible he had not fought with his wife for 12 months and a day. The worthy husband who could make that vow was said to have "brought home the bacon."

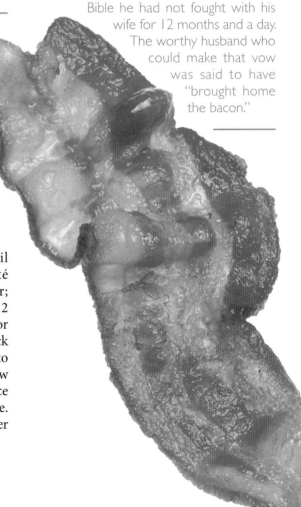

Boston Clam Chowder

Well now, the eternal question arises, cream or tomatoes? Of course everyone knows Manhattan Clam Chowder employs tomatoes and/or tomato juice as the base for their chowder while New Englanders use a dairy product for their chowder. My grandfather researched this extensively, as have I, and we both have found out some basic history on this matter. While the first chowder was made from just clam broth during early colonization, cow's milk was added during the beginning years of the eighteenth century. It wasn't until the late eighteenth century that tomatoes (or some by-product of them) was added to chowder, and it was during this period when Thomas Jefferson began to use them in his chowders and other soups. Therefore, I suppose the question of dating has been answered.

5 slices bacon, cut into 1/2-inch
  pieces
1 lg. onion, minced
4 lg. potatoes, diced
2 1/2 lbs. littleneck clams, shelled
1 qt. milk
2 c. light or heavy cream
Salt and pepper to taste
4 T. butter or margarine

Fry bacon in large heavy saucepan until done but not crispy on medium-high heat. Remove bacon; reserve the fat and fry onion until tender, stirring occasionally. Add potatoes and cover with water 2 inches and cook over medium-high heat for 15 minutes, or until tender but not mushy. Add clams, juice and all, reduce heat to low and continue cooking another 3 to 4 minutes. Add milk, cream, salt and pepper, and butter and stir just a couple of times. Leave it on low heat for another 6 to 7 minutes and remove from heat; serve.

The word chowder actually comes from French. Fishermen on the coast of Brittany threw some of their daily catch in one communal pot on the fire. This pot was called a chaudiere!

Monheggan Salmon Chowder

This is one of the older chowder recipes I own, dating back to the late eighteenth century. I am sure this chowder was served long before that time, however, because of the abundant salmon that was caught by the French and English fisherman on Monheggan Island, even before the colonization of Massachusetts. There are many stories of tremendous hauls of fish off this island.

1 lg. onion, diced
2 lg. potatoes, diced
3 c. water
2 t. salt
1 can (17 oz.) whole-kernel corn,
  drained
1 can (1 lb.) red salmon, flaked
4 c. milk
Salt and pepper to taste

Combine onion, potatoes, water, and salt in medium saucepan; cook on medium-high heat until vegetables are tender. Add corn and salmon and stir until combined. Slowly stir in milk; add salt and pepper to taste. Heat, but do not boil, until hot and serve.

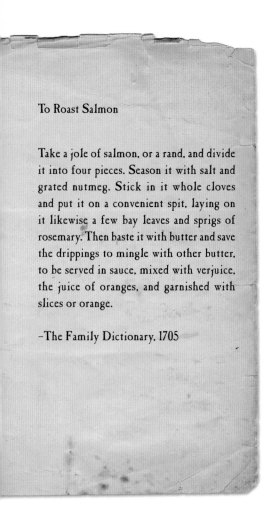

To Roast Salmon

Take a jole of salmon, or a rand, and divide it into four pieces. Season it with salt and grated nutmeg. Stick in it whole cloves and put it on a convenient spit, laying on it likewise a few bay leaves and sprigs of rosemary. Then baste it with butter and save the drippings to mingle with other butter, to be served in sauce, mixed with verjuice, the juice of oranges, and garnished with slices or orange.

–The Family Dictionary, 1705

Oyster Chowder

Not many know that along with the mounds of clam shells Europeans found on American soil when they first arrived, they found oyster heaps as well. Native Americans were fond of this mollusk to the point that these shell heaps often rose more than 20 feet high. Many centuries before this, however, oysters were so well desired that Julius Caesar packed large quantities of "superb British oysters" in snow and delivered them back to his banquet halls in Rome when he conquered Britain.

1/2 sm. onion, chopped
3 T. butter or margarine
1 c. water
1 c. celery, minced
2 c. diced potatoes
1 T. salt
1/2 t. pepper
1 pint oysters, including liquor
4 c. milk

Sauté onion in butter or margarine until slightly brown; add water, celery, potatoes, salt, and pepper. Cover and cook over medium-high heat until vegetables are tender. Reduce heat to low and add milk; simmer 10 minutes. In the meantime, simmer oysters in their liquor in a separate saucepan for 6 to 7 minutes, or until edges start to curl. Drain and combine with milk and vegetables. Serve.

Delicious Cauliflower Crab Chowder

Cauliflower is meant to marry crab. The two tastes go hand-in-hand in this colorful and tasty dish. I do! Now you may eat the chowder.

3 T. flour
4 T. butter or margarine, melted
2 c. cauliflower florets
1 can (14 1/2 oz.) chicken broth
1/2 c. finely chopped
   yellow bell pepper
1 1/2 t. grated lemon peel
2 c. half and half
1/2 lb. frozen crabmeat, thawed
2 t. dried chives

Combine flour and melted butter or margarine until smooth paste is formed; set aside. In a large saucepan combine cauliflower, broth, bell pepper, and lemon peel. Bring to a boil; reduce heat to low and simmer for 8 to 10 minutes until cauliflower is tender. Add half and half and flour/butter mixture. Stir well to incorporate butter mixture into milk/cauliflower mixture. Add crab meat with any liquid that is with it and heat through. Season to taste and top with chives. Serve.

CHAPTER 5

Vegetables

It is said that in a small cemetery in Newport, Rhode Island, there stands a tombstone that bears this legend:"To the first man to eat a tomatoe."

–Michele F. Corne

Oven Roasted Tomatoes

The scent of herbs and garlic roasting with the tomatoes will surely whet your appetite for the coming meal.

2 lbs. tomatoes
3 t. minced garlic
2 T. fresh rosemary, chopped
2 T. fresh thyme, chopped
5 T. olive oil

Bring small saucepan of water to rapid boil. Place one tomato at a time into water and rotate it with a spoon for 1 minute. Immediately remove and set on plate. Repeat with all tomatoes. Under very cold running water, with a sharp kitchen knife, peel tomatoes. Place tomatoes in roasting pan and preheat oven to 200°F. In small bowl, blend all other ingredients and salt and pepper to taste. Slowly pour over tomatoes. Bake for 4 hours; remove and enjoy.

Cheese and Bacon Stuffed Tomatoes

A veritable salad in a tomato and an intriguing start to a brunch.

2 medium tomatoes
6 bacon slices, cooked till chewy
1/4 c. onion, chopped
1/4 c. green bell pepper, chopped
1 c. Cheddar cheese, shredded
1 T. chopped lettuce
1 T. crushed cheese crackers
2 t. butter or margarine

Cut the top off each tomato; scoop out pulp and set aside. Drain tomatoes upside down on a rack. Meanwhile, in a large skillet, cook bacon, onions, and pepper over medium heat until vegetables are done. Remove from heat and blend in cheese, lettuce, and tomato pulp. Fill each shell with half the mixture. Sprinkle with cracker crumbs and dot each with 1 t. butter. Place in buttered baking dish and bake in preheated 350°F oven for 25 to 30 minutes.

Very Old-Fashioned Scalloped Tomatoes

3 c. diced tomatoes
1/2 onion, sliced thin
2 t. sugar
Salt and pepper to taste
3 c. bread cubes
4 T. butter or margarine
1/2 c. shredded Parmesan cheese

Preheat oven to 350°F. In large bowl mix tomatoes, onions, and seasonings. Lightly toss tomatoes and 2 c. bread cubes and place in nonmetallic, buttered baking dish. Top with 1 c. bread cubes, dot with the butter, and sprinkle cheese over the top. Bake for 20 to 25 minutes or until tomatoes are bubbling.

Carrots Au Gratin

A rich casserole recipe that has that distinctive, familiar crunch of a corn flake topping—something every casserole should have.

5 T. butter or margarine, divided
2 c. corn flakes, crushed
   to make about a cup
1/3 c. onion, minced
3 T. flour
1 t. salt
Pinch black pepper
1 1/2 c. milk
1 1/2 c. (6 oz.) American cheese,
   shredded
4 c. sliced carrots,
   cooked and drained
1 T. dried parsley (optional)

Melt 2 T. butter and when just melted, mix with crushed corn flakes; set aside. Melt remaining 3 T. margarine in large saucepan over low heat. Add onion. Cook, stirring frequently, until onion is softened, but not browned. Stir in flour, salt and pepper. Add milk gradually, stirring until smooth. Increase heat to medium and cook until mixture is bubbly and thickened, stirring constantly. Add cheese, stirring until melted and remove from heat.

Stir in carrots and parsley flakes. Spread mixture evenly over top. Preheat oven to 350°F and bake for 20 to 25 minutes or until thoroughly heated and bubbly. Remove from oven and let set for 5 minutes before serving.

Parsley was called "smallage" in colonial America. Here are a few more ingredients you may find in some ancient "receipt" books.

Scummings: skimmings from scum.
Sloths: the wasted skins of peeled fruit or vegetables.
Souse: a pickle made with salt; something steeped in pickling juice or spices, as fish, pigs feet, or hogs ear.
Sweet Bone: bone from fresh meat, not salted, pickled, cured, or corned.
Treacle: obsolete term for molasses; sometimes specifically the molasses which drains from refining sugar. Hence called "refiners syrup" and "sugar house molasses."

Glazed Carrots and Onions

Believe it or not, this side dish is great with grilled steak. Add a cocktail and awaaayyyy you go.

1/4 c. butter or margarine
1 lb. carrots, peeled and sliced
1 1/2 c. chicken broth
1 T. brown sugar
1 1/2 c. cooked pearl onions,
   rinsed and drained
Salt and black pepper to taste

In large skillet melt butter over medium-high heat; add carrots. Cook 5 minutes, stirring frequently. Add the chicken broth and bring to a boil. Reduce the heat to medium-low and simmer until the carrots are tender. Remove the carrots and add the sugar to the liquid in the skillet. Bring the liquid to a boil. Reduce the liquid to about 1/4 cup. Return the carrots and add the onions to the skillet and coat with the glaze. Continue cooking for 4 to 5 minutes longer, stirring frequently. Remove from heat and serve.

Green Bean Casserole

Some people call this classic recipe bland. I have to disagree, but if you want more *oomph*, add some diced, cooked bacon or sour cream to the mix. Either way, how can you not like green bean casserole?

1 can cream of mushroom soup
1/2 c. milk
1 t. soy sauce
Dash pepper
4 c. cooked, cut green beans
1 1/3 c. French fried onions

Preheat oven to 350° F. Mix soup, milk, soy, pepper, beans, and 2/3 c. onions in 1 1/2-quart casserole. Bake for 25 minutes or until heated through. Stir; sprinkle with remaining onions. Bake 5 minutes longer.

Crispy Old-World Asparagus

Again, a very simple dish that has just enough accent not to spoil the great flavor of the asparagus. This side dish is especially great when using batter. Simply dip dry asparagus stalks into pancake batter, tapping the side of your bowl to rid yourself of excess batter. Carefully hold them in the oil for 2 to 3 seconds before dropping them slow and easy into the hot oil to fry for 2 to 3 minutes, or until golden brown.

- 1 bunch fresh asparagus
- 1 c. seasoned bread crumbs
- 3 eggs, beaten well
- 2 T. grated Parmesan cheese
- 1/4 c. vegetable oil

If the asparagus stem is large, slice a 1/4 inch off the end and peel the length of the woody stem with a vegetable peeler. If thin, there is no need. Boil or steam until almost tender, about 10 minutes. Drain in a colander. Combine the bread crumbs and Parmesan cheese. Place eggs in a large bowl. Dip the asparagus into the egg and then immediately into the bread crumbs. Heat oil in large skillet over medium-high heat. Gently place asparagus into oil and brown on all sides—about 2 to 3 minutes. Remove onto paper towel to dry and serve immediately.

Caesar Green Beans

When hard boiling eggs, here is a tip or two. Do not cook them any longer than needed. When they are hard boiled, immediately immerse them in ice cold water. This will prevent the grayish coloration that surrounds the yolk that oftentimes is seen. Also, salt the boiling water you are cooking them in. This will greatly aid in peeling the eggs.

- 1 T. olive oil
- 1 lb. cooked green beans
- 3 T. minced onion
- 1 c. seasoned croutons
- 1 T. cider vinegar
- 3 hard boiled eggs, cooled and chopped
- Salt and pepper to taste
- 4 T. shredded Parmesan cheese

On medium heat and in a large skillet, heat olive oil until hot. Add green beans and onion; sauté until onion is tender and beans are heated through, about 4 to 5 minutes. Add croutons, vinegar, and chopped eggs. With large spoon blend all ingredients and continue cooking for 1 minute; remove from heat and salt and pepper to taste. Dish onto serving platter and top with Parmesan cheese; serve immediately.

4-,7-,and 9-Minute Boiled Eggs.

"Rheumatism is cur'd by the persistant [sic] use of Lemon juice, either diluted or in the form of lemonade. Suck half a Lemon evr'y [sic] morning before breakfast and ocassionally [sic] during the day and partake of Lemonade when thirsty in preference to any other Drinke [sic]." so says our forefathers of the eighteenth century.

-The Yankee Chef Archives

Lemon Asparagus Amandine

2 T. sliced almonds
1 t. cornstarch
3/4 c. chicken broth
1 lb. fresh asparagus
2 t. grated lemon peel
Pinch black pepper

Lightly grease nonstick skillet; cook almonds over medium heat, stirring frequently, 3 to 5 minutes or until light gold in color. Set aside. Blend cornstarch into 2 T. chicken broth; set aside. Break tough ends from asparagus and discard. Add asparagus and remaining chicken broth to skillet; bring to a boil. Reduce heat, cover, and cook 3 to 4 minutes or until asparagus is crisp-tender. Remove asparagus to serving plate with slotted spoon; cover to keep warm.

Stir cornstarch mixture, lemon peel, and pepper into liquid in skillet. Cook, stirring sauce, 1 minute more or until sauce is slightly thickened. Garnish with additional sliced almonds, if desired.

When children and adults alike wanted a cooling drink during the summer, such as lemonade, and lemons were not available, sumac berries were used in place of lemons. Our ancestors would steep these tiny red berries in hot water for at least 2 hours. The berries were removed and the resulting liquid was cooled in the brook or stream before drinking.

Belgian Endives and Walnuts

You don't have to sacrifice taste for lightness. This dish is both light and very satisfying to your taste buds. And here in New England, we say "N-DIVE," not "ON-DEEVE"!

4 heads Belgian endive, sliced crosswise
Lettuce leaves
2 pears, cored and diced
2 T. olive oil
1/4 c. walnuts, chopped
3 T. red wine vinegar

Trim endive stems and slice into narrow strips crosswise. Arrange atop lettuce leaves on 4 salad plates. Add pears. Heat oil in skillet over medium-high heat and add walnuts, cook until lightly browned. Add vinegar. Pour mixture over endive and pears. Season with salt and pepper.

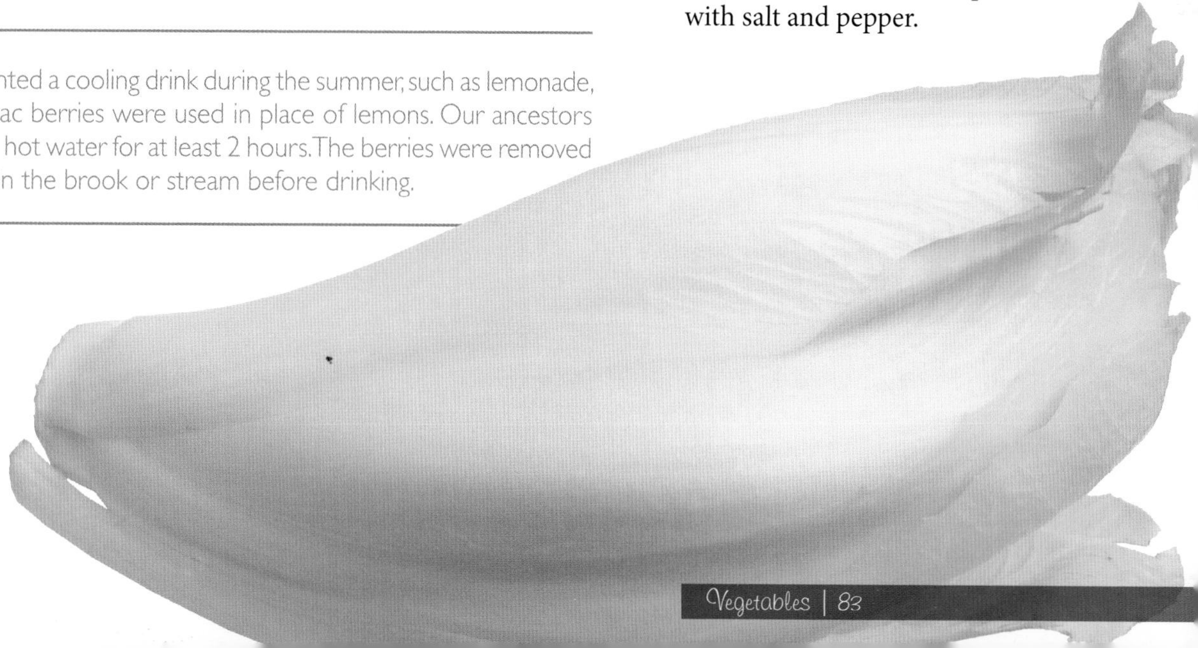

Broccoli with Bacon Salad

You have to make this for your next picnic. Add some plump golden raisins for that sweet and salty combination everyone loves so. Omit the grease and butter altogether and mix in some mayonnaise for yet another flavor combination.

    1 bunch broccoli
    8 slices of bacon
    6 T. butter or margarine
    Salt and pepper to taste
    Seasoned croutons

Rinse the broccoli, pull off the leaves, and cut off the tough lower part of the stalks, leaving about 2 to 3 inches of stalk below the point at which it branches into smaller stems holding the florets. Cut off the florets, and cut the larger florets small. Peel the skin from the remainder of the stalk and chop the same size as your florets. Steam or blanch the broccoli until just tender; drain. Cook the bacon in a large skillet until just done. Drain well on paper towels and dice into small pieces. Using same bacon skillet, add butter and melt on medium heat; add broccoli and bacon bits, toss or mix well, season to taste and heat through. Serve with croutons.

Broccoli with Cashews

As a substitute, broccoflower is a cross between cauliflower and broccoli. It has more vitamin C than oranges and more vitamin A than either broccoli or cauliflower.

    1 pkg. (10 oz.) frozen
      broccoli spears
    1/2 c. cashews, coarsely chopped
    1 T. butter or margarine
    2 t. grated lemon rind

Cook broccoli; drain. In a small skillet, cook and stir cashews in hot butter for 1 to 2 minutes or until golden brown. Remove from heat; stir in lemon rind. Pour over broccoli spears.

Golden Cauliflower

Not eaten nearly as much as broccoli and cheese, cauliflower has been overlooked for far too long, so let's change that, shall we?

    2 T. butter or margarine
    1/3 c. water
    4 c. thinly sliced cauliflower
    1 c. shredded Cheddar cheese
    1 t. paprika (optional)

Melt butter or margarine in large skillet; add cauliflower and water. Cover and steam over high heat for 3 minutes. Sprinkle with cheese and paprika; cover and continue steaming until cheese melts and cauliflower is tender, about 2 minutes.

Harvard Beets

If you want to use fresh beets with this recipe, boil fresh beets, let them cool and don't forget to peel them first before slicing or dicing.

    2 c. (13 oz.-can) sliced beets
    1 t. cornstarch
    1/3 c. sugar
    1/4 c. cider vinegar
    1/2 t. salt
    2 T. butter or margarine

Drain and reserve beet juice. In medium saucepan combine cornstarch and sugar, add the beet juice, vinegar, and salt. Bring to a boil over medium-high heat until thickened and smooth; stirring almost constantly. Reduce heat to low and add sliced beets, stirring gently until beets are warmed through, adding the butter at the last minute.

Yale Beets

Yeah, there is even a rivalry in cookbooks between Yale and Harvard. For those who want more sweet than sour, try these beets. Follow recipe for Harvard Beets but substitute 1/4 c. orange juice for the vinegar.

Peas in Cream

You will not find lettuce in other peas in cream recipes. The addition of lettuce really gives it body and the textural enjoyment is amazing.

3 T. butter or margarine
1/2 c. water
1 1/2 c. fresh shelled peas,
    about 2 lbs. in the shell
2 c. finely shredded lettuce
2 T. minced onion
1 t. sugar
Salt and pepper to taste
1/2 c. light cream

In saucepan, heat butter and water to boiling over medium-high heat. Add peas, lettuce, onion, sugar, salt, and pepper. Cover; reduce heat to medium-low and simmer 12 to 15 minutes until the peas are tender. Remove from heat, do not drain; add cream and serve immediately.

To Keep Green Peas till Christmas

Take young peas, shell them, put them in a colander to drain, then lay a cloth four of five times double on a table. Then spread them on, dry them very well, and have your bottles ready. Fill them, cover them with mutton suet fat when it is a little soft; fill the necks almost to the top, cork them, tie a bladder and a leather over them and set them in a dry cool place.

–American Cookery, 1796

Smoky Peas and Potatoes

For some reason this vegetable dish is my all-time favorite. I think the smokiness of the bacon combined with the sweetness of the peas and potatoes lends itself to be an accompaniment for just about any meat dish you may prepare. Be it summer, winter, autumn, or spring, dry Cheddar cheese can be enjoyed no matter what you do with it.

2 lbs. small potatoes
2 lbs. fresh peas (about 3 1/2 lb.
    peas in the shell)
3 T. butter or margarine
3 T. flour
2 c. milk
1 c. shredded Cheddar cheese
6 slices bacon, cooked
    crisp and crumbled

Cook potatoes in boiling water until just tender; drain. In the meantime, cook peas in 2 c. water until tender; drain. In small saucepan, melt butter over medium heat. Add flour and whisk until smooth. Add milk and continue cooking until milk has thickened; add cheese and the crumbled bacon and stir until cheese has melted. Combine hot potatoes and peas in serving dish; top with cheese sauce and serve while hot.

Cashew-Orange Peas

The pear shaped cashew has two shells that surround the kernel. Between these two shells is a toxic oil that can blister skin. Fortunately, these shells and oil are removed during processing.

1/3 c. orange juice
1 T. honey
Pinch salt
1 t. cornstarch
1 lb. frozen peas, thawed
1/2 t. grated orange rind
1/4 c. cashews, broken into pieces

In medium saucepan, whisk together the orange juice, honey, salt, and cornstarch. Bring to a boil over medium-high heat. Whisk constantly until thickened and syrupy. While on the heat, add the peas, orange rind, and cashews. Stir to blend, cooking an additional 1 minute. Remove and serve.

Easy Minted Peas

I cannot think of one reason why anyone would not want to try this dish. I made it as simple as possible. Use frozen peas if you aren't a fan of canned. Either way, you will not be disappointed.

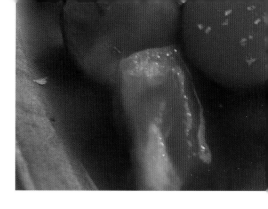

1 can (16 oz.) peas in liquid	1/2 t. salt
1/4 c. mint jelly	Pinch black pepper
1 t. butter or margarine	

Drain liquid from peas into a saucepan. Cook on medium-high heat until only a 1/2 c. of liquid remains. Add peas, jelly, butter, salt, and pepper and heat through, stirring frequently. Serve.

Herbed Vegetable Skillet

Many herbed vegetable skillets add a liquid. Not here! Let the herbs shine through in this vitamin-packed recipe.

2 t. oil
1 clove garlic, minced
1 1/2 c. fresh cauliflower florets,
    cut quarter-sized
2 c. cabbage, chopped quarter-sized
1/2 c. thinly sliced carrots
1/2 t. dried marjoram
Pinch red pepper flakes
Salt and pepper to taste

Heat oil in large skillet over medium heat. Add garlic; cook and stir 30 seconds. Add cauliflower, cabbage, carrot, marjoram, and red pepper flakes; cook and stir 3 minutes.

Stir in salt and pepper and add 1/4 c. water. Cover; reduce heat to medium-low and cook 4 to 5 minutes or until cauliflower and carrots are crisp-tender.

Vermont Maple-Caramelized Vegetables

Although not truly caramelized, the sweetness of maple syrup adds flavors comparable to caramelization. You can almost taste the "forest through the trees" in this recipe.

2 carrots, peeled
2 parsnips, peeled
1 sweet or white potato, peeled
1 fist-sized celery root, peeled
1 zucchini
1 T. butter
1/4 c. maple syrup
1/2 c. roasted and chopped almonds
Salt and pepper, to taste
Pieces of maple sugar, to taste

Cut vegetables into julienne strips and steam all, except for zucchini, for 5 minutes. Add zucchini strips and steam for 2 more minutes. Remove from heat. Melt butter in frying pan. Add maple syrup and cook for 1 minute while stirring. Add vegetables and coat in maple sauce. Season with salt and pepper. Remove from heat. Serve vegetables with chopped almonds. Sprinkle with maple sugar pieces, if desired.

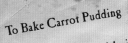

To Bake Carrot Pudding

A coffee-cup full of boiled and strained carrots, five eggs, sugar and butter of each two ounces, cinnamon and rose-water to you taste, baked in a deep dish without paste, one hour.

—New American Cookery, 1805.

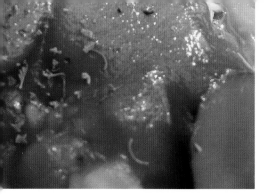

Zucchini and Tomato Sauté

This vegetable dish is best prepared in the fall in New England, when the zucchini, summer squash, and tomatoes are all at their finest. Don't be afraid to add the same amount of golden yellow summer squash either with, or in place of, the zucchini in this dish.

```
1 med. onion, minced
2 T. olive oil
1 clove garlic, minced
3 medium tomatoes, chopped
1/2 t. salt
3/4 t. basil
1/2 t. sugar
3/4 t. oregano
1/4 c. chicken stock
1 1/2 lb. zucchini, unpeeled
    and sliced 1/4 inch thick
```

Cook onion in oil in a skillet until soft over medium-high heat. Mix in garlic, tomatoes, salt, basil, sugar, oregano, pepper, and chicken broth. Bring to boiling, cover, and reduce heat to low. Simmer 20 minutes.

Uncover. Mix in zucchini. Continue cooking over low heat, stirring frequently, until tomato sauce is reduced and thickened and zucchini is crisp-tender, about 10 minutes; salt and pepper.

Maple-Glazed New Potatoes

Italian Balsamic vinegar is aged in wooden barrels for at least 10 years. Some vinegars are aged 50 years while 100 year old Balsamic vinegar is not unheard of. The true stuff is from Treddiano, Italy, and made with white grape juice that has been transferred, during the aging process, from one barrel to another—all of the different woods give it that distinct flavor.

```
3 lb. tiny new potatoes
1/4 c. butter, melted
Salt and black pepper (cracked
    black pepper is best here)
3 T. white balsamic vinegar
2 T. pure maple syrup
3 cloves garlic, thinly sliced
1/4 c. chopped green onions
2 T. chopped fresh thyme
1 T. finely shredded lemon peel
```

Preheat the oven to 350°F. Halve or quarter any large potatoes. In shallow dish large enough to hold potatoes in a single layer, toss potatoes with butter; season with salt and pepper. Spread in single layer. Roast potatoes, uncovered, for 45 minutes, stirring once or twice during roasting.

Meanwhile, in small dish, stir together vinegar, maple syrup, and sliced garlic. Drizzle potatoes with vinegar mixture, gently tossing with a spoon or spatula to coat. Continue to roast about 10 to 20 minutes more, until potatoes are fork-tender and glazed, stirring once or twice. To serve, sprinkle potatoes with green onions, thyme, and lemon peel.

Dilled Potatoes

If you use new red potatoes in this dish, remember that all it takes is a strong wind to "peel" these red wonders. Their skin is so fragile that merely rinsing them under cold water and rubbing gently with your hands is sufficient.

3 T. butter or margarine
8 very small potatoes, cut quarter
   size, cooked, and cooled
2 T. dried dill
3 T. minced onion
Salt and pepper to taste

Over medium-high heat, melt butter in large skillet. Add all ingredients and cook for 8 to 9 minutes or until potatoes are heated through. Toss with slotted spoon while cooling to evenly distribute dill seasoning onto all potatoes. Remove and serve immediately, season with salt and pepper.

Oven-Roasted Rosemary Potatoes

As late as the 1850s, potatoes were considered food for livestock by many New Englanders. *The Farmers Manual* from this time recommended potatoes be "grown near hog pens as a convenience towards feeding the hogs."

2 T. butter or margarine
2 lbs. small potatoes,
   cut into quarters
1 T. olive oil
1 t. dried rosemary, crumbled
1/2 t. dried thyme
3/4 t. salt
1/4 t. black pepper

Preheat oven to 450°F. Place butter in large roasting pan; place in oven until butter melts. Remove pan from oven and add potatoes, oil, rosemary, thyme, salt, and pepper; toss until evenly mixed.

Roast potatoes until tender and browned, stirring occasionally, about 50 minutes. Transfer potatoes to platter and serve.

Caramelized Potatoes

Caramelizing these tubers almost reminds you of the holidays, but please enjoy these during the summer as well, especially with lamb.

1/4 c. sugar
1/4 c. butter or margarine
1 1/2 lbs. small potatoes,
   peeled, cooked, and cooled

In large nonstick saucepan, cook the sugar over medium heat until clear, stirring with a fork. Add butter and potatoes, turn heat up to medium-high and continue cooking about 8 minutes longer, constantly rolling the potatoes around to evenly coat. They will be done when the potatoes are glistening with darkened sugar syrup that clings. Remove and enjoy.

Caramelizing has been given a bad rap as of late. Everyone says by searing this and burning that, you are actually caramelizing. Wrong! Using half the amount of sugar to water and boiling it down to syrup, thereby reducing, is caramelizing. Remember, the darker the caramel, the more bitter. You can stop the caramelizing by immediately deglazing with butter or lemon juice.

Potato Pancakes

Serve with sour cream and chives or applesauce for something different.

3 lbs. potatoes
1 small onion, minced
2 eggs, beaten
1/3 c. flour
2 t. salt
Pinch black pepper
Vegetable oil

Peel and rinse potatoes in very cold water. With a handheld grater, shred potatoes into large bowl quickly before they brown. Add onion, beaten eggs, flour, salt, and pepper; mix very well. In large skillet heat 1/3 c. vegetable oil until hot over medium-high heat. Drop potato mixture by 1/4 cups into 4 mounds, a couple of inches apart. With spatula, flatten each out about 1/2 to 3/4 inches high. Cook pancakes until golden brown on 1 side, about 4 minutes; turn and brown other side. Remove pancakes to serving platter and cover to keep warm. Repeat and add more oil as needed.

Ambered Gratin Potatoes

Cooking spray
1 red onion, thinly sliced
4 oz. cream cheese, cubed
1 1/4 c. chicken broth
1/2 c. milk
4 slices cooked bacon, crumbled
1/4 c. maple syrup
2 lbs. potatoes, cut into 1/4-inch
   slices
1 c. shredded Cheddar cheese

Heat oven to 400F°. Cook onions in large skillet with cooking spray over medium-high heat (3 to 5 minutes), or until crisp-tender, stirring frequently. Remove onions from skillet and add cream cheese, broth, and milk. Cook and stir over medium-low for 5 minutes or until cheese has melted and the whole is blended well. Remove from heat and stir in the syrup and bacon. Spray a 13 × 9-inch baking dish with nonstick cooking spray. Place half the potatoes in the prepared baking dish, cover with half the cheese sauce and shredded cheese. Repeat with the remaining potatoes, cheese sauce, and shredded cheese. Cover and bake 45 to 50 minutes or until potatoes are almost done. Remove cover and continue baking until the top is golden brown. You may also sprinkle additional cheese and parsley on top of casserole when uncovering.

Gratin Potatoes

Follow recipe for "Scalloped Potatoes" but add 1 c. Cheddar cheese to milk mixture and cook until cheese has melted. You may also sprinkle additional cheese and parsley on top of casserole when uncovering to bake the additional 20 minutes.

Sweet Potato Gratin

Here we go again with the salty-sweet aspect that so many have come to love lately. It took me awhile to hop on board, but am I glad I did.

I T. olive oil
2 cloves garlic, minced
I 1/2 lbs. sweet potatoes, peeled
   and sliced 1/4 inch thick
2/3 c. chicken broth
Salt and pepper to taste
3/4 c. almonds, chopped
3/4 c. bread crumbs
4 T. butter or margarine, melted
I c. Swiss cheese, shredded

Grease 8-inch square baking pan with olive oil. Sprinkle baking pan with garlic. Layer sweet potato slices in baking pan. Pour in broth. Season with salt and pepper to taste. Cover and bake at 350°F for 30 minutes.

Meanwhile, combine almonds, bread crumbs, cheese, and melted butter. Sprinkle over hot sweet potatoes and bake, uncovered, 20 minutes or until top is golden brown.

Grilled Potato Wedges with Malt Vinegar-Tarragon Dip

Although designed to be cooked on an outdoor grill, you can also grill these potato wedges in a nonstick skillet. The mayonnaise mixture is also delicious with chicken fingers or any type of deep-fried fish.

3/4 c. plus I t. malt vinegar
I 1/2 c. mayonnaise
I T. chopped tarragon
5 Russet or all-purpose potatoes,
   scrubbed
1/4 c. canola oil
2 T. finely chopped parsley

Bring 3/4 c. vinegar to a boil over high heat in small saucepan and continue boiling until reduced by half. Remove saucepan from heat and let cool 5 minutes. Combine mayonnaise, cooled vinegar, remaining 1 t. vinegar, and tarragon in medium bowl. Season, if desired, with salt and pepper. Cover and refrigerate at least 30 minutes.

Cover potatoes with water in 4-qt. saucepot; bring to a boil over medium-high heat. Reduce heat and simmer 15 minutes or until potatoes are tender, but still firm. Drain and cool slightly. Cut each potato lengthwise into 8 slices. Brush potatoes with oil and season, if desired, with salt and pepper. Grill, turning once, 4 minutes or until golden and cooked through. Arrange potatoes on serving platter, then sprinkle with parsley. Serve with dip.

New Potatoes and Cream

There's something about simmering these potatoes in milk that brings out the very delicate flavor of new potatoes. If it were up to me, I would just run the potatoes under cold water briefly, leaving as much of the skin on as possible.

12 small new potatoes
Flour
1 c. milk
1 c. heavy cream
1 T. butter or margarine
Salt and pepper to taste
1 c. chopped scallions

Scrub new potatoes, leaving some skin on. Cut into quarters and place them in a saucepan; dust with flour. Add milk and cream, butter, salt, and pepper to taste. Cook, covered, over low heat for 20 to 30 minutes, stirring occasionally, until tender.

Maine Scootin' 'Long the Shore

For years, Maine fishermen's wives prepared this dish whenever the men came back from their day of fishing. When asked what they wanted to sup on at the end of the day, the men often remarked, "Well, make it scootin' 'long the shore." One can only venture a guess as to exactly what that meant. Salt pork was often "tryed out" and placed directly on top of this dish when it was done cooking.

4 T. bacon fat
1 medium onion, sliced thin
4 medium potatoes, sliced

Heat bacon fat in a skillet over medium-high heat until oil is hot. Reduce heat to low and stir in onions and potatoes. Cover and cook, stirring occasionally, until the fat is absorbed and the potatoes are tender. Uncover when brown and crusty on the bottom and serve browned side up.

Grilled Sweet Potato Steaks With Maple Pecan Butter

4 lg. sweet potatoes
Olive oil
Salt and pepper
Maple Pecan Butter, *recipe below*
1/2 c. (1/2 stick) butter

1/4 c. maple syrup
3 T. chopped pecans
Pinch ground cinnamon
Pinch cayenne pepper
Pinch salt

Wash sweet potatoes and wrap each in a single sheet of aluminum foil. Build a charcoal fire for indirect cooking by situating the coals on only one side of the grill, leaving the other side void. When the temperature is approximately 400°F, place wrapped sweet potatoes on the grill over the side void of charcoal. Close lid and cook for 1 hour and 15 minutes with indirect heat, or until sweet potatoes soften.

While potatoes cook, prepare Maple Pecan Butter. Melt butter in small saucepan. Add maple syrup, pecans, cinnamon, cayenne pepper, and salt. Heat mixture on low for less than one minute or until a layer of bubbles forms over the surface. Remove from heat, and set aside until needed.

Remove sweet potatoes from grill, unwrap, and halt cooking process by dipping them into a bowl of cold water. Place sweet potatoes on a countertop and let them cool for at least 30 minutes before cutting into 1/2-inch-thick medallions.

Coat each sweet potato steak with olive oil and lightly season with salt and pepper. Grill each steak directly over the coals (approximately 400°F) for 3 to 4 minutes on each side. Remove potato steaks from grill and serve drizzled with warm maple pecan butter.

Arizona Baked Corn

Arizona? Yup! My brother lives next door to this hot, arid state and gave me a recipe for a very tasty corn dish. I tweaked here and touched it there—Arizona Baked Corn is the result.

1 onion, minced
1/2 rib celery, minced
2 T. butter or margarine
2 T. chili powder
2 c. tomato sauce mixed with 3 T.
  tomato paste until smooth.
3 c. whole kernel corn
2 c. Monterey Jack cheese, shredded

In large skillet over medium heat, cook onion and celery in butter until tender but not browned, about 5 minutes. Add chili powder, tomato sauce mixture, corn, and salt and pepper to taste. Pour into 1 quart casserole dish and top with cheese. Bake in preheated 425°F oven for 10 to 12 minutes, or until cheese is browned and bubbly.

Corn Oysters, aka Corn Fritters

Oh man, a plate full of fritters with some warm maple syrup for dunking. Where's my remote?

Vegetable oil
1 1/2 c. flour
3 t. baking powder
3/4 t. salt
1 c. milk
1 egg, beaten
5 ears corn, scraped of their kernels
  (Yes, you can use 1 c. canned or
  frozen corn)

Heat oil to 350°F in a deep fat fryer or heat 2 inches of oil on a stove-top to 350°F. Sift together dry ingredients, and then mix wet into dry just until moistened. Add the corn and mix well. Drop by the tablespoonful into oil and fry 4 to 5 minutes or until golden brown. Serve with warm maple syrup if desired, as they did generations ago.

If you drop fritter batter as directed above, their shape after cooking led to the name Corn Oysters. If you were to shape them into ovals before frying—as they did long ago—then they were called Corn Fritters.

Acorn Squash

Buttercup Squash

Spaghetti Squash

Keep maple butter on hand in the fridge for that extra touch on hot veggies, sweet breads, and even your breakfast toast. Simply beat 1/2 cup of softened, unsalted butter with a pinch of salt until creamy. Beating constantly, slowly drizzle in 1/4 cup pure maple syrup.

Maple Butternut Squash

2 medium butternut squash,
  about 2 lbs. each
1/2 c. maple syrup
6 T. unsalted butter or margarine

Cut each squash lengthwise in half; discard seeds. Then cut each squash half crosswise and peel. Cut into slices about 1 inch thick.

In 4 to 5-quart saucepan, heat 1 inch water to boiling. Add squash; heat to boiling. Reduce heat to low; cover and simmer until squash is fork-tender, about 15 minutes. Drain.

In large bowl, with mixer at low speed, beat squash, maple syrup, and margarine until smooth. Spoon into warm bowl.

Spaghetti Squash with Avocado Pesto

Something different yet quite tasty and refreshing. "A symphony of notes to enjoy," as Dad would say.

1 medium spaghetti squash
  (1 1/2 to 2 lbs.) washed,
  halved lengthwise, and seeded
1/2 ripe avocado (4 ounces),
  pitted and diced
1/4 c. fresh basil leaves
1 T. chopped chives
2 T. grated Parmesan cheese
1 t. minced garlic
1/2 t. salt
1/4 t. black pepper
1/3 c. hot water
2 t. chopped parsley or basil (optional)

Preheat oven to 375°F. Lightly coat a baking sheet with olive oil cooking spray. Pierce outside of each half of squash a few times with a fork. Place squash cut side down on baking sheet and bake for about 45 minutes, or until very tender with a fork. Cool slightly.

Meanwhile, place avocado, basil or parsley, chives, Parmesan, garlic, salt, black pepper, and hot water in blender and process until smooth, turning blender off and on occasionally and adding a tablespoon or two of additional hot water if needed. There will be between 1/2 and 3/4 cup of pesto.

When squash has cooled, use fork to rake the spaghetti-like threads of squash into a serving bowl. Discard skin. Drizzle pesto over squash and garnish with fresh basil or parsley if desired.

Spinach with Mushrooms

Want something texturally different? Chopped, toasted pecans add some crunch to this earthy dish.

4 T. olive oil
1/2 lb. mushrooms, thinly sliced
1 lb. spinach, stemmed
1 T. cider vinegar
1 T. prepared mustard
1 t. sugar
3/4 t. salt

In 4-quart saucepan, heat oil until hot over medium-high heat. Add mushrooms and cook until tender, about 5 minutes, stirring often. Remove saucepan from heat and add spinach, vinegar, mustard, sugar, and salt; gently toss to coat well. Serve warm.

Metro Simmered Spinach

Originally called Downtown Spinach, I brought this recipe up to date with the addition of sun-dried tomatoes, which really give this dish color, texture, and taste.

2 t. olive oil
1 c. sliced mushrooms
1/2 thinly sliced leek or
  4 sliced green onions
1 clove garlic, finely chopped
1/4 c. reduced-sodium
  chicken broth
1 package (10 oz.) fresh spinach
1 T. thinly sliced sun-dried tomatoes,
  drained
1 t. soy sauce

In large skillet heat oil over medium heat; cook mushrooms and leeks about 5 minutes, stirring, until tender. Add garlic; cook 30 seconds. Add broth, bring to a boil; add spinach, cover and reduce heat to medium. Simmer 3 to 5 minutes, until spinach wilts and is tender. Stir in tomatoes and soy sauce. Season to taste with salt and pepper. Serve warm.

In colonial America, if you mistakenly ate poisonous mushrooms, you were in good hands with the local *physick*. This doctor would have prescribed an emetic of ground mustard seed or sulphate of zinc, followed by frequent doses of Epsom salts and large stimulating clysters to clear the stomach and bowels. After the poison had been evacuated, sipping on water or brandy frequently would make you good as new. Rest assured that when the word "stimulating" and "clyster" are in the same sentence, doctors of old were trying to make it sound more fun than it actually was. Just picture the largest syringe you could possibly imagine. Then know that it sure wasn't going to be for the injection of a liquid in your vein...but somewhere else.

Potato and Corn-Stuffed Mushroom Caps

2 T. butter or margarine
1/4 c. chopped red bell pepper
1 garlic clove, minced
1/2 t. salt
1 med. sized potato, peeled, cooked,
   and mashed with a fork
1 c. frozen corn
1/4 c. sliced green onions
3/4 c. Cheddar cheese, shredded
8 large Portobello mushroom caps
Salt and pepper to taste

Melt margarine in medium saucepan over medium heat. Add bell pepper and garlic; cook and stir 1 to 2 minutes or until bell pepper is crisp-tender. Add salt, mashed potatoes, corn, onions, and cheese; mix well. Continue heating another minute or so until cheese is melted and mixture is hot throughout, stirring constantly.

Preheat oven to 350°F. With spoon, scrape underside of caps to remove gills and stems. Place on baking sheet, scraped side up. With tablespoon fill each cap with potato mixture. Place in oven for 8 to 10 minutes or until mushroom caps begin to soften and filling is crisp.

Kosher Dill Refrigerator Pickles

Now how can a Yankee have a vegetable section without a recipe for the most well-liked of all pickles? I can't! Halve this recipe or even quarter it if you aren't "putting up."

4 qts. long red, green,
  or yellow peppers
1 1/2 c. canning and pickling salt
2 garlic cloves
2 T. prepared horseradish
10 c. vinegar
2 c. water
1/4 c. sugar

Prepare and process home canning jars and lids according to manufacturer's instructions for sterilized jars. Wash cucumbers and remove blossoms; drain. Leave whole, cut into spears, or slice. Combine pickling salt, vinegar and water into a large, non-reactive pot. Do not use aluminum. Bring mixture just to boil over medium heat, stirring constantly until mixture dissolves.

Pack cucumbers into sterilized jars, leaving 1/2-inch headspace. Evenly divide hot pickling liquid among the packed jars, leaving 1/2-inch headspace. Remove air bubbles and cap each jar as it is filled. If more liquid is needed for proper headspace, add a mix of 1 part vinegar and 2 parts water. If shelf-stable pickles are preferred, use the hot water bath method, processing pints (20 minutes) and quarts (30 minutes).

Cool to room temperature, label and store in refrigerator. Product is ready to eat after 24 hours. When properly processed and sealed, unopened refrigerator product can be stored up to 6 months, and shelf-stable product up to 18 months.

Homemade Pickling Spice

Now, if you want to make your own pickling spice, use the recipe below. The great thing about making your own pickling spice is that if you wanted to make a spicy pickle you could add some more red pepper flakes. Or, if you don't want any spice, you could leave them out.

6 T. mustard seed
3 T. whole allspice
6 t. coriander seed
6 whole cloves
3 t. ground ginger
3 t. red pepper flakes
3 bay leaves
3 cinnamon sticks

Crush the cinnamon sticks into pieces and crumble the bay leaves. Combine all ingredients and store in an airtight container.

Makes approximately 1 cup and these ingredients can be adjusted according to taste.

Peter Piper picked a peck of pickled peppers,
A peck of pickled peppers Peter Piper picked;
If Peter Piper picked a peck of pickled peppers,
Where's the peck of pickled peppers Peter Piper picked?

The earliest version of this tongue twister was published in *Peter Piper's Practical Principles of Plain and Perfect Pronunciation* by John Harris (1756–1846) in London in 1813, which includes one name tongue twister for each letter of the alphabet in the same style. However, the rhyme was apparently known at least a generation earlier. Two other tongue twisters from the book are:

Enoch Elkrig ate an empty Eggshell:
Did Enoch Elkrig eat an empty Eggshell?
If Enoch Elkrig ate an empty Eggshell,
Where's the empty eggshell Enoch Elkrig ate?

Jumping Jackey jeer'd a Jesting Juggler:
Did Jumping Jackey jeer a Jesting Juggler?
If Jumping Jackey jeer'd a Jesting Juggler,
Where's the Jesting Juggler Jumping Jackey jeer'd?

To Make Cheddar Cheese

Take the new milk of twelve cows in the morning and the evening cream of twelve cows, and put to it three spoonfuls of rennet 'tis come, break it, and whey it: and when 'tis well whey'd, break it again, and work in three pounds of fresh butter, and put it in your press, and turn it in the press very often for an hour or more and change the cloth, and wash them every time you change them. You may put wet cloths at first to them; but towards the last put two or three fine dry cloths to them, let it lie thirty or forty hours in the press, according to the thickness of the cheese; then take it out and wash it in whey, and lay it in a dry cloth till 'tis dry; then lay it on your shelf, and turn it often.

– *The Compleat Housewife*, 1730

Pickled Peppers

4 qts. long peppers (red, green, or yellow)
1 1/2 c. canning and pickling salt
2 garlic cloves
2 T. prepared horseradish
10 c. vinegar
2 c. water
1/4 c. sugar

Wash and drain peppers. Cut 2 small slits in each pepper. Dissolve salt in 1 gallon water. Pour over peppers and let stand 12 to 18 hours in a cool place. Drain, rinse again, and drain thoroughly.

Combine remaining ingredients. Simmer 15 minutes. Remove garlic. Pack peppers into jars, leaving 1/2-inch headspace. Bring liquid to a boil. Fill jar to within 1/2-inch of top with boiling liquid. Remove air bubbles. Tighten lids. Boil 10 minutes in a boiling water bath.

CHAPTER 6
Snacks, Appetizers, Dips, and Spreads

A common kitchen spice can stop a case of the spins. Simply drop a pinch of cayenne into a glass of warm water and sip. The warmth of the water and the heat of the cayenne cause your body to pump more blood and oxygen to your brain, which makes you feel clear-headed and steady. If you continue to experience bouts of dizziness, see your doctor.

Crunchy Meatballs

There is just something about the crunchiness of water chestnuts in meatballs along with teriyaki sauce that makes it impossible for me to eat just a few of these Asian-inspired meatballs.

1 lb. ground beef
1/2 lb. ground pork
2 eggs, slightly beaten
1/2 t. salt
1/4 c. dry bread crumbs
1 T. soy sauce
1/4 t. garlic salt
1 can (8 1/2 oz.) water chestnuts, drained, finely chopped
1 c. teriyaki sauce, warmed

Preheat oven to 375°F. In a medium bowl combine beef, pork, eggs, salt, bread crumbs, soy sauce, garlic salt, and water chestnuts. Shape into 1-inch balls. Arrange on a rack in broiler pan. Bake 15 to 18 minutes in oven or until meatballs are browned throughout. Drain and discard drippings. Pour teriyaki sauce into a small bowl. To serve, spear warm baked meatballs with small wooden picks; dip into teriyaki sauce or simply pour sauce over the meatballs and have at it.

Sweet and Sour Meatballs

My grandfather, the first Yankee Chef, always made Porcupine Meatballs using this recipe. For every pound of hamburger, he added 1 c. cooked, long-grain white rice, 1/2 c. tomato sauce, 1 egg, minced onion, nutmeg, salt, black pepper, and Worcestershire sauce.

1 egg, slightly beaten
1/3 c. milk
1/2 c. soft bread crumbs
1 t. salt
Pinch white pepper
1/4 t. rubbed sage
1/4 c. minced onion
1 lb. ground beef
Sweet and Sour Sauce, below

Preheat oven to 350°F. In a medium bowl, combine egg, milk, bread crumbs, salt, pepper, sage, and onion. Stir in ground beef. Shape into 1-inch balls. Arrange on a rack in broiler pan. Bake 15 to 20 minutes until lightly browned; drain. Prepare Sweet and Sour Sauce. To serve, arrange meatballs in a chafing dish or heat-proof bowl on a hot tray. Pour sauce evenly over meatballs.

Sweet and Sour Sauce:
1 can (8 oz.) sliced pineapple
2 T. cornstarch
2 T. soy sauce
1 c. chicken broth
1 green bell pepper, chopped
1/4 c. vinegar
1/4 c. honey

Drain pineapple; reserve juice in a small saucepan and set aside. Cut pineapple into 3/4-inch pieces; set aside. Stir cornstarch into reserved pineapple juice until dissolved. Stir in soy sauce, broth, green peppers, vinegar, and honey. Cook and stir over medium-low heat until thickened and translucent. Stir in pineapple chunks and cook one minute longer.

To Ragout Hog's Feet and Ears

If they are raw or fowled, boil the feet and ears till they are tender, after which cut them into thin bits about two inches long and a quarter of an inch thick. Put them into a stew pan with half a pint of good gravy, a glass of red wine, a good piece of butter rolled in flour, a little pepper and salt, a good deal of mustard, and half an onion. Stir all together till it becomes of a fine thickness and then pour it into a dish, meat and gravy together.

– *The Frugal Housewife*, 1772

Teriyaki Roll-Ups
Pass the Mai Tai please!

1/3 c. soy sauce
3 T. honey
1/2 t. ground ginger
1 garlic clove, crushed
2 t. grated onion
1/4 c. dry white wine
3/4 lb. top sirloin
1 can (6 oz.) whole water chestnuts, drained

In a shallow medium bowl, combine soy sauce, honey, ginger, garlic, onion, and wine; set aside. Cut meat into very thin, long slices. Cut water chestnuts in half. Wrap 1 slice of meat around each water chestnut half. Secure with a wooden pick. Marinate in soy sauce mixture 1 hour. Preheat broiler if necessary. Place oven rack 5 to 8 inches from heating element. Remove marinated roll-ups from marinade; arrange on broiler pan. Discard marinade. Turning once or twice, broil meat 3 to 4 minutes until evenly browned. Serve hot.

Edam cheese

Stuffed Edam

This creamy appetizer can only be enhanced with the crunchiness of slivered almonds scattered on top. And don't wait for the holidays to get your Snuggie® on, curl up on the couch, and dig in.

1 whole Edam cheese (1 lb.), room temperature
1/4 c. mayonnaise
2 t. chopped chives
2 T. dry white wine
2 t. chopped parsley
2 oz. Swiss cheese, cut into quarter-sized pieces

Cut a 2 1/2-inch circle from top of Edam cheese. Remove and discard circle of red coating. Scoop out center of cheese, leaving about 1/4-inch shell; leave coating intact. Place removed cheese in food processor or blender. Add mayonnaise, chives, wine, parsley, and Swiss cheese. Process until smooth. Spoon about 2/3 of the cheese mixture evenly into cheese shell. Refrigerate remaining cheese mixture; use to refill shell.

To make mayonnaise, beat 3 yolks at room temperature until thick and lemony with the electric mixer on high. Stop mixing and add 1/2 t. salt, 1/2 T. lemon juice, 1/2 T. vinegar, and add 1/4 t. mustard for some extra flavor. Beat thoroughly and add 2 cups of vegetable oil very slowly; continue to beat on high until well incorporated. After 1/2 c. of oil has been drizzled in, pour a little quicker.

Peppered Cheese

Fines herbes is a French phrase meaning a combination of finely chopped herbs. Ages ago, both chopped mushrooms and truffles were part of *fines herbes*, but this term now denotes a mixture of parsley, tarragon, basil, thyme, and chives, all in equal proportions. If you can't find it at a store, make your own, altering some while adding others if you wish. It will keep as other spices do.

2 c. grated Monterey Jack cheese
1 pkg. (8 oz.) cream cheese, room temperature
1 t. *fines herbes*
1 t. minced chives
2 t. Worcestershire sauce
1 garlic clove, minced
3 T. seasoned pepper
Plain or bacon-flavored crackers

In a medium bowl, combine Monterey Jack cheese, cream cheese, *fines herbes*, chives, Worcestershire sauce, garlic, and pepper. Shape cheese mixture into a 5-inch ball; slightly flatten one side. Cut a 12-inch square of waxed paper. Roll cheese ball in pepper until completely covered. Refrigerate 6 hours or overnight. Cheese ball can be stored in refrigerator several days before serving (which will only enhance the flavor). Cut into thin slices; serve on crackers.

Cheese Fritters

These fritters will literally melt in your mouth. Soft and piping hot, they pair well with...a movie.

1/4 c. butter or margarine
1/2 c. water
1/2 c. flour
1/2 t. baking powder
Pinch salt
2 eggs
1/2 c. grated Cheddar cheese
1/4 c. Parmesan cheese
2 egg whites
Oil for deep frying
Additional grated Parmesan cheese

In a medium saucepan, heat butter and water to a rolling boil. In a small bowl, combine flour, baking powder, and salt. Add to water mixture all at once. Beat vigorously over low heat about 1 minute until mixture becomes smooth and leaves side of pan. Remove from heat. Beat in eggs, one at a time. Continue to beat until mixture has lost its sheen. Beat in Cheddar cheese and 1/4 c. Parmesan cheese. In a medium bowl, beat egg whites until stiff but not dry. Fold into cheese mixture.

Pour oil into a deep-fryer to depth recommended by manufacturer or pour oil 2 inches deep in a heavy medium saucepan.

Heat oil to 350°F. Carefully drop heaping teaspoonfuls of cheese mixture into hot oil. Fry until puffy and golden brown, 40–50 seconds. Use a slotted spoon to remove cooked fritter from oil; drain on paper towels. Sprinkle with additional grated Parmesan cheese and serve warm.

Did you know?: Consuming cheese directly after a meal, and in between meals, helps reduce tooth decay.

Turophilia is the love or obsession with cheese.

Mexican Pizza

Serve with a side of warm salsa* to dip this "kick-in-the-pants" appetizer into.

1/4 c. flour
1/2 t. salt
1/4 c. butter or margarine, melted
4 eggs, slightly beaten
1 can (4 oz.) chopped green chilies
1 c. cottage cheese
2 c. grated Monterey Jack Cheese,
    or Pepper Jack cheese

Grease a 12-inch pizza pan; set aside. Preheat oven to 375°F. In a medium bowl, combine flour, salt, and melted butter. Stir in eggs, chilies, cottage cheese, and Monterey Jack cheese. Pour evenly into greased pan and bake 15–20 minutes until firm and lightly browned. Cut into thin wedges.

*Wanna try your own Yankee Salsa? Turn the page!

Harvest Apple Salsa

What do us Yankees know about salsa? You are about to find out.

2 apples, cored and diced
2 c. tomatoes, peeled and diced
1 celery rib, diced
1 onion, diced
1 green pepper, diced
1 1/2 t. salt
1 T. cider vinegar
1 T. sugar
1 green chili pepper, chopped
1 t. chopped, fresh cilantro

Combine all ingredients. If finer texture is desired, put through food grinder using fine blade. Cover tightly and chill overnight. Serve with chips or as a topping for cheese quesadillas, tacos, or nachos.

Deviled Eggs, Recipe 1

I know, many of you are thinking that this dish is too old fashioned. If you are in that group, then try the variations I put forth below.

6 hard-cooked eggs
3 T. mayonnaise
1/2 t. prepared mustard
2 t. vinegar
1/4 t. salt
Pinch black pepper
1/8 t. celery seed (optional)

Cut hard-cooked eggs in half lengthwise. Remove egg yolks; set egg whites aside. In a small bowl, use a fork to mash egg yolks. Stir in mayonnaise, mustard, vinegar, salt, pepper and celery seeds. Spoon egg yolk mixture evenly into egg white halves.

Deviled Eggs, Recipe 2

6 eggs, hard-cooked and peeled
1/4 c. mayonnaise
2 T. celery, finely chopped
2 T. sweet pickle, finely chopped
1/2 t. mustard (Dijon-style or brown mustard works well)
Salt and black pepper to taste
Paprika (optional, for added color)

Slice eggs in half. Scoop out yolks and place in a small bowl. Mix mayonnaise, finely chopped celery and pickle, 1/2 t. mustard, salt, and pepper in with the egg yolks. If it is at all dry, add a tiny bit of the pickle juice to thin it out. Carefully spoon the yolk and mayonnaise mixture into the hollows in the egg whites. Sprinkle the tops with a touch of paprika for added color. Serve.

Variations:

Curried Chutney Eggs: Cut 6 hard-cooked eggs in half lengthwise. Mash egg yolks, stir in 3 T. mayonnaise, 1 T. finely chopped chutney, 1/2 t. curry powder, and 1/4 t. salt; fill egg white halves.

Rosy Eggs: Cut 6 hard-cooked eggs in half lengthwise. Mash egg yolks; stir in 2 T. sour cream, 4 t. juice from pickled beets, 1/2 t. minced tarragon, 2 t. salt, and a pinch of celery seed. Fill egg white halves.

Bacon and Cheese Eggs: Cut 6 hard-cooked eggs in half lengthwise. Mash egg yolks; stir in 2 slices cooked and finely crumbled bacon, 1/4 c. grated Cheddar cheese, 3 T. mayonnaise, 2 t. vinegar, and a pinch of salt. Fill egg white halves.

Smoky Deviled Eggs: Add 1/4 c. smoky cheese spread to basic Deviled Egg recipe above.

Asian Chicken Satay

Fragrant skewers of chicken marinated with traditional South Asian satay. You can also substitute strips of sirloin as well, or do both.

2 T. vegetable oil
1 garlic clove, crushed
1 tomato, peeled, seeded,
  and chopped
1/4 c. chunky peanut butter
1 c. chicken broth
1/2 t. salt
1/2 t. crushed red pepper
1 lb. boneless,
  skinless chicken breast
Bamboo or metal skewers

In a small skillet, heat oil and garlic. Stir in tomato, peanut butter, broth, salt, and red pepper. Simmer about 10 minutes, stirring occasionally; set aside to cool. Cut chicken into 1-inch pieces. Thread 3 or 4 pieces on each of twelve to sixteen 4-inch skewers. Arrange in a large baking pan. Pour peanut butter marinade over skewered chicken; cover and refrigerate 6 hours or overnight. Preheat broiler (or you can use an outdoor grill) and have oven shelf 3–4 inches below broiler. Cook until browned, brushing with marinade; turn and broil other side until browned and tender.

Tahitian Roll-Ups

India is generally recognized as the origin of chutney. It accompanies curry and other highly seasoned dishes, helping to tone down the spice. On the other hand, though, chutneys are generally made from exotic fruits that are found predominately in Hawaii, Tahiti, and other sun-drenched regions. This recipe is aptly named after Tahiti because of the use of coconut, not the chutney. Mango chutney, currant chutney, pear chutney, and apricot chutney are widespread in the market as sweet chutneys while tomato and pumpkin chutneys are great savory relishes.

2 whole, boneless, skinless chicken
  breasts, cut in half
2 c. chicken broth
4 t. curry powder
24–32 green leaf lettuce leaves,
  small
Tahitian Dip, *below*
1 c. toasted coconut

Tahitian Dip:
1 c. sour cream
2 t. finely chopped peanuts
1/4 c. finely chopped chutney

In a medium saucepan, combine chicken breasts, broth, and curry powder. Bring to a boil; simmer on low heat about 20 to 30 minutes or until chicken is tender and done. Refrigerate chicken in broth until cool. Remove chicken breasts from broth. Cut each half breast into 6 to 8 lengthwise strips. Place each strip of chicken across one side of each lettuce leaf. Fold ends of lettuce over chicken; roll up. Secure with a wooden toothpick if necessary. Refrigerate at least 1 hour. Prepare Tahitian Dip. Spoon coconut into small bowl. On a tray or large platter, arrange lettuce-wrapped chicken around dip and coconut. To serve, dip chicken rolls into Tahitian Dip.

Tahitian Dip: In a small bowl, combine sour cream, peanuts and chutney.

Many families in colonial America had chickens roaming their yard, pecking at the ground for any scrap they could find. However, they did not often eat these chickens because of the importance of their eggs. Every day, children would hunt to find fresh eggs. Although not eaten for breakfast as we do today, they were roasted, boiled, fried, or baked in custards called White Pots. Leftover eggs, after the baking, were pickled in vinegar or buried in baskets of fat and straw. These methods of preserving kept them good to eat for a long time.

Avocado Carpaccio with Blueberry Cheese

Every time you turn on any cooking channel, every chef, or chef wannabe, is preparing carpaccio in some obscene manner. Now it's my turn. Carpaccio is a dish of raw meat or fish (such as beef, veal, venison, salmon, or tuna) generally thinly sliced or pounded thin and served as an appetizer. According to Arrigo Cipriani, the present-day owner of Harry's Bar, carpaccio was invented at Harry's Bar in Venice, where it was first served to the countess Amalia Nani Mocenigo in 1950, when she informed the bar's owner that her doctor had recommended she eat only raw meat. It consisted of thin slices of raw beef dressed with a mustard sauce. The dish was named carpaccio by Giuseppe Cipriani, the bar's former owner, in reference to the Venetian painter Vittore Carpaccio, because the colors of the dish reminded him of paintings by Carpaccio. The term is now used to refer to the preparation of meat or fish served raw and sliced thinly—some restaurants have taken to naming any dish of thinly sliced food "carpaccio."

4 small avocados
2 T. lime juice
Salt to taste
1 1/4 c. blueberries
1 c. cottage cheese
1 t. honey
Pinch cayenne pepper (optional)
1 c. alfalfa sprouts

Cut avocados in half and remove pits. Remove peel and slice thinly. Place slices on large plate. Drizzle with lime juice and sprinkle with salt.

In bowl, combine blueberries, cottage cheese, and honey. Add cayenne, if using. Dollop over avocado and top with sprouts before serving.

Cheap Remedy

When your sinuses are full and the pressure from sinusitus is unbearable, Dr. Howard Druce, M.D, Professor of Internal Medicine and Director of The Nasal and Paranasal Sinus Physiology Laboratory at the St. Louis University School of Medicine recommends garlic, Cajun spice, and horseradish. Garlic contains the same chemical found in a drug that makes mucus less sticky. Cajun spice, made with cayenne peppers, contain capsaicin, a substance that can stimulate the nerve fibers while acting as a nasal decongestant. Horseradish contains a chemical similar to one found in decongestants.

Monterey Artichokes

Take it easy with this recipe. It's easy to fill yourself and leave no room for anything else...what the heck, go ahead and fill up. I have many times.

2 jars (6 oz.) marinated artichoke
   crowns or bottoms,
   drained and finely chopped
1 small onion, minced
1 garlic clove, crushed
4 eggs
1/4 c. bread crumbs
2 c. grated Monterey Jack cheese
1/4 t. salt
1/4 t. dried, crushed basil
1/4 t. dried oregano
Pinch black pepper
2 T. finely chopped,
   canned green chilies

Drain artichoke hearts, reserving 1 T. liquid in a small saucepan. Set artichoke hearts aside. Add onion and garlic to reserved liquid. Sauté until onions are soft over medium heat. Preheat oven to 350°F. Grease an 8-inch square baking pan or equivalent; set aside. Finely chop artichoke hearts; set aside. In a medium bowl, heat eggs until foamy. Stir in chopped artichoke hearts, breadcrumbs, Monterey Jack cheese, salt, basil, oregano, pepper, green chilies, and sautéed onion mixture. Spoon into prepared baking pan. Bake 25 to 30 minutes or until mixture is firm. Cut into 25 to 30 small bars or squares. Serve warm or cold.

Stuffed Cucumber Slices

Summertime just screams for anything with cucumbers and this cucumber appetizer just screams for you!

1 large cucumber
1 pkg. (3 oz.) cream cheese,
   room temperature
1 T. crumbled bleu cheese
1 t. grated onion
2 t. chopped parsley
1/2 t. dried dill
20–25 pimiento strips

Score cucumber by pressing tines of a fork about 1/16 inch into peel and pulling tines lengthwise, leaving grooves. Turn cucumber and continue scoring until grooves are lengthwise over entire surface. Cut 1-inch slice from one end. Use an iced tea spoon or parfait spoon to scoop seeds from inside cucumber. Stand cut end on paper towels to drain, about 10 minutes. In a small bowl, combine cream cheese, bleu cheese, onion, parsley, and dill weed. Spoon mixture into hollowed-out center of cucumber. Wrap in foil or plastic wrap; refrigerate 3 to 4 hours. Slice crosswise into 1/4-inch slices. Garnish slices with pimiento strips. Refrigerate 3 to hours. Slice crosswise into 1/4-inch slices. Garnish each slice with a strip of pimiento.

Chew on a small handful of anise, dill, or fennel seeds when you feel bloated. The compounds in these seeds relax the muscles in your digestive tract, which allows trapped gas to pass. You can buy the seeds in the spice aisle of grocery stores or the bulk section of natural food stores. Bonus: they freshen your breath, too.

Stuffed Snow Pea Pods

I think beef and pea pods go so well together that I created this recipe to whet my hunger for those sweet, edible pea pods. The pods are just as tasty as the peas themselves believe it or not.

1/2 lb. snow pea pods
1 pkg. (3 oz.) thinly sliced
  cooked beef
1 t. prepared horseradish
1 c. sour cream
1/2 t. prepared mustard
Pinch black pepper

Trim ends from pea pods. In a medium saucepan, bring 3 c. water to boil. Carefully lower trimmed pea pods into boiling water and simmer over medium heat about 1 minute or until crisp-tender; drain. Immediately immerse pods in cold water. Drain again and refrigerate at least 30 minutes until well chilled. Chop sliced beef very fine. In a small bowl, combine chopped beef, horseradish, sour cream, mustard, and pepper. With a sharp knife, carefully slit one side of pea pod. Use a demitasse spoon or other small spoon to fill each pod with beef mixture. Arrange filled pods on baking sheet with raised sides, with pea pods touching to keep them upright. Refrigerate at least 1 hour, serve cold.

Brie en Croute

Jazz up this Holiday favorite with the addition of dried cranberries (that have been soaked and drained) and slivered almonds inside. The colors, when sliced into, remind you of holly berries.

3/4 c. flour
1 pkg. (3 oz.) cream cheese, room temperature
1/4 c. butter, room temperature
1/2 t. rosemary
1 pkg. (4 1/2 oz.) Brie cheese
1/2 t. sesame seeds

In a medium bowl, cut flour, cream cheese, butter, and rosemary with a pastry blender until particles resemble small peas. Shape into a ball. Wrap in foil or plastic wrap; refrigerate at least 1 hour. Divide dough into 2 pieces. On a lightly floured surface, roll out each piece about 1/8 inch thick. Cut each into a 6-inch circle, reserving excess dough for trim. Place 1 circle of dough on an ungreased baking sheet. Place whole Brie cheese in center of dough; top with other pastry circle. Pinch pastry edges together to seal. Preheat oven to 400°F. Roll out excess dough. Cut 1 decorative design with a cookie cutter and about 10 small designs with knife resembling any fashion you choose. Place large cutout on top of Croute and small cutouts around side. Sprinkle with sesame seeds. Bake 15 to 17 minutes until golden brown. Let stand 5 to 6 minutes before cutting into small wedges and serve warm

Open-Faced Tacos

In Mexico, the word taco is as generic as the word sandwich is here in America. A taco is simply a tortilla wrapped around a filling. Like a sandwich, the filling can be made with almost anything and prepared in many ways. Anything that can be rolled inside a tortilla becomes a taco.

1 lb. ground beef
1 pkg. (1 1/4 oz.) taco seasoning
1 c. water
1 pkg. round, flat tortilla chips,
  2 1/2-inch rounds
2 c. grated Cheddar cheese
2 medium tomatoes, chopped
1 avocado, pitted, peeled,
  and thinly sliced
1/2 c. sour cream

In a medium skillet, cook beef until browned, stirring with a fork or spoon to crumble meat. Drain and discard drippings. Stir in taco seasoning mix and water. Bring to a boil. Simmer 10 to 15 minutes, stirring occasionally. Arrange a single layer of tortilla chips on an ungreased baking sheet. Preheat broiler if necessary. Place oven rack 5 to 8 inches from heating element. Spoon about 2 t. meat mixture on each chip. Sprinkle cheese evenly over chips. Place under broiler until bubbly. Top each chip with about 2 pieces tomato and 1 avocado slice. Top with sour cream.

Zesty Cheese Sticks

Make some of these and bring to work to snack on. Your co-workers will make you bring more in the next day. Better yet, keep them for yourself at home.

1/4 c. butter or margarine,
    room temperature
1 c. shredded sharp Cheddar cheese
3 T. grated Parmesan cheese
1 t. Worcestershire sauce
1/4 t. chili powder
1/4 t. celery salt
1/2 c. flour

In a small bowl, combine butter, Cheddar cheese, Parmesan cheese, Worcestershire sauce, chili powder, and celery salt and beat until smooth. Stir in flour until blended. Wrap dough airtight in foil or plastic wrap. Refrigerate at least 1 hour.

Preheat oven to 350°F. Pinch off walnut-size pieces of chilled dough. Roll each piece between your palms to make 4 inch, pencil-like ropes, about 1/4 inch thick. Arrange on an ungreased baking sheet and bake 8 to 10 minutes until golden brown. Don't forget the warmed tomato sauce for dipping.

Prosciutto Wrapped Watermelon and Brie Fingers

My take on prosciutto and melon. I think you will agree that all three ingredients complement each other enough to compliment you, the host!

16 thin slices of Brie, about the same dimensions as the watermelon fingers
16 seeded watermelon cubes, pinky finger sized
16 slices prosciutto ham

Place a piece of Brie on top of each watermelon and wrap each with a slice of the ham. Secure with a toothpick.

Baked Brie with Peach-Zinfandel Chutney

Peach-Zinfandel Chutney is available in the gourmet aisles of some supermarkets and at many gourmet stores. Apricot preserves can be substituted if necessary. To still achieve the wine effect, stir 2 tablespoons white zinfandel into the preserves.

1 round (15 oz.) Brie cheese
1 jar (8 oz.) peach-zinfandel chutney
1/2 c. drained jarred or canned peaches in juice
1/4 c. slivered almonds
Plain or wheat crackers, for serving

Preheat oven to 350°F. Line 9-inch pie pan with aluminum foil. Coat with nonstick cooking spray. Place cheese in pan. Top with chutney, peaches, and almonds. Bake for 30 minutes, or until chutney is bubbly and cheese is heated through. With large spatula, carefully transfer cheese to serving dish. Spoon sauce over top. Serve with crackers.

Prosciutto and Melon

Prosciutto is the Italian word for "ham." It has been seasoned, salt-cured (but not smoked), and air-dried. Italian prosciuttos are designated prosciutto cotto, which is cooked, and prosciutto crudo, which is raw but ready to eat because of its curing. Prosciutto should be golden-pink and moist-looking; its fat should be pure white.

It is classically served as this recipe states, or with figs, but use other types of sweet melons, star fruits, Asian pears or any good, stout fruit to offset the saltiness of this great Italian ham.

    I small honeydew melon or
        cantaloupe, chilled
    4 oz. thinly sliced prosciutto
    Freshly ground black pepper

Cut melon in half and remove seeds. Slice each half into 4 wedges, cut off rind. Arrange 2 melon wedges on each of 4 salad plates; arrange prosciutto alongside melon, arrange decoratively on top one another or wrap melon with prosciutto. Serve with pepper.

Watermelon Cucumber Shrimp Cocktail

I know...why screw around with a classic? Well, because I can! Although a few extra ingredients are used, as compared to the classic shrimp cocktail, I just think clean, fresh flavors blend well with the freshest shrimp you can find. See if I am right.

    2 T. extra virgin olive oil
    I bunch scallions, trimmed and chopped
    I t. toasted sesame oil
    2 T. fresh lime juice
    1/2 c. water
    1/4 c. sugar
    I t. salt
    I clove garlic, minced
    I serving cracked pepper or hot pepper sauce to taste
    I lb. cooked, cleaned, and chilled cocktail shrimp
    I cucumber, peeled, seeded, and chopped
    1/4 c. chipped cilantro leaves
    4 pieces of 3-inch watermelon circles
    I piece thin breadsticks, sugar cane swizzles, or celery sticks for garnish

Heat the oil in a sauté pan over medium high heat. Add the scallions and sauté. Remove from heat and stir in sesame oil. Set aside. Whisk together the lime juice, water, sugar, salt and garlic. Spice to taste with pepper or pepper sauce. Stir in the shrimp, cucumber and cilantro. Mix well then chill. Divide the watermelon among 4 small dishes. Divide the shrimp and cucumber mixture over the watermelon and drizzle the scallion mixture over the top of each cocktail.

Monterey Turkey Appetizers

Turkey is high in gamma-amino butyric acid (GABA), a calming amino acid which balances the flow of dopamine and scrotomin. These are two mood-monitoring neurotransmitters that help bring you to a relaxed state of mind.

8 oz. thinly sliced turkey ham
8 oz. sliced smoked turkey breast
8 slices (1 oz.) Monterey
   Jack cheese
16 slices whole grain bread
Vegetable oil for frying
4 eggs, slightly beaten
3/4 c. milk
2 T. flour
1 c. sour cream
1 c. strawberry jam

Place 1 slice each turkey ham, turkey breast, and cheese on each of 8 slices of bread. Top with remaining bread slices. Cut sandwiches into quarters; secure with wooden toothpicks. Pour oil into large skillet, 2 inches depth, and heat to 375°F.

Combine eggs, milk, and flour. Dip each mini-sandwich into egg mixture. Fry them, a few at a time, 50 to 60 seconds until golden brown, turning half way through frying time. Drain on paper towels and serve with sour cream and jam.

Spicy Honeyed Chicken Wings

For those of you who want chicken wings but want to enjoy them without heat, picante sauce is available mild and very flavorful, so keep dipping these wings in that bowl of picante sauce.

2 lbs. chicken wings
1/2 c. picante sauce
1/2 c. honey
1/4 c. soy sauce
2 T. Dijon mustard
2 T. vegetable oil
2 t. grated fresh ginger
1/4 t. grated orange peel
Additional picante sauce

Cut off and discard wing tips on the chicken wings; cut each wing in half at joint. Place in 13 × 9-inch baking dish. Combine picante sauce, honey, soy sauce, mustard, oil, ginger, and orange peel in small bowl; mix well. Pour over chicken wings. Cover and refrigerate at least 6 hours. Preheat oven to 400°F. Place chicken wings and sauce in single layer on foil-lined baking pan and bake 40 to 45 minutes or until brown. Serve warm with additional picante sauce.

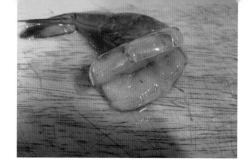

Butterfly Shrimp

You will be surprised at the taste of this bacon-filled, tempura-style shrimp recipe. The salt from the bacon gives this dish just the right amount of seasoning.

1 1/2 lb. large shrimp, shelled and
   deveined, leaving tails on
3 egg yolks
1 1/2 t. cornstarch
1/2 t. salt
Black pepper to taste
2 slices bacon, cut lengthwise
   in half and then cut crosswise
   every 1 1/2-inches
Vegetable oil for frying

Heat oil in large skillet over medium-high heat to 375°F. Cut deep slit down back of each shrimp. Flatten cut side slightly with fingers. Beat egg yolks, cornstarch, salt, and pepper with fork in medium bowl. Place a bacon strip on cut side of each shrimp; closing back up again. Dip each shrimp into egg mixture and carefully drop and cook the shrimp, a few at a time, until golden, 2 to 3 minutes. Drain on paper towel and serve.

Just as we Americans are fond of and familiar with ketchup or other condiments for our daily fare, shrimp paste is favored in Asian cuisines. Known as *Chiu Chow* in Southern China and *Belachan* in Malayasia, as well as *Kapee* in Thailand, this paste of tiny shrimp is packed in jars with salt to retard spoilage. It is made by mashing the shrimp, salting it, and allowing it to ferment, making it extremely pungent before putting it into jars.

Shrimp Toast

I got this idea when I was making "Toad in a Hole" one morning at the restaurant. I made it once that afternoon and put it on the menu that night. I heard not one complaint and everyone thoroughly enjoyed this prelude to a great meal, as I think you will as well.

12 large shrimp, shelled and
   deveined, leaving tails intact
1 egg
2 1/2 T. cornstarch
1/4 t. salt
Black pepper to taste
3 slices white sandwich bread,
   crustless and quartered
1 hard cooked egg yolk,
   cut into 1/2-inch pieces
1 slice cooked ham,
   cut into 1/2-inch pieces
1 green onion, finely chopped
Vegetable oil for frying

Cut down back of shrimp; press gently to flatten. Beat the 1 egg, cornstarch, salt, and pepper in large bowl until blended. Add shrimp to egg mixture; toss to coat well.

Place 1 shrimp cut-side down on each bread piece. Press shrimp gently into bread. Brush or rub small amount of egg mixture over each shrimp. Place 1 piece each of egg yolk and ham and a scant 1/4 t. onion on top of each shrimp.

Heat oil in large skillet over medium-high heat to 375°F. Cook 3 or 4 shrimp/bread pieces at a time until golden, 1 to 2 minutes on each side. Drain on paper towels.

Cut cancer with cabbage. It contains isothiosyanates, compounds that stimulate apoptosis, the process by which the body eliminates cancerous cells.

Spring Rolls

1 lb. medium shrimp,
  shelled and deveined
1 lb. boneless lean pork
4 oz. fresh mushrooms
8 green onions
1 red bell pepper
8 oz. bok choy or napa cabbage
  (about 1/2 head)
1 can (8 oz.) water chestnuts,
  drained
3 T. dry sherry (optional)
1 1/2 T. soy sauce
2 t. minced fresh ginger
1 t. sugar
1/2 t. salt
24 egg roll wrappers
Vegetable oil for frying
1 1/2 T. cornstarch
1/4 c. water

Finely chop shrimp, pork, mushrooms, onions, red pepper, cabbage, and water chestnuts. Transfer all chopped ingredients to large bowl and add sherry, soy sauce, ginger, sugar, and salt; mix well.

Place about 1/4 cup pork mixture evenly across one corner of each wrapper. Mix cornstarch with the water and brush mixture evenly over all edges of wrappers. Carefully roll wrappers around filling, folding in corners to seal. Heat oil in large skillet or wok over medium-high heat to 375°F. Cook 3 or 4 rolls at a time until golden, 3 to 5 minutes each. Drain on paper towels.

The "Hold Me Over 'til Supper" Dip

Want something for the kids after school that they will love but won't fill them to the point of side stitches while playing? Trust me, they'll love it.

1 pkg. (8 oz.) fat-free cream cheese
1 T. fat-free milk
1/2 t. pumpkin pie spice
4 T. brown sugar
1/2 c. raisins
Fruit wedges, such as apples, or veggie sticks

In a food processor or blender, combine cream cheese and milk. Blend until creamy and then add the pumpkin pie spice and brown sugar; blend until creamy. Pour into a small bowl and mix in the raisins. Serve with fruit wedges or veggie sticks.

Ranch-Style Bean Dip

Make sure you have something stout to dip with. This rich and thick dip will break any wimpy potato chip.

1/4 c. butter or margarine
1 small onion, chopped
1 jalapeno pepper,
  seeded and chopped
1 garlic clove, crushed
1 can (16 oz.) pinto beans
  or kidney beans, drained
1 1/2 c. grated
  Monterey Jack cheese
Corn chips

In a medium skillet, melt butter. Add onion, jalapeno pepper, and garlic; sauté until tender. In a medium bowl, use a fork to mash beans. Stir into onion mixture. Cook and stir over low heat until hot but not boiling. Stir in cheese until melted; do not boil. Spoon into a small bowl on a hot tray. Serve hot with corn chips to dip.

Cheese Dunk

Roquefort cheese is considered the "King of Cheeses." With its tingly pungent taste, it is made only from the milk of specially bred sheep and ripened in limestone caverns in Roquefort-sur-Soulzon, France. Ripe Roquefort is creamy, thick, and white on the inside and has a burnt-orange skin. The distinct smell is enhanced by the sweet burnt-caramel taste of sheep's milk and the sharp, metallic tang of the blue mold.

2 c. cottage cheese
1 c. grated sharp Cheddar cheese
2 oz. Roquefort cheese or bleu cheese, crumbled
3 T. mayonnaise
2 t. prepared horseradish
1 T. prepared mustard
3 green onions, minced
1/4 t. salt
Pinch black pepper
2 apples, sliced
2 pears, sliced

Drain cottage cheese by inverting into a strainer and letting it sit for 10 minutes. In a medium bowl, combine drained cottage cheese, Cheddar cheese, Roquefort cheese, mayonnaise, horseradish, mustard, onions, salt, and pepper, stirring to blend ingredients. Spoon into a medium serving bowl and serve with apples, pears, and chips for dipping.

Bacon and Avocado Dip

I know, you are thinking there is a lot of fat in this recipe, with the bacon and avocado, but it sure tastes good. Go ahead and splurge once, but remember your manners—no double dipping!

2 avocados, peeled and pitted
1 T. lemon juice
2 green onions, chopped fine
1 small tomato, seeded and chopped
2 small green chili peppers, seeded and chopped fine

3 slices bacon, cooked and crumbled
1/4 t. salt
Tortilla chips or corn chips

In a medium bowl, use a fork to mash avocados. Stir in lemon juice, onions, salt, tomato, chili peppers, crumbled bacon, and salt. Cover and refrigerate 2 hours. Serve with chips for dippers.

Hot Crab Dip

Buy a small round loaf of bread, hollow it out, and serve this dip poured inside this bread for a festive gathering.

1 can (6 oz.) crabmeat or frozen crabmeat, thawed
1/2 c. sour cream
1 pkg. (3 oz.) cream cheese, room temperature
1 T. lemon juice
1 t. prepared horseradish
3 T. minced green peppers
1 t. minced pimiento
French bread, sliced
Tortilla chips

Drain and flake crabmeat; set aside. In a medium saucepan, combine sour cream, cream cheese, lemon juice, and horseradish, stirring to blend. Add green pepper, pimiento, and flaked crabmeat. Stir over low heat until bubbly. Serve with slices of French bread or tortilla chips.

Cayenne Pepper Salt

Wear glasses to save your eyes from being incommoded by them. Dry ripe chilies before the fire the day before. Trim the stalks, pound the pods in a mortar until powdered, add one-sixth their weight in salt.

—Directions for Cookery, 1837

Guacamole

True Guacamole uses mortar and pestle (called *molcajete* in Spanish) to pound Hass avocado with just a little sea salt, tomato, chile, and onion. The lumps should be very prevalent in sight and texture. I have added additional ingredients I think you will find very well balanced and absolutely delicious.

1 large ripe avocado
2 t. lemon juice
1/4 t. salt
1 canned green chili, minced
1/2 t. Worcestershire sauce
1 t. grated onion
3 to 4 drops hot pepper sauce
1 garlic clove, crushed
1 small tomato, chopped
Tortilla chips

In a small bowl, use a fork to mash avocado or use blender for a smoother dip. Stir in lemon juice, salt, green, chili, Worcestershire sauce, onion, hot pepper sauce, garlic, and tomato. Serve with chips.

Nor'east Guacamole

Again, all you need is a little ingenuity to come up with a delicious alternative to recipes. The addition of apples to guacamole is a perfect complement.

3 ripe avocados, halved and pitted
1/2 c. minced sweet onion
1/2 c. snipped fresh cilantro
Juice of 1 lime
Bottled hot pepper sauce, to taste
1 Granny Smith apple, peeled, cored, and finely chopped
Kosher salt or table salt, to taste
Assorted dippers (baked fruit crisps, apple chips, and/or tortilla chips)

Scoop avocado flesh into bowl; add onion, cilantro, lime juice, and hot pepper sauce. Mash with fork until it reaches the desired consistency. Stir in apple and season with salt to taste. Serve with dippers.

Best Spinach Dip

Yup, going prepackaged again on ya' folks. Just a way to simplify this recipe so that more than just a few of you will try this earthy-tasting dip.

1/4 c. butter or margarine
1 pkg. (1.25 oz.) Hollandaise sauce blend
3/4 c. milk
1 pkg. (10 oz.) frozen, chopped spinach, thawed and drained
1 jar (4 oz.) diced pimiento, drained
3/4 c. grated Parmesan cheese
1 t. dried dill
8 oz. sour cream

In a small saucepan, melt butter over medium heat. Stir in Hollandaise sauce blend. Gradually stir in milk. Cook and stir until mixture comes to boiling; reduce heat to low. Simmer, uncovered, about 1 minute or until it has thickened, stirring constantly.

Stir spinach, pimiento, Parmesan cheese, and dill into sauce mixture. Cook until Parmesan cheese is melted and sauce mixture is well blended, stirring often. Remove from heat and add sour cream, stirring until smooth. Transfer to serving bowl and serve with assorted vegetables and/or chips.

Refried Bean Dip

I have always enjoyed the taste of refried beans on their own, but livening up (as I have done) mentally transports me to the Rio Grande.

1 can (8 oz.) refried beans
1 c. grated sharp Cheddar cheese
1/2 t. chili powder
3 t. minced onion
1/8 t. garlic salt
2 to 3 drops hot pepper sauce
Tortilla chips

In a small saucepan, combine beans, cheese, chili powder, onion, garlic salt, and hot pepper sauce. Stir over low heat until cheese is melted; do not boil. Spoon into a small bowl on a hot tray. Serve warm with chips.

Buffalo Dip

If you want bolder flavor, add some chopped jalapenos or any hot peppers.

1/4 c. hot sauce
1/2 t. lemon juice
1/4 t. black pepper
1/4 c. mayonnaise
1/4 c. sour cream

Place all ingredients in bowl and combine.

Ever heard of the Negative Calorie Diet? Some foods contain fewer calories than are needed to digest them. For example, if you are eating a 1 1/2 oz. stalk of celery that contains 7 calories, but maybe your body needs 30 calories to break it down. If true, eating a stalk will burn 23 calories—and if you eat five stalks a day, you'll lose a pound a month. This is based on the 1990s book *Foods that Cause You to Lose Weight: the Negative Calorie Effect*, by Neal D. Barnard, M.D.

Maple Pumpkin Spread

If you closed your eyes and tasted this treat, you'd swear you were eating pumpkin pie.

1 pkg. (8 oz.) cream
    cheese (Neufchâtel),
    at room temperature
1/2 c. pure pumpkin puree
2 T. real maple syrup,
    the darker the better
Pinch ground cinnamon

Stir cream cheese, pumpkin, honey, and cinnamon in medium bowl for 1 minute or until smooth. Serve immediately or refrigerate. Best served with apple slices or whole-wheat crackers.

Bleu Cheese Spread

The addition of creamy mascarpone cheese balances perfectly with the sharpness of the bleu cheese.

1/2 c. mascarpone cheese, softened
1 T. heavy cream
2 t. lemon juice
1/2 t. dried thyme
1/4 t. salt
1/2 t. black pepper
1/4 t. cayenne pepper
1 c. crumbled bleu cheese

Mix the mascarpone, heavy cream, lemon juice, thyme, salt, pepper, and cayenne together in a medium bowl; gently stir in the bleu cheese and serve.

Smoked Salmon Spread

This recipe was created for those of you who don't want to break the bank when using salmon. Canned salmon is quite appropriate and very good.

I pkg. (3 oz.) cream cheese,
   room temperature
I T. lemon juice
1/2 t. prepared horseradish
I t. grated onion
1/4 t. salt
Pinch black pepper
1/4 t. liquid smoke
I can (7 1/2 oz.) salmon
Crackers

In a medium bowl, combine cream cheese, lemon juice, horseradish, grated onion, salt, pepper, and liquid smoke. Thoroughly drain salmon; remove and discard bones. Use 2 forks to flake drained salmon. Stir flaked salmon into cream cheese mixture. Refrigerate about 1 hour. Shape into an 8 × 2 1/2-inch roll. Cut a 12-inch square of plastic wrap or foil. Wrap salmon roll in plastic wrap or foil. Refrigerate 6 hours or over night. Spread onto crackers.

Hummus

Referred to as garbanzo beans, Spanish beans, or ceci peas, chickpeas come in black, red, or white. They are a major ingredient in Mediterranean, Middle Eastern, Latin American, and Indian cuisine. In addition to hummus, falafel is another Middle Eastern dish that includes chickpeas. Having tried this spread for the first time a couple of years back, I have included this in my cookbook because of its growing popularity and also because I can't find myself enjoying any other dish that includes chickpeas besides this tasty recipe.

2 c. cooked or canned chick peas,
   drained
2/3 c. tahini (sesame paste)
3/4 c. lemon juices
2 cloves garlic
I t. salt

Place the chickpeas, tahini, lemon juice, garlic, and salt in a blender or food processor and blend until smooth. Mound into a bowl and serve.

If you find the price of tahini too steep, it is very cheap to make a version of the sesame paste yourself using sunflower seeds. Simply put I c. sunflower seeds (salted or unsalted) into a food processor or blender and add 1/2 c. olive oil. I do not use extra-virgin olive oil because it is too overpowering. Grind both together until a paste is formed. It will make about 2/3 cup of tahini paste.

CHAPTER 7 Salads and Slaws

Barbecued Chicken Salad

Not your "run of the mill" barbecued chicken salad but one with gusto and accents from all regions of this great country. You'll love it.

2 c. chopped Romaine lettuce
2 c. chopped iceburg lettuce
1/2 c. chopped red cabbage
1 tomato, sliced
3 chicken breasts, cut in half
1/2 c. barbecue sauce
1/2 c. refried black beans
1/2 c. shredded Cheddar cheese
1/4 c. fried onion rings
3 avocado slices
1/4 c. ranch dressing

Toss chopped lettuces and cabbage; arrange on large platter. Arrange tomato slices on lettuce in a mound. Grill chicken either on barbecue grill or in sauté pan until done, 4 to 5 minutes per side. Brush generously with barbecue sauce while cooking.

Heat beans in microwave for 1 minute, remove to stir and continue to microwave another minute. Spread beans over lettuce next to the tomatoes. Slice warm chicken into bite-sized pieces and arrange on lettuce, next to the beans. Mound shredded cheese in another stack on lettuce. Do the same with the onion rings. Garnish with avocado slices and serve with ranch dressing on the side.

Orange and Cucumber Salad

What a great complement to a hot summer day without being weighed down. Add other fruits and vegetables if you like. Also, here's a recipe for Pumpkin Vinaigrette you may want to try with this salad or any that you throw together. Combine 1 clove garlic, minced; 1 t. honey or maple syrup; 1/2 t. salt; 1/8 t. black pepper; 2 T. pumpkin puree; and 2 T. of rice vinegar. Slowly pour in 4 T. extra-virgin olive oil and blend very well.

1 head Boston or bibb lettuce
1 cucumber, thinly sliced
3 oranges, peeled, halved,
  seeded, and thinly sliced
1/4 c. frozen orange juice
  concentrate, thawed
2 T. white wine vinegar
2 T. salad oil
2 T. honey
1 T. snipped fresh mint or
  1/2 t. dried mint, crushed

Line 6 salad plates with lettuce. Arrange orange and cucumber slices in circles atop lettuce.

For dressing, in a screw-top jar combine thawed concentrate, vinegar, salad oil, honey, mint, and a dash of pepper. Cover and shake well and drizzle over salads.

I remember when I was a child in the 60s and early 70s, Dad made sure there was always an orange in our Christmas stocking. We kids never did give much thought or much enthusiasm to this seemingly trivial gift, but we knew it had to have been a special orange because (of course) Santa put it there. A few years before Dad died, we were speaking of Christmases past and he told me that when he was a child, as well as his father, they only ate oranges once in a very great while. Why? Because they were just too expensive to buy on a regular basis. It had held special memories for him and now the same holds true for me.

Marinated Green Bean and Potato Salad

This salad is not only delicious and holds up well on a picnic, but you can use any dressing of your choice, such as flavored vinaigrettes or Catalina. Check the market for any oil and vinegar-based dressing that may add some extra zing.

1/2 t. salt
8 to 10 small red potatoes, quartered
1 lb. fresh green beans, cut in half
1 small onion, thinly sliced, separated into rings
1/2 c. Italian salad dressing
Black pepper

Fill large saucepan half full of water; add salt. Bring to a boil. Add potatoes and cook 8 to 10 minutes or until tender. Meanwhile, in a medium saucepan, bring 1 c. water to a boil. Add green beans; return to a boil. Reduce heat; cover and simmer 6 minutes.

Add onion to beans; cook an additional 1 to 2 minutes or until beans are crisp-tender. Drain; rinse with cold water and place in a large bowl. Drain potatoes; add to beans and onion. Add salad dressing and pepper to salad; mix well. Serve immediately or cover and cool until serving time.

Try this great topping for any fruit: 1 cup marshmallow creme mixed well with 1/4 c. softened cream cheese and 4 T. lemon, orange, or pineapple juice.

Honey Lime Fruit Salad

1/2 c. coleslaw dressing
4 T. honey
1 t. grated lime peel
2 t. lime juice
8 c. fresh fruit, deli fruit salad

In small bowl, combine coleslaw dressing, honey, lime peel, and lime juice; blend well. Just before serving, in large serving bowl, combine fruit salad and dressing mixture; toss gently to mix.

Forms of Honey

Comb honey is a honey-filled beeswax comb as stored directly by the bees.

Liquid honey is prepared by cutting off the wax cappings and whirling the comb in a honey extractor, where centrifugal force moves the honey out of the cells.

Granulated honey, called creamy honey, is produced by blending one part finely granulated honey with nine parts liquid honey to spreadable consistency.

Chunk honey is comb honey in a jar with liquid honey poured around it.

Raw honey is honey as it exists in the beehive or obtained by extraction, settling and straining without the heat. It contains some pollen and may contain small particles of wax. Allergy sufferers seek raw honey, as the pollen impurities are thought to lessen the sensitivity to hay fever.

Southwest Layered Salad

This quick, inexpensive salad looks as good as it tastes. Dig into the multiple layers of fun and take what you want.

6 c. torn Romaine lettuce
1 can (15 oz.) black beans, drained and rinsed
1 c. frozen corn, thawed
1 c. salsa
3/4 c. shredded Cheddar jack cheese
1/4 c. ranch dressing
1 c. tortilla chips, crushed

Arrange lettuce in bottom of serving bowl or plate. Layer beans, corn, salsa, and cheese evenly over top. Drizzle with dressing; sprinkle with chips.

Chicken BLT Salad

Chicken and bacon go so well together that I had to incorporate both into a simple and filling salad. Add some plain croutons if you want more crunch.

8 c. torn Romaine lettuce
3 c. sliced cooked chicken breast
2 c. cherry tomatoes, halved
1/2 c. sliced red onions
1 c. Cheddar cheese crumbles,
  or shredded
1/4 c. ranch dressing with bacon
2 slices cooked bacon, crumbled
1/4 c. pine nuts

Toss lettuce, chicken, tomatoes, onions, and 1/2 c. of the cheese in large bowl. Add dressing; mix gently. Top with remaining 1/2 c. cheese, crumbled bacon, and pine nuts.

"Maturity" of Cheddar Cheese

White House historians aver that President Andrew Jackson had a 1,400-lb. block of Cheddar cheese served as a refreshment.

A 7,000-lb. block was immortalized in the poem "Ode on the Mammoth Cheese Weighing over 7,000 Pounds," by James McIntyre.

In 1893, a 22,000 lb. cheese crashed through the floor of the Chicago World's Fair, still garnering the bronze medal.

The largest of all Cheddar cheeses ever was a 56,850-lb. wheel produced in Oregon by the Federation of American Cheesemakers in 1989.

Coastal Shrimp and Pea Salad

Have you noticed how simple I am keeping all the salads? By all means, add some nuts, other raw vegetables, or other herbs as you like. I am simply giving you a foundation on which to work.

1 lb. large cooked shrimp,
  peeled and cooled
2 c. frozen peas, thawed
3 c. shredded iceburg lettuce
3 c. shredded green leaf lettuce
1/2 c. thinly sliced red onions
1/4 c. creamy cucumber dressing

Place shrimp and peas in large bowl; set aside. Arrange shredded lettuce on 4 plates. Add onions and dressing to shrimp mixture; toss lightly. Spoon onto mounds of lettuce.

Mandarin Chicken Salad

Replace the spinach with Romaine or Boston Bibb if you want a heartier salad. I love this salad because of the mandarin oranges and baby spinach, they go so well together.

8 c. baby spinach leaves
3 c. chopped, cooked chicken breast
1 can (11 oz.) Mandarin orange
  segments, drained
1 c. fresh sliced mushrooms
4 slices cooked bacon, crumbled
1/4 c. balsamic vinaigrette dressing
1/4 c. pecan pieces

Toss spinach, chicken, oranges, mushrooms, and bacon bits in large bowl. Drizzle with dressing just before serving.

Spinach was first cultivated in Persia for the enjoyment of cats! Many centuries later, Catherine de Medicis, an Italian noblewoman from Florence who married King Henry II, is said to have eaten it at every meal, thus any dish using spinach is called Florentine.

Picnic Macaroni Salad

What can you say about macaroni salad that hasn't been said before. I have kept the same basic ingredients that have been passed down and I think you will enjoy this summertime treat.

1 1/2 c. uncooked spiral pasta
1 c. mayonnaise or salad dressing
1/4 c. chopped red onion
2 T. sugar
2 T. sweet pickle relish
2 t. prepared mustard
3/4 c. frozen peas, thawed
2 eggs, hard-cooked and chopped

Cook spiral pasta to desired texture as directed on package. Drain; rinse with cold water and drain again. In large bowl combine mayonnaise, onion, sugar, pickle relish, and mustard; blend well. Stir in cooked pasta, peas, and eggs. Cover; refrigerate at least 2 hours before serving.

Let's dispel two myths about pasta cooking. Adding salt to boiling water only lowers the boiling point of the water, thereby bringing the water to boiling faster, in order to cook the pasta faster. Adding oil does not prevent the pasta from sticking together. It only helps to prevent droplets of water from flying out of the pot during the boiling of the pasta. Frequent stirring and plenty of water prevents clumping.

Potato Salad

What could be more satisfying than bringing potato salad to a picnic. The taste of a seasoned potato salad such as this one combines well with anything cooked outside.

1 lb. small red potatoes, cooked
 cooled, skinned (if desired), and
 cubed
1/2 c. mayonnaise
2 t. dried basil
3 peeled, chopped, hard-cooked
 eggs
1 carrot, shredded
1 small green bell pepper, chopped
1 t. dried parsley (optional)

Add basil to mayonnaise and whisk until well incorporated. Combine remainder of ingredients in large bowl and mix well with the potatoes. Cover with plastic wrap and let sit for at least one hour before serving.

Potato Salad with Bleu Cheese and Bacon

The addition of bleu cheese gives this salad a great tang, maybe even converting those diehard fans to add vinegar to their potato salad.

3 medium potatoes, cooked,
 peeled, cubed
1 c. sliced celery
1/2 c. peeled, diced cucumbers
1/3 c. half and half
1/3 c. salad dressing or mayonnaise
1/4 c. crumbled bleu cheese
4 slices bacon,
 cooked and crumbled
1 t. dried parsley (optional)

In large bowl, combine potatoes, celery, and cucumbers; mix well. In small bowl, combine half and half and salad dressing; mix well. Stir in bleu cheese, parsley, and 2 T. of the bacon. Add to potato salad; mix well. Sprinkle with remaining bacon.

Potato Salad with Bleu Cheese and Bacon

Antipasto Salad

4 c. torn mixed salad greens
6 oz. sliced salami, wedged
6 oz. sliced provolone, wedged
1 c. thinly sliced zucchini
1 medium green or red bell
   peppers, cut into strips
8 cherry tomatoes, quartered
1/4 c. sliced ripe or black olives
1/2 c. shredded mozzarella cheese
1/2 c. drained garbanzo beans

In a large bowl, combine all ingredients and toss. Serve topped with Roasted Garlic Dressing.

Roasted Garlic Dressing:
1/3 c. vegetable oil
8 garlic cloves, peeled
4 T. vinegar
4 T. grated Parmesan cheese
Black pepper to taste

In a small skillet, cook 2 T. of the oil and garlic over medium heat about 10 minutes, stirring frequently, until garlic is golden brown. Cool. In a blender or food processor bowl, combine garlic mixture and remaining oil and dressing ingredients. Cover and blend on high speed until smooth.

Antipasto sandwiches are gaining popularity as of late. Simply sprinkle wine vinegar and olive oil inside a fresh sub roll, then a couple of pinches of dried oregano topped with any Italian ham and cheese, green peppers, onions, canned pimientos, shredded lettuce, tomato slices, hard cooked egg slices, and top with anchovies.

Salmon Salad with Two Melons

If you'd like to use salmon fillets instead of the less expensive canned salmon, simply cook skinned, boned salmon, cool, and cut into bite-sized portions before gently mixing.

1 can (7 1/2 oz.) red salmon,
   drained and flaked
3 c. torn mixed greens
1 c. cantaloupe balls
1 c. honey dew melon balls
3 kiwifruit, peeled, sliced, and halved

Mango Dressing:
1 can (5 oz.) evaporated milk
1 ripe mango, peeled and cubed
3 t. sugar

In blender or food processor, combine all dressing ingredients. Cover; blend until smooth. In large bowl, combine all salad ingredients and toss gently. Spoon salad mixture into serving bowls; drizzle each with 2 T. dressing. Serve with remaining dressing.

Raw kiwifruit is rich in the protein-dissolving enzyme actinidin, which is commercially useful as a meat tenderizer. People with latex allergies, though, are likely to be allergic to kiwifruit. The actinidin also makes this fruit unsuitable for use in desserts containing milk or any other dairy products because the enzyme begins to digest milk proteins.

Warm Chicken Salad with Roasted Red Pepper Dressing

Roasted Red Pepper Dressing:
1 lg. red bell pepper
1/3 c. olive oil
2 T. lime juice
2 T. lemon juice
3 t. fresh cilantro, chopped
1/4 t. salt

Salad:
4 boneless, skinless chicken breasts
2 c. torn spinach leaves
2 c. torn romaine lettuce
1 medium yellow or red bell pepper,
   diced
1 c. cubed Jicama

For the dressing, cut red bell pepper in half lengthwise and remove seeds. Place pepper halves, cut side down, on broiler pan. Broil 4 inches from heat for 5 to 10 minutes or until skin is evenly blistered. You may also char pepper on outdoor grill. Place in paper bag, close, and let stand 15 to 20 minutes. In blender or food processor, combine pepper halves and remaining dressing ingredients. Cover; blend until almost smooth. Place chicken breasts on same broiler pan; broil 4 inches from heat for 18 to 22 minutes or until chicken is no longer pink and juices run clear, turning once.

In large bowl, combine spinach leaves and remaining salad ingredients; toss. Arrange on 4 individual plates; set aside. Gently remove and discard skin from roasted red bell pepper.

To assemble salads, cut chicken on the bias into 1/2-inch slices. Arrange over salad ingredients on plates and drizzle with dressing.

Steak and Fruit Salad with Pineapple Dressing

Don't think the man in your life will eat a fruit salad? Set this main-dish salad in front of him and watch. The creamy dressing is given a jump start in taste with the mustard and blends very well with steak.

Pineapple dressing:
1/2 c. pineapple yogurt
1 t. Dijon-style mustard
2 t. honey
1 T. reserved pineapple liquid
  (*see below*)

Salad:
1 can (20 oz.) pineapple chunks,
  drained, reserving liquid
3 T. sliced green onions
1 t. Dijon-style mustard
1 1/2 lb. boneless beef sirloin steak
6 c. torn mixed greens
1 medium apple, cored and chopped

In small bowl, combine all dressing ingredients; blend well. Cover; refrigerate until serving time.

For the salad: In a 2-quart baking dish or strong plastic bag, combine pineapple liquid (less the 1 T. used in the dressing) green onions and 1 t. mustard; mix well. Add steak; turn to coat and cover dish or seal bag; refrigerate 6 hours or overnight.

Place steak on broiler pan and broil 4 inches below heat source for 8 to 20 minutes or until desired temperature, turning once. Cut steak into thin strips.

In large bowl, combine pineapple chunks, salad greens, and apple; arrange on 6 individual salad plates. Arrange warm beef strips on top; drizzle with dressing.

Jicama is a root vegetable that resembles a large turnip, although it's actually a legume that has a thin brown skin and white crunchy flesh, reminiscent of water chestnuts. With a sharp knife, peel off the brown skin along with the white fibrous layer. The flesh is crisp, sweet, and nutty and has been described as a cross between a pear and an apple or an apple and a potato. Try sprinkling slices of jicama with lime juice and a little chili powder to snack on or replace water chestnuts with jicama in Chinese dishes. In addition, you could thinly slice this vegetable for sandwiches, use in stir-fries, boil, mash as potatoes, or use in soups (add toward the end in order for it to retain its crunchy texture).

Crunchy Broccoli Salad

3/4 c. salad dressing
2 T. sugar
2 T. cider vinegar
1 bunch broccoli, cut into florets
8 slices bacon,
  cooked and crumbled
1 small red onion, chopped
1/4 c. sesame seeds
1/2 c. raisins

Mix dressing, sugar, and vinegar in large bowl. Add remaining ingredients and lightly mix. Refrigerate at least one hour before serving.

Remember the phrase, "Open Sesame" from *Arabian Nights*? When sesame seeds are mature in the pod, they burst open, hence the phrase.

Waldorf Salad

This is delicious enough to enjoy as an entrée by adding strips of chicken breasts, smoked turkey, or grilled salmon flaked over the top.

4 medium red delicious apples,
  cored and sliced thin
4 stalks celery, thinly sliced
1/2 c. raisins
3 T. lemon juice
6 T. mayonnaise
2/3 c. chopped walnuts
Whole walnuts for garnish

Combine all in large bowl and toss until thoroughly mixed. Chill at least 1 hour and serve.

If Cole Porter mentions Waldorf Salad in his song "You're the Top" then it must be famous. Right? How about the cookbook entitled *Oscar of the Waldorf*? Anything yet? Well, at least know that the Waldorf-Astoria Hotel in New York City employed a maitre d'hotel by the name of Oscar Tschirky who created this dish in 1894, as well as many other signature dishes that made this hotel the finest place to dine in all of New York for many years.

Maine Fiddlehead Salad

The flavor of fiddleheads has been described as a cross between asparagus and mushrooms. This sprout of the fern family can be picked along most stream edges in northern New England and Canada. Pick when the curled frond (leaf) is about 2 inches above the ground. You will find a brown dried "skin" which can easily be rinsed off before cooking. Just fill a bowl of cold water, soak the fiddleheads for 10 minutes, and skim off the brown layer on the water before removing the greens.

1 c. plain yogurt
1 c. mayonnaise
1 t. Dijon-style mustard
Salt and pepper to taste
1 c. cooked fiddleheads,
  coarsely chopped and cooled
3 scallions, sliced thin
1 medium cucumber, peeled
3 T. minced red bell pepper

In small bowl, combine yogurt, mayonnaise, mustard, salt, and pepper; mix well. In separate bowl, combine remainder of ingredients; toss with mayonnaise mixture. Refrigerate 1 hour before serving.

> To Stew Cucumbers. Pare twelve cucumbers and slice them, as for eating and put them to drain and lay them in a coarse cloth until they are dry. Flour them, and fry them brown in butter. Then put to them some gravy, a little claret, some pepper, cloves and mace and let them stew a little. Then roll a bit of butter in flour, and toss them up. Put them under mutton and lamb roasted.
>
> —*The Compleat Housewife, 1730*

Yankee Spinach Salad

You will find this version of Spinach Salad soaring above all others. The tanginess of the cranberries and the smoke-flavored bacon just turn this salad into a keeper.

6-oz. package of salad spinach
1/2 c. sweetened dried cranberries
4 thin slices of red onions

Dressing:
4 slices bacon or turkey bacon, cooked crisp and crumbled
1/2 c. plain or orange-flavored honey
1/2 c. lime juice
2 T. Dijon mustard

Salad:
Wash and clean spinach. Divide evenly among 4 salad plates. Top each with 2 tablespoons sweetened dried cranberries and onion slices.

Dressing:
Combine dressing ingredients in a small glass mixing bowl using a wire whisk. Heat in the microwave on high for 1 minute or until warm. Pour over salad and toss.

Papaya-Kiwi Salad with Orange Dressing

Want to add a little spice? Sprinkle some cayenne pepper in the dressing or mince some chilies to dot the top of the finished salad.

1 papaya
4 kiwis
6 T. frozen orange juice concentrate, thawed
3 T. honey
1 c. sour cream
1 T. grated orange peel
1 T. grated lime peel

Peel and remove seeds from papaya. Slice lengthwise into thin slices. Peel kiwi and cut crosswise into thin slices. Arrange papaya and kiwi on 4 salad plates. Combine orange juice concentrate and honey in a small bowl. Stir in sour cream. Spoon dressing over salads; sprinkle with grated peels.

Don't throw those orange peels away once you've gotten your fill of citrusy goodness. Try some of these uses.

- Add to meat dishes to enhance the flavor. Put peels in braising liquid or into the cavity of a whole chicken before roasting.
- Infuse your liquor, especially vodka, for excellent cocktails.
- Dry and save for black tea.
- Add orange peels to aging olive oil to add an extra zest that's great on salads and pastas.
- Set some orange peels around areas where ants are a problem—it works as a great ant repellent, which makes it helpful while on a picnic or camping.
- Deodorize garbage cans by dropping a couple of orange peels in the bottom of the can before inserting the trash bag.

Watermelon Hawaiian Salad

Imagine yourself on the beach in Oahu. What's the first food item that comes to mind? Chances are, it's one of the following ingredients you'll find in this scrumptious salad.

1 c. macadamia nuts
2 bananas
1 small papaya
Juice of 4 limes
3 c. seedless watermelon
    balls or small squares
2 c. fresh pineapple chunks
1 c. freshly grated or
    unsweetened coconut
3 c. low-fat vanilla flavored yogurt
1/3 c. papaya seeds

Place the macadamia nuts in a food processor fitted with a steel blade and pulse them a couple of times just to chop them into large pieces. Then, place them in a non-stick heavy sauté pan and toast them over medium heat just until they turn golden, stirring constantly. Remove them to a heatproof dish or bowl and allow them to cool.

Peel and cut the bananas and papaya flesh into small chunks and toss them in the lime juice. Place the banana and the papaya chunks in a large glass bowl with the watermelon, pineapple, and coconut. In another bowl, mix together the yogurt and the papaya seeds. Pour over the fruit and coconut. Toss to combine. Place in a serving bowl or coconut shells. Sprinkle the toasted macadamia nuts over the top and serve immediately.

Coleslaw

The old fashioned way of serving coleslaw (yes, one word) was to pile shredded cabbage in individual bowls and then ladle the dressing over the top. The reason being that cabbage will soften within minutes, shrinking the portion. However to make it easier for your friends and family to enjoy, just mix the dressing and cabbage together yourself and serve immediately.

1 1/2 lb. cabbage
1/2 c. shredded carrots
1 c. mayonnaise
1/2 c. plain yogurt
1 t. horseradish (optional)
2 T. sugar
3 scallions, sliced thin
1 T. cider vinegar
Black pepper to taste

Finely shred or chop cabbage. In separate bowl, combine remainder of ingredients and whisk until smooth and well combined. Add shredded cabbage to the mayonnaise mixture and toss until evenly distributed. Chill and serve. To serve the old fashioned way, divide the shredded cabbage into serving bowls and ladle coleslaw dressing over the top of each. Serve.

Apple Celery Slaw

Try using wedged pears in place of apples, pineapple juice in place of apple and lemon juices, honey and Parmesan cheese in place of ginger, or red and yellow bell peppers and carrots in place of celery.

2 c. each shredded red
    and green cabbage
1 rib celery, thinly sliced
2 red apples, cored
    and thinly wedged
1/4 c. golden raisins
1 c. Miracle Whip®
1 t. dried ginger
3 T. apple juice
2 T. lemon juice

Toss cabbage, celery, apples, and raisins together in large bowl. In separate bowl, mix Miracle Whip, ginger, apple, and lemon juice until well blended. Toss all together.

A Curious and simple manner of keeping apricots, peaches, plums, etc. fresh all the year. Beat well up together equal quantities of honey and spring water; pour it into an earthen vessel. Put in the fruits all freshly gathered and cover them up quite close. When any of the fruit is taken out, wash it in cold water, and it is fit for immediate use.

-*The Universal Receipt Book, 1814*

Beef and Pepper Slaw

This actually could be classified as a salad because it is so hearty. A broken piece of crusty bread should round this meal off just fine.

2 medium red, yellow, and/or green bell peppers
4 c. finely shredded cabbage with carrot
2/3 c. cucumber ranch dressing
1/4 c. frozen orange juice concentrate, thawed
12 oz. cooked beef, turkey, chicken, or pork
4 oranges, peeled, sectioned, and seeded

Cut bell peppers into bite-sized strips. In a salad bowl combine peppers and cabbage. In a bowl combine salad dressing and thawed concentrate; toss with cabbage mixture.

Cut meat or poultry into thin bite-sized strips or shred. Fold meat and orange sections into cabbage mixture.

Four-Veggie Slaw

If you sneak this delightfully creamy slaw into your picnic basket, maybe the kids will have a go at it.

3 c. shredded green cabbage
1 c. shredded red cabbage
1 c. shredded carrots
2 c. shredded zucchini or cucumber

3/4 c. creamy cucumber dressing
1/4 c. plain yogurt
1/2 t. celery seed
1/4 t. salt

In large bowl, combine all ingredients and mix well.

Your afternoon snack can also soothe your sunburn. Smearing yogurt on your skin as soon as it turns pink cools your skin and reestablishes its pH balance so it heals faster. Use plain, full-fat yogurt that contains few additives. Let it sit on your skin until it warms up and then rinse it off with tepid water. Apply as often as needed.

Beachcombers Slaw

This is a beautiful presentation. Although called a slaw, serving this as a main-dish salad will please even the hungriest.

3 c. finely shredded cabbage
1/2 c. minced yellow bell pepper
1 small red onion, thinly sliced
1/4 c. chopped fresh parsley
2 c. cooked lobster, chopped
1 c. cooked artichoke hearts, (rinsed if canned) halved and thinly sliced
1 c. Lemon Vinaigrette, *recipe below*
1 cantaloupe melon
1 lb. shrimp
Mint sprigs for garnish

Combine all ingredients in a large mixing bowl and toss gently to blend. Chill at least 2 hours; occasionally tossing. Make Lemon Vinaigrette.

Lemon Vinaigrette:
3 T. lemon juice
1 T. red wine vinegar
2 T. extra-virgin olive oil
3 T. honey
1/2 t. dried basil
1/4 t. celery seeds

Place all ingredients in a blender and puree until smooth and emulsified.

Cut melon in half and scrape out seeds. Slice melon into large to small whole circles, removing rind after; place on individual serving plates. Mound slaw in center of each melon circle and gently place cooked shrimp over the top of each, letting it spill haphazardly.

CHAPTER 8

Poultry

THE COUNTRY EDITOR—PAYING THE YEARLY SUBSCRIPTION.—[DRAWN BY F. S. CHURCH.]

A newspaper depiction of a man paying for his subscription to the Podunk Weekly Bugle with chickens

From time immemorial, many a family has had to live off poultry, be it home raised or shot in the forests of New England, but the simple fact is that poultry has always had a close place next to our dry witted Yankee hearts. So enjoy these delicious recipes with a touch of international flair. And, yes, goose is still available in supermarkets.

Beer-Braised Goose

The English are more familiar with cooking goose than Americans and I don't know why. It may be because goose is all dark meat, but it is so flavorful and the fat of the goose is unequaled.

Half goose, skinned and filleted
4 medium potatoes, scrubbed
4 carrots, cut into 1/2-inch slices
1 onion, peeled and thinly sliced
1 can beer
1/4 c. barbecue sauce
2 T. brown sugar
1/2 t. garlic salt

Cut the goose into 2- or 3-inch cubes. Scrub and halve the potatoes. Cut carrots into 1-inch pieces. In a crockery cooker, place potatoes, carrots, and onion; place the meat on top. Combine beer, barbecue sauce, brown sugar, and garlic salt. Pour over the meat. Cover and cook for 2 hours at 350°F.

Corned Goose

Goose fat will collect on top while cooking in the crock pot. Be sure to check often and skim.

One large goose breast and legs,
  skinned
1 medium onion
1 T. pickling spice mix
4 c. water
1 c. pickling salt

Place goose meat in a nonmetallic container. Chop onion, sprinkle over meat. Sprinkle the spices over the meat. Mix water and pickling salt, and pour over the meat. Be sure the meat is submerged, and let the goose soak for 48 hours while refrigerated. The meat should now be drained and rinsed several times. Soak in fresh water for about 4 hours before cooking. Cook in a crock pot with about 1 cup of onion soup on low for 6 to 8 hours.

Apple Sweet Barbecued Chicken

I think this recipe is probably the simplest I have in this cookbook. I almost didn't add it, but because of the addition of apple juice in the barbecue, it is a great baste for the chicken. Use apple cider for an even deeper, richer flavor.

1 c. barbecue sauce
1/3 c. frozen apple juice
  concentrate, thawed
2 (3 to 3 1/2-lb.) frying chicken, cut
  into quarters, or more if you like

Grill Directions: Heat grill. In small bowl, combine barbecue sauce and apple juice concentrate; mix well. When ready to grill, place chicken, skin side down, on gas grill over low heat or on charcoal grill 4 to 6 inches from medium coals. Cook 40 to 50 minutes or until chicken is fork tender and juices run clear, turning often and brushing frequently with sauce during last 15 minutes of cooking. Heat any remaining sauce to a boil; serve with chicken.

Oven Directions: Heat oven to 375°F. Prepare sauce as directed above. Place chicken, skin side down, in ungreased baking pan and bake for 30 minutes. Using spoon, remove most of the pan juices. Turn chicken over; brush with sauce. Return to oven; bake an additional 15 to 20 minutes, or until chicken is fork tender and juices run clear, brushing frequently with sauce. Heat any remaining sauce as above.

Jamaican Jerk Chicken and Fettuccine

The cuisine of Jamaica and New England are worlds apart, but my brother once owned a sandwich shop in Maine and his best seller was a Jamaican jerk chicken sandwich. I adapted his recipe for a main course I believe you will love.

4 skinless, boneless chicken breast
  halves, about 1 lb.
2 c. chicken broth
1/4 c. whipping cream (or heavy)
12 oz. dried fettuccine

Jerk Seasoning Paste:
1/2 c. firmly packed fresh cilantro
5 T. each of water and minced fresh
  ginger
3 T. whole black peppercorns
2 T. each ground allspice and brown
  sugar
3 cloves garlic
1 t. crushed red pepper flakes
1/2 t. each of coriander and nutmeg

In a blender or food processor, combine ingredients for the jerk seasoning. Whirl until smooth and reserve 2 T. and refrigerate. Coat the chicken with the remainder of the seasoning rub. Cover and refrigerate at least 1 hour. If overnight, that's even better. In a frying pan, boil reserved seasoning, broth, and cream over high heat, stirring, until reduced to about 1 1/2 cups; keep warm. Arrange chicken on baking sheet and bake for 20 to 25 minutes on 350°F, or until done and the juices run clear. You can also cook these on an outdoor barbecue grill just as easily.

While the chicken is cooking, bring 3 qts. water to a boil over high and cook fettuccine according to box instructions. Drain well and add back to the pot. Add broth and continue cooking pasta over medium heat until broth is absorbed. In the meantime, when chicken is done, remove chicken from oven and add the juices from the chicken to the broth/noodle mixture. Spoon pasta onto a plate and top with chicken that has been sliced on the bias.

Chili-Rubbed Chicken Legs

My favorite part of poultry is the dark meat. I just love the taste of dark meat chicken and you will be converted once you try this Southern-inspired dish. Use chicken thighs if you prefer.

Spice Rub:
1/4 c. paprika
1 T. brown sugar
2 t. chili powder
1 t. cumin
1 t. garlic salt
1/2 t. salt

Potatoes and Chicken:
4 baking potatoes
1 onion, sliced thinly
4 T. butter or margarine
8 chicken legs

Spice Rub: In a small bowl, stir paprika, brown sugar, chili powder, cumin, garlic salt, and salt together and set aside.

Potatoes: Heat oven to 350°F. Cut each potato in half lengthwise and place 1/4 of the onion, 1 T. of the butter, and 1/2 t. of the spice rub on one exposed surface of each potato. Reform 2 halves of a potato to make a whole and wrap tightly in tin foil. Bake potatoes for about 45 minutes or until, when gently squeezed, are soft. In the meantime, coat all sides of the chicken legs with the remaining spice rub, or remove skin and coat thoroughly. Place the chicken on a baking sheet and cook until the juices run clear and are done, about 30 to 35 minutes. Turn the legs once during cooking. Serve together.

To drive flies from a room in 1818, this concoction was used by the Emery Family of Massachusetts:

Take a 1/2 t. of well pulverized black pepper, 1 t. of brown sugar, 1 T. cream, mix them well together and place them in a room on a plate where the flies are troublesome and they will soon disappear.

Stuffed Chicken with Apricot Glaze

Again, I am taking a shortcut. But who doesn't like the packaged stuffing now-a-days?

1 (3 1/2 to 4-lb.) frying chicken	1/4 c. raisins
1/2 t. salt	1/4 c. thinly sliced celery
1/4 t. pepper	1/2 t. grated lemon peel
2 T. vegetable oil	1/2 c. apple jelly
1 pkg. (6-oz.) chicken-flavored stuffing mix	1 T. lemon juice
1 c. chopped apple	1/2 t. cinnamon
1/4 c. chopped walnuts	

Preheat oven to 350°F. Sprinkle inside of chicken with salt and pepper; rub outside with oil. Prepare stuffing mix according to package directions in a large bowl. Add apple, walnuts, raisins, celery, and lemon peel; mix thoroughly. Stuff body cavity loosely with stuffing. Place chicken in baking pan; cover loosely with tin foil and roast for 1 hour.

Meanwhile, combine jelly, lemon juice, and cinnamon in small saucepan. Simmer over low heat for 3 minutes or until blended. Remove foil from chicken; brush with jelly mixture. Roast, uncovered, brushing frequently with jelly glaze, 30 minutes or until meat thermometer inserted into the thickest part of thigh registers 185 °F. Let chicken stand for 15 minutes before carving.

Plum Sweet and Spicy Chicken

Reading through some old cookbooks in my library, I found our ancestors used prunes so often in recipes it's a wonder they stayed in the kitchen long enough to cook without having to run outside to that crescent moon door. I decided to use plums because of their sweetness and overall taste. The cider vinegar truly adds a special taste profile to this sweetened chicken entrée.

1/2 t. white pepper
1/2 t. ginger
1/2 t. cinnamon
1/2 t. ground cloves
1 (3 1/2 to 4-lb.) frying chicken
4 T. soy sauce, divided
3 T. honey
1/2 c. plum jelly
1/4 c. your favorite chutney
2 t. sugar
2 t. cider vinegar

Combine white pepper, ginger, cinnamon, and cloves in a small dish. Rub the inside of chicken with half of the spice mixture; rub on outside of chicken. Cover chicken and refrigerate for 1 hour.

Preheat oven to 350°F. Put chicken in a baking pan and bake for 45 minutes; increase oven temperature to 450°F. Combine remaining 3 T. of soy sauce and the honey; brush on the chicken. Combine plum jelly, chutney, sugar, and vinegar; spread on chicken. Bake an additional 15 minutes or until brown and tender.

Monterey Chicken

An aged version of Monterey Jack cheese is available, called Dry Jack. It resembles Parmesan cheese in texture and is great crumbled on top of salads.

    6 bacon strips, halved
    6 boneless, skinless chicken
       breast halves
    1/2 c. olive oil
    1/4 c. red wine vinegar
    1/4 c. soy sauce
    1 t. minced garlic
    1/2 t. salt
    1/2 t. oregano
    1/2 t. black pepper
    6 thin slices onion
    6 thin slices tomato
    6 thin slices avocado
    6 slices Monterey Jack cheese

Cook bacon according to package directions; drain. Meanwhile, flatten chicken to 1/4 inch thick. In a large resealable plastic bag, combine the oil, vinegar, soy sauce, garlic, salt, oregano, and pepper; add chicken. Seal bag and turn to coat; refrigerate for at least 60 minutes. Drain and discard the marinade. Grill chicken, uncovered, over medium heat for 4 to 6 minutes on each side or until meat is no longer pink. Move chicken to edges of pan and add bacon pieces and one slice of onion, tomato, avocado, and cheese. Cover and grill 4 to 6 minutes longer or until cheese is melted. To serve, stack the veggies and cheese on top of the chicken.

David Jack (1822–1909), American businessman and one of the creators of Monterey Jack cheese

Oven Crispy Orange Chicken

If you don't want the fat, just peel off the skin on each segment of chicken before dipping the chicken. The flavor will not be lost.

    1 beaten egg
    1/2 of a 6-oz. can (1/2 c.) frozen
       orange juice concentrate, thawed
    2 T. soy sauce
    1/2 c. bread crumbs
    1 t. paprika
    1/4 t. salt
    3 T. butter or margarine
    One 2 1/2 to 3-lb. fryer chicken,
       cut up

Combine beaten egg, orange juice concentrate, and soy sauce; stir to mix well. In a small bowl, thoroughly combine bread crumbs, paprika and salt. Melt butter in a 13 × 9 × 2-inch baking pan. Dip chicken pieces in the orange-soy mixture, then coat with crumbs. Place chicken, skin side up and so pieces don't touch, in the pan. Sprinkle with any remaining crumb mixture. Bake, uncovered, in a 375°F oven for 50 minutes or until done. Do not turn.

Dr. Zerobabel Endecott of Salem during the 17th century provides the following cure:

For Vometing & Looseness in Men Women & Children. Take an Egg break a Little hole in one end of it & put owt ye white then put in a bout 1/2 spoonfull of baye salt then fill up the egg with strong Rum or spirits of wine & sett it in hott ashes & Lett it boyle till ye egg by dry then take it & eat it fasting & fast an hour after it or drink a Litle distilled waters of mint & fennill which waters mixed together & drank will help in most ordinary Cases.

Bleu Buffalo Chicken

Why the name Buffalo? No idea! My brother had Bleu Buffalo this and Bleu Buffalo that at his sandwich shop. Regardless of the origin, these drumsticks have a rich flavor and are a great alternative to your basic fast food fare.

    1 bottle (8 oz.) bleu cheese
       salad dressing
    2 c. bread crumbs
    1/2 t. celery salt
    1/2 t. dried dill
    1/4 t. black pepper
    12 chicken drumsticks
    Cooking spray

Preheat oven to 350°F. Spray baking sheet with cooking spray; set aside. Pour dressing in a medium bowl. Combine bread crumbs, celery, salt, dill, and pepper in a shallow dish. Dip chicken into the dressing; roll in bread crumb mixture. Place chicken in a single layer on prepared baking sheet. Bake, uncovered, 50 minutes or until juices run clear, turning once.

Grilled Mango Chicken

Honestly, I can't think of any other side dish that I would want served with this delicious chicken so why even try? Enjoy this all by itself but not by yourself.

Chicken:
    1/2 c. mango nectar
    6 T. olive oil
    1/4 c. lime juice
    2 garlic cloves, minced
    1 T. sugar
    1/2 t. salt
    6 boneless, skinless
       chicken breast halves

Mango Salsa:
    1 mango
    1 cucumber
    1 avocado
    1 jalapeno chile, seeded
    1/4 c. diced red onion
    2 T. olive oil
    2 T. lime juice
    1/2 t. salt
    1 T. chopped fresh
       cilantro leaves (or 1 t. dried)

Chicken: In a medium-sized bowl, combine mango nectar, oil, lime juice, garlic, sugar, and salt. Place chicken breast halves and mango mixture in a large plastic food storage bag; seal. Marinate in refrigerator for 3 hours.

Mango Salsa: Meanwhile, peel and dice mango, cucumber, and avocado. Finely chop jalapeno. In a large bowl, combine mango, cucumber, avocado, jalapeno, red onion, oil, lime juice, cilantro, and salt. Refrigerate until serving.

Remove chicken from marinade, discard the juice. Grill over medium-high heat for about 6 minutes per side or until juice runs clear. Serve with the Mango Salsa.

Beer Can Chicken

Propping a whole chicken on an open can of beer and slow-roasting it on the grill may seem a bit unusual, but the result is incredible. The beer vapors do little to moisten the chicken; rather, the vertical position of the bird allows its juices to flow down over the breast, keeping it succulent.

2 T. Garlic Barbecue Marinade, recipe follows
1 four-pound chicken
2 T. Seven-Spice Dry Rub, recipe follows
One can (12-oz.) of beer
1 c. hickory or other hardwood chips, soaked in water
Cider Mop Spray, recipe follows
1/2 c. your favorite barbecue sauce

Rub the marinade all over the chicken and refrigerate overnight or let stand for at least 4 hours at room temperature. Bring the chicken to room temperature and sprinkle the dry rub all over the skin. Light a charcoal fire in a covered grill and set it up for indirect grilling. When the temperature reaches 225°F, carefully push the hot coals to one side and place a drip pan filled with 1 cup of water on the opposite side. Discard (or drink) half the beer. Stand the chicken upright on the can, with its legs pointing down. Transfer the chicken on the beer can to the grill, setting it over the drip pan, and cover the grill; you will need to cook the chicken for about 3 hours total. To maintain the temperature inside, you will have to replenish the charcoal with a fresh batch of burning coals every hour. Add more water to the drip pan when half of it is evaporated. After the first 45 minutes, rotate the chicken, then drain 1/2 cup of the wood chips and scatter them over the coals. After another 45 minutes, drain and scatter the remaining wood chips over the coals. Rotate the chicken again, and spray the chicken with the mop spray. Rotate and spray the bird twice more, at 45 minutes intervals.

The chicken is done when the internal temperature of the chicken reads 170°F. Remove and discard beer can and transfer the bird to a carving board. Remove the drip pan from the grill and stoke the coals and spread them in an even layer. Replenish with fresh coals to make a moderately hot fire. Cut the chicken in half though the backbone and brush it all over with the diluted barbecue sauce. Grill the chicken, skin side down, until lightly charred. Turn and brush it with more sauce. Continue grilling, brushing, and turning until the chicken skin is crisp and glazed.

Garlic Barbecue Marinade:
10 garlic cloves, coarsely chopped
1/4 c. Worcestershire sauce
2 T. soy sauce
1 onions, chopped
1/4 c. water

Put all ingredients in a blender and pulse until thoroughly combined.

Seven-Spice Dry Rub:
1/2 c. brown sugar
1/2 c. paprika
2 T. salt
1/4 c. chili powder
1/4 c. dry mustard
1 T. black pepper
2 t. Old Bay® seasoning
1/2 t. ginger

In a small bowl, whisk together the brown sugar, paprika, salt, chili powder, dry mustard, black pepper, Old Bay, and ginger.

Cider Mop Spray:
1 c. apple juice
1 c. water
1/4 c. cider vinegar

In a large glass measuring cup, combine all ingredients and pour into a spray bottle; refrigerate.

Mahogany Chicken

This is a popular, quick chicken dish with pieces of chicken glazed with a sweet and tangy marinade. Many people add a hint of soy sauce to the glaze, but I think the balsamic vinegar does the trick.

One 3 1/2-lb. chicken
1/4 t. salt
1/2 t. coarse black pepper
2 T. balsamic vinegar
2 T. dry vermouth
2 T. brown sugar
1/4 c. water

Preheat oven to 350°F. With breast side up, lift wings up toward neck and fold the wing tips under back of chicken so they stay in place. Tie the legs together. Place chicken, breast side up, on rack in roasting pan; sprinkle with salt and pepper and roast chicken for 45 minutes.

Meanwhile, prepare glaze; in small bowl, stir vinegar, vermouth, and brown sugar, until sugar has dissolved. After chicken has roasted 45 minutes, brush with some glaze. Turn oven to 400°F and roast chicken, brushing with glaze, until chicken is a deep brown color, about 30 minutes longer. Chicken is done when temperature inside is 170°F and the juice runs clear when pricked.

Remove rack from roasting pan after you have transferred chicken to a platter, and add water to pan juices. Heat to boiling over medium heat, stirring to loosen browned bits from the bottom of the pan. Remove pan from heat; skim and discard fat from pan juices if you like and carve chicken. Serve with the pan juices.

40 Clove Chicken

If you love the taste of garlic, I mean really love, then this recipe is right up your alley. Full of taste and scent, combine this with something a little tamer such as buttered pasta or a medley of steamed vegetables.

One 3 1/2-lb. chicken
6 thyme sprigs
1/2 t. salt
1/4 t. coarse black pepper
40 garlic cloves, about 3 heads,
    unpeeled, with loose
    papery skin removed
1 c. chicken broth

Preheat oven to 450°F. With fingertips, gently separate skin from meat on the chicken breast. Place 4 thyme sprigs on meat under skin of chicken breast. Place remaining 2 sprigs inside cavity of chicken. Sprinkle with salt and pepper. With breast side up, lift wings up toward neck, and then fold wing tips under back of chicken so they stay in place. Tie legs together with string if needed. Place chicken, breast side up, on rack in roasting pan.

Roast chicken for 30 minutes. Add garlic cloves to pan and roast about 30 minutes longer. Chicken is done when thermometer inserted in thickest part of thigh reaches 170°F and juices run clear when pricked. Transfer to platter and let rest.

Meanwhile, remove rack from pan and, with a slotted spoon, remove garlic cloves to small bowl. Skim and discard fat from pan juices if you like. Discard skin from 6 garlic cloves; add peeled garlic and broth to roasting pan. Heat broth mixture to boiling over medium heat, stirring to loosen browned bits from the bottom of the pan, and mashing garlic with spoon, until well blended. Carve chicken, arrange on platter, and serve with pan juices and remaining garlic cloves.

Country Captain Casserole

A mild casserole usually served over white rice but I like it as a stew. The great thing about this is the fact that you only dirty one pot.

2 T. plus 1 t. vegetable oil	3 T. curry powder
2 chickens (3 1/2 lb. each), skinned and cut into 8 pieces	1/2 t. black pepper
	1/4 t. cumin
2 onions, chopped	1 can (28 oz.) tomato puree
1 apple, peeled, cored, and chopped	1 can (14 1/2 oz.) chicken broth
1 green bell pepper, cored and chopped	1/2 c. raisins
3 cloves garlic, minced	1 t. salt
1 T. minced fresh ginger (or 1 t. dried)	

In a 2-gallon pot, heat 2 T. oil over medium-high heat until hot. Add chicken, cook until chicken is browned all over and remove. Preheat oven to 350°F. In same pot, heat 1 t. oil over medium-high heat. Add onions, apples, green pepper, garlic, and ginger and cook, stirring frequently, about 2 minutes. If using dried ginger, add after this mixture is done cooking. Reduce heat to medium and cover, cook an additional 5 minutes. Stir in curry powder, pepper, and cumin; cook, stirring, 1 minute. Add tomato puree, broth, raisins, salt, and chicken pieces and any juices from the chickens. Heat to boiling over high heat; boil 1 minute. Cover and place in the oven for about 1 hour, or until chicken is done.

Think about this the next time you complain about a hair in your food.

The New England Journal of Medicine reported that in November of 2007, doctors took out a 10-pound hairball from an 18-year-old woman after she came to them with pain and a 40-pound weight loss. She had had stomach pains for months before the doctors found the mass with a small camera. The hairball took up almost her entire stomach content. She had developed trichophagia, a compulsion to eat her own hair.

Other obsessions and compulsions. See if you know what they are. Answers found at the end of the chapter:

a. Mycophobia	**d.** Phogophobia
b. Mageirocophobia	**e.** Sitophobia
c. Dipsophobia	

My Chicken Cordon Bleu

Not swaying too far from the classically prepared dish, I find the presentation of this recipe worthy of any formal gathering, or just to show off, either way.

1 T. butter or margarine
4 boneless, skinless chicken
   breast halves
2 T. balsamic vinegar
Pinch black pepper
4 thin slices of cooked ham
4 thin slices Pepper Jack cheese
1 bag washed and
   stemmed baby spinach

In a nonstick skillet, melt butter over medium-high heat. Add chicken breasts and cook until golden brown, about 6 minutes. Turn chicken, cover, and reduce heat to medium. Cook chicken until chicken loses its pink color, about 5 more minutes. Increase heat to medium-high and stir in vinegar and pepper to the pan juices; cook 1 additional minute. Remove skillet from heat; top with slices of ham and cheese and cover skillet until the cheese melts.

To serve, place the baby spinach on a large platter; top with chicken breasts and drizzle with the pan juice mixture so that the baby spinach begins to wilt.

Chicken Pot Pie with Cornbread Crust

A delicious pot pie made from scratch. This budget-friendly version is heart warming and made even more delectable with the addition of the cornbread crust.

Chicken Filling:
1 T. butter or margarine
2 carrots, peeled and sliced
1 onion, chopped
1 can (14 1/2 oz.) chicken broth
1/4 t. each of salt and black pepper
1/4 t. dried thyme
3 T. cornstarch
1 1/2 c. milk
3 c. chunked, cooked chicken
1 pkg. (10 oz.) frozen
    whole-kernel corn
1 pkg. (10 oz.) frozen green beans

Cornbread Crust:
1/2 c. flour
1/2 c. yellow cornmeal
2 T. sugar
1 1/2 t. baking powder
1/2 t. salt
2 T. cold butter or margarine
3/4 c. milk

Preheat oven to 350°F. Prepare Chicken Filling: In a large saucepan, melt butter over medium-low heat and add carrots and onion; cook, stirring occasionally, for 5 minutes. Add the broth, salt, pepper, and thyme; heat to boiling over high heat. Reduce heat to low; cover and simmer until vegetables are tender, about 10 minutes.

Meanwhile, in a small bowl, with wire whisk, mix cornstarch and 1/2 c. milk until well blended. Stir cornstarch mixture and remaining 1 c. milk into saucepan with the carrots; heat to boiling over high heat, stirring constantly. Boil, stirring for 1 minute. Stir in chicken, corn, and beans. Transfer mixture to a shallow 2 1/2 qt. casserole dish.

Prepare Cornbread Crust: In medium bowl, stir flour, cornmeal, sugar, baking powder, and salt. With a pastry knife or two knives used scissor-fashion, cut in the butter until mixture resembles peas. Stir in the milk until blended and mixture thickens slightly. Pour mixture over the filling; spread to form an even layer. Bake casserole until the filling is bubbling and the top is golden brown, about 40 minutes.

Arroz con Pollo

Traditionally, this dish is flavored and colored with saffron threads, but since they are far too expensive for us cheap Yankees, turmeric is used in its place. If you would like, add 1/2 t. saffron in place of turmeric with the oregano. I omit them when cooking this dish because I prefer it without these spices.

6 skinless chicken thighs
1 t. salt
1/2 t. black pepper
1/3 c. flour
2 T. vegetable oil
1 onion, chopped
4 cloves garlic, skinned and chopped
2 c. white rice, uncooked

5 c. chicken broth
1 t. fajita seasoning
1 t. oregano
1/2 t. turmeric
1 lb. frozen peas
10 pitted green olives, sliced
1 jar (4 oz.) diced pimiento, drained

Season chicken with 1/2 t. salt and 1/8 t. black pepper. Coat with flour. In large heavy pot, heat 1 T. oil over medium-high heat and brown the chicken, in batches, for about 3 minutes per side. Add the remaining tablespoon of oil as needed. Remove from pot. Reduce heat to medium and add the onion; cook, stirring occasionally, about 5 minutes or until softened. Add garlic, cook 1 minute. Stir in uncooked rice to coat with oil. Add chicken, broth, seasoning, oregano, turmeric, and the remaining salt and black pepper; simmer, covered, for 20 minutes. Stir in the peas, olive slices, and pimiento; simmer for 10 minutes.

Tandoori Chicken Sticks with Blueberry-Fig Sauce

I "Yanked" (yes, "Yanked"...not "Yankeed" or "Yankeefied", i.e. deconstructed to fit the New England cuisine) this dish with the addition of blueberries and the elimination of turmeric which ordinarily gives this dish the classic orange color. Not knowing what to expect on my palate (although it sounded good on paper) I made it, tasted it, and loved it.

2/3 c. blueberries	1/4 t. coriander
1/2 c. blueberry jam	1 1/2 lbs. boneless,
1/2 c. chopped, fresh figs	skinless chicken breast
(or substitute pears)	1 package Tikka or
1/2 t. grated orange zest	Tandoori Chicken marinade*
2/3 c. cooked red lentils	1/2 c. plain yogurt
1/4 t. salt	1 T. of oil or cooking spray
1/4 t. black pepper	Skewers

Chop chicken breast into bite-sized chunks. Stir together Tandoori Tikka and yogurt in medium bowl and add chicken. Cover and let marinate for at least 1 hour.

Blueberry Dipping Sauce: Stir together blueberries and jam in a small saucepan. Rinse and chop figs. Add figs and orange zest. Cook sauce, stirring until it just comes to a simmer. Remove from heat, cool slightly, add lentils and season with salt, pepper, and coriander.

Sticks: Pre-heat oven to 425°F. Remove chicken from the marinade and drain in a colander. Place chicken pieces in an oiled 11 × 13-inch glass baking dish, without allowing them to touch. Roast 8 to 10 minutes until done. Place chicken on skewers. Serve with the Blueberry Dipping Sauce. Traditionally accompanied by rice as an entrée.

You can also make a simple Tikka marinade by mixing together 2 t. paprika, 2 t. ground coriander seed, 2 t. cumin, and 1 1/2 t. ground ginger. Add 2 or 3 drops of orange or red food coloring to give it the classic color.

Chicken Tagine with Sweet Potatoes

Although lamb is the most common meat for a tagine, there are many versions made with chicken. You can substitute dates or pitted prunes for the sweet potatoes used here.

1/4 c. plus 1 T. olive oil	3/4 lb. white or yellow sweet potatoes,
One 4-lb. chicken, cut into 8 pieces	peeled and sliced on the bias very thin
Salt and black pepper	2 tomatoes, chopped
1 onion, chopped	2 cloves garlic, minced
1 t. ginger	1/2 c. water
1 t. cinnamon	1 T. chopped fresh parsley (optional)

Traditional Moroccan tajine pot, much like our clay bean pots and serving the same function

In a large casserole pan (or tagine), heat 2 T. olive oil over medium-high heat. Season the chicken with salt and pepper and cook the chicken until lightly browned on all sides, about 3 minutes per side. Transfer chicken to a platter.

Add the remaining olive oil to the casserole pan along with the onion, ginger, cinnamon, and 1 t. black pepper. Cook over low heat, stirring occasionally, until the onion is soft, about 6 minutes. Arrange the chicken pieces in the pan in an even layer. Spread the sweet potatoes over the chicken and season with salt and pepper. Sprinkle evenly with the tomatoes, garlic, and parsley. Add the water to the casserole and bring to a simmer. Cover and cook the tagine over low heat until the chicken and sweet potatoes are tender, about 50 minutes.

Using a spatula, transfer the sweet potatoes to a large bowl, add the chicken pieces to the bowl and keep warm. Boil the sauce over high heat until slightly thickened, about 5 minutes. Season with salt and pepper. Pour the sauce over the chicken and sweet potatoes and serve.

Chicken and Vegetable Risotto

Risotto is considered a *primi piatti* in Italian cooking, meaning it is served as the first course. Hard to believe something as creamy and hearty as this recipe would start any meal, so why let it? Serve as the main course, the meat and vegetables are in it already.

Nonstick cooking spray
2 c. sliced mushrooms
1/2 c. chopped onions
4 cloves garlic, minced
1 T. parsley
1 T. basil
6 c. chicken broth
1 1/2 c. uncooked Arborio rice
   or converted rice
2 c. broccoli florets, cooked
1 lb. boneless, skinless chicken
   breast, cut bite-sized
4 plum tomatoes, seeded and
   chopped
1/2 t. salt
1/2 t. black pepper
2 T. grated Parmesan
   or Romano cheese

Grill chicken until done; let cool. Meanwhile spray large nonstick saucepan with cooking spray; heat over medium heat until hot. Add mushrooms, onion, and garlic. Cook and stir 5 minutes or until mushrooms are tender. Add parsley and basil. Cook and stir 1 minute. Place chicken broth in medium saucepan; bring to a boil over high heat. Reduce heat to medium-low; simmer.

In a separate pot, cook broccoli until barely done. Strain. Add rice to mushroom mixture, cook and stir over medium heat 1 to 2 minutes. Stir 1/2 c. hot chicken broth into rice mixture; cook until broth is absorbed, stirring constantly. Stir remaining hot chicken broth into rice mixture with the broccoli, cooked chicken, plum tomatoes, salt, and pepper. Cover and simmer for 15 to 20 minutes or until rice is fully cooked and the liquid has absorbed. Remove from heat and ladle onto a serving platter, sprinkle cheese over the top.

Chicken Croquettes

One of the best croquettes I ever had (besides mine of course) were the devilled crabs I had near Ybor City in Florida. They were shaped as they should have been, like a bell, and made with blue crab. Maybe in my next cookbook I will give you the recipe, but in the meantime, enjoy these crispy bells.

3 T. butter or margarine
1/4 c. flour
1/2 c. milk
1/2 c. chicken broth
1 t. lemon juice
2 t. grated onion
Dash paprika
Dash nutmeg
1 1/2 c. cooked, minced chicken
3/4 c. dried bread crumbs
1 beaten egg

Melt butter; blend in the flour well. Add the milk and broth. Cook and stir till mixture bubbles; cook and stir one additional minute. Add lemon juice, onion, paprika, dash of black pepper, nutmeg, and 1/4 t. salt. Cool mixture and then add chicken; chill. You can use your blender or food processor to make life a little easier if you would like.

With wet hands, shape chicken mixture into 8 balls, a scant 1/4 c. each. Roll in crumbs. Shape these balls into cones, bell shapes, cylinders, or balls, handling lightly so the crumbs remain on the outside. Dip into mixture of egg mixed with 2 T. water; roll in crumbs again. Fry in deep fat fryer at 350°F for about 3 minutes or until golden brown. Remove and let drain. Serve with white or chicken gravy.

Sweet and Sour Chicken

This is a Chinese style version of the dish with pineapple and bell peppers; you can use red wine vinegar and a dash of lemon juice for an alternate taste.

1/4 c. vinegar
2 T. soy sauce
2 T. water
2 T. brown sugar
1 T. cornstarch
1/2 t. salt
3 T. vegetable oil
1 onion, sliced
1/2 green bell pepper, chopped
1/2 red bell pepper, chopped
4 boneless, skinless chicken breast
   halves, cut into bite-sized pieces
1 can (20 oz.) pineapple
   chunks in juice

In a small bowl, stir together vinegar, soy sauce, water, brown sugar, cornstarch, and salt until the sugar has dissolved. In a large skillet, heat oil over medium heat. Add onion and peppers and cook, stirring occasionally, until tender. Increase to medium-high heat and add the chicken; cook, stirring, until chicken loses its pink color, about 5 minutes. Add pineapple chunks with the juice, cornstarch mixture; cook, stirring often, till juices boil and it has thickened. Serve over white rice.

Crispy-Honeyed Fried Chicken

Panko is just a fancy (if you can call it that) Japanese word for bread crumbs. What sets it aside from what us Americans are used to is that it is coarser than normal bread crumbs and doesn't contain the crust of the bread it is made from. Light, airy, and crisp, they are perfect for fish as well.

Chicken:
2 T. hot pepper sauce
2 T. Dijon-style mustard
1/2 c. honey
8 chicken breast halves,
   pounded till 1/2 inch thick
2 c. Panko (Japanese) bread crumbs
1 1/2 t. oregano
1 1/2 qts. vegetable oil for frying
1/2 t. salt
1/4 t. black pepper
1/2 t. baking powder

Honey-Mustard Sauce:
4 T. honey
2 T. Dijon-style mustard
1 T. white wine vinegar

For the marinade, in a large glass bowl, whisk together first 3 ingredients. Add pounded chicken and submerge. Cover with film wrap or add chicken in a large resealable bag with the marinade. Refrigerate at least 2 hours. In a shallow dish, toss together bread crumbs, oregano, salt, and black pepper; set aside. Heat oil to 350°F.

One at a time, remove chicken from marinade and let excess marinade drip off. Coat in crumbs. Throw away the marinade. Deep fry chicken until moderately browned on both sides, about 4 to 5 minutes total. Drain on paper towels or rack and serve with the Honey-Mustard Sauce for dipping.

Honey-Mustard Sauce: Simply add all ingredients together and whisk well.

Beer Batter Chicken

If you really want to taste the beer from the onset, use stout or lager beer. The darker the beer is, the more flavorful. But remember that the darker the batter, the darker the crust will be when you're finished cooking. Don't use this batter just for chicken, it is also great with fish as well.

Vegetable oil for frying
2/3 c. flour
I t. salt
1/2 t. black pepper
1/3 c. beer
I egg
I chicken (3 lb.), cut into 8 pieces

In a heavy skillet, at least 2-inches deep, heat 1/2-inch of oil over medium heat until the temperature reaches 350°F, about 10 minutes. Meanwhile, in a medium bowl, stir together all dry ingredients. In a separate bowl, combine beer, egg, and 2 t. of oil; stir into the dry ingredients, leaving very few lumps. Dip half of the chicken into the batter, coating well. Carefully place chicken, skin side up, into the hot oil. Cook until the outside is deep golden brown, about 5 minutes. Reduce heat to low and cook an additional 5 minutes or when the juices run clear. Drain chicken, skin side up, on paper towels or rack and transfer to a platter. Keep warm and repeat with the remaining chicken.

Cornmeal Batter-Fried Chicken

Add a little Southwest influence by chopping one jalapeno pepper, removing the white part (pith) and the seeds. Add to batter and mix well. If you like it hotter, add another, or a more potent, pepper.

3/4 c. flour
1/2 c. yellow cornmeal
I t. salt
1/2 t. black pepper
1/4 t. poultry seasoning
Pinch garlic powder
Pinch cayenne pepper
I egg
I 1/4 c. buttermilk
I chicken (3 lb.), cut into 8 pieces
2 T. vegetable oil

In a large bowl, combine all dry ingredients. In a separate bowl, combine all wet ingredients. Blend together both wet and dry until no lumps are apparent. Dip half of the chicken into the batter, coating well. Carefully place chicken, skin side up, into the hot oil. Cook until the outside is deep golden brown, about 5 minutes. Reduce heat to low and cook an additional 5 minutes. Drain chicken, skin side up, on paper towels or rack and transfer to a platter. Keep warm and repeat with the remaining chicken.

Apple Curry Chicken

Yellow, red, and green curries are the most widespread. Yellow (which is found in most supermarkets) is the mildest of the three. Green curry has the flavor of lemon grass, lime leaves, and chilies. Red curry powder is very spicy, especially red Thai curry.

4 chicken breast halves
I c. apple juice or cider, divided
1/4 t. salt
Pinch black pepper
I 1/2 c. croutons
I apple, chopped
1/2 c. minced onion
1/4 c. raisins
2 t. brown sugar
I t. curry powder
3/4 t. poultry seasoning
1/8 t. garlic powder

Preheat oven to 350°F. Lightly grease a baking dish and arrange chicken in a single layer in this prepared pan. Combine 1/4 c. apple juice, salt, and pepper in a small bowl. Brush all of the mixture over chicken. Combine croutons, apple, onion, raisins, sugar, curry powder, and garlic powder in a large bowl. Stir in the remaining 3/4 c. apple juice and spread over the chicken. Cover and bake for about 45 minutes or until tender.

Chicken Picante

This very quick dish is just spicy enough to open your eyes to a marvelous taste. The lime juice adds "depth," as we chefs say.

3/4 c. hot chunky taco sauce
1/4 c. Dijon-style mustard
3 T. lime juice
1 t. hot pepper sauce
6 chicken breast halves
3 T. butter or margarine
Chopped cilantro
Plain yogurt for garnish

Combine taco sauce, mustard, lime juice, and hot pepper sauce in a large bowl. Add the chicken, turning to coat. Cover and marinate in the refrigerator for at least 1 hour. Melt butter in a large skillet over medium heat until foamy. Remove chicken from the marinade; reserve. Add the chicken to the skillet; cook until brown on both sides, about 10 minutes. Add the marinade and cook about 5 minutes or until chicken is tender and glazed. Remove to platter and boil leftover marinade over high heat for 1 minute; pour over chicken. Serve with chopped cilantro sprinkled over the top and yogurt on the side.

Stir-Fried Chicken

The trick to a stir-fry is the heat. Cooking everything over high heat ensures a crisp, caramelized texture as long as you constantly stir. In no time at all you will have a dish as good as any Asian restaurant can produce.

4 chicken breast halves
2 T. vegetable oil
1 c. sliced celery
1 carrot, sliced
1 green bell pepper, thinly stripped
1 c. sliced mushrooms
1/2 onion, thinly sliced
1 t. salt
1/4 t. dried ginger
1 can (16 oz.) bean sprouts, drained
1 can (5 oz.) water chestnuts,
   drained and sliced
1/4 c. water
2 T. soy sauce
2 t. cornstarch
3 c. hot cooked rice
3/4 c. peanuts

Slice chicken on the bias in strips. Heat oil in wok or large skillet over high heat. Add celery, carrot, green pepper, onion, salt, and ginger. Stir fry about 3 minutes or until veggies are crisp tender; remove from pan and keep warm. Add the chicken and stir fry 3 to 5 minutes or till tender. Return vegetables to pan along with bean sprouts, water chestnuts, and water.

Blend cornstarch with soy sauce until smooth then slowly stir it into the chicken and veggie mixture. Cook, constantly stirring, until thickened slightly. Mound rice on a serving patter; spoon stir-fry chicken over rice and sprinkle with peanuts.

Did you know that 1/2 c. peanut butter and two slices of 100 percent, whole wheat bread equals the protein of a 16-oz. steak?

Indonesian Chicken Breasts

1/2 c. orange juice
1/4 c. peanut butter
2 t. curry powder
4 chicken breast halves
1 red bell pepper, cut in half
1/4 c. shredded coconut
1/4 c. currants
Hot cooked rice

Beat orange juice, peanut butter, and curry powder in a medium non-metallic bowl and add chicken, turning to cover. Refrigerate at least 2 hours, turning once. Remove chicken and discard marinade. Over medium-high heat, in an oiled skillet, cook chicken about 6 to 8 minutes per side or until nicely browned and done.

To serve, cut chicken breasts and raw bell pepper into 1/2-inch slices. Top chicken and bell pepper with coconut and currants. Serve over rice.

Peanut oil is great for making your own infused oils. It is bland to the taste and picks up whatever essence you combine with it. For example:

To make Onion Oil, take 1 lb. yellow onions very thinly sliced and simmer them in 2 c. peanut oil for 30 minutes. Drain oil into container, pressing onions on the side of the sieve.

To make Garlic Oil, add 2 c. peanut oil to 3 c. thinly sliced garlic. Simmer 15 minutes, strain, and bottle.

To make Shallot Oil, use 1 1/2 c. peanut oil and 1 lb. shallots, thinly sliced. Prepare just as the Garlic Oil.

Ricotta-Stuffed Chicken Breast for the Grill

Once you slice into this stuffed chicken, every bite will have just that perfect amount of herbed-flavored ricotta. A glass of white wine and you've got an elegant entrée.

8 oz. ricotta cheese
1/4 c. grated Parmesan cheese
1 egg yolk
2 T. parsley
1 t. basil
1 t. tarragon
1 clove garlic, minced
8 chicken breast halves
2 t. olive oil

In a small bowl, combine ricotta, Parmesan cheese, egg yolk, parsley, half the basil, half the tarragon, and garlic. With a mallet or flat-bottomed pan, pound each breast between plastic wrap until they are about 1/8 inch thick.

Spread cheese mixture evenly over each breast and start rolling, starting on the long side and tucking in the edges as you go. Fasten with toothpicks and brush with olive oil. Sprinkle each with the remaining basil and tarragon and arrange on your cooking grate. Close lid and cook for 14 to 16 minutes, turning once, cutting open to ensure doneness. Remove toothpicks and slice to serve.

Mustard Baked Chicken Breasts

The use of nonfat dry milk with a small amount of water gives a thick, creamy coating that will stick perfectly.

1/3 c. Dijon-style mustard
1/4 c. nonfat dry milk
2 T. water
3 slices of bread, crumbled
1/4 t. tarragon
6 chicken breast halves

Preheat oven to 350°F. Arrange oven rack to the highest point in the oven. In a small bowl, combine mustard, dry milk, and water; mix well. Stir in the bread crumbs and tarragon. With a rubber spatula, spread this mixture over the top of each chicken breast, which are arranged on a nonstick baking pan. Bake, uncovered, for 20 to 25 minutes or until done, cutting open to ensure doneness.

Tarragon is said to contain chemicals that help prevent cancer and possibly some viruses. Add 1 t. tarragon to tea and steep for 15 minutes. It is also said that by chewing on tarragon leaves, a toothache can be relieved. For people on salt-restricted diets, tarragon can be used in place of salt.

Chicken Schintzel with Mustard Sauce

If you find that veal for Schnitzel is out of your financial range, there's nothing wrong with adapting a recipe to your circumstance. Chicken Schnitzel is an inexpensive (I didn't use the word "cheap" this time) alternative, and tweaking a few ingredients, its flavor is right on the money...that you saved.

1/2 c. Greek yogurt
1/4 c. whole-grain mustard
1 c. dried bread crumbs
3/4 t. marjoram
Salt and black pepper to taste
1/2 c. flour
2 eggs
4 chicken breast halves,
   pounded thin
Vegetable oil for frying

Whisk yogurt and mustard together until smooth. In a separate bowl, combine bread crumbs, marjoram, salt, and pepper to taste. Put flour in another separate bowl and in a third bowl, beat the eggs. Season the chicken breasts with salt and pepper. Dredge each breast in flour and shake off excess. Dip them into the eggs and then the bread crumbs, pressing to coat well; set aside and repeat with remaining breasts.

Heat 1/8-inch oil in large skillet over medium-high heat until hot. Add 2 breasts at a time and cook till golden brown on both sides, about 6 minutes total. Repeat with remaining breasts and serve with mustard sauce.

Chicken Fricassee

This is so sinfully sloppy to eat, but you can't stop once you get that taste of spiced tomatoes and chicken. It's not nearly as spicy as many recipes out there, but who needs heat all the time?

One 2 1/2 to 3 lb. fryer chicken, cut
   into 6 pieces
3 T. vegetable oil
1 c. flour
Salt and black pepper to taste
2/3 c. white wine
1/2 onion, thinly sliced
1 green bell pepper, seeded and cut
   into strips
1 carrot, thinly sliced
1/2 stalk celery, thinly sliced
1 clove garlic, minced
2/3 c. diced Italian tomatoes

Heat oil in a large skillet over medium-high heat until hot. Dredge chicken in flour and shake off the excess. Brown all chicken, 2 pieces at a time, on both sides for about 3 to 4 minutes per side. Transfer to a platter and salt and pepper to taste. Now very carefully add the wine to the pan and raise the temperature to high. Boil until reduced by half. Scrape bottom of pan to loosen brown bits. Lower heat to medium and add onion. Cook 5 minutes, stirring occasionally. Add the chicken (except the breasts) sliced pepper, carrot, celery, garlic, and tomatoes with the juice. Bring to a boil, reduce to low, cover, and simmer for 10 minutes. Add the breasts, cover and continue cooking for an additional 20 minutes or until chicken is done, basting frequently. Transfer to a platter to serve. If the sauce is too thin, boil it on high until it thickens.

Quaking Custard is a Yankee dessert, originally from England, of custard enveloped in egg whites and baked or steamed. The whole thing jiggled, hence the name. According to Shakespeare, "A most strange custom prevailed before and about the time of Charles I of England. This was to have a huge 'quaking custard' on the table, into which, at a private signal, the City Fool suddenly leapt over the heads of the astonished feasters, who were instantly bespattered with this rich and savory mud."

Chicken Divan

You will find all the famous television chefs rating their Divan dishes as the best. Try mine! And by the way, I love to annoy people. Take the word pecan for example. I pronounce it "pee-can". And with Divan, I pronounce it "Die-van." When I make my first million, I will say "pe-cahn" and "de-vahn."

Two pkgs. (10 oz. ea.)
   broccoli florets
1/4 c. butter or margarine
1/3 c. flour
Pinch nutmeg
1 c. light cream or milk
1 c. chicken broth
1/4 c. white wine
1/3 c. shredded Swiss cheese
10 oz. cooked chicken, sliced
   or chunked
1/4 c. Parmesan cheese

Cook vegetables according to package directions, drain. Arrange crosswise in a 12 × 7 × 2-inch baking pan. For the sauce, melt butter over medium-high heat in a small saucepan. Stir in the flour and add nutmeg, 1/2 t. salt, pinch of black pepper, and combine well. Add the cream or milk and broth at once. Cook, stirring constantly, until bubbling and thickened, about 4 to 6 minutes. Stir in the wine and add the Swiss cheese; whisking until melted. Remove from heat and pour half of the sauce over the broccoli, top with cheese and pour the remaining sauce over it all. Sprinkle Parmesan cheese and bake at 350°F for 20 minutes or until heated through.

Scalloped Chicken

With a side of fresh green beans or peas, you can sit on the couch, wrap up with your favorite afghan and enjoy dinner once, twice, or heck, go back for thirds.

2 c. dried bread crumbs
2 T. butter or margarine
1 T. minced onion
1 1/2 t. poultry seasoning
1/4 t. salt
2 c. diced cooked chicken

Custard Gravy:
4 T. butter or margarine
4 T. flour
3 c. hot chicken stock
Salt to taste
2 eggs, lightly beaten

Melt the butter over low heat and mix in the bread crumbs. Add the onion, poultry seasoning, and salt. Remove from heat.

Layer the crumbs, chicken, and custard gravy in a shallow casserole dish beginning and ending with the bread crumbs. Bake in a preheated 350°F oven for about 30 minutes or until bubbly and heated through

Making Custard Gravy: Melt 4 T. butter or margarine and mix in the chicken stock. Cook, stirring, until thickened. Season to taste with salt and pepper. Stir about 1 c. of the hot gravy into the eggs. Return egg mixture to the gravy and cook an additional 2 minutes. Cool.

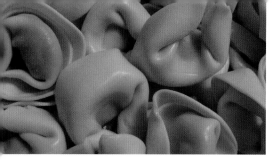

Spring Chicken Tortellini Casserole

Yes, I have jarred Alfredo sauce here. Although I would much rather have you make it from scratch from my cookbook, there's no reason why you can't take a shortcut. Heaven knows I take them as much as possible.

1 pkg. (19 oz.) frozen
  cheese tortellini
1 pkg. (9 oz.) frozen asparagus, cut
1 T. butter or margarine
1/4 c. Italian-style bread crumbs
8 to 10 oz. cooked chicken, cubed
1 jar (16 oz.) Alfredo sauce
2 T. shredded Parmesan cheese

Bring 4 quarts water to a boil in a large pot. Add tortellini and bring to a boil, reduce heat to low, and add asparagus; simmer 3 minutes or until tortellini is tender. Drain.

Meanwhile, melt the butter in a small skillet over medium-high heat. Add the bread crumbs and stir to coat. Cook 1 to 2 minutes or till golden brown, constantly stirring. Remove from heat. Place tortellini and asparagus in a 2-qt. casserole dish and gently stir in the chicken and Alfredo sauce. Top with bread crumbs and sprinkle with Parmesan cheese. Serve.

Chicken A La King

1 1/2 c. frozen mixed vegetables
1 c. water
1 T. granulated chicken bouillon
1 T. white wine or
  Worcestershire sauce
1/2 t. basil
Pinch black pepper
2 c. milk
1/2 c. flour
2 c. chopped, cooked chicken
  or turkey
4 frozen patty shells, baked,
  or 4 cooked biscuits

In a large saucepan, combine vegetables, water, bouillon, white wine, basil, and pepper. Bring to boiling, reduce heat to low, cover and simmer for 5 minutes. Meanwhile, combine milk and flour. Stir into the vegetable mixture. Cook and stir until thickened and bubbly, cook and stir 1 additional minute after that. Stir in the chicken and heat through. Serve in a patty shell or over biscuits.

Maple-Glazed Turkey Breast

I know it would be much less expensive to buy imitation maple syrup, but don't. Find yourself real maple for this dish. I suggest Grade A Dark Amber. I believe it to have the most robust flavor, although many chefs choose Grade B.

1 skinless turkey breast (5 to 6 lbs.)
1/4 c. pure maple syrup
2 T. butter or margarine, melted
1 T. bourbon (optional)
2 t. grated orange peel

Preheat oven to 350°F. Place turkey in a large baking pan. Bake for 50 to 55 minutes or until almost done in the center. In the meantime, combine maple syrup, butter, bourbon, and orange peel in a small bowl; brush half of mixture over the turkey. Continue to cook for an additional 15 minutes or until internal temperature reads 170°F, brushing occasionally with remaining mixture. Transfer turkey to carving board; tent with foil and let stand for 10 minutes before carving.

Hotel cook William King of Philadelphia died on March 4, 1915. and here is a reprint of his obituary:

The name of William King is not listed among the great ones of the earth. No monuments will ever be erected to his memory, for he was only a cook. Yet what a cook! In him blazed the fire of genius which, at the white heat of inspiration, drove him one day, in the old Bellevue, in Philadelphia, to combine bits of chicken, mushrooms, truffles, red and green peppers and cream in that delight-some mixture which ever after has been known as "Chicken a la King."

Pomegranate Glazed Turkey

This tangy glaze, made from pomegranate juice and cranberry sauce, doubles as a sauce at the table.

1 (14 to 16-lb.) turkey, thawed
4 c. water
Vegetable cooking spray

Glaze:
2/3 c. pomegranate juice
1/4 c. cranberry mustard
   (or use Dijon-style)
2 c. jellied cranberry sauce
1/4 c. sugar
1/2 t. black pepper
4 sprigs of fresh thyme,
   or 1/4 t. dried, crushed

Preheat oven to 350°F. Place turkey, breast side up, on a roasting rack in a roasting pan. Add water to pan and spray turkey with cooking spray. Place turkey in oven and roast for 2 1/2 hours. While bird is roasting, make the glaze. In a medium saucepan, combine pomegranate juice, mustard, cranberry sauce, sugar, and pepper. Bring to a simmer over medium heat and whisk until smooth, about 3 minutes. Remove from heat and add sprigs of thyme. Set aside.

Baste turkey with the cooking juices while roasting. After 2 1/2 hours, generously baste with glaze and set aside remaining glaze. Bake another 20 minutes then check internal temperature, it should be 170°F. Keep cooking and checking every 10 minutes if not. Remove turkey from oven, loosely wrap it in foil and let it rest for 20 minutes. Reheat glaze over medium heat until warmed, about 4 minutes. Remove thyme sprigs and discard. Transfer glaze to a small pitcher to serve on the side.

In Aneta, North Dakota, with a population less than 250 people, they hold the World's Largest Turkey Barbecue. The third Saturday in June, for over 50 years, more turkeys are barbecued than the population. They feed more than 3,000 people in three hours.

Turkey Bolognese and Polenta

You have a choice here. Either use the jar of marinara sauce listed here or make your own tomato sauce as listed in this cookbook. I only added the jarred item to make it a little easier on you. Traditional Bolognese uses beef, but the taste of ground turkey is a nice change.

2 T. olive oil
1 pkg. (4 oz.) sliced
   mixed mushrooms
1 1/2 lb. ground turkey
1 t. basil
1/4 t. salt
1/4 t. black pepper
1 jar (24 oz.) marinara sauce
1/3 c. heavy cream
1 pkg. (24 oz.) heat and serve
   polenta, cut into 1/2 -inch slices
6 T. shredded Parmesan cheese

In a large nonstick skillet, heat oil over medium-high heat. Add mushrooms and cook for 3 minutes. Crumble in the ground turkey and add the dried basil, salt, and pepper. Cook for 5 minutes longer, stirring occasionally. Stir in the marinara sauce and cook over medium heat, stirring occasionally, for 5 minutes longer, stir in the cream. While sauce is cooking, heat a grill pan and grill the polenta slices until heated through. Serve sauce with the polenta slices. Sprinkle each serving with shredded cheese.

Sweet and Sour Turkey Meatballs

These are equally delicious as an appetizer, over noodles, or in a sandwich.

1 can (20 oz.) pineapple chunks with juice
1 can (14 oz.) chicken broth
1 green bell pepper, seeded and cut into strips
1 red bell pepper, seeded and cut into squares
1 c. ketchup
1/4 c. brown sugar
1/4 c. cider vinegar
About 2 lbs. turkey meatballs, recipe below
6 scallions, cut into 1-inch segments
2 1/2 c. instant rice, cooked

In a large skillet, combine pineapple and juice, broth, green pepper strips, red pepper squares, ketchup, brown sugar, and vinegar. Bring to a simmer over medium-high heat, stirring to dissolve sugar. Add the meatballs; simmer covered for 10 minutes. Stir in the scallions and serve over the rice.

Turkey Meatballs:

Heat 1 t. vegetable oil over medium heat and add 1 small onion, minced, and 1 crushed garlic clove. Cook, stirring frequently, for 5 minutes or until onion is tender. Transfer to large bowl and add 1 lb. ground turkey, 1 egg, 2 T. milk, 1 slice of bread (crumbled), 1/2 t. salt, and 1/2 t. black pepper. You can add 4 T. favorite fruited chutney (such as mango chutney) at this point if you would like. Combine until well blended and shape into small meatballs. Bake in a 350°F oven for about 20 to 30 minutes, or until done throughout.

Good Luck!

Ever pull on the collarbone (wishbone) of a turkey for luck? It started when ancient civilizations thought the wishbone resembled a human groin, thereby believing it to have special powers. The Romans introduced the custom of two people pulling on the wishbone to see who was the lucky one, with the winner being said to have gotten "the lucky break," hence the origin of that phrase as well. Just remember, you can never tell anyone your wish.

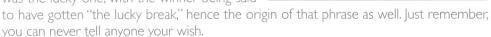

Turkey Cranberry Loaf

By looking at this moist, glazed goodness, it's hard to believe that ground turkey was used. The cranberry sauce baked on top just brings the flavor of the turkey to the forefront.

1 can whole cranberry sauce
1/2 c. orange juice
1 1/2 c. ground turkey
1 1/2 c. dried bread crumbs
1/4 c. lemon juice
2 eggs
1 T. chicken bouillon powder
2 t. poultry seasoning

Preheat oven to 350°F. In small bowl, mix the cranberry sauce and orange juice well; reserve half cup. In a large bowl, combine remaining ingredients and mix well. Turn into a 9-inch pie pan. Pack and smooth the top. Bake 30 minutes or until set. Top with reserved cranberry-orange sauce and continue cooking an additional 20 minutes. Let stand 5 minutes before slicing to serve.

Answers (to questions on page 136)
a. the fear of mushrooms;
b. the fear of cooking;
c. the fear of drinking anything, especially alcohol;
d. the fear of eating anything;
e. the fear of food;
f. the fear of cemeteries;
g. the fear of ghosts;
h. the fear of tombstones; and
i. the fear of the unknown

An 1880 advertisement for the Melville Garden Clambake, a public clambake in Hingham, Massachusetts. Courtesy of the American Antiquarian Society.

CHAPTER 9 *Fish and Seafood*

Shipping operations in Salem, Massachusetts, during the 1770s, by Balthasar Friedrich Leizelt

Reverse side of advertisement for the Melville Garden Clambake

Finnan Haddie

Originally simmered in milk for breakfast, this smoked haddock takes a breakfast item and serves it at dinner. The egg sauce cuts through the smoky flavor so well it shouldn't be made just by our grandparents anymore.

1 lb. finnan haddie,
   cut into large chunks
2 T. margarine or butter
2 T. flour
1 c. milk
1/2 c. heavy cream
2 hard-cooked eggs
Toast wedges (points)

In large, shallow baking dish, place finnan haddie chunks in enough cold water to cover. Soak 1 hour, then drain. In 12-inch skillet, melt margarine over medium heat and then stir in flour; blend until smooth. Gradually stir in the milk and cream, and cook, stirring almost constantly until mixture has thickened slightly and boils; add fish. Cover, simmer, stirring occasionally, until fish flakes easily when tested with a fork, about 15 minutes.

Reserve 1 hard-cooked egg yolk. Chop whites and other egg yolk. Using a fork, coarsely flake fish; stir in chopped eggs, and pour into warm serving dish. Press reserved egg yolk through coarse sieve over top of dish. Serve warm with toast points.

Here is a good rule of thumb when dealing with large or small bones when buying, cooking, and eating fish. Haddock, cod, or flounder (saltwater fish) need larger bones because salt water provides more buoyancy, thereby fish need to be heavier. Freshwater fish (such as catfish and trout) have hundreds of minuscule, filament-thin bones; they needn't be so heavy in order to navigate the streams. So, if you don't want to fight those tiny bones be sure to choose saltwater species when buying whole fish or filets.

Codfish Balls

This codfish dish was a mainstay on many Yankee tables for generations, but if you want to spice things up, add 2 T. dried cilantro and a teaspoon or two of hot pepper sauce.

1 1/2 c. salt codfish
3 c. diced potatoes
1 1/2 T. butter or margarine
Black pepper to taste
1 egg
Vegetable oil for frying

Soak codfish in cold water for 30 minutes; repeat. Drain and flake. Boil fish and potatoes together until potatoes are tender; drain. Mash, being sure there are no lumps; add butter and pepper and beat with electric mixer until mixture is fluffy. Add egg and continue beating mixture until it is smooth.

Meanwhile, heat 1 1/2 to 2 inches of vegetable oil in deep-fat fryer or over medium-high heat until temperature reaches 350°F. Drop by the tablespoonful into hot fat and fry no more than 4 or 5 at a time, flattening slightly if you prefer, until golden brown. Drain on paper towels and serve the old fashioned way, with sweet gherkins or sliced green tomato pickles.

Cod Lore

Throwing the first cod caught over your shoulder while you were out to sea was good luck on a fishing trip.

Right up until the early twentieth century, fishermen who drank a cup of gurry from the barrel of codfish livers every morning were said to have good health.

Contemporary Codfish Cakes

I have named this as such because our forefathers used the most basic of ingredients, along with salted cod, in this dish. In revamping this authentic New England dish, I hope to get people to give it a try; it is so succulent and satisfying!

1/2 small onion, sliced
1 rib celery, thinly sliced
1 small carrot, peeled
    and diced small
1 lb. boneless, skinless cod
2 c. peeled, diced potatoes
4 T. butter or margarine
3 scallions, minced
2 eggs, beaten
Black pepper to taste
Cracker crumbs
4 T. vegetable oil

In large saucepan over medium-high heat, cover onion, celery, carrot, and cod with 2-inches of water and boil for 35 minutes. Carefully remove cod and discard liquid and vegetables. Set aside. Cover potatoes with water, in another pot, and boil until tender; mash with butter. Mix mashed potatoes with cod and add scallions, eggs, and pepper to taste. Let cool enough to handle. Form into thick patties, adding cracker crumbs to mixture, just enough so that mixture almost falls apart but is wet enough to hold together.

Heat vegetable oil on medium-high in large sauté pan and grill codfish cakes until well browned on each side, about 5 to 6 minutes per side.

Imperial Cod

Many Imperial recipes use peppers and onions, with slight variations of the other ingredients. I give you an original Imperial recipe that will blow the socks off your fins.

2 c. chopped tomatoes
1/4 c. chopped onion
1/4 c. chicken broth
2 t. grated orange peel
2 t. dried thyme, crushed
3 cloves garlic, minced
1/4 t. red pepper flakes
3/4 lb. cod fillets,
    cut into 4 serving size pieces

In a large nonstick skillet, combine tomatoes, onion, broth, orange peel, thyme, garlic, and red pepper. Bring to a boil. Place fish pieces on top of tomato mixture. Cook over medium heat, covered, for 6 to 9 minutes or until fish flakes with a fork. Remove fish; keep warm. Simmer tomato mixture, uncovered, for 2 to 3 minutes or until desired consistency. Serve fish with sauce. Season to taste with salt and pepper.

Crab Spinach Stuffed Flounder

1 lb. fresh crabmeat	Garlic salt
Juice from 1/2 lemon	Black pepper
1/2 bag fresh spinach	Oregano
1/2 stick Cheddar cheese (4 oz.)	Approximately 1 lb. flounder, cut into 4 pieces
2 sticks butter or margarine, divided	Paprika

Preheat oven to 375°F. Drain crabmeat and squeeze 1/2 lemon on top. Clean, remove stems and slightly chop spinach. Grate the cheese, and then melt 2 T. butter in sauté pan. Add spinach and cook until melted. Season to taste with garlic, pepper and oregano. Add crabmeat and cook until heated thoroughly. Let mixture cool slightly and then add grated cheese. Stir enough to be able to mold mixture when needed. Set aside.

Place 3 T. butter on a cookie sheet or other flat pan with sides and allow to melt in oven. Pull out pan and rub both sides of flounder in butter. Line up flounder next to each other, skin side up in pan. Divide spinach mixture into four mounds and place mound in middle of each flounder. Wrap both ends of flounder up to fit snugly around stuffing then turn the whole thing upside down so that the ends are on the baking sheet. Place dabs of butter and sprinkle paprika on top of each piece. Bake at 375°F for approximately 20 minutes. Check at 15 minutes. Fish is done when it is white and flakes easily when pried with a fork.

Did you know that the flounder has two eyes on one side of its head? Born with an eye on each side, as it matures, one eye migrates to the other side. That's because when a predator comes along, the flounder lies on its side on the ocean floor so that both eyes can see where the danger is and when it passes. They are also unequalled at changing their appearance when hiding from enemies.

Lobster-Stuffed Flounder

Hey, buying canned Cream of Shrimp soup is a whole lot less time consuming than making it, trust me!

1/4 c. chopped onion
3 T. butter or margarine
5 slices bread, torn into small pieces
1 c. cooked lobster meat, diced small
Pinch thyme
Salt and pepper to taste
6 flounder fillets
2 c. Cream of Shrimp soup
Milk

Saute onion in butter over medium-high heat. Add bread, lobster meat, thyme, salt, and pepper to taste and blend until well incorporated. Preheat oven to 350°F. Spread mixture on each fillet and roll up. Place seam side down in baking sheet lined with foil. Heat soup and, while stirring, add enough milk to thin. Pour over stuffed flounders and bake 20 to 25 minutes or until fish is done.

Haddock with Shrimp Sauce

There are so many recipes for Shrimp Sauce and I have yet to taste one that I thoroughly enjoy, until now. My father and I equally created this dish and I think you will taste the decades of experience brought to you through our collaboration.

2 green onions, thinly sliced
1 clove garlic, minced
4 T. olive oil
3 tomatoes, chopped
1 1/2 t. chopped jalapeno
  or Serrano pepper
1/2 c. small shrimp, cooked, peeled,
  and deveined
4 haddock fillets (4 to 5 oz.)
Hot cooked couscous or white rice

In a large saucepan over medium-high heat, cook onions and garlic in oil until onions are opaque. Stir in tomatoes, pepper, and shrimp; heat through. With slotted spoon, remove vegetables to separate bowl. Place haddock fillets into same saucepan and top with shrimp mixture. Cover and reduce heat to medium. Continue cooking for 12 to 15 minutes or until haddock flakes easily with fork. Serve over hot couscous or rice.

Outdoor Quick and Easy Grilled Tuna

When I was in South Beach, Florida, I saw many complicated recipes for tuna. When I returned to Maine, I made my own Yankee recipe and I think you will find this more than satisfying, while keeping it simple.

1/4 c. soy sauce
1 T. maple syrup
1 T. prepared horseradish
4 tuna steaks (3/4 inch thick,
  about 1 1/2 lbs.)
Garnish: lemon rind strips

Combine first 3 ingredients in a heavy-duty zip-top plastic bag; add tuna. Seal and chill 1 hour, turning occasionally. Remove tuna from plastic bag, discard marinade.
Grill tuna, covered with grill lid, over high heat (400°F to 500°F) 2 minutes on each side or to desired temperature. Garnish, if desired and serve with a light salad.

In the fishing industry, scrod has come to mean haddock under 2 1/2 lbs. The correct definition of scrod is a small fish prepared for planking.

Nicoise Tuna Sandwich

The correct pronunciation is "Nee swa." It must have taken me 20 years to remember this, and to this day, I take a moment to pronounce it correctly.

1 small tuna fillet (or 1 can
    yellow fin tuna, drained)
2 T. olive oil
1 deli roll of your choice
Green leaf lettuce
2 slices tomato
1 small red potato, boiled,
    cooled, and sliced
1 small red onion, sliced
1 small red bell pepper, sliced
3 to 5 fresh green beans,
    cooked and cooled
2 t. white wine vinegar

Cook tuna fillet over medium-high wheat with olive oil until clear and flaky, about 4 to 5 minutes per side. Remove to paper towel to dry.

Slice open roll and place a lettuce leaf and 2 tomato slices on roll. Top this with sliced potatoes and onion slices, separated into rings. Chunk canned tuna on top or place warm grilled tuna fillet over top. Add sliced red bell pepper and green beans. Sprinkle with white wine vinegar over the top before closing sandwich.

Spicy Salmon Steak

What a gorgeous looking dish. I would proudly offer this succulent recipe to my patrons, complete with a side of cooked vegetable.

6 salmon steaks
2 t. cumin
1/2 t. cayenne pepper,
    or more to taste
1/4 c. olive oil plus
    some for the skillet
3 yellow bell peppers, cored,
    seeded, and halved
3 red bell peppers, cored,
    seeded, and halved
1 T. balsamic vinegar

Rub both sides of salmon with cumin and cayenne. Marinate for at least 3 hours. In large skillet, over medium-high heat, fry the salmon steaks in 3 T. olive oil, covered, for 4 to 5 minutes per side or until light pink throughout. Cut bell peppers into strips and toss with vinegar and oil. Add to skillet with salmon and cover again. Cook an additional 3 minutes or until peppers are crisp yet slightly cooked.

Grilled Salmon with Grapefruit Sauce

I am a lover of anything fruited. If you can add fruit to a dish without ruining it, do it! The Grapefruit Sauce adorning the salmon is balanced very well, without overshadowing the fish.

3 T. olive oil, divided
2 oz. shallots, minced
6 oz. salmon fillet
1 qt. ruby-red grapefruit juice
1/4 c. sugar
1/2 t. cardamom
2 lb. unsalted butter
Salt and pepper to taste

Prepare sauce first: In large sauce pan, place 1 T. olive oil and shallots over medium-high heat for 3 minutes, stirring constantly. Add grapefruit juice, sugar, and cardamom and continue boiling, uncovered, until reduced by a little more than 75 percent, stirring occasionally, about 30 minutes. Remove from heat and add butter slowly, whisking until butter has completely melted. Makes about 2 1/2 cups.

To prepare salmon: In medium sauce pan, heat 2 T. olive oil over medium-high heat. Gently place salmon fillet into pan and sauté 4 to 5 minutes per side until done; serve with sauce over top.

Teriyaki Salmon Burgers

Why should hamburgers have all the fun in a bun? No need for cheese, ketchup, or mustard on these bad boys, they are delicious as is.

5 hamburger buns
1 skinless salmon fillet (1 lb.),
   all bones removed
3 T. teriyaki sauce
3 medium green onions, chopped
1/2 t. dried ginger
1 c. dried bread crumbs
Hamburger rolls

Tear one hamburger bun into very small pieces. Set aside. Finely chop salmon and place in medium bowl. Add teriyaki sauce, green onions, ginger and 1/3 c. of the bread crumbs. On waxed paper, shape salmon mixture into four 3-inch round patties. Use reserved bread crumbs to coat patties, patting crumbs to cover.

In nonstick large skillet, cook patties over medium-high heat 5 minutes per side, until about opaque throughout.

Parmesan Baked Salmon

1/4 c. mayonnaise
2 T. Parmesan cheese
1/8 t. cayenne pepper
4 salmon fillets (1 lb. total)
   with skins removed
2 t. lemon juice
15 butter-flavored crackers, crushed

Heat oven to 400°F. Mix mayonnaise, cheese, and pepper until well blended. Place fish in shallow, foil-lined pan; drizzle with lemon juice. Cover with mayonnaise mixture and cracker crumbs. Bake 12 to 15 minutes or until fish flakes easily with fork.

Did you know that folklore states that salmon always come back to the exact spot where they were born to spawn? In the past few decades, with a number of scientific studies, researchers have found this to be true.

New England Fried Smelts

One of the cleanest fish flavors there is, it should be prepared in one of the simplest ways you can. I believe my recipe is the only way smelts should be cooked. With only about 100 calories for a half pound of these tiny fish, make these smelts as often as possible, not merely a one-hit wonder.

1 lb. fresh smelts
1 c. yellow cornmeal
1 t. salt
1/2 t. black pepper
1/2 c. light cream
4 T. butter or margarine
Tartar sauce
Lemon juice

Clean smelts by slitting the belly and, under cold running water, use your thumb to run it the length of the slit to remove the innards. I leave the heads intact, but those of you from out of state can go ahead and cut the head off before slicing the belly to clean; pat dry. Combine cornmeal, salt, and pepper in a bowl. Dip smelts in the cream, then coat well in the cornmeal mixture. Let set for 10 minutes while you heat the butter in a large frying pan over medium high heat. Place the smelts in the pan, cook for about 5 minutes per side or until nicely browned. Remove and enjoy with tartar sauce or lemon juice.

Halibut with Orange-Ginger Sauce

Being a very firm white fish, halibut is ideal to use with any type of marinade or sauce. It holds up very well on outdoor barbecue grills as well.

1 lb. fresh or frozen halibut steaks, about 1-inch thick
Salt and black pepper to taste
3/4 c. frozen orange juice concentrate, thawed
1 T. soy sauce
2 t. cornstarch
1/4 t. ground ginger
1/3 c. water
1/2 c. coarsely chopped water chestnuts
2 c. hot cooked couscous or rice

Thaw fish, if frozen. Rinse fish; pat dry. Sprinkle fish with salt and pepper if desired. Place fish on a broiler pan. Broil 4 inches from heat for 9 to 12 minutes or until fish flakes easily, turning once.

Meanwhile, in a small saucepan, stir together thawed concentrate, soy sauce, cornstarch, ginger, and 1/3 c. water. Cook and stir until thickened and bubbly. Cook and stir for 2 minutes more. Stir in water chestnuts. Place fish atop couscous or rice. Spoon sauce over halibut.

Halibut was once called "Buttfish" and was once eaten during holy days in medieval England, thereby the name "Holy-but," thence halibut.

An Alaskan fisherman filleting a Pacific halibut

Halibut with Scallops and Peas

With minimal effort, you will have a summer treat on your hands here. I stay true to my Yankee roots with simplicity and ease of preparation here, which I am sure everyone will appreciate.

1 1/2 lbs. halibut fillets
1/2 lb. scallops
1/2 c. dry white wine
1/4 c. sliced scallions, including green
1 c. cooked peas
Salt and black pepper to taste
2 t. dried ginger
Parsley to garnish

Place halibut fillets in a large, shallow, buttered baking dish. Spread the scallops on top of the halibut and pour the wine over the top. Distribute the scallions and peas over this and salt and pepper to your liking. Sprinkle the ginger over the entire dish and bake in a preheated 375°F oven for about 10 minutes or until halibut is done. Garnish with parsley when ready to serve.

Trout with Italian Crumb Topping

Trout is considered an oily fish, but it contains one of the lowest amount of dioxins (an environmental contaminant) of all oily fishes.

1/2 c. Italian seasoned bread crumbs
4 T. shredded Parmesan cheese
3 T. butter or margarine, melted
1 clove garlic, minced
1 1/2 t. grated lemon rind
2 T. pine nuts
4 trout fillets (4 to 5 oz.)

Preheat oven to 350°F. In large bowl, combine all ingredients except trout; mix well. Coat each trout fillet with bread crumb mixture and bake for 25 to 30 minutes, or until browned nicely and fish flakes easily.

Herbed Perch

With less than a gram of fat per serving, perch is considered a lean fish. Three ounces of perch yields only 80 calories, 90 mg. of calcium, 16 g. of protein, and 36 mg. cholesterol. But that doesn't come without a price. They are loaded with bones, so be extra careful and vigilant when eating.

3 bunches flat-leafed parsley
5 cloves garlic
3/4 c. olive oil
1/2 c. white wine vinegar
1/2 t. red pepper flakes
1/2 t. black pepper
2 to 3 lb. whole cleaned perch
1/2 t. Bells® brand seasoning

Measure 4 c. parsley; set aside. In blender, puree remainder of ingredients, except perch, until smooth. Preheat oven to 350°F. Place perch in large, covered, oven-safe, casserole dish. Pour parsley mixture over perch and bake for 20 to 25 minutes or until fish flakes easily with fork.

Sam's Fried Clams

The first Yankee Chef, Samuel Bailey, owned Sam's Clam Shack in Lincoln, Maine, during the beginning of the depression. This was one of his featured items and the way clams should be deep fried. I have not changed this recipe one bit because the succulence of the clams bursts through the crispy, perfectly seasoned coating.

Vegetable oil for frying
3 eggs
1/2 c. heavy cream
3 c. finely ground cracker crumbs
    or cracker meal
3 c. flour mixed with 1 t. salt
    and 1/2 t. black pepper
1/2 qt. whole belly clams

Heat oil to 350°F in either a deep-fat fryer or bring 3-inches of oil to same temperature in a 4-qt. stock pot. Mix eggs and heavy cream thoroughly in large bowl. Have cracker crumbs in another large bowl with the flour in a third large bowl. Dredge 1 cup of clams at a time in the flour mixture first. Gently dip in egg wash and make sure they are separated before dredging them in cracker crumbs. One by one, gently dip the battered clams in hot oil and fry about 2 minutes each, until they are golden brown. Remove and drain on paper towels. Repeat process quickly until all clams are cooked.

True and original clam cake recipes contain only four ingredients: shucked clams, cracker crumbs, clam juice (or liquor), and eggs. They were formed and fried in lard or vegetable oil.

New England Steamers, Pure and Simple!

In the United States, this dish is commonly prepared with a kind of shellfish called steamers, a somewhat generic name that usually refers to a small soft-shell clam harvested and served along the East Coast and in New England. Steamers are so named because of the way they are most often prepared.

Hard shell clams, sometimes known as quahogs, can also be steamed. They are categorized by size—the smaller ones are called littlenecks, medium-sized ones top necks, and the larger ones cherrystones.

Place 1 cup water in large stockpot. Bring to a boil over high heat. Add 2 lbs. steamer clams. Cover stockpot; steam 5 to 7 minutes or until clams open. Strain clams and reserve broth to dip your clams into before dipping in melted butter.

Steamers can also be cooked in beer, garlic, shallots, parsley, and wine and served with lemon juice. Steamers can be held by the siphon or "neck" when eaten. Pull away and remove the black skin covering before eating.

Clams are steamed according to many different recipes in different regions:
In China, steamed clams can be served with eggs.
In Thailand, steamed clams are served with lemongrass, ginger, or herbs.
In France, they are often cooked with white wine, onion, garlic, shallots, and butter.
Steamed clams are also eaten in Japan. They are known as Oosari and are somewhat larger than our steamers in the Northeast.
Steamers are praised by many chefs, for instance Jacques Pépin says of these Yankee favorites: "Plentiful and inexpensive during the summer, especially in the Northeast, steamers are one of the great treats of the season."

New England Clam Bake

This has been called the Shore Dinner, Clam Boil, and the Lobster Bake. In my files, and according to the first and second Yankee Chefs, the shore dinner included chicken, chowder, and watermelon. Whatever moniker you wish to give it, the same basic ingredients are used. This will feed 6 people.

3 lbs. clams, cleaned
3 lbs. mussels, cleaned
6 baking potatoes
6 onions, peeled
12 ears of corn (husk left on but silk removed)
12 live lobsters
Lemons cut into wedges
Lots of melted butter
A large piece of canvas or tarp

Dig a shallow, circular hole in the ground, from 6 to 8" deep and about 2 feet in diameter (for 6 to 10 people). The diameter will depend on the number of persons to be fed. (For example, a 5-foot circle is needed for 50 people.) Line the hole with hard, clean, round or oval shaped rocks about the size of footballs, taking care that the tops are about the same level and as close together as possible. Build a fire and keep it going over the entire surface of the circle of rocks, keeping it as hot as possible. When rocks are hot enough, water will immediately sizzle and turn into steam instantly, a process that takes about two hours. When rocks are hot enough, remove all burning wood with a steel rake or hoe and clean ashes from rocks with a live green tree branch. Place a layer of wet seaweed about 6" deep to cover all rocks on top and around the edges to prevent the canvas

Stereoscopic view of a clambake at Old Orchard Beach, Maine, many years ago.
From the collection of Robert N. Dennis

cover from burning. Working quickly to prevent loss of steam, spread a layer of clams on top of the seaweed. Place lobsters directly on top of clams. On top of lobsters, place corn, onions, and potatoes. Cover all with a piece of canvas that completely protects the whole bake, taking care that as little steam as possible escapes around the edges. Many experts agree that no seaweed should be placed on top of the bake. Small stones can be placed on top of the canvas around edges; make sure canvas does not touch hot rocks around the edges. Keep stones covered with seaweed and make sure the canvas does not burn by adding a very small amount of water on top every now and again. After being well covered, the bake can remain for about one hour and a half. Lift the edge of canvas and if the lobster nearest the edge is done, you are ready. If not, continue cooking a little longer until done.

Some Variations: If you would like to have an easier time at doling out the spoils, wrap individual servings of all the ingredients in cheesecloth and tie the corners together or simply place items in wire baskets to dump out when done. Once the rocks are hot enough to spit a drop of water back at you, rake off the coals from the fire and cover the rocks with seaweed. Place the food packets on the seaweed and cover with more seaweed. Cover this with the canvas or tarp. That's how you hold a traditional clambake. Of course there are regional differences, but you get the general idea.

If you don't want the hassle of digging a hole and heating the rocks, you can also make this using a charcoal or gas grill. Cut way down on the seaweed. You will only need a small amount soaking in water. Wrap individual servings in cheesecloth with a little seaweed inside, tying the corners, and then wrap tightly in aluminum foil. Place the packages on a hot grill and close the lid. In an hour you can eat.

Of course you can add almost anything you want to your clambake. The secret is that the seaweed steams the food, so it's important that you have something sitting with the food to provide moisture. If you don't have access to seaweed you can add about 1/4 c. of water to the food packages as long as they are sealed completely. If there isn't enough moisture then the food won't cook properly.

If you truly want to make this a shore dinner, add an assortment of side dishes as well, such as macaroni and potato salad, cole slaw, etc. Also, you can add some eggs inside your bundles to cook with the lobster, too; like they did in the old days. Have some watermelon,

creamy chowder, biscuits, and some cold beverages at the ready and you've got yourself a cookout that "hollah's" Yankee Cooking!

Originally, cole slaw would be chopped or shredded cabbage, with a mixture of cream, sugar, and vinegar poured over the top. I remember my father serving that very same coleslaw at his restaurant in the early 1970s.

Crab Meat Scampi

I have chosen lump crabmeat for this recipe only because it holds together better than other crab. If desired, use local crabmeat, being careful to buy a good proportion of claw meat to body meat though.

2 T. olive oil
1 T. chopped garlic
8 oz. lump crabmeat
1/4 t. flaked red pepper
2 t. Worcestershire sauce
1 T. lemon juice
1/2 c. white wine (optional)
2 T. cold butter, cut small
Salt and pepper to taste
Cooked pasta or rice (optional)

Place oil in large skillet on medium heat, add garlic, and cook until garlic browns. Quickly add crab meat and toss. Add red pepper, Worcestershire, and lemon juice. Add wine and stir to lift any cooked pieces on bottom of skillet. Whip in cold butter until melted. Add salt and pepper and serve over rice or pasta.

Maryland Crab Reuben

Here are some variations (as this recipe is one) of the famous Reuben Sandwich.

The Rachel, which uses pastrami and cole slaw. The Bleu Reuben, which uses bleu cheese instead of Swiss, and the Virgin Reuben, a vegetarian's delight.

1 lb. Maryland crabmeat
1/4 c. mayonnaise
1 T. chili sauce
2 t. sweet relish
10 slices rye bread
5 oz. Swiss cheese
2 eggs, beaten
1/4 c. milk
Pinch salt and black pepper
2 T. butter or margarine

Combine crab, mayonnaise, chili sauce, and relish in a medium mixing bowl. Spread over five slices of bread. Top each with a slice of cheese. Close sandwich with another slice of bread.

Blend together eggs, milk, and salt in another medium mixing bowl. Dip both sides of sandwich into the egg mixture. Melt 2 T. butter or margarine in large skillet over medium heat. Cook sandwiches on both sides until browned.

Maryland Crab Cakes

Why Maryland crabmeat in both recipes? Because even though I am a true "Mainah," Maryland has been, and will always be, the front-runner of crab cuisine.

1 lb. crab meat
1 egg
1 t. Worcestershire sauce
1 t. lemon juice
1/4 t. dry mustard
1 T. mayonnaise
1 t. prepared mustard
2 slices bread
3 t. butter or margarine

Place crabmeat into large mixing bowl. Beat egg, Worcestershire sauce, lemon juice, dry mustard, mayonnaise, and prepared mustard in a separate bowl. Break the slices of bread into very small pieces and gently fold into bowl of crab meat along with egg mixture. Shape into slightly flattened patties and chill for 1 hour.

In medium saucepan, melt butter over medium-high heat until melted. Place crab cakes in skillet and grill until well browned and slightly crispy. Turn and repeat on other side. Serve hot.

Sam's Clam Shell Lobster Salad

I may be biased but I truly believe this recipe to be the best lobster salad roll you can make. My grandfather, Sam, sold this roll at his clam shack, called Sam's Clam Shell. Many chefs put relish, grated onion, minced pickles, celery and just use mayonnaise or miracle whip. This is not too much or too little. Enjoy!

2 c. cooked lobster meat, roughly
    chopped and squeezed dry
1/4 c. mayonnaise
1/4 c. minced cucumber, seeds
    removed with a spoon
Pinch black pepper

Mix all together and stuff into grilled hot dog rolls.

Real Maine Piccalilli

1 peck green tomatoes, sliced; 3 lb. onions, sliced; 3 lg. green peppers, julienned; 3 red peppers, julienned; 1 c salt; 2 c. sugar; 1 1/2 qts. vinegar; 1 c. whole mixed pickling spices; and 2 c. water. Put vegetables into a kettle, in layers, with salt sprinkled between the layers. Let stand overnight, drain, rinse with cold water and drain again. Cook vegetables with sugar, vinegar, pickling spices, and water until mix has thickened slightly. Turn into sterilized jars and seal. Makes about 7 quarts.

-So says the first Yankee Chef.
 Samuel Bailey

To Dress Cold Crab: Empty the shells, and mix the flesh with oil, vinegar, salt and a little white pepper and cayenne. Then put the mixture into the large shell and serve. Very little oil is necessary.
-*The American Domestic Cookery, 1822.*

Lobster Thermidor

Lobster Thermidor classically should be prepared as below but instead of baking in the oven as is, it was and still is, in some restaurants, stuffed into the split back of a live lobster before baking.

4 T. butter
1/4 c. green onions, chopped
4 T. flour
1 t. dry mustard
1 1/2 c. light cream
1 t. dried tarragon, crushed
1 t. oregano
Salt and pepper to taste
1/2 c. cooking sherry
2 c. lobster meat,
    cooked and chunked
1/2 c. Parmesan cheese

Preheat oven to 400°F. Melt butter in medium-sized saucepan and sauté onion until translucent; about 4 to 5 minutes. Mix in flour and mustard and stir until well blended. Add cream and cook, stirring constantly, until mixture thickens. Stir in tarragon, oregano, salt, pepper, and sherry. Stir until smooth. Add lobster meat to the sauce and place the mixture in a shallow baking dish; sprinkle with cheese. Bake for 15 to 20 minutes or until bubbly and lightly browned.

Lobster Newburg

We can give credit to Ben Wenburg for this beautifully created dish. He was a sea captain in the last quarter of the  nineteenth century. Originally called Lobster Wenburg, and after a long story, argumentative in nature, the name was changed to Newburg, an anagram of Wenburg's last name, by the chef at Delmonico's Restaurant in New York City.

5 T. butter
2 c. cooked lobster meat, chunked
2 T. sherry
1 T. flour
1 c. all-purpose cream
2 egg yolks, beaten
1 t. lemon juice
Salt to taste
Paprika for color

In a large skillet, melt 3 T. butter over medium-high heat until melted. Add lobster and sherry and continue cooking until lobster is heated through. Be careful not to brown butter, remove from heat. In another pan, melt the remainder of the butter and blend in the flour, whisk until smooth. Add cream and stir constantly until the sauce boils and thickens over medium-high heat.

Remove from heat and add egg yolks, lemon juice, and seasonings. Stir well, add lobster mixture and liquid and stir again. Serve with toast points or egg noodles.

Lobster Cakes

Not as old of a recipe as crab cakes, it is nonetheless just as succulent. No sauce is required for this dish though. These cakes, as well as crab cakes, should be dry but not too dry.

2 slices bread, crustless
1 to 2 T. milk
2 c. cooked lobster meat,
    cut into small pieces
1/4 t. sage
1/2 t. salt
1 T. mayonnaise
1 T. Worcestershire sauce
1 T. baking powder
1 egg, beaten
3 T. olive oil

Break bread into small pieces and moisten with milk. Add lobster meat and mix with remaining ingredients. Shape into cakes and chill at least one hour. Sauté cakes in olive oil over medium-high heat until browned on both sides and heated through, about 4 to 5 minutes per side.

Batter Fried Lobster

Although I may be partial to Maine lobsters (I honestly believe they are the best), lobster meat from any coast would be just as welcome in this recipe. Don't forget the cole slaw though.

1/2 c. flour
1/4 t. salt
1/2 t. paprika
1/4 t. curry powder
1/4 t. baking powder
1 egg
1 t. lemon juice
1/2 c. milk
2 c. cooked lobster meat,
    cut into quarter sized pieces
Vegetable oil for frying

Heat deep-fat fryer to 350°F according to manufactures instructions or heat 3 inches vegetable oil in large stock pot over medium-high heat until it reaches 350°F.

Mix together flour, salt, paprika, curry powder, and baking powder. Beat the egg and then add the lemon juice and milk. Beat the liquids into the flour until smooth using a whisk or electric beater. Add a little more milk if batter is too heavy and thick.

Dip pieces of cooked lobster meat into the batter until coated completely and drop gently into hot fat. Fry only until golden brown in color and remove to drain.

Try using 1/2 cup stout, lager, or any dark beer mixed in with this batter for beer battered lobster, it's a great touch of flavor.

This batter works great with shrimp as well.

Seasoned Naked Lobster

The "Naked" refers to the fact that we take its hard-shelled "clothes" off before beginning this dish. The tarragon is a taste that not all people enjoy, so make sure you truly want that flavor before preparing. If not, just omit.

2 lobsters (1 1/4 lb. ea.) or 1/2 lb. lobster meat (ask for 3 ounces of tomalley)
2 T. butter or margarine, plus extra for the baking dish
2 t. chopped shallot
1/2 c. dry white wine
1/2 t. dried tarragon or 2 t. fresh tarragon
1 1/2 T. chopped, fresh parsley
Salt and black pepper to taste
1/2 c. bread crumbs or crushed cheese crackers
3 T. butter or margarine, melted

If using live lobsters, heat two inches of water in a large pot, add 2 T. of salt and place lobsters on a steamer rack after water comes to a boil. Steam for 11 minutes, then remove from heat. Remove meat from lobsters, reserving liquid from the shells, the green tomalley, and the roe from the females. The roe is red when cooked, but may be inky black in undercooked lobsters. It will turn red quickly in the sauté pan and adds a mild flavor and its color to the dish. Peel the thin dorsal layer off the tails to remove the intestinal vein. Cut the meat into 1 inch pieces, but leave claw meat whole. Season lightly with salt and pepper and add tarragon. Place meat into a buttered, shallow baking dish, sized so that the meat will make a layer 2 1/2 to 3 inches thick. Pour some of the reserved lobster liquid into baking dish to a depth of 1/2 inch. If using lobster meat, bring the extra 1/2 c. white wine to a boil and add to meat.

Melt butter in a sauté pan over medium heat and add shallots, stirring until they are soft but not browned. Add tomalley and roe, and cook until roe is deep red. Mash the roe with a spoon and add white wine and parsley, boiling until reduced slightly. In small bowl, combine the crumbs with the melted butter and spread mixture evenly over the lobster meat. Cover and refrigerate for up to 24 hours if you are preparing this to be served later. Remove from refrigerator 1 hour before cooking.

Heat oven to 350°F. Place baking dish, tightly covered with foil, into the oven on a middle rack and cook for approximately 30 minutes. When juices are bubbling, cook uncovered for 8 to 10 minutes and serve immediately.

Baked Stuffed Maine Lobster

You have the ocean's bounty in one dish here. We let the natural flavor of all the seafood come out with minimal ingredients. Go ahead and splurge.

One 1 1/2-lb. live lobster
1 egg
1/2 c. crushed Ritz crackers
1/2 stick butter, melted
1 T. grated Parmesan cheese
1 oz. scallops, cooked
2 oz. shrimp, cooked
3 oz. haddock, cooked

Preheat oven to 450°F. Split live lobsters with a sharp, pointed knife from head to tail lying on its back. Open flat and remove intestinal vein, stomach, and tomalley. Crack claws, remove meat, and cut into pieces.

Moisten crumbs with butter and egg. Add Parmesan cheese and seafood. Spread stuffing generously in cavity and split tail to prevent curling. Place on cookie sheet or baking sheet and bake for 20 minutes, or until browned on top.

Crab Stuffed Maine Lobster

Replace 2 c. drained crabmeat instead of seafood in Baked Stuffed Lobster recipe and follow baking instructions.

Lobster Fra Diablo

Fra Diablo means "brother devil" because of the spicy sauce. The name is Italian but the dish is rarely served in Italy.

4 live lobsters (1 1/4 lb. ea.)
3 T. butter or margarine
1 T. minced garlic
3 T. olive oil
4 c. canned whole tomatoes, drained and chopped
1/2 t. oregano
1/2 t. hot pepper sauce

Preheat oven to 350°F. Boil lobsters, cool, and pick out the meat. Cut meat into bite-sized pieces. Reserve body cavity shells.

Sauté lobster meat in butter until heated through; drain. Sauté garlic in olive oil over medium heat for 3 minutes. Add tomatoes, oregano, and hot pepper sauce; sauté an additional 4 minutes. Add lobster meat and heat throughout.

Split lobster body shells by cutting halfway through them from top to bottom. Put the mixture into the body shells and place on foil-lined baking sheet. Bake 12 to 14 minutes or until heated and bubbling. Remove and serve.

Spicy Lobster Gumbo

Now I have given Maryland her due, Maine's turn is here and now. There is no better lobster in the world than Maine "lobstah"...period, end of story, over and out, ciao, aloha!

1/4 lb. Andouille sausage, diced
2 stalks celery, minced
1 green pepper, diced
3 cloves garlic, minced
1 medium onion, minced
2 scallions, diced
8 okra pods, sliced
4 tomatoes, diced
2 qts. chicken stock
2 bay leaves
2 c. white rice, cooked
1 T. file powder
12 oz. lobster meat, diced
Hot pepper sauce to taste
Salt and pepper to taste

In 4-qt. stock pot, sauté sausage over medium-high heat until hot. Add celery, green pepper, garlic, onion, scallions, okra, and diced tomatoes, stirring until vegetables are soft. Add stock, bay leaves, rice and file powder, stirring until ingredients are blended. Simmer gently for 15 minutes over medium heat, stirring to avoid scorching rice. Stir in lobster. Add hot sauce, salt, and pepper to taste.

Grilled Shrimp with Tropical Rice

Tropical fruits and shrimp just seem to go together so naturally, as in this colorful and sunny dish. Take a break and treat yourself.

    1 1/4 c. water
    3/4 c. coconut milk
    1 c. uncooked long grain rice
    1 t. dried ginger
    1/2 c. crushed pineapple, drained
    1/3 c. coconut, toasted in 350°F
        oven for 4 to 5 minutes
    1 t. dried cilantro
    3 T. olive oil
    1/3 c. minced red bell pepper
    1/3 c. minced red onion
    1/2 c. chopped cashews
    10 to 12 medium-sized shrimp,
        peeled, deveined

Bring water and coconut milk to boil over medium-high heat in medium stock pot. Stir in rice and ginger. Cover and reduce heat to low; simmer 20 minutes until liquid is absorbed. Transfer to bowl.

Add pineapple, coconut, and cilantro to rice; stir to combine. Heat olive oil in sauté pan and add vegetables and shrimp, sauté until softened. Add cashews and cooked vegetables to rice and stir to blend. Place cooked shrimp on bed of ice and serve.

Barbecued Shrimp

I wouldn't add any more hot pepper sauce than what is called for here. Although only 1 T., it does give you the nudge that it's there.

    5 to 6 large, uncooked shrimp
    1/4 c. butter or margarine, melted
    1 T. your favorite hot sauce
    2 cloves garlic, minced
    1/2 t. black pepper (cracked black
        pepper is desired here)
    Parsley, to your liking
    Dried rosemary, to your liking
    Salt, to your liking
    Lemon wedges

Preheat oven to 400°F. Shell and devein shrimp. In small baking dish, combine butter with hot sauce, garlic, salt, rosemary, black pepper, and parsley; stir to combine. Dip and evenly coat each shrimp with your spice mixture and arrange shrimp side by side on baking dish. Bake 6 to 8 minutes, or until shrimp is barely done. Remove and broil for 3 to 4 minutes, or until shrimp has taken on an almost barbecued glaze and crispness. Remove and squeeze lemon wedges over the top, serve.

Cooking with Beer

High alcoholic beer is good for deglazing because some of the alcohol can be evaporated and the flavor of the beer won't be overpowering. Lighter beer and wheat beer is better for poaching preparations, especially with shrimp and other seafood. Try it sometime.

Kung Pao Shrimp

This Shanghai preparation means "crown prince." There is a tale told of a crown prince, while travelling through the Shanghai region of China long ago, who was presented with this dish in his honor. He was so happy it is said that he brought the cooks back to the imperial court.

1/2 lb. medium-sized shrimp,
    peeled and deveined
1 egg white, beaten (for the sauce)
3 t. chili sauce
1 t. soy sauce
2 t. sugar
1 t. Chinkiang vinegar
    (or red wine vinegar)
3 T. ketchup
Pinch Szechuan peppercorns,
    crushed (or use white pepper)
3 c. peanut oil
1/2 c. peanuts
2 fresh Thai chilies, minced
1/2 c. chopped scallions, white part
    only, sliced on the diagonal

Place shrimp in a bowl with the egg white, mix well to coat. Combine the next 6 ingredients in a bowl and whisk well, set aside. Heat wok on high heat for 1 minute. Add the peanut oil and cook peanuts for 1 to 1 1/2 minutes, or until they turn golden dark brown. Turn off the heat and remove peanuts with a strainer. Drain and transfer hot oil to a heat-proof bowl. Return 1 T. of the hot oil to wok and heat over high for 20 seconds. Add the chilies, stir, and cook for 30 seconds. Add scallions, shrimp, and continue cooking and stirring for 2 minutes. Make a well in the middle of shrimp and add the sauce mixture. Stir and cook 45 seconds longer. Add peanuts, turn heat off, and transfer to platter.

Shrimp Wiggle from the Turn of the Twentieth Century

James Beard said, "For many years this was in the repertoire of every coed with a chafing dish and every girl who had a beau to cook for." The recipe below was my grandfather's, who, indeed, made it in college. "Combine 1 T. butter, 1 T. minced onion, 1 c. cooked rice, 1/2 can tomato soup, salt, and pepper in a double boiler. Add some red pepper, 1 c. cream, some cooked Maine shrimp, and 2 c. peas. Serve on crackers, toast, or pastry shells."

Shrimp, Fiddlehead, and Asparagus Stir-fry

I know many of you have never seen, let alone tasted, fiddleheads before, but they are a long time treat here in New England. You can find them in cans outside of New England but if you can't, simply opt for snap peas or fresh green beans in its place.

3 T. vegetable oil
1/2 lb. shrimp, peeled
35 to 40 fiddleheads, cleaned
    (see page 166)
1/2 t. ginger
1/2 c. water, divided
4 scallions, both green and white
    part sliced
8 to 10 stalks asparagus, trimmed,
    peeled, and cut into 1-inch
    segments
1 t. sesame oil

In a large skillet or wok, over medium-high heat, stir fry fiddleheads in 2 T. vegetable oil for 2 minutes. Add 1/4 c. water and lower heat to medium; cover. Continue cooking 4 to 5 minutes or until water has been absorbed. Add asparagus and remainder of water. Cover and steam, cook another 4 to 5 minutes or until tender. Add rest of oil, shrimp, and ginger and continue cooking 2 to 3 minutes more until shrimp are just done. Stir in sesame oil and serve over rice.

Fiddleheads: A New England Delicacy

New Englanders are a frugal bunch. Mention "free" and we'll come in a hurry. Free food falls into this category—as in "free for the picking." When spring arrives in northern New England, the free food abundant in the woods is fiddleheads.

While the best fiddleheads spots are often a guarded secret (akin to French truffles in Provence), finding them is a special treat. These sprouts, in the shape of the top of a fiddle, are actually the young coiled leaves or shoot of the ostrich fern. While nearly all ferns have "fiddleheads," those of the ostrich fern are unlike any other—they are delicious!

According to the University of Maine Cooperative Extension, fiddleheads (which appear during April and May) should be harvested as soon as they appear within an inch or two from the ground. Brush out and remove the brown scales.

Wash and cook the "heads" in a small amount of lightly salted boiling water for ten minutes or steam for 20 minutes. Serve at once with melted butter. The quicker they are eaten, the more delicate their flavor.

But before you run out to collect these little delicacies, be forewarned that the Center for Disease Control has found a number of outbreaks of food-borne illness associated with fiddleheads (nothing is simple, right?) But the outbreaks occurred when the ferns were eaten raw or lightly cooked (as in sautéed, parboiled, or microwaved). So…cook your fiddleheads thoroughly before eating them…boil them for at least 10 minutes. Then you can eat them right away, or freeze or pickle them.

If you're unsure of what a fiddlehead looks like (make sure you know what an edible fiddlehead looks like because some ferns can be poisonous) or have no desire to muck through the woods during mud season to pick them, you can sometimes find them in your produce section if you live in New England or Canada. If you can't find them, ask your grocer (if he or she knows what they are!)—fiddleheads can be special ordered.

Shrimp and Cashew Stir-Fry

Don't be intimidated with the ingredient list. Although you do need a large frying or sauté pan, you'll have plenty of room for everything. The spinach quickly cooks down and is a nice addition to this hearty stir-fry.

1/2 c. dry roasted cashews
3 T. peanut or vegetable oil
1 medium onion, cut in half and sliced julienne style
1/2 c. thinly sliced celery
6 oz. mushrooms, sliced
1 clove garlic, minced
1 lb. medium-sized shrimp, peeled and deveined
1 t. cornstarch
2 T. soy sauce
1/4 c. chicken broth
2 c. spinach leaves, chopped
1/4 lb. snow pea pods, strings removed
Salt and pepper to taste
Cooked brown rice

Stir cashews in heated oil in large frying pan, over medium-high heat, until they give off a nutlike aroma and begin to brown. Remove with a slotted spoon and reserve. To same oil, add onion and celery. Cook, stirring occasionally until onions are transparent, about 3 minutes. Add mushrooms and cook until they begin to brown. Mix in garlic and shrimp, stirring until shrimp turn pink.

Mix cornstarch smoothly with soy sauce and chicken broth. To shrimp mixture add spinach and peas; stir 30 seconds. Mix in cornstarch mixture, stirring just until thickened. Taste; add salt, if needed. Sprinkle with reserved cashews. Serve over brown rice.

Pan Seared Maple Scallops

I can't think of any recipe that uses maple syrup and scallops, so I came up with this. Thank you, Vermont! I am sure you readers will agree with me that maple does enhance the flavor of the scallops.

2 T. soy sauce
1/4 t. fried ginger
1 lb. scallops
2 T. maple syrup
1 T. butter or margarine
2 T. water to thin sauce
Lemon for seasoning and garnish

Mix together soy and ginger. Heat butter in non-stick skillet until smoking brown. Add scallops, patted dry. Turn after 30 seconds or until well browned. Remove to serving platter. Add the syrup and bring to a boil. If you would like a thinner sauce, dilute with water. Add soy and ginger mixture to deglaze the pan; don't scrape the bottom of the pan. Pour over scallops and garnish with lemon slices.

Eastern Broiled Scallops

Not Eastern U.S., but far-Eastern. The influence of India is obvious with the addition of curry. If you dare to make it more fiery, add a little more curry if needed, the pear and raisins help even out the heat.

1 lb. bay scallops
2 t. olive oil
2 t. curry powder
1/2 c. chopped onion
1 c. chicken broth
1 medium pear, peeled,
    cored, and diced
1/2 c. raisins or dried fruit pieces
1 c. couscous, cooked

Preheat broiler. Rinse scallops and pat dry. In a medium saucepan, combine oil and curry powder. Remove 1 T. of the oil mixture and set aside. Add onion to oil mixture in saucepan. Cook over medium heat until onion is tender. Add broth, pear, and fruit pieces. Bring to a boil. Stir in couscous. Remove from heat; cover and let stand 5 minutes.

Toss scallops in reserved oil mixture. Place scallops onto broiler-safe baking sheet and broil until scallops are opaque in color; 6 to 8 minutes per side. Make sure heat source is 4 inches from scallops. Serve scallops over couscous.

Spicy Orange Scallops and Pasta

Originally I didn't add the Scotch bonnets to this meal, but after tasting (and although very good in its own right) I decided it needed a little pizzazz, so here it is. I think you'll agree, it's just what the...pepper farmer ordered.

8 oz. of fettuccine
12 oz. of scallops
1 red bell pepper, diced
1 t. Scotch Bonnet chili pepper,
    minced
1 T. olive oil
1 c. frozen orange juice concentrate
1/2 c. chicken broth
6 t. cornstarch

Cook pasta according to package directions. Drain and keep warm. In a large skillet over medium high heat, sauté scallops, bell pepper, and Scotch peppers in olive oil 3 to 4 minutes, until scallops are almost done and opaque. In a large mixing bowl, combine orange juice concentrate, broth, and cornstarch until well mixed and add to skillet. Cook until thickened and bubbling. Remove and serve over pasta.

Stir-fried Scallops and Peas

Found in all the world's oceans, scallops can be prepared in just as many ways. My father used to eat them raw, but I prefer this recipe. The snow peas add a great snap to this dish.

10 to 12 bay scallops
Cornstarch for dredging
1/4 c. peanut oil
4 scallion bulbs (white part) sliced 1/2-inch long
3/4 t. minced garlic
1/4 t. dried ginger
1/4 c. sliced water chestnuts
6 oz. snow peas
3 oz. bean sprouts

Sauce:
2 T. soy sauce
1 t. white vinegar
1/4 t. red pepper flakes
1/4 t. sesame oil

In small bowl, whisk the sauce ingredients together well; set aside. Toss the scallops and cornstarch to evenly coat in a bowl; set aside. Heat a wok on medium-high heat until a drop of water fizzles and dissipates quickly. Add the peanut oil and carefully add the scallops, one at a time, and stir fry for 2 to 3 minutes, continuously stirring, until done throughout. Remove the scallops onto a paper towel-lined platter. Turn up the heat to high and add the scallions, stir frying for 15 seconds. Add the garlic, ginger, and water chestnuts, stir fry 15 additional seconds, constantly stirring. Add the peas and bean sprouts and stir fry 15 seconds longer. Add prepared sauce and scallops and stir well. Add the sesame oil lastly and remove from heat. Serve over white rice or Asian noodles.

Oyster Crisp

This easy-to-prepare dish uses oysters, crackers, bacon, and cream to make a creamy baked side dish or an entrée. You can substitute light cream for the heavy without losing any flavor.

1 pint shucked oysters, in juice
1/4 t. salt
Pinch black pepper
Pinch nutmeg
6 strips bacon,
    cooked crisp and crumbled
1 c. shredded Swiss cheese
1 c. whipping cream
1/2 c. crushed saltine crackers
2 T. butter or margarine

Preheat oven to 350°F. Grease a shallow 2-qt. baking dish. Arrange oysters evenly in dish; pour their juice over the top. Sprinkle salt, pepper, and nutmeg evenly over oysters. Scatter crumbled bacon over oysters; then top with cheese. Pour cream evenly over all; then cover evenly with cracker crumbs and dot with butter. Bake, uncovered, for 20 minutes or until bubbly and browned.

The Original Pigs in Blankets

To purchase live, healthy oysters remember to reject any with broken shells or that don't have tightly closed shells, or with shells that don't snap shut when tapped with your finger. The smaller an oyster is for its species, the younger and more tender it will be. You can safely store live oysters in your refrigerator (larger shell down), covered with a damp towel, for up to 3 days. If any shells open during storage, tap them—if they don't close, throw them out. Oyster shells will also open easier if they have been frozen for 15 to 20 minutes.

12 large oysters, shelled
Salt and pepper to taste
1 T. minced garlic, mixed with 4 T. melted butter or margarine
6 strips raw bacon
Toast, cut into rounds as a bed for the cooked oysters

Sprinkle oysters with salt, pepper and garlic butter. Cut each strip of bacon in half and encircle each oyster in a half-strip of the bacon. Secure bacon firmly with a toothpick. Broil 8 minutes or until bacon is crispy. Serve on toasted rounds of bread, buttered if you wish.

Oysters Rockefeller

The country's oldest family-run restaurant, Antoine's, is noted for being the originator of Oysters Rockefeller. The richness of this dish is the reason why this recipe was named after the richest man in the world at the time, John D. Rockefeller.

6 oz. butter or margarine
1 t. minced onion
1 t. dried parsley
Pinch salt
Pinch cayenne pepper
3 slices bacon, cooked and crumbled
1/4 c. packed, fresh spinach, minced
1/2 c. dried bread crumbs
12 fresh oysters, opened

Preheat oven to 475°F. Cream the butter with all ingredients except oysters. Separate oysters from their shells by cutting the muscle underneath. Spread butter mixture onto each oyster on the half shell, discarding unused half of each oyster shell. Place on a baking sheet and bake for 10 minutes or until plump and done. Remove and broil additional minute or so until browned on top. Serve.

Yankee Mussels

So named as a spin-off of Oysters Rockefeller. Just as delicious as Oysters Rockefeller but much cheaper…just like a Yankee!

3 T. butter or margarine
1 small onion, chopped
1 clove garlic, minced
1 c. chicken broth or white wine
1/8 t. black pepper
2 to 3 qts. live mussels in shells, cleaned
Melted butter

In a large stock pot, about a 4-qt. size, melt the 3 T. butter over medium heat. Add onion and garlic and cook, stirring occasionally, until soft. Add broth or wine and pepper; bring mixture to a boil. Add mussels, cover, and simmer gently until mussels have opened, about 7 to 8 minutes.

With a slotted spoon, transfer mussels to individual serving bowls, pour cooking liquid evenly over servings. Serve with melted butter.

CHAPTER 10
Beef, Lamb, and Pork

Steak and Potato "Stir-Fry"

This dish is for that meat and potato kind of person everyone seems to know. The addition of the balsamic vinaigrette dressing gives this dish an Italian flare.

1 lb. boneless sirloin steak,
  cut into strips
1 T. oil
2 c. cubed potatoes
2 c. sliced carrots
1/4 c. water or beef broth
2 c. sliced mushrooms
1 small onion, chopped
1/4 c. balsamic vinaigrette dressing

Cook and stir meat in oil in skillet on high heat for 2 minutes, or until browned. Remove from skillet; set aside. Add potatoes, carrots, and water to skillet and bring to a boil; cover. Reduce heat to low and simmer 15 minutes. Stir in mushrooms, onions, dressing, and meat; cook and stir on high heat for 5 minutes or until heated through.

Tenderloin Dijon with Pepper

Dijon mustard usually contains both red and white wines and complements meat very well. Go ahead and try American beer mustard if you can find it. It incorporates beer instead of an acid. Whole grain mustard works especially well, too.

1/2 t. celery salt
2 t. black peppercorns,
  crushed with side of large knife
4 beef tenderloin steaks,
  each 1-inch thick
2 T. vegetable oil
1/3 c. brandy or beef broth
2 T. Dijon-style mustard

On waxed paper, mix celery salt and pepper; use to rub on steaks. Heat nonstick, 12-inch skillet with oil over medium-high heat until hot. Add steaks and cook 4 to 5 minutes per side for medium-rare or until desired temperature. Remove steaks to plate; keep warm.

Remove skillet from heat; add brandy or beef broth and mustard and stir to combine. Return skillet to medium-high heat and cook, stirring frequently, until sauce boils; boil 30 seconds. Pour sauce on plates and place steaks on top of sauce.

Tequila Steaks

Le encantara este filete hace de la manera mexicana. You will love this steak done the Mexican way. Hey, we have a town called Mexico in Maine.

1 c. tequila, or less if desired
2 T. olive oil
1 1/2 T. black pepper
2 t. grated lemon zest
1 t. grated lime zest
1 clove garlic, minced
4 sirloin steaks, 1 to
  1 1/2 inches thick
Salt to taste

Combine tequila, oil, pepper, lemon, lime zest, and garlic in a large heavy duty plastic bread bag or large shallow bowl, nonmetal. Add steaks and seal bag or cover bowl. Rotate bag to evenly distribute marinade or turn meat occasionally to evenly saturate steaks. Refrigerate 2 hours or over night.

Remove steak and drain, reserving marinade. Cook steaks either on outdoor grill or in skillet, brushing with marinade often. Cook to your liking and serve.

Chefs from bygone days used to "lard" tough cuts of meat. With a hollow, elongated needle (larding needle) they would first inject the needle into lardons (pork fat) to retrieve a length of lard. They then would inject it into the meat to melt for a more tender meat.

Seared Rosemary Steak

I remember Dad used to cook Black and Blue steaks many times at his restaurants. This means blackened on the outside but rare, very rare, on the inside.

1 beef flank steak (1 lb.),
   trimmed of fat
2 T. peanut oil
1/2 t. salt
1/4 t. black pepper
1 t. dried rosemary, crushed
4 c. watercress

Pat meat dry with paper towels. Heat a large cast iron skillet with peanut oil over high heat until very hot. Sprinkle salt, pepper, and rosemary on steak. Add steak to hot skillet; reduce heat to medium-high heat, and cook 6 to 7 minutes per side for medium-rare or longer for desired temperature. Remove from pan and place steak on cutting board. Add 1/2 c. water to skillet and let cook 1 minute; remove from heat.

To serve, arrange watercress on large warm platter. Thinly slice steak on the bias and place on watercress. Pour any meat juices from cutting board and pan over the top.

Beef with Cashews

True Chinese Beef and Cashews has oyster sauce and Chinese chili sauce. Although you may not be able to find Chinese chili sauce, substitute any brand of chili sauce, it will be just as delectable.

1 lb. beef rump steak, trimmed
4 T. vegetable oil, divided
1/2 c. water
4 t. cornstarch
5 t. soy sauce
1 t. sesame oil
2 t. oyster sauce
1 t. chili sauce
8 green onions,
   cut into 1-inch segments
2 cloves garlic, minced
1 t. dried ginger
2/3 c. roasted cashews

Cut beef across the grain into thin slices about 2-inches long. Heat 2 T. of the vegetable oil in wok or large skillet over high heat. Stir-fry half the beef until brown, 3 to 5 minutes. Remove and set aside; continue with remaining beef. Combine water, cornstarch, soy sauce, sesame oil, oyster sauce, and chili sauce in small bowl; mix well. Heat remaining 2 T. vegetable oil in wok over high heat. Add onions, garlic, ginger, and cashews. Stir-fry 1 minute. Add meat and cornstarch mixture. Cook and stir until liquid boils and thickens.

Try these Steak Sauces:

For Lamb: **Mint Sauce**—Mince 1 bunch of mint, mix with 2 T. sugar. Chill 30 minutes. Combine 1 1/2 c. water with 1/2 c. sugar; stir until dissolved and boil 2 minutes. Pour onto mint mixture, stir, and cool. Season with lemon juice, salt, and pepper.

For Steak: **Bordelaise Sauce**—Bring 1 1/2 c. demi-glace to a boil. Meanwhile, in separate bowl, add 2 minced shallots, 1 t. white pepper, 1 thyme sprig, bay leaf, and 3/4 c. red wine; reduce to half. Strain and add to demi-glace. Mount with a few knobs of ice cold butter and stir.

For Steak: **Pepper-Cream Sauce**—Fry steak in pan over medium-high heat with butter. Remove meat and add green peppercorns. Cook for 3 minutes and add 3/4 c. heavy cream. Cook until thickened.

And here's the classic l'Orange sauce, but it is equally as good on any steak. **Duck A l'Orange**—Bring 1 1/2 c. demi-glace to gentle boil, add 2 T. tomato paste, 1/2 c. orange juice, 3 T. lemon juice, 5 T. corn syrup, and boil for 20 minutes. Add julienned orange peel, orange liqueur, salt, and pepper

Caramelized Onion Steak Sandwich for a Crowd

And I do mean a crowd. Grab some beverages, slaws, and salads and invite everyone you can to come and taste how caramelized onions share the spotlight with tenderloin.

4 1/2 lb. beef tenderloin
4 Spanish onions, thinly sliced
2 sticks of butter or margarine
2 1/2 t. salt
1 t. black pepper
2 t. thyme
12 slices very sharp Cheddar cheese
12 thick slices bread
3/4 c. Dijon mustard
24 Boston Bibb lettuce leaves
24 slices tomatoes

Grill or bake steak to desired temperature; set aside to cool. Sauté onions with butter in sauce pan over medium heat for 10 minutes. Add salt, pepper, and thyme; continue cooking for an additional 15 to 20 minutes until onions are translucent, tender, and golden brown.

Slice cooled tenderloin very thin and separate. Arrange thin meat into 12 stacks and broil, turning once. Add cheese to each stack and broil until melted. Toast bread slices. Arrange toasted bread on individual plates. Spread each slice with mustard. Add lettuce leaves, tomato slices, and broiled meat to each. Top with caramelized onions and serve open faced.

Other Steak Sandwich Options:

Steak Toast: Grill marinated steak slices and top with Fontina cheese, cooked mushrooms, roasted peppers, and horseradish on your favorite roll.

Sabana Steak Sandwich: Grilled marinated steak slices topped with cooked onions, Gouda cheese, and pickled vegetables on your favorite roll.

Sweet Steak Sandwich: Spicy marinated steak slices cooked and topped with grilled green tomatoes, arugula lettuce, and mango chutney.

Steak Supermelt: Cooked, sliced tenderloin slices with grilled onions, peppers, and portabella mushrooms topped with melted Pepper Jack cheese on grilled rye.

The Cuban Joe: Philly-style shaved beef on a Cuban roll with chimichurri sauce and black bean aioli.

Chimichurri Sauce: 3/4 c. extra virgin olive oil, 2 T. chopped fresh parsley, 1 T. chopped cilantro, 1/2 t. minced garlic, 1/4 t. salt, 1/4 t. cumin, and pinch of black pepper; mixed well.

Black Bean Aioli: 1 c. mayonnaise, 3 oz. drained canned black beans, chopped. Mix together well.

Smoked Brisket Sandwich: Sliced, smoked brisket stacked on a toasted jalapeno bun with BBQ sauce, raw onion, sliced dill pickle, and garlic butter

Steak and Gravy Sandwich: Sliced, cooked marinated steak of your choice topped with bleu cheese, sautéed mushrooms, and beef gravy. Served open faced atop toasted Italian bread.

California Steak Sandwich: Sliced, cooked marinated steak topped with shredded, raw spinach, sliced avocados, sliced red onion, sliced mushrooms, and Dijon-style mustard, served on sour dough rolls.

English Flips: Sliced, cooked steak served on a toasted English muffin with horseradish sauce, chopped tomato, cooked bacon, and very sharp Cheddar cheese.

Pepper Steak Sandwich: In a toasted French roll, add cooked, sliced steak, oregano, sliced onion, minced garlic, red and yellow bell pepper strips, and slice of Monterey Jack cheese.

Open-Faced Italian Steak Sandwich: On top of garlic Texas toast, add sliced, cooked sirloin steak, pesto, sun-dried tomato spread, and toasted pine nuts.

Steak Fajita Sandwich: On hard rolls, add slices of cooked green, bell peppers, hot pepper sauce, taco seasoning, and hot pepper Monterey Jack cheese.

Ranch Steak Sandwich: Coat sliced sirloin with flour, dry mustard, Worcestershire sauce, and black pepper. Pile into sub roll with cooked onions, mild Cheddar cheese, and just a sprinkle of ranch dressing.

Veal Parmigiana

This delectable Italian classic is generally served with a pasta of your choice, but why only pasta? A comfortable mashed or baked potato or a side of rice goes equally as well. And for the scaloppini? It is simply meat (in this instance, veal) that has been pounded thin either by you, the butcher, or purchased as such.

4 large slices veal scaloppini
1 egg, beaten
Seasoned bread crumbs
3 T. butter or margarine
1/2 c. tomato paste
1 T. vermouth (optional)
Grated Parmesan cheese
4 slices mozzarella cheese

Preheat oven to 350°F. Dip Scaloppini (very thin slices of veal) in beaten egg, then in seasoned breadcrumbs. Add butter to large sauté pan and cook veal on medium-high heat on both sides until done, about 2 minutes per side, or until well browned but not burnt. In shallow baking pan, add tomato paste; spread evenly over bottom. Place veal over paste. Drizzle vermouth over top and sprinkle Parmesan cheese generously on top. Place in center of oven for about 6 to 7 minutes or until tomato sauce is bubbling. Remove from oven and place a slice of Mozzarella cheese over the top of each. Return to oven and cook until cheese has completely melted.

Old Dutch Wiener Schnitzel

This Austrian Schnitzel is best served with boiled red potatoes sprinkled with melted butter and parsley, or add a scoop of your favorite potato salad.

2 lbs. veal cutlets, pounded no more
   than 1/2-inch thick
1/2 c. flour
Salt and pepper to taste
1 egg, beaten
1 c. bread crumbs
3 T. butter or margarine
1 T. paprika
1/2 c. chopped onions
1/2 c. beef broth
1 t. lemon juice
1/2 c. sour cream
1 T. dried parsley

Dredge the meat in flour seasoned with salt and pepper. Dip each piece of meat into beaten egg and then into bread crumbs. Place meat on platter and refrigerate for an hour or more. Heat butter in skillet over medium heat and stir in the paprika. When bubbling, sauté onions until transparent. Push onions to one side of skillet and add meat, turning it so that it is brown on all sides. Add broth, reduce heat, cover and simmer for about a half an hour.

Remove veal to a hot dish. Add lemon juice and sour cream to pan. Heat but do not boil. Pour sauce over meat and garnish with parsley.

The Best American Veal Pie

I came up with this recipe because one of my favorite savory pies is Canadian Pork Pie. I am declaring this Veal Pie to be my number one choice. Adding just those pinches of thyme and ginger complements the veal very well.

1 lb. ground veal
1/4 c. minced onion
2 bay leaves
1 c. water
1 T. flour
1 t. salt
Pinch black pepper
Pinch crushed thyme
Pinch dried ginger
1 egg, slightly beaten
1 single pie shell, uncooked
2 T. butter or margarine
2 T. flour
1/2 c. milk
1 c. shredded Cheddar cheese
2 eggs, separated

Preheat oven to 425°F. Brown ground veal in large skillet over medium-high heat. Add onion, bay leaves and water. Simmer uncovered for 15 minutes, stirring occasionally. Stir in flour, salt, pepper, thyme, ginger and egg. Pour into unbaked pie shell and bake for 15 minutes while preparing cheese soufflé. Reduce oven temperature to 375°F. Pour soufflé over partially baked pie, sealing to edge of crust and continue baking for 20 to 25 minutes, or until soufflé is nicely browned.

To make cheese soufflé: Melt butter in medium saucepan. Blend in flour; whisk to smooth. Add milk and cook over medium heat, stirring constantly, until thickened. Add cheese, stir until melted. Remove from heat. Add egg yolks. Blend in thoroughly. Beat egg whites until stiff and gently fold into cheese mixture.

Sheep were not eaten widely during the seventeenth century because of their value for wool. One seventeenth-century cookbook attempted to satisfy the craving for lamb with a recipe for turning a pig into a lamb through an extensive process of boiling and baking: "this metamorphosis may at first seem somewhat strange," said Dr. Salmon, the cookbook's author, "though we can assure you it has been much in esteem, viz. to make a Lamb out of a Pig...".

Venetian Veal Pie

Normally I abhor using so many ingredients but this recipe demands the complex nature of every spice. When you pull it from the oven, you'll see why.

1 lb. veal round steak, cut in strips
1/3 c. flour
3 T. olive oil
1/2 c. white wine (optional)
1 can (8-oz.) tomato sauce
1/4 c. minced onion
2 T. sugar
1 t. basil
1/2 t. salt
1/2 t. garlic salt
1 t. oregano
1/4 t. black pepper
1 flaky pie crust, unbaked
1/4 c. grated Parmesan cheese
1 t. oregano
1/2 t. garlic salt
1 c. shredded Mozzarella cheese
6 T. grated Parmesan cheese

Preheat oven to 450°F. Coat veal with flour and brown in oil in large skillet over medium-high heat. Reduce heat to low; add wine. Mix well. Add tomato sauce, onion, sugar, basil, salt, garlic salt, oregano, and pepper. Simmer, covered, for 30 minutes or until meat is tender. Meanwhile, prepare recipe for 8-inch pie shell, adding cheese, oregano, and garlic salt to flour in recipe. Bake as directed. Remove from oven; reduce oven temperature to 350°F. Pour hot filling into crust. Sprinkle with mozzarella and Parmesan cheese. Bake for 10 minutes until cheese is melted. Let cool 10 minutes before cutting into wedges to serve.

Roast Beef with Pan Gravy

I know, you're asking, "Who doesn't know how to make Roast Beef?" Well, I have come across a great many younger people who don't even know how to hard boil an egg, let alone make a roast beef. And since this is a complete book on Yankee cooking, let me help those less fortunate.

2 T. Worcestershire sauce	2 t. salt
1 rump roast (4 to 5 lb.)	3 T. flour
1 t. garlic powder	1/2 c. melted butter or margarine
1 t. onion powder	2 c. beef broth
1 T. plus 1/4 t. black pepper	

Preheat oven to 425°F. Rub the Worcestershire sauce over the entire roast and allow to marinate for 30 minutes. Combine the powdered garlic, onion powder, and 1 T. pepper in a small bowl; sprinkle the seasoning mixture evenly over the roast, pressing it and let the roast stand for an additional 30 minutes. Rub the meat with 2 t. salt and place fat side up in a shallow roasting pan; roast 15 minutes.

Reduce oven temperature to 325°F and continue to roast until the meat's internal temperature reaches 130°F, about 2 hours. Let roast stand for 20 minutes before carving. If you want this meat well done, cook an additional hour, or until internal temperature reaches 180°F.

Make the gravy. Skim any fat from the liquid that remains in the roasting pan. Whisk the flour and 1/2 c. melted butter or margarine together to a paste; set aside. Scrape the drippings from the bottom of the roasting pan, add the beef broth and stir over medium heat until the mixture begins to simmer. While continuously whisking, add the flour/butter mixture and bring to a boil.

Reduce heat to medium-low and let simmer for 4 to 5 minutes. If needed, add a little water to thin the gravy. Add remaining salt and pepper and serve warm.

To Boil Beef or Mutton. When your meat is put in, and the pot boils, take care to scum it very clean, otherwise the scum will boil down, stick to your meat, and make it look black. Send up your dish with turnips, greens, potatoes or carrots. If it be a leg or loin of mutton, you may also put melted butter and capers in a boat.

—The Frugal Housewife, 1772

Yankee Pot Roast

As with any popular dish, there is no single "correct" recipe for Yankee Pot Roast, and we each remember our family's recipe and consider it the best.

Common to all is the combination or braising and roasting at moderate heat, which slowly tenderizes less expensive cuts of meat. True to Yankee practicality, vegetables appearing in the recipe depend upon what is available and economical, most commonly onions, potatoes, and carrots, but turnips, parsnips, and even celeriac are not out of place. Economical cuts of meat are actually essential to this slow cooking; the connective tissue breaks down leaving moist and tender pieces which are full of flavor. I prefer bone-in chuck roast and cook it whole. Small pieces of "stew beef" frequently are trimmings from several cuts, some of which are too lean to be cooked this way, and the larger piece better maintains its moistness.

1 boneless chuck roast (4 to 5 lbs.), trimmed of excess fat
Salt and black pepper
Vegetable oil
4 to 5 cloves garlic, sliced
1 large carrot, chopped
1 onion, chopped
1 celery stalk, chopped
2 t. dried thyme
2 bay leaves
3 T. flour
3 1/2 c. beef stock.
2 T. tomato paste
8 to 10 small onions
5 carrots in 1 to 2 inch pieces
1 lb. red potatoes or larger white potatoes, in chunks

Over high heat, pour sufficient oil to cover the bottom of a large Dutch oven or other large heavy pot, generously salt and pepper both sides of the roast and sear meat until well browned on both sides. Remove meat and pour off oil. Return pot to medium heat and add chopped carrot, celery, onion, and the garlic. Cook, stirring and adding a small amount of oil if necessary, until softened but not browned. Sprinkle flour over vegetables and stir for 2 to 3 minutes. Return meat, adding water, tomato paste, and herbs.

Bring to a simmer on top of the stove, cover (use aluminum foil under cover if it does not fit tightly). Place into preheated 325°F oven and cook for 2 hours.

Check at 1 hour and turn meat if it is not covered by liquid; add additional water if liquid is too thick—it should be the consistency of thin gravy.

At 2 to 2 1/4 hours, add remaining vegetables; the time varies according to size. Cook for a total of 3 hours. If the vegetables are not quite cooked, cover and let sit—cooking will continue with the retained heat. Check for seasoning, adding salt or pepper to taste.

Skim excess fat from the liquid, cut meat into serving size pieces, arrange on a heated platter, and surround with vegetables. Moisten with some of the liquid, pass around the remainder of the liquid at the table and enjoy a true New England tradition.

New England Boiled Dinner

Traditionally served on either Monday nights or Wednesday night in the old days.

By the way, black pepper was often referred to as Black Gold because of its importance in trading, and the fact that it was used as money in many societies in ancient times. The term "peppercorn rent" is still widely used throughout the world to mean a place where the rent is minimal.

5 lbs. beef brisket	1 sm. cabbage, quartered
6 peppercorns	6 onions, peeled
6 fresh beets, unpeeled but rinsed	8 potatoes, peeled
6 carrots, unpeeled but rinsed	2 small turnips, peeled and cut into quarters

Place the meat in a large pot with the peppercorns. Cover with cold water and simmer for 3 1/2 to 4 hours, or until the meat is tender and done. During the last hour of cooking, remove the peppercorns floating on top and add the turnips and carrots. Cook the beets separately in water over high heat for 15 to 20 minutes, or until tender; drain. Cool and peel the skin from the beets. In the last half hour, add the cabbage, potatoes, and onions. Continue cooking until all the vegetables are tender. Add the corned beef back into the pot if there is room and let cook for 10 minutes, just to heat up again. Arrange the meat in the center of a large platter and place all the vegetables around the corned beef.

Red Flannel Hash

There is a rumor circulating that the name Red Flannel Hash first began in 1907, when a woman, angry with her husband, threw his red flannels into the dinner hash one evening. He liked it so much that he asked her to make it again. Of course, with the missing flannels, she had to use another red product, hence the introduction of beets. Still another story began when the Green Mountain Boys and Ethan Allen were starving during a particularly brutal campaign in the Revolutionary War, so they decided to shred their red flannels and add them to the meager ration of potatoes.

6 fresh beets, cooked, peeled and
  sliced (or use leftover beets)
4 potatoes, cooked
  (with or without the skin)
2 c. cooked cabbage, chopped
  (optional)
2 c. chopped, cooked turnip
  (optional)
1 c. cooked, peeled
  and chopped onions
3 T. butter or margarine
2 T. heavy cream
2 c. cooked, chopped corned beef
Salt and pepper to taste

In a large, sturdy bowl, chop the beets, potatoes, cabbage, and turnip to a fine dice. In a separate bowl, chop the corned beef the same way. Add the corned beef to the vegetable mixture along with the cream and mix well. In a large skillet, cast iron works best, melt the butter over medium-high heat. Scoop out the hash into the skillet and flatten to about an inch thick. Brown both sides very well and enjoy. Many enjoy this dish baked. If so, simply scoop out the hash into a greased 9-inch square baking pan and bake at 375°F for 40 to 45 minutes, or until browned and crisp on top.

Beef Stroganoff

The first Stroganoff recipe I can find is in an 1861 Russian cookbook that uses mustard in a sauce instead of sour cream. My recipe varies from the norm as well. Adding cauliflower, carrots, and broccoli brightens it up and tastes great as well.

1 lb. beef round steak,
    thinly sliced to 1-inch chunks
1 T. vegetable oil
1 medium onion, chopped
1 clove garlic, minced
2 c. sliced fresh mushrooms
1/2 c. beef broth
2 T. red wine (optional)
1 t. black pepper
2 c. egg noodles
2 c. frozen cauliflower,
    broccoli, and carrots
2 c. sour cream
2 T. flour

In a large skillet, over medium-high heat, brown half of the meat in oil. Remove meat and brown remaining meat with onion and garlic, adding more oil if necessary. Drain off fat. Return all meat, onion and garlic to skillet. Stir in mushrooms, beef broth, red wine, and pepper. Bring to a boil; reduce heat to low and simmer, covered, for 30 to 45 minutes or until meat is tender.

Meanwhile, cook noodles and vegetables in a large amount of boiling water for 6 to 8 minutes or till tender. Drain; keep warm. Combine sour cream and flour. Stir into meat mixture. Cook and stir over medium heat until bubbly. Cook and stir 1 minute more. Serve over noodles and vegetables.

Sloppy Joes

What can one say about Sloppy Joe sandwiches? If ever there was a comfort food for children and adults alike, it would be this. I know my parents used to open a can of sauce and pour it into cooked hamburger. This recipe is indistinguishable from those memories at the supper table.

3/4 lb. ground beef
1/2 c. minced onion
1/2 c. minced celery
1 clove garlic, minced
1 can (8 oz.) tomato sauce
1/4 c. chili sauce or ketchup
1 1/2 T. brown sugar
2 t. prepared mustard
2 t. Worcestershire sauce
1/2 c. shredded Cheddar cheese
4 hamburger buns

In a large skillet, cook ground beef, onion, celery, and garlic until meat is no longer pink and onion is tender. Drain off fat. Stir in tomato sauce, chili sauce (or ketchup), brown sugar, mustard, and Worcestershire sauce. Bring to a boil; reduce heat and simmer, covered, for 10 minutes.

To serve, spoon meat mixture over buns and sprinkle with cheese.

Shepherd's Pie

Now, some New Englanders swear by a different recipe for Shepherds Pie. The beginning layer of cooked hamburger is covered by either half and half cream-style corn and whole kernel or just cream style corn. This is then topped with mashed potatoes and slid under the broiler to brown and baked in the oven until browned. Although quite, well, filling, I think you will find this recipe to be more appealing and less sloppy.

1 lb. ground beef
2 cloves garlic, minced
2 c. hot mashed potatoes
4 oz. cream cheese, cubed
2 c. shredded Cheddar cheese
4 c. frozen mixed vegetables, thawed
1 c. beef gravy

Cook ground beef and garlic in a large skillet until done, separating as you cook. Drain excess grease from the skillet. Preheat oven to 375°F. Layer meat into a 9-inch square baking pan, top with cooked vegetables. Pour gravy evenly over this mixture and top with cream cheese. Lastly, add the mashed potatoes and Cheddar cheese. Bake for 20 minutes or until heated through and slightly browned on top.

Burger and Frank Barbecue

This recipe may seem like a backwoods kind of recipe, but I always have children in mind when I put together a cookbook, and this is no exception. Although we adults may not fancy a hamburger and hot dog barbecue, you just might find yourself dipping into it behind their backs.

I package dry yeast	I egg
1/4 c. warm water	I 1/2 to 2 c. flour
I envelope onion soup mix	I lb. ground beef
2 c. hot water for soup mix	1/2 lb. hot dogs, sliced
I T. sugar	1/2 c. BBQ sauce
2 T. vegetable oil	Celery seeds
1/2 t. salt	

Preheat oven to 375°F. Add yeast to warm water in small bowl. Measure 1/4 c. onion soup and blend into yeast water along with sugar, vegetable oil, salt, and egg. Add 1 c. flour; beat at medium speed with electric mixer for one minute. Gradually stir in remaining flour by hand with wooden spoon to form a soft dough. Cover; let rise in warm place for 45 minutes.

While dough is rising, prepare filling by breaking ground beef into small pieces in a 9-inch square baking pan or casserole dish. Bake for 30 minutes. Remove from oven and drain off excess fat. Add hot dogs, barbecue sauce, water, sugar, and remainder of onion soup. Mix well. Return to oven until dough is ready.

After yeast dough has risen, punch down until the air is deflated entirely. Drop by the tablespoonfuls on top of hot meat mixture. Sprinkle with celery seed and let rise for 15 more minutes. Bake for 15 to 20 minutes or until golden brown.

In honor of National Hot Dog Day, the midtown east ice cream parlor Serendipity III introduced a fancy new menu item: the "Haute Dog," a 12-inch frank that sells for $69, setting the world record for the most expensive hot dog. This restaurant also holds the record for the world's most expensive ice-cream sundae ($1,000) and the largest hot chocolate at four gallons. The world's most expensive hot dog is grilled in white truffle oil, placed in a salted pretzel bread bun toasted with white truffle butter, topped with medallions of duck foie gras, and black truffles with side condiments of black truffle Dijon mustard, caramelized Vidalia onions, and heirloom tomato ketchup.

Burger Pockets

Your children won't have regular hamburgers again. These Burger Pockets can be reheated in a snap without losing moistness or flavor.

2 c. flour
I t. salt
2/3 c. shortening
3/4 c. shredded Cheddar cheese
2 t. caraway seeds (optional)
I t. vinegar
1/2 c. milk
I lb. ground beef
I package onion soup mix
1/2 c. chili sauce
2 T. flour
2 T. relish
1/2 t. salt

Preheat oven to 400°F. Combine flour and 1 t. salt. Cut in shortening. Stir in cheese and caraway seed. Add vinegar to milk. Stir into flour mixture until dough clings together. Divide in half on floured surface and roll out half of dough to a 10-inch square. Cut into four 5-inch squares. Place on ungreased cookie sheet. Roll out remaining dough to an 11-inch square. Cut into four 5 1/2-inch squares.

Filling: Combine ground beef, onion soup mix, chili sauce, flour, pickle relish, and salt

Divide filling mixture in fourths; shape each to within 1/2 inch of edge of pastry on cookie sheet. Moisten edge and top with remaining square of pastry. Seal with a fork. Prick top of each pocket with a fork as vents. Bake for 25 to 30 minutes or until golden brown.

Italian Pancake Bake

I really should call this a French Pancake Bake because there are no noodles. By using these thin pancakes, or crepes, the texture is rich and satisfying, and you won't even miss the noodles.

Pancake Batter:
2 eggs
2/3 c. milk
1/2 c. flour
1/4 t. salt

Filling:
1 lb. ground beef
1 can (6 oz.) tomato paste
1/2 c. minced onion
1 t. basil
1 t. garlic salt
3/4 t. oregano
1/4 t. black pepper
3 c. shredded mozzarella cheese
1/2 c. grated Parmesan cheese
1 c. cottage or ricotta cheese

Preheat oven to 375°F. Combine eggs and milk in medium mixing bowl with electric mixer. Add flour and salt; beat until smooth. Heat a 9-inch skillet over medium-high heat. Grease lightly before cooking each pancake. Pour batter, 1/3 c. at a time, into skillet, tilting pan to spread evenly over bottom. When pancake is light brown and set, turn to brown other side. Prepare 4 pancakes.

Brown ground beef in medium skillet over medium-high heat until done. Add tomato paste, onion, basil, garlic salt, oregano, and pepper. In the bottom of a 10-inch pie pan or cake pan, place 1/4 of the meat mixture. Spread with 1/4 c. shredded Mozzarella cheese, 1/4 c. cottage cheese, and 1 T. grated Parmesan cheese. Repeat with remaining pancakes ending with the remainder of the cheese on top. Bake for 30 to 35 minutes, until it's nice and bubbly and browned on top. Cut into wedges to serve.

Yankee Meatloaf

Next to macaroni and cheese, nothing says comfort more so than moist, succulent meatloaf that just teases your senses while cooking, and plays with your palate when eating.

2 medium onions
2 lbs. ground beef
2 eggs
2 c. fresh bread crumbs
1/2 c. beef broth
1/4 c. ketchup
1 t. salt
1/4 t. black pepper
1/2 t. dried basil
2 T. butter or margarine

Preheat oven to 350°F. Finely chop half an onion and slice remaining 1 1/2 onions; wrap sliced onions and refrigerate. In large bowl, combine chopped onion, ground beef, eggs, bread crumbs, broth, ketchup, salt, pepper, and basil, until well blended. Place meat mixture into a 9 × 5-inch loaf pan,

shaping the meatloaf and pressing firmly. Bake meatloaf 1 hour and 30 minutes. When meatloaf is done, let stand for a few minutes before slicing into it.

About 15 minutes before being done, melt margarine in large skillet over medium heat. Add reserved sliced onions and cook, stirring occasionally, until tender. Serve atop sliced meatloaf.

Glazed Meatloaf: 1 cup ketchup mixed with 1/2 c. honey and whisk until smooth. Pour over meatloaf before baking.

Meatloaf Tips

Using ground round means using less fat (which would be absorbed by breadcrumbs) than regular ground beef and more fat than ground sirloin, which would produce a dry meatloaf.

Use coarsely ground meat instead of finely ground for a more moist and tender meatloaf.

Try adding 1/3 c. vegetable juice per pound of ground meat for a more flavorful meatloaf.

Using soft fresh breadcrumbs instead of dry breadcrumbs will produce a moister, more tender meatloaf.

Add fiber and nutrition by substituting 1/3 c. oat bran for 1/3 c. breadcrumbs.

To reduce your red meat intake, try substituting a cup of finely grated potato or carrot for a quarter pound of meat.

Rubbing the top of a meatloaf mixture smooth with cold water will minimize cracking.

Stuffed Cabbage

You can also use this same stuffing for stuffed green peppers.

I large head green cabbage
   (4 to 4 1/2 lb.) outer
   leaves discarded
I lb. ground beef
I medium onion, chopped
I green bell pepper,
   seeded and chopped
I garlic clove, minced
I t. salt
1/2 t. black pepper
I c. cooked rice
I can (28 oz.) tomato
2 1/2 c. water

Carefully remove 2 large leaves from cabbage; set aside. With sharp knife, carefully cut out stem and center of cabbage, leaving a 1-inch-thick shell. Discard stem; coarsely chop cutup cabbage. In 5-quart stock pot, cook ground beef, onion, green pepper, garlic, salt, pepper, and 1 c. chopped cabbage, over medium-high heat, stirring frequently, until meat is browned and cabbage is tender, about 15 minutes. Stir in rice and 1 c. tomato sauce; remove from heat.

Spoon beef mixture into cabbage shell. Cover cabbage opening with reserved 2 large cabbage leaves. It's not necessary, but you can use kitchen string to tie the cabbage securely to hold leaves in place. In same pot, pour in water; stir until browned bits on bottom are loosened. Add remaining chopped cabbage and remaining tomato sauce. Place stuffed cabbage, stem end down, in sauce. Heat to boiling over high heat. Reduce heat to low; cover and simmer, basting occasionally with pan juices, until cabbage shell is fork-tender, about 1 hour and 30 minutes.

This recipe for Farmer's Cabbage was found on a slip of paper being used as a book mark in the vegetable section of an old cookbook. I thought it sounded great so here it is.

Preheat oven to 350 °F. Put 1 small cabbage through the food processor until coarsely chopped. Place in a well oiled or buttered baking dish. Season with salt and pepper. Add 2 cups medium white sauce and mix well. Cover with buttered bread crumbs and bake until browned all over, about 20-25 minutes.

Crockpot Grape Jelly Meatballs

All the rave now are meatballs with a grape jelly sauce over them. Having tried a few of them, I came up with my own recipe to make this new-fangled fad more palatable. I think you will find these meatballs have the perfect amount of sweet combined with a dab of tart.

I 1/2 c. chili sauce
I c. grape or currant jelly
I to 3 t. Dijon mustard
I lb. lean ground beef

I egg, lightly beaten
3 T. fine dry bread crumbs
1/4 t. salt
1/4 t. black pepper

Combine chili sauce, grape jelly, and mustard in crock pot and stir well. Cook covered on high while preparing meatballs to bake. Combine remaining meatball ingredients and mix thoroughly. Shape into 30 meatballs. Bake meatballs in a preheated 400°F oven for 15 to 20 minutes or until done; drain well. Add meatballs to sauce, stir to coat, cover, and cook on low for 4 to 6 hours.

Swedish Meatballs

Many recipes call for the addition of sour cream instead of heavy cream to this dish; either is great. Try mixing in 1/4 c. cranberry jelly into the sauce, incorporating well, before adding the meatballs. The flavor will have you digging in again and again. Serve over cooked fettuccine if you like.

2 slices fresh white bread
1/4 c. milk
3 T. butter or margarine, divided
1/2 c. finely chopped onion
Pinch plus 1 t. kosher salt
3/4 lb. ground chuck
3/4 lb. ground pork
2 large egg yolks
1/2 t. black pepper
1/4 t. ground allspice
Pinch nutmeg
1/4 c. flour
3 c. beef broth
1/4 c. heavy cream

Preheat oven to 200°F. Tear the bread into pieces and place in a small mixing bowl along with the milk. Set aside. In a 12-inch, straight sided sauté pan over medium heat, melt 1 T. of the butter. Add the onion and a pinch of salt and sweat until the onions are soft. Remove from the heat and set aside.

In the bowl, combine the bread and milk mixture, ground chuck, pork, egg yolks, 1 t. of kosher salt, black pepper, allspice, nutmeg, and onions. Mix thoroughly with your hands.

Using a scale, weigh meatballs into 1-ounce portions and place on a sheet pan. Using your hands, shape the meatballs into rounds.

Heat the remaining butter in the sauté pan over medium-low heat. Add the meatballs and sauté until golden brown on all sides, about 7 to 10 minutes. Remove the meatballs to an ovenproof dish using a slotted spoon and place in the warmed oven.

Once all of the meatballs are cooked, decrease the heat to low and add the flour to the pan or skillet. Whisk until lightly browned, approximately 1 to 2 minutes. Gradually add the beef stock and whisk until sauce begins to thicken. Add the cream and continue to cook until the gravy reaches the desired consistency. Remove the meatballs from the oven, cover with the gravy and serve.

True Italian Meatballs

There is no chef in the world, Iron Chefs included, that can make a better meatball than The Yankee Chef!

1 lb. ground beef
1/2 lb. ground veal
1/2 lb. ground pork
2 cloves garlic, minced
2 eggs
1 c. grated Romano cheese
1 1/2 T. parsley
Salt and black pepper to taste
2 c. stale Italian bread, crumbled
1 1/2 c. beef broth
1 c. olive oil

Combine beef, veal, and pork in a large bowl. Add garlic, eggs, cheese, parsley, salt, and pepper. Blend bread crumbs into meat mixture. Slowly add the beef broth 1/2 c. at a time. The mixture should be very moist but still hold its shape if rolled into meatballs. (I usually use about 1 1/4 c. of broth). Shape into meatballs.

Heat olive oil in a large skillet. Fry meatballs in batches. When the meatball is very brown and slightly crisp, but done on the inside, remove from heat and drain on a paper towel. (If your mixture is too wet, cover the meatballs while they are cooking so that they hold their shape better.)

You can also bake these meatballs in a 350°F oven for 20 minutes or until done.

Greek-Style Roasted Lamb

This dish is Greek, through and through. If you only tolerate lamb, this dish will convert you to a lamb lover, or at least a lover of this recipe. The lamb shines here but is not overpowering.

1/2 lb. ground sausage
1 onion, chopped
4 cloves garlic, minced
1 lb. fresh spinach,
  washed and stemmed
1 t. dried basil
1/4 lb. feta cheese
3-lb. boneless leg of lamb
Whole Kalamata olives (optional)
Oregano

Sauté sausage in a large frying pan. When nearly done, add onion and garlic and sauté until onion is limp but not browned; pour off excess grease. Add spinach and basil and cook until the spinach is limp. Add feta cheese and mix well. Pound meat slightly with a mallet to flatten. Place stuffing in the center of the meat, roll up, and tie securely. Roast meat uncovered at 325°F for 1 1/2 hours. Serve with olives dotting the platter and dust with oregano.

Alphonso olives are huge, dupe purple olives from Chile. They are brine-cured in red wine and are slightly bitter.

La Catalan olives are also brine-cured and marinated with curry, celery, and pepper. These Spanish olives have an assertive curry flavor.

Cerignola olives are enormous, blue-green or jet-black. From Southern Italy, they have a mild, sweet flavor but are difficult to pit.

Moroccan Dry or Salt-Cured olives are jet-black and wrinkled. Being moist, they have a woodsy, almost smoky flavor with a hint of cinnamon.

Bleu Cheese Stuffed Lamb Chops

The sweetness of the sugar, the saltiness of the soy, and the rustic flavor of the bleu cheese heightens these lamb chops so they are pleasantly favored by many who have never tried lamb before.

8 small lamb chops, 1" thick
1/2 small onion, chopped
1/2 c. soy sauce
3 T. brown sugar
3 T. lemon juice
2 cloves garlic, peeled
1/2 c. pine nuts
1/2 c. crumbled bleu cheese
Black pepper to taste

With a sharp knife, cut a horizontal slice in each chop, in a blender, puree onion, soy sauce, brown sugar, lemon juice and garlic until smooth. Pour into a large plastic food bag and add chops; seal securely. Marinate for up to 6 hours or overnight, occasionally rotating to evenly distribute marinade over entire chops.

Toss pine nuts in a small frying pan over medium heat, shaking pan often until golden, 3 to 5 minutes. Transfer nuts to a small bowl and stir in bleu cheese; season to taste with pepper. Remove chops and drain, reserving marinade. Using a spoon, stuff cheese filling into each pocket.

Arrange chops on outdoor grill or place in preheated 375°F oven in a shallow baking sheet. Cook chops, without turning, until done, frequently brushing marinade over tops, about 10 minutes for medium rare or longer. Cut to test for desired temperature.

Lamb with Green Beans

The first Yankee Chef always told my father that lamb's best friend isn't mint, it's green beans. I never really gave it much thought until I sampled this dish many years ago when the Second Yankee Chef made it for his diners. Now the third Yankee Chef realizes just how right he was. Confused yet?

    2 T. olive oil, divided
    2 lbs. boneless lamb, trimmed
        and cut into 1 1/2-inch cubes
    1 lg. onion, chopped
    1 t. salt
    1/2 t. black pepper
    3/4 t. allspice
    1/2 t. ground nutmeg
    1 can (28 oz.) whole tomatoes
        in juice
    2 lbs. fresh green beans, snipped
        and cut into 2-inch segments

In 5-quart stock pot or Dutch oven, heat 1 T. oil over medium-high heat until very hot. Add half the lamb and cook, stirring occasionally until browned, about 5 minutes. Using slotted spoon, transfer meat to bowl as it is browned. Repeat with remaining lamb. In same pot, heat remaining 1 T. oil. Add onion, salt, pepper, allspice, and nutmeg; cook, stirring frequently, 5 minutes. Add tomatoes with their juice; heat to boiling, breaking them up with side of spoon. Return lamb and any juice in bowl to pot; add green beans and heat to boiling. Reduce heat to low; cover and simmer until meat is fork-tender, about 1 hour.

Celebrity chef Hubert Keller has created the world's most expensive hamburger for his Fleur de Lys Restaurant at the Mandalay Bay Hotel and Casino in Las Vegas. Topping out at $5,000, the so-called FleurBurger 5000 is made with Kobe beef and topped with a slab of foie gras, truffle sauce, and black truffle shavings, all served on a brioche truffle bun. You get a complimentary bottle of Chateau Petrus 1995 from Bordeaux.

Slow-Cooked Orange Barbecue Pulled Pork Sandwich

As with other barbecued dishes, use whatever shredded cheese is to your liking. Add freshly made coleslaw and sweet pickles (even inside the sandwich) and top off with strawberry shortcake to make an ideal summer picnic. This is great served over white rice without the cheese as well.

    1 pork shoulder (3 lbs.)
    18 oz. your favorite BBQ sauce
    Juice from 2 oranges
    1/2 c. mayonnaise
    12 sandwich rolls, split and toasted
    Shredded Cheddar cheese

Place meat in slow cooker; top with BBQ sauce and orange juice. Cover with lid and cook on low for 8 to 10 hours. Remove meat from slow cooker; cut into small pieces or shred with fork. Return meat to slow cooker; stir until meat is evenly coated with the BBQ sauce mixture. Spread mayo onto rolls and fill with meat mixture. Top with shredded cheese and place in oven at 350°F for a few minutes, long enough for the cheese to melt.

BBQ Boston Butt Roasts (Pork Shoulder)

Boston butt is a cut of pork that comes from the upper part of the shoulder, from the front leg, and may contain the blade bone. This pork cut and the way it is prepared and served makes a distinctly American dish. Smoked or barbecued Boston butt is a southern tradition. As a mainstay of cuisine from the Deep South, particularly Alabama, Georgia, South Carolina, and North Carolina, it is often smoked and sold as a fundraiser on roadside stands by charities and local organizations.

Spicy Pork Medallions

So tender you can enjoy it without a knife. The red currant jelly can be substituted with apricot or even plum jelly if desired.

2 pork tenderloins (10 to 12 oz. each), trimmed
1 t. salt
1/4 t. black pepper
1/2 t. dried thyme
1/2 t. cinnamon
1/4 t. nutmeg
1/4 t. ground cloves
1 T. vegetable oil
1/2 c. red currant jelly
1 c. chicken broth

Cut each pork tenderloin into 4 pieces on the bias. With a meat mallet or rolling pin, pound each piece of pork to 1/2-inch thickness between waxed paper or plastic wrap.

In medium bowl, combine salt, pepper, thyme, cinnamon, nutmeg, and cloves. Add pork medallions to spice mixture and toss to coat. In large skillet, heat oil over medium-high heat until very hot. Add pork medallions; cook 5 minutes per side or until they are no longer pink inside. Transfer pork to warm platter, into drippings add jelly and stir until melted; stir in chicken broth and heat to boiling. Spoon sauce over pork and serve.

Chinese Spiced Pork

As you may have noticed throughout this cookbook, I have added many other recipes that have zero to do with New England. I have chosen, what I think, are the best of the best recipes. I'm sure you'll agree this amazing dish is in a class all its own.

3 T. soy sauce, divided
2 T. cornstarch
2 T. dry sherry
1 t. minced, fresh ginger
1/2 t. Chinese five-spice powder
Pinch pepper
2 lbs. boneless lean pork, cut into large pieces
Vegetable oil for frying
1/4 c. water
1 t. instant chicken bouillon granules

Combine 2 T. of the soy sauce, cornstarch, sherry, ginger, five-spice powder and pepper in large bowl. Add pork, one piece at a time, turning to coat well. Refrigerate 1 hour, stirring occasionally.

Pour 1 1/2 inches of oil in large skillet and heat until it reaches 350°F. Cook half the pork until brown and cooked through, about 4 minutes; remove to drain and repeat with remainder of pork.

In small saucepan combine water, bouillon granules, and remaining 1 T. soy sauce and bring to a boil. Pour mixture over cooked pork. Serve.

Sweet and Sour Pork

One colonist, William Byrd (1539–1623), commented that people ate so much pork, they began to show pig tendencies, as shown by this entry in his journal: "The truth of it is, these people live so much upon the swine's flesh that it don't only incline them to the yaws and consequently to the downfall of their noses, but makes them likewise extremely hoggish in their temper, and many of them seem to grunt rather than speak in their ordinary conversation."

The combination of sweet and sour, salty and sweet, and crunchy and moist for some reason entices us. This dish is sure to lure you in like, well, pig to slop.

1/4 c. soy sauce
1 1/2 T. dry sherry
2 t. sugar
1 egg yolk
2 lbs. boneless pork, cubed
10 T. cornstarch, divided
3 c. plus 3 T. vegetable oil
1 can (20 oz.) pineapple chunks in syrup
1/4 c. white vinegar
3 T. tomato sauce
1 c. water
1 onion, thinly sliced
8 green onions, cut into 1-inch segments
1 red bell pepper, chopped
4 oz. fresh mushrooms, quartered
2 stalks celery, sliced
1 medium cucumber, seeded and sliced 1/4 inch wide

For marinade, combine soy sauce, sherry, sugar, and egg yolk in large bowl. Add pork; mix to coat well. Cover and refrigerate at least 1 hour, stirring occasionally.

Drain pork, reserving marinade. Place 8 T. of the cornstarch into large bowl. Add pork pieces; toss to coat well. Heat 3 c. of the oil in wok or large skillet over high heat. Add half of the pork pieces until brown, about 5 minutes. Drain on paper towels. Repeat with remaining pork.

Drain pineapple, reserving syrup. Combine the syrup, reserved soy sauce marinade, vinegar, and tomato sauce in small bowl. Blend remaining 2 T. cornstarch and the water in another small bowl. Heat remaining 3 T. oil in wok over high heat. Add all vegetables and stir-fry 3 minutes. Add pineapple syrup mixture and cornstarch mixture; cook and stir until sauce boils and thickens. Add pork and pineapple; stir-fry until heated through.

Blueberry-Rhubarb Pork Chops

4 pork chops (about 5 oz each)
Nonstick cooking spray
2 c. chopped rhubarb
2 c. blueberries
2 T. honey
2 T. brown sugar
1/8 t. cinnamon
1/4 c. flour
Salt and pepper to taste

Dredge chops in flour, salt, and pepper to coat. Spray skillet with cooking spray, and brown the pork chops on each side, without cooking through. Mix rhubarb, berries, honey, brown sugar, and cinnamon in a bowl and add to chops in skillet. Cook at medium-low heat for 20 to 30 minutes, covered.

By gently simmering blueberries in milk during the colonial period of New England, our forefathers made gray paint for their fences while the Shakers of "Yankee-land" made blue paint for their homes by mixing blueberries, indigo, and sage blossoms with milk. My word, I would be going around licking every Shaker house and fence for miles around if I had lived then.

Honey Glazed Spareribs

Spareribs are the least expensive cut of beef or pork ribs so grab a few racks and invite friends and family over. If you've never had Chinese five-spice powder, you and your friends are in for a treat.

1 side of pork spareribs (2 lbs.)
1/4 c. plus 1 T. soy sauce
4 T. hoisin sauce
3 T. dry sherry, divided
1 T. sugar
1/2 t. dry ginger
2 cloves garlic, minced
1/4 t. Chinese five-spice powder
3 T. honey
1 T. cider vinegar

Cut between bones to make single ribs. Place ribs in heavy bag for the marinade. Combine 1/4 c. of the soy sauce, the hoisin sauce, 2 T. of the sherry, sugar, ginger, garlic, and five-spice powder in small bowl; mix well. Pour marinade over ribs. Seal bag tightly and place in large bowl. Refrigerate 8 hours or overnight, turning bag occasionally.

Foil-line a large baking pan. Place rack in pan and place ribs on rack; reserve marinade. Bake in preheated 350°F oven for 30 minutes. Turn ribs over, brush with marinade and bake until ribs are tender when pierced with a fork, about 40 minutes longer.

For the glaze: Combine honey, vinegar, and remaining sherry in small bowl; mix well. Brush 1/2 of the mixture over ribs; place under broiler 4 to 6 inches from heat source and broil until ribs are glazed, 2 to 3 minutes. Turn ribs over, brush with remaining honey mixture and broil until glazed.

Although honey has more calories than table sugar (65 calories per tablespoon vs. 46) it has a range of flavors unlike its counterpart. The tastes of alfalfa, clover, tupelo, and wild flower come through, just to name a few. The flavor depends on the source of the nectar. On the flip side of pleasurable experiences though, honey obtained by certain types of rhododendrons, especially in the Pacific Northwest and Northeast, can cause sudden illness mimicking a heart attack.

Here are four rubs for pork that I think you might find tasty. Mix ingredients well and simply rub onto roasts, chops, or steaks and then grill or bake as usual.

Cajun Rub
1/4 c. coarse salt
2 T. onion powder
2 T. oregano
1 T. black pepper
3 t. cayenne pepper
2 T. garlic powder
2 T. dried thyme
2 T. paprika
1 T. white pepper.

Nicoise Rub
1/2 c. dried parsley
3 T. dried coriander
3 t. cracked black peppercorns
2 T. garlic powder
2 t. coarse salt
1 1/2 T. red pepper flakes

Greek Rub
1/4 c. coarse salt
1/4 c. dried oregano
2 T. olive oil
1/4 c. cracked black peppercorns
2 T. dried dill.

Memphis Rub
1/4 c. paprika
1 1/2 T. sugar
1 1/2 t. celery salt
1 1/2 t. garlic powder
1 T. brown sugar
2 t. coarse salt
1 t. black pepper
1 1/2 t. dry mustard
1 1/2 t. onion powder

Tourtiere (French Canadian Pork Pie)

We overlook our neighbor's contribution to world cuisine much too often. Here is, I believe, the best tasting pork pie you can find anywhere. Why eat it just for dinner? Heated for breakfast, this dish is a great way to start a cold winter's day.

    I onion, minced
    I clove garlic, minced
    2 T. butter or margarine
    I 1/2 lb. ground pork
    1/2 t. ground cloves
    1/2 t. cinnamon
    1/2 t. ground savory
    3/4 c. water
    Salt and pepper to taste
    Double Flaky Pie Crusts, unbaked,
        see recipe or buy prepared
    I egg mixed with 2 T. milk

Cook the onion and garlic in butter until wilted. Add the pork and continue cooking over medium-high heat, breaking up the meat and stirring frequently. Add the cloves, cinnamon, savory, water, salt, and pepper to taste. Continue cooking, stirring occasionally, about 30 minutes. Place the filling in the refrigerator and chill thoroughly.

Preheat the oven to 350°F. Line a pie pan with one crust and spoon in the filling. Cover with the remaining pastry, pressing to seal the edges. Prick the top to allow steam to escape. Brush with the beaten egg/milk mixture. Place in the oven and bake for 40 to 45 minutes or until bubbling and browned.

Yankee Pork Roast

The jelly holds the corn chips on so that each bite will have that crunch along with a taste of spicy glaze.

    I boneless rolled pork loin roast
        (4 to 5 lbs.)
    1/2 t. salt
    1/2 t. garlic salt
    I t. chili powder
    3/4 c. apple jelly
    3/4 c. ketchup
    I T. vinegar
    I t. chili powder
    2 c. crushed corn chips
    Water

Place pork, fat side up, on rack in shallow roasting pan. Combine the salt, garlic salt, and 1 t. chili powder; rub into roast. Roast, uncovered, at 325°F for about 2 1/2 to 3 hours or until internal temperature reaches 165°F.

In small saucepan, combine jelly, ketchup, vinegar, and 1 t. chili powder. Bring to boiling over medium-high heat. Reduce heat to low and simmer, uncovered, for 2 minutes. Brush roast with glaze. Sprinkle top with corn chips. Continue roasting until thermometer registers 170°F, about 10 to 15 minutes longer. Meanwhile, measure pan drippings, including any corn chips. Add water to drippings to make 1 cup. Heat to boiling and pass the sauce with the meat.

Pork Loin with Apple Butter

Large copper kettles of apple butter were made in centuries past, each child taking a turn at stirring this great pot. We don't eat nearly the amount our ancestors did and maybe we should. It goes perfectly with the pork here.

    I boneless pork loin (5 to 6 lb.),
        rolled and tied
    3/4 c. apple butter
    3 T. peanut butter
    1/2 t. grated orange rind
    1/2 t. grated lemon rind
    3 T. orange juice

Heat oven to 350°F. Place pork in roasting pan and bake until thermometer registers 150°F, about 2 1/2 hours. Gradually stir apple butter into peanut butter; add orange peel and lemon peel and combine. Add orange juice a tablespoon at a time so it is not too thick. Brush pork with marinade and continue cooking pork until the internal temperature reaches 170°F, about a half hour longer; continue brushing with marinade a couple more times during this cooking.

Ginger Pork Stir-Fry

Here is a little Asian feast for the eyes, tongue, belly, and whatever other senses might perk up from the aroma of this stir-fry. Add some water chestnuts or bamboo shoots for more crunch.

I pork tenderloin (12 oz.)
I T. dried ginger (or 3 T. peeled, grated fresh ginger)
I c. chicken broth
3 T. teriyaki sauce
3 t. cornstarch
2 t. vegetable oil
8 oz. snow peas, strings removed
I medium summer squash, cut in half lengthwise, sliced thinly
3 green onions, cut into 3-inch segments

In medium bowl, toss pork and ginger, coating evenly. In bowl, stir together broth, teriyaki sauce, and cornstarch. In nonstick 12-inch skillet, heat 1 t. oil over medium-high heat until very hot. Add snow peas, summer squash, and green onions and cook, stirring frequently, until lightly browned and tender-crisp, about 5 minutes. Transfer to bowl.

In same skillet, heat remaining 1 t. oil, add pork mixture and cook, stirring quickly and constantly, until pork just loses its pink color throughout. Transfer pork to bowl with vegetables. Stir cornstarch mixture; add to skillet and heat to boiling, stirring constantly. Boil 2 minutes until sauce thickens. Stir in pork and vegetables and any juice in bowl; heat through.

Here is a recipe that dates back many generations. My ancestor, Josiah Bailey of Topsfield, Maine, and his wife Charlotte ate this dish many times according to family notes.

Salt Pork and Milk Gravy

Cube and fry until crisp a pound of salt pork. Remove from fat but leave fat in pan. Add flour or cornmeal and blend until smooth. Add a cupful of milk. Cut up salt pork and add to sauce. Serve over bakers [baked potatoes].

Baked Ham with Pink Champagne

This recipe contains all the elements of a holiday centerpiece. You will love the addition of the subtle taste of champagne married with the fruits of the orchard.

14 to 16 lb. smoked, pre-cooked ham
I bottle pink champagne
4 T. orange juice
2 T. pineapple juice
2 T. honey
1/2 c. brown sugar
24 whole cloves
I lg. can pineapple rings
Maraschino cherries
2 T. peach brandy

Score fat on top of ham in a diamond pattern, then marinate with champagne overnight in refrigerator. Next day, remove ham from refrigerator and let stand at room temperature for half an hour. Place on platter and reserve champagne. Meanwhile, mix orange and pineapple juice with honey and brown sugar. Rub this liquid all over ham and decorate with cloves, sticking them at the cross sections of your pattern.

Place ham on rack in roasting pan and add enough champagne to cover bottom (about 1 cup). Place in cold oven and turn heat to 325°F. Bake for 1 hour. Pour another cup of champagne over ham, adding more if bottom of pan is not covered. Bake 15 minutes and baste with pan drippings and champagne. Return to oven and continue cooking for 30 minutes. Now place pineapple rings over ham and put a cherry in center of each. Baste well with pan drippings and additional champagne and cook for 15 minutes. Just before serving, heat brandy and dribble it over all, flame if desired.

Maple Orange Glazed Ham

You can also substitute Maple Orange with Maple-Apricot flavored syrup. Simply combine 3/4 c. maple syrup with 1/4 c. apricot preserves and 1 T. butter or margarine. Heat through and glaze.

1 precooked ham (5 lb.)
1 t. whole cloves
1/4 c. Dijon-style mustard
1/2 c. brown sugar
1/2 c. real maple syrup
1 1/2 c. chicken broth
Juice from 2 large oranges
1/2 t. dried thyme, crushed
1 t. grated orange rind
1/4 t. salt

Preheat oven to 325°F. Trim all fat and skin from ham. Score ham to a diamond pattern with a sharp knife. Insert a whole clove into each intersection of lines, layer mustard over the top and sides of the ham; sprinkle with brown sugar. Pour the maple syrup and chicken broth into a 12 × 17-inch roasting pan. Add the ham. Bake, basting every 30 minutes, for 1 1/2 hours. Add orange juice and thyme to the pan. Bake for 30 more minutes and remove.

Prepare the sauce. Strain the pan juices and skim the fat off the top. Add the orange zest and salt; boil for about 10 minutes on the stove top on medium-high heat. Serve hot, poured over slices of ham.

Honey of a Ham Steak

When you take the ham from the oven, you will see the honey magic. Glistening with these simple ingredients, how can you go wrong?

3 T. prepared mustard
3 T. honey
2 T. butter or margarine
1 fully-cooked center-cut ham steak, 1/2-inch thick

In large skillet, over medium heat, warm mustard, honey, and margarine, stirring until blended. Add ham steak; cook 5 minutes per side or until heated through. Remove ham to warm medium platter; pour pan juices over ham and serve.

World's Most Expensive Ham

A leg of Iberico ham, which weighed in at only 15 lbs. costs $2,947 and was produced by pig farmer and ham expert Manuel Maldonado. The pig hailed from Extremadura, Spain, where pampered pigs roam free while gorging themselves on the fruits of the Encina, or Holm Oak. After the pigs are slaughtered, the meat is salted and cured for three years before going on sale in a handmade wooden box in an apron made by one of Spain's most exclusive tailors.

Iberico ham hanging from shop rafters in Spain

Brats and Beans
with Mustard Biscuits

Bratwurst literally means "frying sausage" in German. It is zestfully seasoned with coriander, ginger, mustard, sage, and thyme. These make a great picnic food when cooked and cooled before hand, a perfect meat to serve with potato salad.

1/2 c. chopped onion
1/4 c. water
1 clove garlic, minced
1 can (15 oz.) navy beans
1 can (8 1/2 oz.) red kidney beans, drained
3/4 c. ketchup
1/2 c. honey or maple syrup
1 T. cider vinegar
1/4 t. black pepper
12 oz. fully cooked bratwurst, sliced
2 large apples, cored and chopped

Prepare mustard biscuits first (ingredients below). Preheat oven to 400°F. Combine flour, baking powder, sugar, and cream of tartar. Cut in shortening or butter until mixture resembles coarse crumbs. Add milk and mustard and stir just until dough clings together. Drop dough from a tablespoon into 8 mounds on a greased baking sheet. Bake for 10 to 12 minutes or until browned.

In a saucepan, combine onion, water, and garlic. Bring to boiling; reduce heat. Cover and simmer 5 minutes or until tender. Stir in navy beans, kidney beans, ketchup, honey or syrup, vinegar, and pepper. Stir in bratwurst and bring to a boil; reduce heat. Cover and simmer for 5 minutes. Uncover and simmer an additional 5 minutes or to desired consistency. Stir in apple. Cover and cook 2 minutes longer or until apple is tender. Top with mustard biscuits and serve. Try these Mustard Biscuits with any ham dish as well as Boston Baked Beans for a twist on your tongue!

Mustard Biscuits:
3/4 c. flour
1 t. baking powder
1 t. sugar
1/4 t. cream of tartar
1/4 c. shortening or butter
1/3 c. milk
1 T. prepared mustard

Sausage and Pepper Grill

Ever wander through the fair grounds and wish you could replicate that same smell? Here it is folks, and far better than the greasy mess (although decadently greasy) you pay for at the fair.

1/2 c. balsamic vinegar
2 t. brown sugar
1/2 t. salt
1/4 t. black pepper
2 medium red bell pepper, cut in half, seeded and cut into strips
2 medium green bell peppers, cut in half, seeded and cut into strips
1 lg. red onion, cut into 6 wedges
1 T. olive oil
1 lb. hot Italian sausage links
1 lb. sweet Italian sausage links

In cup, mix vinegar, brown sugar, salt, and pepper. In large bowl, toss red and green pepper and onions with olive oil to coat.

In large skillet, place sausages in pan first and cover with oiled vegetables. Cook, covered, over medium heat until sausages are done, about 25 to 30 minutes. Remove the lid and add vinegar mixture over sausage and peppers and toss to coat, cooking an additional 5 minutes. Remove from heat and serve.

Polish Reuben Casserole

As much as I hate using canned soup mixes, I am adding them here for the ease of preparation for those of you on the run. It really is a remarkably Reuben-tasting casserole.

2 cans (11 oz. each) cream of mushroom soup, condensed
1 1/2 c. milk
1/2 c. chopped onion
2 T. prepared mustard
2 lbs. sauerkraut, rinsed and drained
8 oz. uncooked rotini noodles
2 lbs. Polish sausage, sliced
3 c. shredded Swiss cheese
1 c. bread crumbs
4 T. melted butter or margarine

Preheat oven to 350°F. Combine soup, milk, onion, and mustard in medium bowl; blend well. Spread sauerkraut in greased 12 × 9-inch pan. Top with uncooked noodles. Spoon soup mixture evenly over top. Top with sausage and cheese. Combine crumbs and butter in small bowl; sprinkle over top. Cover pan tightly with foil and bake for 1 hour or until noodles are tender.

CHAPTER 11

Pasta, Rice, Grains, and Legumes

Cream Sauce or Béchamel

3 T. butter or margarine
3 T. flour
2 c. milk
Salt and white pepper

Over low heat in medium sized saucepan, melt butter. Add flour and whisk until smooth. Add milk and continue cooking, raising the heat to medium; stirring almost constantly to prevent lumps and scorching on bottom of pan. When thickened, about 10 to 12 minutes, remove from heat. Season to taste.

Cheese Sauce

1 c. shredded yellow
  Cheddar cheese
2 c. Cream Sauce

After cream sauce has thickened, add cheese and continue stirring until cheese has melted. Of course, use this with Baked Macaroni and Cheese.

A wide variety of cheeses may be used, such as:
1 cup cubed American cheese
1 c. grated Gruyere cheese

Brown Sauce

3 T. butter or margarine
3 T. flour
1 1/2 c. beef stock or broth
1/2 c. tomato puree
Salt and pepper to taste

Melt butter over low heat in medium saucepan until melted. Add flour and whisk until smooth. Raise heat to medium and add beef broth and whisk until smooth. Continue cooking and whisking frequently until thickened and heated throughout. Remove from heat and add tomato puree; blend well. When you fill manicotti or ziti, use this sauce for a topping, a great treat. Makes 2 cups

Mushroom Sauce

1/4 lb. sliced mushrooms
2 T. butter or margarine
2 c. Brown Sauce

In large skillet over medium heat, melt butter. Add mushrooms and cook until soft, stirring frequently, about 8 to 10 minutes. Remove from heat and add brown sauce; mix well. Goes great with linguine, fettuccine, and gnocchi.

Burgundy Sauce

2 c. Brown Sauce
1/2 c. Burgundy wine
1 t. dried coffee

Add all together in medium saucepan and blend well. Great accompaniment for spaghetti, stuffed manicotti, and ravioli.

Tomato Sauce

2 c. canned tomatoes
2 T. olive oil
1/2 small onion, minced
1 clove garlic, minced
1/2 small green pepper, minced
1 t. sugar
1 t. dried basil
1 t. dried oregano
1 c. tomato puree
3 T. tomato paste

In large bowl, break up canned tomatoes with a potato masher, keeping liquid. In 1 qt. saucepan, over medium heat, combine oil, onions, garlic, and green pepper. Sauté until tender; drain. Reduce heat to low and add remainder of ingredients, whisk well to blend, and continue to simmer for 1 hour. Makes 2 cups

Meat Sauce

2 c. Tomato Sauce
1/4 lb. ground beef

Brown ground beef, drain excess fat and add to one serving of Tomato Sauce.

A good rule of thumb when determining which pasta goes with which sauce: Remember that thin or smooth noodles require a light, smooth sauce that won't overpower or weigh down the pasta. Sturdy shapes like rotini can handle chunkier sauces.

American Chop Suey

American Chop Suey (also sometimes known as American Goulash, Macaroni Goulash, or Macaroni and Beef) is an American pasta dish. The name American Chop Suey is most prevalent in New England. Commercial preparations of this dish are commonly marketed as Macaroni and Beef. Classic American Chop Suey consists of elbow macaroni and bits of cooked ground beef with sautéed onions and green peppers in a thick tomato-based sauce. Though this decidedly American comfort food is clearly influenced by Italian-American cuisine, it is known as a "chop suey" because it is a sometimes-haphazard hodgepodge of meat and vegetables. It is also known as "Johnny Marzetti" in the Ohio valley.

The recipe is quite adaptable to taste and available ingredients. Elbow macaroni can be substituted with any pasta of similar size, such as ziti, conchiglie, or rotelle. The onions or green peppers may be omitted, or replaced with other vegetables or mushrooms. While some recipes call for a smooth prepared tomato sauce, some chefs (the first and second Yankee Chefs to name two) prefer to add crushed or diced tomatoes along with tomato paste for a chunkier, more intensely flavored dish. Black pepper, Italian herbs, and Worcestershire sauce are sometimes used in preparation.

1 box (16-oz.) elbow macaroni, cooked according to directions on box
2 T. olive oil
1 c. chopped celery
2 green bell peppers, small dice
2 medium sweet onions, small dice
1 to 2 garlic cloves, minced (depending on your taste for garlic)
1 1/2 lbs ground beef
2 T. sugar
1 t. dried basil
1 t. dried oregano
Salt and pepper, to taste
3 cans (14 1/2 oz. ea.) stewed tomatoes in juice

In a very large skillet, heat the olive oil. Add the chopped celery and cook a few minutes. Add the cut-up green bell pepper, and cook a few more minutes. Add the onion and continue to cook until celery, peppers, and onions are tender, about 5 minutes. Add the minced garlic and mix into the vegetables. Then add the ground beef, breaking up with a wooden spoon. Continue to cook until the ground beef is browned, about another 5 minutes, mixing the beef up with the vegetables. Sprinkle the mixture with the sugar, basil, oregano, and parsley and mix. Add the stewed tomatoes, juices and all. Add salt and pepper, to taste. Let simmer, covered, stirring occasionally.

Meanwhile, cook the elbow macaroni according to the directions on box in a very large saucepan. But, don't overcook. The macaroni should be *al dente*, because it will continue to cook a little when added to the beef/vegetable mixture. Drain pasta and put back into the large saucepan in which it was cooked.

Very carefully, add the beef and vegetable mixture, juices and all, to the drained pasta in the large saucepan. Mix well and keep heated, covered, stirring occasionally, on a very low heat.

When ready to serve, just put the pot of "American Chop Suey" along with bowls in the middle of the table, so everyone can help themselves. Serve with a basket of good Italian bread and butter.

Pasta and Chicken with Orange-Basil Sauce

This is my take on the classic and expensive Chicken a l'Orange. So sweet and tangy, you can make this dish in a breeze.

3/4 c. frozen orange juice
   concentrate, thawed
1/2 c. chicken broth
4 t. cornstarch
6 oz. dried rotini
1 pkg. (16 oz.) frozen vegetable
   blend (zucchini, carrots,
   cauliflower or any
   3-vegetable blend)
2 c. cubed, cooked chicken
1/4 c. snipped fresh basil

For sauce, in a small saucepan combine thawed concentrate chicken broth and cornstarch. Cook and stir over medium-high heat until thickened and bubbly; cook and stir 2 minutes more.

In a large saucepan, cook pasta in boiling water for 5 minutes. Add frozen vegetables and return to boiling. Cook, uncovered, 5 minutes more or until pasta and vegetables are tender. Drain; return to saucepan. Add sauce, chicken, basil, and pinch of pepper. Heat and toss until hot.

Taco-Stuffed Pasta Shells

A little "South of the Border" mixed with the land of Nero makes this meal delightfully robust. Comer Bien and Mangiare Bene!

1 1/2 lb. ground beef
1 pkg. (3 oz.) cream cheese,
   cubed and softened
1 t. salt
1 1/2 t. chili powder
18 cooked, cooled jumbo shells
2 T. melted butter or margarine
1 c. taco sauce
1 1/2 c. shredded Cheddar cheese
1 c. Pepper Jack cheese
2 c. crushed tortilla chips
1 c. sour cream
3 green onions, chopped

Preheat oven to 350°F. Cook beef in large skillet over medium-high heat until brown, stirring to separate meat; drain fat. Reduce heat to medium-low. Add cream cheese, salt, and chili powder; simmer 5 minutes. Toss shells with butter; fill with beef mixture. Arrange shells in buttered 13 × 9-inch pan. Pour taco sauce over each shell. Cover with foil and bake for 15 minutes.

Uncover; top with Cheddar cheese, Pepper Jack cheese, and chips. Bake 15 minutes more or until bubbly. Top with sour cream and onions.

During the eighteenth century, young English aristocrats returning home from a tour of Italy became known as "macaronis" for their love of foreign ladies and the land. During the mid-1700s, towering hairstyles of the wealthy were called "macaroni," while "Dandy" was the name of the person wearing it. The word "doodle" comes from the German word meaning "simpleton," which was the same definition of "noodle" at the time. So in summation, the song "Yankee Doodle" was used by the British to ridicule the American colonists. But we turned it around and became proud of our moniker.

Spaghetti Rolls

We've always enjoyed meat on top of the pasta, now let's try it in the pasta. A beautiful dish with the taste that is equally satisfying.

1 1/2 lb. ground beef
1/4 c. minced onion
1 t. salt
1/2 t. pepper
1 1/2 c. shredded mozzarella cheese
2 c. tomato sauce
1 pkg. (8 oz.) uncooked manicotti shells, cooked and cooled

Preheat oven to medium-high (350°F). Cook beef and onion in large skillet over heat until brown, stirring to separate meat; drain fat. Stir in salt and pepper. Stir in 1 c. of the tomato sauce; cool and set aside. Reserve 1/2 c. of the ground beef mixture. Combine remaining beef mixture with cheese in large bowl. Stuff into manicotti. Arrange in greased 13 × 9-inch baking pan. Combine remaining tomato sauce with reserved beef mixture in small bowl; blend well. Pour over manicotti and cover with foil. Bake for 20 to 30 minutes or until hot.

Bailey Family Lasagna

This is the recipe my dad used in all his restaurants. Margaret Chase Smith ordered this delicious lasagna about once a month at the Oak Pond Restaurant in Canaan, Maine.

1/2 lb. ground beef
1/2 lb. sweet Italian sausage, diced
1/2 c. chopped onion
2 cloves garlic, minced
3 c. tomato sauce, see index for recipe
1 can (4 oz.) sliced mushrooms, drained
3 eggs
1 lb. cottage cheese
1 c. grated Parmesan cheese
1/2 t. salt
1/2 t. pepper
8 oz. uncooked lasagna noodles, cooked and cooled
3 c. shredded Cheddar cheese
3 c. shredded mozzarella cheese

Preheat oven to 350°F. Cook meats, onions, and garlic in large skillet over medium-high heat until meat is brown, stirring to separate meat; drain fat. Add tomato sauce and reduce heat to low. Cover; simmer 15 minutes, stirring often. Stir in mushrooms; set aside.

Beat eggs in large bowl; add cottage cheese, 1/2 c. Parmesan cheese, salt, and pepper. Mix well. Place 1/2 the noodles in bottom of greased 13 × 9-inch pan. Spread 1/2 of the meat mixture and 1/2 of the Cheddar and mozzarella cheese. Repeat layers. Sprinkle with remaining Parmesan cheese. Bake 40 to 45 minutes or until bubbly. Remove from oven and let stand for 15 minutes before cutting and serving.

It's Clabberin' Time

Colonists were told that rennet should be high on their list of foodstuffs to bring to the New World during the early 1600s. Rennet is a cheese coagulant used to coagulate milk into cheese—it is very tedious to make.

First a calf's stomach was pickled in brine, then salted, dried, and cut into small pieces, which were kept tightly closed in a container.

Rennet was for producing curds in milk. It was added to a large quantity of milk to produce a sour liquid called clabber. After several hours, the curds separated from the water whey and were then tied in a cloth and allowed to drain. The curds were eaten with cream as a breakfast dish.

Vegetarian Lasagna

A rich, cheesy lasagna loaded with vegetables. You won't even miss the meat.

1 can (14 1/2 oz.) diced tomatoes, reserving liquid
2 c. tomato sauce (see page 196 for recipe)
1 lg. onion, chopped
1 1/2 t. minced garlic
2 T. olive oil
2 small zucchinis, chopped
8 oz. mushrooms, sliced
1 lg. carrot, chopped
1 yellow bell pepper, chopped
2 c. shredded mozzarella cheese
2 c. cottage cheese
1 c. grated Parmesan cheese
8 oz. uncooked lasagna noodles, cooked and cooled

Preheat oven to 350°F. In large saucepan, cook and stir onion and garlic in oil over medium-high heat until onion is translucent. Add zucchini, mushrooms, carrot, and yellow pepper. Cook and stir until vegetables are tender, about 15 minutes. Stir tomato sauce into vegetable and mix well. Simmer for 5 minutes longer. Combine mozzarella, cottage, and Parmesan cheese in large bowl; mix well.

Spoon about 1 c. sauce into the bottom of a 12 × 9-inch pan. Place a layer of noodles over sauce, then half of the cheese mixture and half of the remaining sauce. Repeat layers of noodles, cheese mixture, and sauce. Bake for 30 to 45 minutes or until it bubbles. Let stand 15 minutes before serving.

Spinach Pesto

The combination of spinach and basil make this sauce bright green to the sight and well balanced to the tongue. Add some chopped chicken or shaved prosciutto.

1 bunch fresh spinach,
    rinsed and chopped
1 c. Parmesan cheese
1/2 c. chopped walnuts
6 cloves garlic, minced
1 T. dried tarragon, crushed
1 t. dried basil, crushed
1 t. salt
1/2 t. pepper
1/4 t. celery seed
1 c. olive oil
Your favorite pasta, cooked

Place all ingredients, except oil and pasta, in food processor or blender. Cover and puree until smooth. With contents still pureeing, remove cover and add oil in a thin stream. Add salt and pepper to taste. Pour over hot pasta and toss to serve.

Salmon Fettuccine and Cabbage

The fennel seeds add such flavor to this dish. It really does link the salmon with the cabbage very well.

    1 pkg. (9 oz.) dried
       fettuccine noodles
    1/4 c. plus 2 T. rice vinegar
    2 T. vegetable oil
    1/2 small head of cabbage, shredded
    1/2 t. fennel seeds
    Salt and pepper to taste
    1 can (15 1/2 oz.) salmon,
       drained and flaked

Cook fettuccine according to package directions (about 5 minutes); drain. Heat vinegar and oil in large skillet over medium-high heat. Add cabbage; cook 3 minutes or to crisp tender. Stir in fennel seeds, salt, and pepper to taste and add fettuccine; toss lightly to coat. Add salmon and lightly toss.

Fennel seeds

Fettuccine Carbonara

Add some cooked broccoli, cooked carrots, peas or any cooked vegetable in this dish for a blend of sweet and salty.

    4 oz. pancetta (Italian bacon) diced
    3 cloves garlic, peeled and cut in half
    1/4 c. dry white wine
    1/3 c., heavy cream
    1/2 lb. dried fettuccine
    1 egg plus 1 egg yolk
    1 c. grated Parmesan cheese
    1/8 t. white pepper

Cook and stir pancetta and garlic in large skillet over medium-low heat until pancetta is light brown, about 4 minutes. Discard garlic and all but 2 T. of the drippings. Add wine to skillet; cook over medium heat until wine is almost completely evaporated, about 4 minutes. Stir in cream; cook and stir 3 minutes. Remove from heat.

Cook fettuccine in large saucepan of boiling water just until tender, 6 to 8 minutes; drain well and return to dry saucepan. Whisk egg and egg yolk in small bowl; whisk in 1/3 c. of the cheese and pepper. Pour bacon-cream mixture over fettuccine in saucepan; toss to coat. Heat over medium-low heat just until hot. Stir in egg-cheese mixture and toss to coat evenly. Remove from heat and serve immediately sprinkled with remaining cheese.

Fettuccine All' Alfredo

The key to this dish is not to rinse the pasta. The sauce will stick to the pasta much better and every bite will have the great taste of Parmesan cheese. Very easy to make and quick to boot.

2 T. butter or margarine
1 c. heavy cream
1/2 c. grated Parmesan cheese
1/4 t. salt
1/4 t. black pepper
12 oz. fettuccine noodles, cooked, drained, and cooled

In medium-sized saucepan, place the butter on medium-high heat. When half melted, add cream, Parmesan cheese, salt, and pepper. Bring to a boil, whisking constantly until butter is completely melted. Add cooked noodles and stir constantly over heat until all is hot, thickened, and combined well, about 2 to 3 minutes. Remove from heat and serve immediately.

Down Home Macaroni and Cheese

Now this is how Yankees like their Mac and Cheese, but by all means use other cheeses or a combination, such as fontina, havarti, American just to name a few out of hundreds.

3 T. butter or margarine
3 T. flour
2 c. milk
12 oz. dried elbow macaroni
3 c. (12 oz.) shredded Cheddar cheese*

1 1/2 t. Dijon mustard
1 t. salt
1/4 t. black pepper
1 c. bread crumbs tossed with 2 T. melted butter or margarine (optional)

Preheat oven to 350°F. Melt 3 T. butter over medium heat; add flour and stir until smooth. Add milk and whisk until smooth. Reduce heat to medium-low; add cheese, mustard, salt, and pepper. Simmer 5 minutes, stirring frequently. Meanwhile, cook macaroni according to package directions. Drain and place in large bowl.

Remove cheese sauce from heat and pour over warm macaroni. Stir to combine well. Pour into large baking or casserole dish and top with buttered bread crumbs. Bake until crumbs have browned or bake without the breadcrumbs.

Try using a combination of the following cheeses for a livelier dish:

1 cup shredded Cheddar, 1 c. shredded Fontina, and 1 c. grated Parmesan cheese
2 c. shredded Cheddar with 1 c. Monterey Jack cheese

Rice Pilaf

When cooking rice, remember not to stir rice unless you are using chopsticks to eat it with. Stirring releases the starch, thereby making rice gummy and sticky which is fine when trying to pick up mouthfuls with chopsticks.

1 small onion, minced
1 T. butter or margarine
2 c. basmati or long-grain rice
4 c. chicken broth
1/4 t. pepper

In medium sized saucepan over medium-high heat, sauté onions in butter until translucent. Combine remaining ingredients, stir to combine, cover, and lower heat to low. Simmer 20 to 25 minutes or until rice is tender; do not stir! Remove from heat and blend with long-handled spoon.

Creole Frittata

Creole Frittata

1/3 c. uncooked long-grain
   white rice
2/3 c. water
6 eggs
1/4 c. milk
1 t. dried basil
1/2 t. salt
1/2 t. hot pepper sauce
1 T. vegetable oil
1/2 c. chopped onion
1/2 c. chopped green bell pepper
1/4 c. chopped celery
1 garlic clove, minced
1 medium tomato, chopped
1/2 c. shredded mozzarella cheese

Cook rice in water as directed on package. Meanwhile, in medium bowl, combine eggs, milk, basil, salt, and hot pepper sauce; mix well and set aside.

Heat oil in large nonstick skillet over medium-high heat until hot. Add onion, bell pepper, celery, and garlic; cook and stir 3 minutes. Add cooked rice and tomato; mix well.

Reduce heat to low and pour egg mixture into skillet. Cover loosely; cook 15 to 20 minutes or until center is set, lifting edges occasionally to allow uncooked egg mixture to flow to bottom of skillet. Sprinkle frittata with cheese. Cover; cook 2 minutes longer or until cheese has melted. Cut into wedges.

Rice is the highest yielding cereal grain on earth. One seed of rice produces more than 3,000 grains of rice. With more than 250 million rice farms in Asia, over 65 kilos of rice is produced for every single person on earth each year.

According to *Webster's New International Dictionary*, 1993, a person who is a native or resident of Connecticut is a Connecticuter. There are numerous other terms coined in print, but not in use, such as: Connecticotian (Cotton Mather, 1702) and Connecticutensian (Samuel Peters, 1781). Nutmegger is sometimes used, as is Yankee (the official State Song is "Yankee Doodle"), though this usually refers to someone from the wider New England region (and in the southern United States, to anyone who lives north of the Mason-Dixon Line).

Connecticut Kedgeree

2 c. cooked white rice
2 T. dried parsley
2 c. cooked, flaked white fish
4 hard-cooked eggs, chopped
1/2 c. milk
Salt and pepper to taste

Put all ingredients in top of a double boiler over medium-high heat and cook until all ingredients are hot and thick. Serve with toast points or cover with buttered bread crumbs in an ovenproof casserole dish and bake in a 400°F oven until crumbs are browned.

Rice and Vegetable Curry

Here's an international-style curry dish that fits in with the vegetarian lifestyle but couples with a meat dish as well.

1 c. uncooked long-grain white rice
3 3/4 c. water
2 T. flour
1 T. oil
3 t. curry powder
1/2 t. salt
1/4 t. cumin
Pinch cayenne pepper
1 small onion, chopped
1 clove garlic, minced
6 small potatoes,
    cut into 1-inch cubes
2 medium carrots,
    cut into 1-inch slices
2 vegetable bouillon cubes
2 c. fresh broccoli florets
2 c. cauliflower florets
1/2 medium red bell pepper,
    chopped

Cook rice in 2 cups of the water as directed on package. Meanwhile, in small bowl, combine 1/4 c. of the water and flour; beat with wire whisk until smooth. Set aside. Heat oil in large saucepan over medium-high heat until hot. Add curry powder, salt, cumin, and ground cayenne; cook and stir 1 minute. Add onion and garlic; cook and stir 1 minute. Add potatoes, carrots, bouillon cubes, and remaining 1 1/2 c. water. Bring to a boil. Reduce heat to low and simmer 10 minutes.

Add broccoli, cauliflower, and bell pepper. Cover; simmer 4 to 5 minutes or until vegetables are crisp-tender. Stir flour mixture into ingredients in saucepan; cook over medium heat until the dish boils and thickens, stirring constantly. Boil and stir 1 minute and serve over ice immediately.

Spanish Rice

2 T. oil
1 medium onion, thinly sliced
1/2 medium green bell pepper,
    chopped
1 c. white rice, uncooked
1/2 lb. ground beef
2 c. tomato sauce,
    (see page 196 for recipe)
1 3/4 c. hot water
1 t. prepared mustard
1 t. salt
1/4 t. black pepper

Heat oil in large skillet over high heat. Add onion, green pepper, rice, and beef. Stir and cook until lightly browned. Add tomato sauce and remaining ingredients. Mix well. Cover tightly and reduce heat to low. Simmer 25 minutes or until rice has absorbed all liquid.

Arroz Con Jocqui

I have repeatedly mentioned the presence of foreign dishes in this Yankee cookbook. I am proud that we, as New Englanders, are a diverse culture—we always have been. During the great migration of the seventeenth-century, many different cultures joined our English forefathers in making this land as acceptable as possible. This is a great dish that speaks to that diversity.

1 lb. Monterey Jack cheese
3 c. sour cream
2 cans peeled green chilies, chopped
Vegetable oil
3 c. cooked rice
Salt and black pepper to taste
1/2 c. shredded Cheddar cheese

Preheat oven to 350°F. Cut Monterey Jack cheese in strips. Thoroughly mix sour cream and chilies. Oil a 1 1/2 qt. casserole well. Season rice with salt and pepper. Place a layer of rice, sour cream mixture, and cheese strips in that order until you finish with rice on the top. Bake for 30 minutes. During the last 5 minutes of baking, sprinkle grated Cheddar cheese over rice and allow it to melt before removing from oven.

To Make Savory Rice: Wash and pick some rice. Stew it very gently in a small quantity of veal or rich mutton stock with an onion, a blade of mace, pepper and salt. When swelled, but not boiled to mash, dry it on a shallow end of a sieve before the fire and either reserve it dry or put it in the middle of a dish, and pour the gravy around, having heated it.

–*The New System of Domestic Cookery*, 1807

Lobster Fried Rice

After having eaten many varieties of fried rice at the numerous Chinese restaurants that dot our land, I thought of making a Yankee version of fried rice, something that would go well as the base for a meal with a salad and some crusty sourdough bread. I came up with this. Yes, you will see a little Asian influence, but the addition of lobster is ideally paired with water chestnuts and mushrooms. I think you'll agree.

1 T. vegetable oil
2 c. cooked rice
1 egg, beaten
1 c. cooked, diced lobster meat
1 T. soy sauce
1 T. cooked, diced mushrooms
3 T. minced water chestnuts
1 T. sugar
Salt and pepper to taste

Over medium-high heat, place oil in large skillet. Add rice and stir until blended. Stir about 2 minutes and push aside so you can add egg to bottom of pan. Scramble immediately and stir in the rice. Add remaining ingredients and cook until heated through.

It's hard to believe that lobsters were once a poor man's meal. They used to wash ashore by the hundreds on every beach along the New England coast. It was so looked down upon as food that not only were they used as fertilizer, but many indentured servants made it a stipulation in their contracts that they were to only be fed lobster no more than once a week by their employers.

Orange Rice

For this dish, try brown rice, which is more nutritious than white. The nutty flavor of the brown rice combines with the sweetness of the orange flavor to make it quite worthwhile.

1/4 c. chopped onion
1/2 c. chopped celery
3 T. butter or margarine
3 strips (2 inches) orange peel
2 c. orange juice
2 c. cooked white or brown rice
1/8 t. salt

Sauté onion and celery in butter over medium-high heat until browned. Add orange peel and juice. Bring to a boil and add rice and salt. Cover, remove from heat and let stand 10 minutes before fluffing.

White Cheddar Cheese Grits

I know, grits in a Yankee cookbook? But I have to say that cornmeal of any type is welcome in our fare because of the importance corn has played in our lives since colonization.

1 qt. half and half
2 c. stone-ground grits
5 c. chicken broth
1 1/2 c. grated white Cheddar cheese
Salt and white pepper to taste

Bring half and half to a boil over medium heat in medium saucepan. Stir in grits and simmer, stirring often, until thick. Add 2 cups of broth. Remove from heat and add cheese, salt, and pepper. Add remaining cup of broth and stir, keeping the grits warm until serving time.

Down in the southern states, dried grits were used to kill any invading ants that may find there way into the house during the early years of southern colonization. It was believed that by eating the grits, ants would explode when the dried corn mixed with the fluids inside their bodies. Laboratory tests with fire ants have determined this folk remedy for exterminating ants to be just that, folklore.

Cheese Polenta with Spicy Chili Topping

It is so much cheaper to make Italian polenta instead of buying it. If you have any left over the next day, butter and grill it to have with whatever you're eating—it makes a great side dish.

1 c. yellow cornmeal
3 1/2 c. water
1/2 t. garlic salt
1/8 t. pepper
1 c. shredded sharp Cheddar cheese

In medium saucepan, combine cornmeal and 1 cup of water; beat with wire whisk until well blended. Add remaining 2 1/2 c. water, garlic salt, and pepper; mix well. Bring to a boil over medium-high heat, stirring constantly. Reduce heat to medium-low. Cover; cook 10 to 15 minutes or until very thick, stirring frequently. Remove polenta from heat; stir in cheese. Spread in ungreased 9-inch pie pan; set aside to cool completely.

Heat oil in small saucepan over medium heat until hot. Add onions and chili; cook and stir 3 minutes. Add beans; cook until thoroughly heated. Stir in tomato. Remove from heat. Top serve, cut polenta into wedges; place on individual serving plates and spoon topping over wedges.

Topping:
2 t. oil
1/4 c. chopped onions
1/2 fresh jalapeno chili, seeded and minced
1 can (15 oz.) spicy chili beans, unstrained
1 large tomato, chopped

Thee the soft nations round the warm Levant
Palanta call, the French of course Polante;
E'en in thy native regions how I blush
To hear the Pennsylvanians call thee Mush!
On Hudson's banks, while men of Belgic spawn
Insult and eat thee by the name suppawn.
All spurious appellations; void of truth:
I've better known thee from my earliest youth.
Thy name is Hasty-Pudding!

—*The Hasty-Pudding,* Joel Barlow, 1793

Legumes, which were probably the earliest plant to be cultivated, include lentils, fava, navy, bush, string, lima, soy, peas, chickpeas, and peanuts. Although they contain the same low calorie count as grains, they have 2 to 4 times as much protein. Legumes are fat and cholesterol free with lentils, beans, and peas containing large amounts of fiber. They also lower the rate which blood sugar rises. By blocking certain enzymes that seem to promote cancer, they also protect against breast, colon, and prostate cancer. Soybeans contain a group of compounds called isoflavones that are modified in the body and transform into substances that may block the entry of the female hormone estrogen into cells, which may decrease the risk of breast and ovarian cancer.

Meatless Jambalaya

Instead of using the traditional meat, poultry, and shellfish found in Classic Jambalaya, try this red and butter bean replacement. Together with the spices, vegetables, and cornbread, I think you will agree that this low-fat recipe will please everyone.

1 T. oil
1/2 c. chopped onion
1/2 c. chopped green bell pepper
2 garlic cloves, minced
2 c. water
1 can (14.5 oz.) diced tomatoes
1 can (8 oz.) tomato sauce
1/2 t. Italian seasoning
1/4 t. cayenne pepper
Pinch fennel seed, crushed
1 c. uncooked long-grain white rice
1 can (16 oz.) red beans or kidney
   beans, drained and rinsed
1 can (15.5 oz.) butter beans,
   drained and rinsed

Heat oil in large skillet over medium-high heat until hot. Add onion, bell pepper, and garlic; cook and stir 4 to 6 minutes or until crisp tender. Stir in the water, tomatoes, tomato sauce, Italian seasoning, cayenne, and fennel seed. Bring to a boil and add the rice. Reduce heat to low; cover and simmer 20 to 30 minutes or until rice is tender, stirring occasionally. Stir in the beans. Cover; simmer an additional 8 to 10 minutes or until well heated, stirring occasionally.

Buckwheat-Stuffed Cabbage Rolls

Buckwheat is known as a pseudocereal. It is not a wheat, cereal, or grain, but related to rhubarb and sorrel. Being far less expensive than its sidekick grains, it is lower in calories than rice or corn. This recipe calls for buckwheat groats. These are the whole, raw, and unroasted buckwheat kernels. When roasted, it is called kasha. You can buy both.

1 onion, peeled and minced
1/2 green bell pepper, minced
3 T. oil
2 c. buckwheat groats
4 c. boiling water
1/2 t. salt
1/2 c. finely chopped peanuts
1/4 c. finely chopped
   sunflower seeds
1 head of cabbage
1 can (29 oz.) of tomato puree

In large sauté pan over medium-high heat, sauté the onion and green pepper in oil until tender, about 5 minutes. Add groats and stir until coated with oil. Reduce heat to low, add the water, cover and simmer for 15 minutes or when groats are tender and the water has been absorbed. Season and add the peanuts and sunflower seeds.

Core the cabbage and cook in water until the leaves are pliable. Remove cabbage and let cool to the touch. Separate the leaves and place 3 T. of the groat mixture on each leaf. Roll and tuck in the sides.

Preheat oven to 350°F. Place cabbage rolls in a baking dish and pour tomato puree over rolls. Cover and bake for 1 1/2 hours or until cabbage is tender.

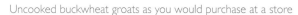
Uncooked buckwheat groats as you would purchase at a store

Bean and Veggie Burgers

Many people scoff at meatless burgers but this is the best that I have tasted. Make it even more flavorful by adding 1/2 c. applesauce or minced apples to this already juicy "burger."

I can (15 oz.) kidney beans,
   drained and rinsed
1/2 c. rolled oats
1/2 c. chopped fresh mushrooms
1/4 c. chopped onion
I small carrot, shredded
1/2 medium red bell pepper,
   chopped
I garlic clove, minced
3 T. ketchup
3/4 t. salt

In food processor with metal blade, combine beans, oats, mushrooms, onion, carrot, bell pepper, garlic, ketchup, and salt; process with pulses until coarsely chopped. Do not puree! Shape mixture into 4 patties and refrigerate for at least 1 hour before cooking.

Boston Baked Beans

Try these baked beans with Baked Boston Brown Bread. Together with coleslaw, sweet pickles, and a slab of ham and you have a meal truly made for a...Yankee!

I qt. navy or pea beans
3/4 lb. bacon, diced
I small onion, peeled and quartered
1/3 c. molasses
I T. salt
3 T. brown sugar
1/2 t. dry mustard

Soak beans overnight in enough water to cover beans at least 6 inches. Next morning, strain beans and place all ingredients in a large baking pan. Cover with water to bring it up to 2 inches above the beans. Stir well to combine all ingredients. Cover and bake at 250°F for 6 hours. The last hour of baking, remove lid to brown on top.

For true New England baked beans, use yellow-eyed beans, and for Vermont Baked Beans, substitute dark maple syrup for molasses.

Chickpea Chili

Tomatillos are referred to as green tomatoes. If needed, replace the tomatillos with green tomatoes.

I lb. fresh tomatillos, outer,
   papery skin removed
1/4 onion, diced
2 T. olive oil
I jalapeno pepper, stem removed
2 garlic cloves
I t. salt
I lb. canned chickpeas,
   drained and rinsed
I t. dried cilantro (or use I T. fresh)
   chopped
1/2 t. black pepper

Preheat oven to 400°F. Place tomatillos in a heavy pan with onion, oil, jalapeno, garlic and salt; roast 20 to 30 minutes or until soft and lightly browned. Remove and puree in blender or food processor until smooth. Pour into a saucepan and add the chickpeas. Simmer over medium heat for 10 minutes and stir in the cilantro, serve.

Vegetable Couscous with Wild Blueberries

Couscous with berries? Yup! another recipe has been Yanked.

1 c. vegetable stock
3 T. olive oil
1 c. couscous
1 t. grated lemon zest
Pinch cumin
2 carrots, peeled and diced
1 small zucchini, diced
1/4 c. walnut halves, chopped
1 1/4 c. blueberries
1/2 c. cooked chickpeas
Salt and pepper to taste
4 sprigs fresh cilantro, chopped

In small saucepan, bring vegetable stock and 2 T. of the oil to boil over medium-high heat. Add couscous, lemon zest, and cumin; stir to combine. Remove from heat and cover; let stand for 5 minutes. Fluff with fork and scrape into large bowl.

Meanwhile, heat remaining oil in skillet over medium heat and cook carrots for 5 minutes or until they begin to soften. Add zucchini and cook for 3 minutes or until softened. Remove from heat and add walnuts. Add to couscous. Add blueberries and chickpeas to bowl. Season with salt and pepper to taste. Add cilantro and stir to combine well.

Hoppin' John and Skippin' Jenny

I love these names. Well before the mid-1800s, Hoppin' John was known throughout the south as a gut busting meal using black-eyed peas, rice, and pig's feet. During the Middle Ages, eating beans during the New Year brought good luck. Peas were substituted for beans, but the lucky superstition stayed with this dish. You must leave three peas on your plate when through. They symbolize luck, fortune, and romance.

So why is a southern dish in a Yankee cookbook? Just because it's delicious and I love the names.

2 c. black-eyed peas
5 to 6 c. water
2 t. salt
3/4 c. chopped onion
1/4 c. chopped celery
2 lbs. pigs feet or a 2 lb. ham hock
1 c. brown rice
1/2 c. frozen peas
1/4 t. black pepper

Soak black-eyed peas in 6 cups water overnight. Next morning add salt, onion, celery, and pig's feet to peas and soaking water. Bring mixture to a boil over high heat, reduce to low and cover. Cook about 45 minutes or until peas are a little firm and still whole. Add the rice, peas, additional salt (if needed), and black pepper. Continue simmering for 45 to 50 minutes or until the rice is tender and water absorbed. Remove pig's feet or ham hock to cool and pick the meat off the bones. Add meat to pot and mix all together; serve.

Skippin' Jenny? Well, that's leftover Hoppin' John that is eaten the next day, bringing even more luck.

CHAPTER 12

Cakes, in one form or another, have been part of our civilization for more years than we can count. Ancient Egyptians recorded over 30 different cakes and breads in use during the Twentieth Dynasty. Romans, as early as the second century B.C., treasured a fruitcake called *satura*, which was made with barley mash, raisins, pine kernels, pomegranate seeds, and honeyed wine.

The origin of many cakes in unknown, but a few can be traced to individual people and places. For example, Sponge Cake originated in the Italian House of Savoy during the eleventh century. The recipe was introduced to many countries during the thirteenth century by the daughters of this house when they married and moved to foreign lands.

Cakes, Cookies, and Confections

Angel Food Cake is another cake with a known history. It was first made in 1890 in a St. Louis restaurant where the chef guarded the secret of this high, light cake by saying that it was a secret powder he had used. This powder turned out to be cream of tartar.

The Chiffon Cake was first introduced in 1949 by a flour milling company.

Basic cake ingredients should be understood so that if a cake fails, the problem will be readily seen and corrective measures will be taken so that your baking can be as easy as possible. A couple of things first though. Remember to follow directions exactly, follow the order of mixing correctly and time your baking according to the recipe.

Flour gives the cake structure by building a framework. Both cake flour and all-purpose flour are used in cakes. Cake flour produces a larger, softer, more velvety cake than all-purpose. However, all-purpose is more nutritious. When a recipe does not specify which type to use, assume that all-purpose flour is to be used. The ratio or substitution is; 1 c. cake flour equals 1 c. all-purpose flour minus 2 tablespoons. Never pack flour into a measuring cup when determining a measurement. Loosely scoop out the flour and level off with a knife.

Granular sugar is always used unless powdered or brown sugar is specified. Only brown sugar is packed into a cup for measuring purposes. All other sugar is to be loosely scooped as flour is.

Another major ingredient is egg, which adds flavor, color, and acts as a binder in most instances. Volume is also attained through the use of eggs.

Leavening, the substance which causes a food to rise, makes the cake lighter, more digestible, and more palatable. Baking powder is normally used, but air incorporated in eggs, steam from liquid in the cake, and the reaction of baking soda and acid in a liquid also leavens the cake.

Several fats are used in the preparation of cakes. Shortening, butter, margarine, and salad oil are among them. Each give flavor and/or tenderness to a cake.

To check for the doneness of a cake, look to see if the sides of the cake are pulled away from the sides of the pan. Touch the top of a cake also, if it springs back in the middle, the cake is done. Or simply use a wooden toothpick or knife inserted in the middle of the cake, if it comes out clean, it is done.

Troubleshooting Tips

Coarse Texture: Insufficient creaming; oven temperature too low; or not enough liquid
Heavy, compact texture: Oven temperature too low; extreme over beating; or too much sugar or shortening
Dry: Over beaten egg whites; over baked; or too much flour or leavening agent
Hump or cracks on the top: Oven temperature too hot; too much flour; or pan placed too high in the oven
Cake falling: Oven temperature too low; insufficient baking; too much batter in pan; cake was moving during baking; or too much shortening
Poor volume: Pan too large; oven temperature too hot; not enough mixing; or not enough leavening

Blueberry Cake with Lemon Sauce

I often think of my grandmother when eating blueberry cake because she used love and pride when baking. With the addition of Lemon Sauce to this recipe, I think she would have lovingly and proudly admired this dessert.

2 eggs, separated
1 c. sugar plus more for dusting top
1/2 c. shortening or butter
1/4 tsp. salt
1 tsp. vanilla
1 1/2 c. flour plus 1/4 c.
1 tsp. baking powder
1/3 c. milk
1 1/2 c. blueberries
Lemon Sauce, *recipe below*

Preheat oven to 350°F. Grease a loaf pan with oil or cooking spray. Beat egg whites until stiff. Add 1/4 c. of sugar. Cream shortening; add salt, vanilla, and remaining sugar. Add 2 egg yolks; beat well. Mix flour and baking powder together. Mix with creamed shortening alternating with milk. Fold egg whites in with rubber spatula. Mix 1/4 c. flour

with blueberries and fold into mixture. Pour into prepared pan and sprinkle sugar on top; bake 45 to 50 minutes or until done. Remove from oven and let cool for a few minutes before removing cake to cooling rack. Serve with warm lemon sauce.

Lemon Sauce:

3/4 c. sugar
2 T. corn starch mixed with 1/4 c. water
1 3/4 c. water
Pinch salt
1/4 c. fresh lemon juice
Grated rind of 2 lemons
1/4 c. butter

Mix all ingredients together in saucepan except butter and bring to a boil over medium-high heat, stirring constantly. When thickened, add the butter, remove from heat, and whisk until smooth.

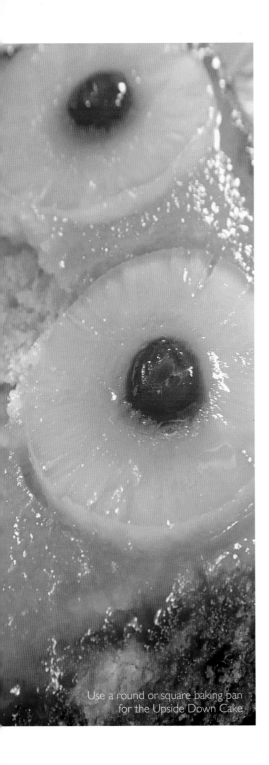

Pineapple Upside Down Cake

Although many people may grimace at the thought of attempting this cake, it isn't any more difficult than most other classic cakes. Very popular during the mid twentieth century, the fascination has waned as of late, probably due to time constraints most families are in nowadays—stop and smell the pineapple!

I frequently use parchment paper as a base for this cake. I cut out a circle of parchment paper a little bigger than the bottom of the cake pan and spray it with nonstick cooking spray before continuing with the recipe. If you don't have parchment paper, just follow the recipe as is and this cake will come out beautifully!

I 1/2 oz. can sliced pineapple
3 T. butter or margarine
1/2 c. brown sugar
4 maraschino cherries, halved
1/3 c. shortening
1/2 c. granulated sugar
I egg
I t. vanilla
I c. sifted, all-purpose flour
I 1/2 t. baking powder
1/4 t. salt

Drain pineapple, reserving liquid. Halve pineapple slices. Melt butter in 9 × 1 1/2-inch round pan. Add brown sugar and 1 T. of the reserved pineapple syrup. Add water to remaining syrup to make 1/2 cup. Arrange pineapple in the bottom of pan. Place a cherry half in center of each slice.

Cream together shortening and sugar until light. Add egg and vanilla; beat until fluffy. Sift together dry ingredients; add alternately with the 1/2 cup reserved pineapple syrup and water mixture, beating after each addition. Spread over pineapple and bake in preheated 350°F oven for 40 to 45 minutes. Cool 5 minutes and then invert onto serving plate. Serve while warm.

Some studies a few years back have shown that bromelin, a chemical found in pineapples, actually cleanses arteries!

Warm Banana Upside Down Cake with Hot Chocolate Sauce

With its long title, you would think this recipe was out of some fancy restaurant in a big city...wrong! I proclaim this to be a true Yankee dish because it was invented by a true Yankee...me! Enjoy.

1 c. vegetable oil
2 c. sugar
5 eggs
7 bananas, mashed
4 c. flour
3 t. baking soda
3 t. baking powder
1 t. salt
1 c. milk
1 T. vanilla
8 oz. semisweet chocolate
1/4 c. heavy cream

Preheat oven to 350°F. In a large bowl, mix oil and sugar together; add eggs and bananas. Sift in flour, baking soda, baking powder, and salt. Add 1/2 c. milk; setting aside remainder for chocolate sauce. Add vanilla and mix well. Spray muffin tins well with nonstick cooking spray. Pour batter into individual muffin tins up to three-quarters full. Bake for 15 to 16 minutes or until done.

While cakes are cooking, melt chocolate in microwave for 35 to 40 seconds, or until melted. Remove from microwave and add remainder of milk and the cream. Serve with chocolate sauce over the warm cakes.

Easy Methods for Distinguishing Fats

Polyunsaturated Fats: remains liquid at room temperature—canola, safflower, and corn oils are examples.

Monounsaturated Fats: remains liquid at room temperature but thickens upon refrigeration—avocado, olive, and many nut oils.

Saturated Fats: either solid or semi-solid at room temperature—butter, hard margarine, lard, and shortening.

Highly Saturated Fats: liquids which include coconut and palm oils.

Orange Cranberry Upside Down Cake

I have taken the classic Pineapple Upside Down Cake and turned it, well, upside down with this fragrant, colorful adaptation. Enjoy.

1/2 lb. fresh cranberries
2 oranges, peeled
2 T. butter or margarine
1 c. firmly packed brown sugar
1 1/4 c. flour
2 t. baking powder
1/4 t. salt
1/4 c. shortening
1 t. grated orange rind
3/4 c. sugar
1 egg
1/4 c. evaporated milk
1/4 c. orange juice

To Make Cheesecake without Curd, beat two eggs very well; then put as much flour as will make them thick. Then beat three eggs more very well, and put to the other with a pint of cream, and half a pound of butter. Set it over the fire, and when it boils put in your two eggs and flour, and stir them well, and let them boil until they be pretty thick. Then take it off the fire, and season it with sugar, a little salt, and nutmeg; put in currants, and bake them in Patti pans as you do others.

—The Compleat Housewife, 1730

Preheat oven to 350°F. Wash cranberries and coarsely chop. Divide oranges into segments. Melt butter and stir in brown sugar. Mix well and spread evenly over bottom of pan. Cover with cranberries then with orange sections. Sift flour, baking powder, and salt together. Cream shortening with orange rind, add sugar gradually, and beat until fluffy. Add egg and beat thoroughly. Mix milk and orange juice and add alternately with dry ingredients in small amounts, beating after each addition. Pour batter over fruit and bake for 40 to 45 minutes, or until cake is done in the middle.

Old Fashioned Dark Gingerbread with Citrus Whipped Cream

Most likely, gingerbread was first made by the ancient Greeks some 5,000 years ago. Although some authorities date this delicious bread as starting to be made in the Middle Ages. Nonetheless, we do know that it was one of the awards given to medieval British knights for winning a tournament. Gingerbread was molded and baked during this time in the shape of birds, animals, and alphabet letters. Some of these molded, cooked gingerbreads are still with us at various museums of the world. Early American settlers also baked these breads, George Washington's mother often made it and served it to her guests. It is said that Abraham Lincoln's favorite cake was the gingerbread.

The marriage of gingerbread making and the holidays in New England probably started when this bread was made for Military Training Days in colonial New England—it took off from there.

1 1/2 c. flour	1/4 c. dark brown sugar
2 t. baking powder	1/2 c. butter or margarine
2 t. ginger	2 eggs
1/2 t. powdered cloves	1/2 c. boiling water
1/2 t. baking soda	3/4 c. dark molasses
1/2 t. salt	1/2 c. chopped walnuts (optional)

Preheat oven to 350°F. Sift flour with baking powder, spices, and salt; set aside. Cream sugar with butter until light and fluffy; add eggs and beat thoroughly. Combine boiling water and molasses; stir in soda until dissolved and add to batter. Add flour mixture gradually, stirring well between additions. Add nuts and pour into a well-buttered (or use nonstick cooking spray) 8-inch square pan or 8-inch loaf pan and bake for 20 to 30 minutes or until toothpick inserted in center comes out clean. Some may wish to let cake set for 10 minutes then remove to wire rack to cool. I prefer to leave cake in original pan, cut into desired serving sizes and top with Citrus Whipped Cream.

Citrus Whipped Cream:

In a small saucepan, beat 2 eggs; add 1 c. sugar, 2 t. grated orange peel, 2 t. grated lemon peel, and 4 T. lemon juice. Cook over low heat until thickened, about 6 to 7 minutes. Cool thoroughly. Whip 2 c. whipping cream to stiff peaks and fold into cooled mixture; chill and top the gingerbread.

How to Make Cinnamon-Scented Gingerbread Men Ornaments

Gingerbread men are a classic cookie seen on holiday platters during the Christmas season. You can recreate the look of these tasty little men without the excess calories and fill your home with the delightful aroma of cinnamon at the same time. These "cookies" can be stored away and used for years without spoiling. If the cinnamon scent fades over time, rub them with a little cinnamon oil to spice them up again.

1 c. cinnamon
1 c. applesauce

Mix one cup of ground cinnamon with one cup of applesauce in a mixing bowl. Stir until the ingredients have formed a dough. Sprinkle additional cinnamon on a clean counter and place the dough on the counter. Roll the dough out with a rolling pin until it is approximately 1/4- to 1/2-inch thick. Cut the dough with gingerbread men cookie cutters. Use a chopstick to make a hole at the top of each cookie cutter so that you can hang the ornaments when they are dry. Allow the ornaments to dry at room temperature until they are hard. This will take at least 24 hours. Apply a coat of decoupage glue to the back of each ornament with a paint brush to strengthen the ornaments. Do not cover the entire ornament with glue as it will conceal the cinnamon aroma. Allow the glue to dry completely before you continue. Decorate the gingerbread men with fabric paints to create buttons, hair, clothing, and facial features. Allow the paint time to dry. Insert a piece of ribbon or yarn through the hole in each ornament and tie it into a loop. Use this loop to hang the ornaments.

Apricot Upside-Down Gingerbread

Oh yeah, the best of both worlds, warm scented gingerbread topped with glazed fruit. You should absolutely give this a try during your fall baking, everyone will ask for more.

3 t. butter or margarine
1 1/2 c. firmly packed brown sugar
1 1/2 c. canned apricots, drained
1/2 c. shortening
2 eggs, beaten
1 c. molasses
2 1/2 c. sifted flour
2 t. baking powder
3 t. ginger
1/2 t. salt
1 c. milk or buttermilk

Preheat oven to 350°F. Spray bottom of 9 × 9-inch baking pan with nonstick spray. Melt butter in bottom of cake pan over medium-low heat. Add 1 c. brown sugar gradually and blend well. Remove from heat. Arrange apricots, cut side up, to cover bottom of pan. Cream shortening; add remaining 1/2 c. brown sugar and cream until fluffy. Add eggs and molasses and beat well. Sift dry ingredients together; add alternately with milk, mixing well after each addition. Pour batter over apricots; bake for 40 to 45 minutes or until done. Cool for 5 minutes and carefully but quickly invert onto serving dish, serve warm.

Colonial Molasses Toast, 1740

"Let molasses boil 5 minutes slowly with a bit of butter to the pint, as large as half an egg. If toast is too dry and hard, dip it quickly in hot water, and then in the molasses...". Boy this brings back memories. Dad told me his father used to make this recipe as such; 1 pint molasses simmered with 3 T. butter was enough for about 10 slices of toast. After the butter had melted and the molasses was hot, the family would dip the toast and enjoy.

Woodsman's Cider Cake

This cake was made in lumber camps of old, a true delight to the lumbermen, river drivers, and bosses alike. Go ahead and make it regardless of its origins. Serve a thick slab with whipped cream dusted with cinnamon.

6 c. flour
1 t. baking soda
1/2 t. salt
1 t. nutmeg
3 c. sugar
1 c. butter or margarine
4 eggs, beaten
1 c. apple cider

Preheat oven to 350°F. Spray or grease a loaf pan. Mix flour, soda, salt, and nutmeg in large bowl. In separate bowl cream together sugar and butter until creamy. Add eggs and beat thoroughly with electric mixer. Add flour mixture alternately with cider into butter/sugar mixture, beating until smooth after each addition. Turn into greased loaf pan and bake for about 45 to 50, or until toothpick inserted in middle comes out clean.

Poke Cake

If you are part of Generation X, ask your parents if they ever had Poke Cake (your grandparents may even remember it). The answer will almost always bring back memories of someone in the family making this childhood favorite. This recipe has been around almost since the beginning of commercial gelatin, around 1930. I remember fondly no icing or frosting was needed on this cake, for the sweetness of the cake combined with the chilled funnels of gelatinized sugar throughout was enough for me as I think it will be for you and yours as well.

1 box gelatin, your choice of flavor
2 c. hot water
2/3 c. butter or margarine
1 3/4 c. sugar
2 eggs
2 t. vanilla
3 c. all-purpose flour
2 1/2 t. baking powder
1 t. salt
1 1/4 c. milk

Mix the box of gelatin with 2 cups of hot water, stir to dissolve. Cool until lukewarm. In the meantime, cream butter and sugar until light and fluffy in a large bowl. Add eggs and vanilla and continue beating until fluffy once more. Sift flour, baking powder, and salt together; add to creamed mixture alternately with milk, beating after each addition. Beat 1 minute longer. Bake in 2 greased and floured 9 × 1 1/2-inch round pans for 30 to 35 minutes at 350°F. Cool in pans for 10 minutes and remove to separate dishes to cool the remainder of the time. Take a long serrated knife and level off one layer of the cake so that the rounded layer can steadily sit on top when the preparation is complete later on.

When the cake has cooled, take something dowel-shaped, such as the ends of beaters that you don't lick and poke holes throughout both layers of cake. Take the gelatin mixture and proceed to pour over and into the tops of the cakes, making sure the holes get plenty of gelatin. Refrigerate immediately.

When refrigerated, stack layers (flat top on bottom) and serve with whipped cream if desired.

Pound Cake

This was one of the first recipes that I attained during my amateur, teenage years while learning to cook. Dad told me his grandmother handed down this dense cake recipe with the following rule of thumb; 1 lb. flour,1 lb. sugar,1 dozen eggs (actually a Yankee dozen, which is 13), and 1 lb. butter. That was it. Although I have never tried his grandmother's recipe, I am sure it isn't much denser than our pound cake of today. Although there are 3 optional ingredients in this recipe, I urge you to gather these items and incorporate them into this batter.

3 1/2 c. flour
1 t. baking powder
1/2 t. salt
1/4 t. mace (optional)
1 3/4 c. butter or margarine
1 lb. powderer sugar
8 eggs
1 t. vanilla
1 t. almond extract (optional)
1/2 t. lemon extract (optional)

Preheat oven to 325°F. Grease a 10 × 4-inch tube pan. Combine the flour with baking powder, salt, and mace and sift together. Cream butter in a bowl until light and fluffy. Add powdered sugar slowly and beat until mixture resembles whipped ream. Add the eggs, one at a time, beating well after each addition. Stir in half the flour mixture, and then add flavorings and remaining flour mixture. Pour into prepared pan and cut through batter several times with knife to break any air bubbles (or you can tap the sides all around with a heavy butter knife). Bake for 1 hour and 10 minutes or until toothpick withdrawn from the middle comes out clean. Remove from pan immediately and cool on cake, or wire rack.

Baptist Cakes

I was unable to find mention of a Baptist Cake in any Yankee bibliography, and the reason being (after days of speculation) was because in Connecticut they were called Holy Pokes and in Maine they were referred to as Huffjuffs. They are not much different then a French beignet. Enjoy!

1 T. butter or margarine
1 T. sugar
1/2 c. scalded milk
1/2 c. boiling water
1/2 pkg. yeast dissolved in
    1/3 c. warm water
3 c. all-purpose flour
1 t. salt

Sizzlers were another name for these Baptist Cakes. Other colloquialisms in the Yankee fashion are:

Drop Cakes: what we today call fritters
Slumps: fruit topped with dumplings
Stifles: Cape Cod talk for meat or fish stew
Emptyin's: settlings of a beer barrel from which yeast is derived

---

Combine butter, sugar and salt in a large bowl. Add the milk and water. Stir and let rest until mixture is lukewarm. Add the dissolved yeast and 1/2 the flour. Mix thoroughly with a spoon (do not whisk or use a mixer!). Add another cup of flour, mix well and gradually add the remaining flour, mixing all the while.

Turn out on a floured board or counter and knead until elastic and smooth. Place in dry, clean bowl and cover with towel to let rise until doubled in size. Return to floured counter or board and roll with a rolling pin to about an 1/8-inch thickness. Cut strips using knife or pizza cutter about 3 inches wide. Cut again to make squares 3 inches across or diamonds the same size. Cover with towel and let rest for 15 minutes while heating 3 inches of frying oil (your choice, but I prefer safflower oil) or heating your deep fat fryer to 350°F. Fry about 4 minutes on the first side and about 2 minutes on the other, or until it is golden brown on both sides. Serve with powdered sugar or maple sugar.

For those who pay attention to detail, these cakes are classically served with milk sauce. Scald 2 c. milk and add 2 T. butter or margarine until it melts. Remove from heat and allow your guests to dunk these Baptist Cakes into the milk.

Election Cake

Beginning in Hartford, Connecticut, this yeast-raised cake slowly came up the coast to Maine and other New England States. Originally called the Hartford Election Cake, it was first made using leftover bread crusts, spices, and fruit and served during election time. Why? Because when the men-folk came home from a day at the local town hall, or office, they were so hyped on their own political views and from arguing politics with their neighbors who didn't agree with them, they often returned home in a sour mood. The wife got to thinking maybe a sweet treat would replace this sour mood! Well not only were they right but a tradition had begun. The original recipe calls for an addition of 1/4 c. sliced citron.

William Hogarth's The Polling, 1758. After voting (shown here), Election Cake was freely handed out.

1 t. dry yeast dissolved in 1/2 c. lukewarm water	2 eggs, well beaten
1 T. butter or margarine	1 c. raisins
1 T. sugar	2 t. lemon rind, zested
1/2 t. salt	3 t. lemon juice
1 1/4 c. flour	1 t. baking soda
1/2 c. butter or margarine	3/4 c. flour
1 c. sugar	1/4 t. salt
	1/2 t. nutmeg

Dissolve yeast in lukewarm water and add 1 T. butter or margarine, 1 T. sugar, salt, and 1 1/4 c. flour, mixing well. Set aside in a warm place for 2 hours, or until almost doubled in bulk (an oven that has been set to warm for 15 minutes and then shut off is perfect for this cake).

In separate bowl add 1/2 c. butter or margarine and 1 c. sugar and beat until light. Add eggs, raisins, lemon rind, and lemon juice. Sift together the baking soda, flour, salt, and nutmeg and add mix thoroughly. Add this mixture to the risen dough that has been punched down. Mix very well.

Return entire dough to the same bowl that it originally rose in and cover with towel. Set aside and let rise for 1 hour. After the 45 minute mark, preheat oven to 350°F. Put the risen dough into a greased bread pan and bake for 50 minutes or until a toothpick inserted in center comes out clean. Let rest in pan for 10 minutes and remove to wire rack to cook. Ice with a mixture of powdered sugar and water. Serve while barely warm.

An old dessert enjoyed along the coast of New England a few generations ago was called the Old Maine Lobster Cake. This was, in reality, a marble cake with the dark part having molasses, cloves, and nutmeg while the other half had raisins and chopped citron.

Old Fashioned Honey Cake

This deliciously sweet cake is a great substitute for coffee cake on your Sunday brunch. Serve a dessert sauce (*see pages 277-279*) in a boat if desired.

1/2 c. butter or margarine
4 egg yolks, beaten well
1 c. honey
4 c. flour
1 t. baking soda
1 t. cinnamon
1/2 t. ginger
1/2 t. nutmeg
1/2 t. salt
1/4 t. ground cloves
1 c. water
4 egg whites, beaten to stiff peaks
1 c. chopped nuts (optional)

Preheat the oven to 350°F. Oil and flour a bread pan; set aside. Cream the butter well and add the beaten egg yolks. Mix well. Stir in the honey and blend. Sift the dry ingredients together and add alternately with the water to the first mixture. Beat well. Fold in the stiffly beaten egg whites. Add the nuts and pour into prepared pan; bake for 50 minutes or until toothpick inserted in center comes out clean.

Grammy Anna's Chestnut Cake (c. 1862)

My great, great grandmother Philinda (Anna) Bailey wrote this recipe down when in her 60s. Notice no oven temperature or time!: "2 c. sugar, 1 c. butter, 6 eggs, 1 c. whiskey, 3 t. baking powder, 4 c. flour, 2 bowls (2 c. each) chestnuts, ground up. Mix like all other cakes and bake."

Grammy Charlotte's Syllabub (1820)

My great, great, great grandmother Charlotte Bailey passed this down through the family: "Sweeten a quart of cyder with sugar and grate a little nutmeg if you can find it and add rich milk, whip. Pour into mug and pour a pint or more of sweet cream over the top of it."

Irish Fruit Cake

This is a traditional Irish fruitcake that utilizes Irish whiskey. Of course, this is optional but it does add a little bit of that lucky charm. This recipe also calls for grinding nuts and blanching almonds. First, to grind, just set your almonds in a food processor and add a little granulated sugar to them so that your blades will not collect all the ground almonds in a ball when pureeing them. A blender works well for this also. For blanching, cover your almonds with just enough water to cover and simmer them for 15 minutes with the cover on. When done, strain and dry them with a paper towel or clean cloth.

1/2 c. maraschino cherries
3/4 c. whole almonds, blanched
2 c. raisins
3/4 c. candied fruit peel
3 T. chopped, peeled apple
3 c. flour
1/2 t. cream of tartar
1/2 t. cinnamon
1/2 t. nutmeg
1 c. butter or margarine
1 c. sugar
6 eggs
Grated rind of 1/2 lemon
1 t. vanilla extract
3 oz. Irish whiskey
Frosting of your choice

Preheat oven to 250°F. Drain cherries and dry carefully. Grind half of the almonds and coarsely chop the other half. Now, in large bowl combine all fruits and nuts and toss to blend. In separate bowl sift dry ingredients together and set aside. In yet another bowl, cream butter and sugar until fluffy. Add eggs, lemon rind, vanilla, and almond extract; beat well. With large wooden or metal spoon, add flour mixture to butter mixture and stir well to incorporate. Add fruits and nuts and half of the whiskey; blend well.

Butter a 9-inch round cake pan that is at least 3-inches deep. If you don't have one, use a 9-inch tube pan. Butter or spray both sides of a piece of waxed paper so that when folded in half, it will be large enough to cover the bottom of your baking pan, place this oiled paper into the bottom of the pan and pour batter into pan.

Bake for 4 hours or until toothpick inserted in middle comes out clean. Pour remainder of whiskey over the top as soon as you remove cake from the oven. Wait one hour before dislodging and transferring the cake to a serving dish. When cooled, add your choice of icing or frosting if desired.

Danish Beer Fruit Cake (Olfrugtbrod)

This recipe is for our family and friends from Denmark who would like to bring a bit of Scandinavia to our lives.

Following the above recipe for Irish Fruit Cake, omit the chopped apple, almond extract, and whiskey. Substitute 3/4 c. chopped figs (available in most supermarkets—even up here in New England). Substitute 1 1/2 c. brown sugar for the 1 c. white sugar. Also, use only 2 eggs in place of the 6 eggs called for and stir in 1/2 c. dark beer (lager or stout) with the fruits and nuts.

Victorian Plum Cake

Sure, there are many ingredients in this recipe, but well worth the time and expense. Store for 1 week before enjoying, as our ancestors did!

1/2 lb. golden raisins
1/2 lb. dark raisins
1 lb. currants (optional)
1 c. coarsely chopped
  candied cherries
1 c. candied fruit peel, diced
1/2 c. crushed almonds
3 c. flour
1/4 t. each allspice, cinnamon,
  nutmeg, ginger, and cloves
1 c. butter or margarine
1 c. brown sugar, firmly packed
2 T. molasses
Grated rind of 2 oranges
Grated rind of 2 lemons
5 eggs
1/2 c. brandy, rum,
  sherry, or Madeira
White Icing (below)

Preheat oven to 350°F. Combine all fruits, peels, and nuts; toss with 3 T. flour. Sift remaining flour with spices. Cream butter with sugar until light and fluffy. Add molasses, grated rind of lemons and oranges, and eggs, one at a time, beating well between additions. Add flour and spices into mixture and add fruit. Mix well; then stir in brandy, rum, or wine, adding enough to make a soft batter that can be dropped from a spoon.

Bake in an 8- to 9-inch round pan that is 3 to 4 inches deep. Butter the pan (or use nonstick spray); lining the bottom with sprayed waxed paper. On top of that, place a double lining of waxed paper that comes 2 inches above the sides of the pan. Pour in the batter and gently tap to remove air bubbles.

Bake in oven for 1 1/2 hours, reduce heat to 225°F for 3 additional hours longer, or until a toothpick inserted comes out clean. Let cake get cold in pan, put onto a plate and remove paper. Sprinkle with additional rum or brandy and place in an airtight container for at least one week before icing.

White Icing:
2 c. powdered sugar
1/2 c. orange juice

Mix the two together well until icing is smooth and thick. If too thick, thin down with a teaspoon at a time of orange juice until the consistency is that of molasses. If too thin, add more confectioner's sugar, a tablespoon at a time, until desired consistency is found.

Plain Cake (c. 1870)

To be eaten with some fruit. Break an egg into a mug; fill halfway with fat and the rest with milk. Mix 1/2 dipper sugar, one of flour, 1/2 spoonful of powder and stir. Add all together and stir. Add some flavoring. Pour into Dutch oven that has been greased and bake. Eat with cob syrup.

Cob Syrup

Boil fifteen corn cobs about two hours or until you have about 1 pint of liquid when done. Strain and add about two pounds of brown sugar and boil until thick. This is good on cake, mush or flaps [pancakes].

–The Yankee Chef Archives

A standard loaf pan also works for Pain D'Epice

Pain D'Epice

This recipe comes from the various French settlements that dot our New England countryside. Brought over with their other cherished family recipes, the list of ingredients has not changed since the origination of this holiday treat in Dijon, France. Pairing well with a hot mug of your favorite beverage, Pain D'Epice is simple to make and simply a great ending to a chilly evening.

1 c. honey
1/2 c. hot water
1 1/2 t. crushed anise
1 t. grated lemon rind
2 1/2 c. flour
1/2 t. cinnamon
1/4 t. ground cloves
1 t. baking soda
2 T. sugar

Preheat oven to 350°F. Grease and flour a 9 × 9 × 2-inch pan. Stir together honey, water, anise, and grated lemon rind. Sift together flour, cinnamon, cloves, and baking soda; gradually add flour mixture to honey mixture along with the sugar, mixing well. Spread in prepared pan. Bake for 35 to 40 minutes; cool 10 minutes when done. Remove from pan onto a serving dish and garnish with candied fruit or peel or with cherries if desired. Slice thinly to serve.

Festive Egg Nog Cake

With the rum glaze drizzled over the top, you'd think it was snowing outside and the Yuletide has just begun.

Use Poke Cake Recipe
   (excluding gelatin portion)
1/4 c. rum
1/2 t. nutmeg

Preheat oven to 350°F. Grease and flour fluted tube pan. In large bowl, prepare poke cake. Add the rum and nutmeg. Bake for 35 to 40 or until done.

Glaze:
1/2 c. sugar
1/4 t. nutmeg
1/4 c. butter or margarine
2 T. water
3 t. rum

In small saucepan, heat sugar, nutmeg, margarine and water until mixture boils and sugar is melted over medium-high heat. Remove from heat and add rum. Pour half of glaze around edges of hot cake. Cool upright in pan 5 minutes; turn onto serving plate. Pour remaining glaze over top of cake and serve warm.

Sweet Apple Dumpling Cake

This is probably my favorite cake not only to make, but to eat. I love the addition of apples and cinnamon in the cake mix, but the topping of apples and raisins just gives it the extra incentive to make another when the first is gone.

2 c. chopped apples
1 c. raisins
8 green apples, peeled and cored
Juice of 1 lemon
1 c. butter or margarine
1 c. sugar
5 eggs, separated

2 c. flour
2 t. baking powder
4 T. chopped walnuts
1/2 c. chocolate chips
2 c. water
1/2 c. dark brown sugar

Preheat oven to 350°F. Grease, bottom only, a 13 × 9-inch square pan or 2 round cake pans. Spread 1 c. chopped apples and raisins evenly over bottom of pan.

Grate apples in a blender or food processor until shredded. Sprinkle at once with lemon juice; set aside. Beat the butter and sugar until creamy; gradually add the egg yolks. Combine the flour, baking powder, walnuts, and chocolate chips. Drain the apple and stir into the creamed mixture alternately with the flour mixture. Beat egg whites until stiff peaks form and gently fold into cake batter. Pour into cake pan.

In small saucepan over medium-high heat, place 2 c. water with brown sugar and bring to boiling. Boil one minute; remove from heat and pour in thin streams over cake batter. Bake cake for 40 to 50 minutes or until toothpick inserted comes out clean. Let rest for 10 minutes and invert onto serving dish. Serve warm with dollop of whipped cream.

Many old homesteads in New England, and elsewhere, had what were called fruit cellars. These cellars were often a cave like affair dug out of the side of a hill for fruit storage. Likewise, vegetable cellars were a separate section of a cellar for vegetable storage. A milk cellar was an entire building almost completely underground with a stone floor and a small window to the north to keep milk cool in the summer.

Colchester Apple Crumb Cake

This is aptly named for Old Colchester, Massachusetts (now Salisbury), because of the addition of molasses. Molasses was so important to this old town that my family did without pumpkin pie for a year because they couldn't get their hands on any molasses in the year 1671. Molasses is also important to this cake as well. Without it, it would just be the run of the mill apple crumb cake. Although it would be good to eat in and of itself, it is the molasses that crosses that line between good and great, and indeed this is a great cake!

2 1/4 c. flour
1/2 t. salt
2 t. cinnamon
1 c. light brown sugar
1/2 c. sugar
3/4 c. vegetable oil
1 egg
1 t. baking soda
1 t. baking powder
1/2 c. molasses
1 c. whole milk
1 1/2 c. chopped green apple, peeled
1/2 c. oatmeal
1/2 c. chopped nuts
1/4 c. butter or margarine, melted

Preheat oven to 350°F. Grease a 9 × 13-inch square baking pan. In a large mixing bowl combine flour, salt, 1 t. cinnamon, brown sugar, and granulated sugar. Remove 3/4 c. of the mixture and set aside for the topping. To the remainder add 1/2 t. cinnamon, oil, egg, baking soda, baking powder, molasses, milk, and apple. Mix well. Pour into prepared pan. To the reserved 3/4 c. topping add 1/2 t. cinnamon, oatmeal, chopped nuts, and melted butter or margarine. Stir to combine and sprinkle evenly over the batter. Bake for 30 minutes or until toothpick inserted in center comes out clean. Serve warm as a breakfast treat or with chipped cream, ice cream, or candied fruit on top for dessert.

Oatmeal, as everyone has heard, is a good way to lower your risk of heart disease and increase your soluble fiber intake, but soaking in an oatmeal bath can be great for soothing the itch of poison ivy, poison oak, bee stings, hives, insect bites, and sunburn. Simply fill your tub with tepid water and add one to two cups of oatmeal, suggests UCLA Medical Center's Dr. Kakita. It's also good for relieving dry, irritated skin.

Autumn Carrot Cake

2 c. flour	1 1/2 c. vegetable oil
2 c. sugar	5 eggs
2 t. baking soda	3 c. grated carrots
3 t. cinnamon	1 c. chopped nuts (optional)
1 t. salt	

Preheat oven to 350°F. Grease and flour a 13 × 9-inch pan. Stir together dry ingredients in large bowl. Add oil and mix well; add eggs, one at a time and mix just until combined. Fold in carrots. Pour into prepared pan. Bake for 25 to 30 minutes or until springy to the touch. Remove from oven and cool in same pan. Frost with cream cheese frosting.

Cream Cheese Frosting:

1/2 c. butter or margarine	3 t. vanilla
1 kg. (8 oz.) cream cheese	1 c. chopped pecans (optional)
1 lb. powdered sugar	

Cream together butter and cheese until smooth. Add sugar, vanilla, and nuts and combine until thoroughly mixed.

Believe it or not, carrots are a member of the parsley family, which relates it to dill, parsnip, Queen Ann's lace, and the deadly hemlock. Afghanistan is where historians believe carrots originated more than 800 years ago. Not only was it enjoyed as a food by the Chinese and Japanese during the thirteenth century, it was also used for reasons other than for ordinary food purposes. For example, the Germans minced and browned carrots for a coffee substitute. The bright green leaves of the carrot were also worn by English ladies as a hair adornment. In 1609, the carrot was introduced by the English in Virginia and has been utilized ever since.

Blueberry Applesauce Cake

The cinnamon and cloves lend an appetizing aroma to this cake. Although a very old cake by itself, I have added a little of the Maine countryside with the addition of blueberries, and I think you'll agree the taste is phenomenal.

2 1/2 c. flour
1 t. baking powder
1 t. baking soda
2 t. cinnamon
1/2 t. ground cloves
1/2 t. salt
1/2 c. shortening, softened
2 1/2 c. sugar
2 eggs
2 c. applesauce
2 c. blueberries

Preheat oven to 350 °F. Grease a 13 × 2-inch pan. Sift together dry ingredients in one bowl and cream shortening and sugar in another. Beat in both eggs, one at a time, until well incorporated. Add applesauce and blueberries into shortening/sugar mixture. Add both dry and wet together and mix until well blended. Pour into prepared pan and bake for 45 to 55 minutes, or until done. Let set in original pan and cool. Great with sweetened cream, cinnamon ice cream, or fresh fruit.

Angel Food Cake

Although one should truly sift all dry ingredients in any cake mix, you really don't need to. But this cake is the exception. If you want this cake to be as light and airy as possible, sift everything as directed.

1 1/2 c. egg whites
1 1/2 c. sifted powdered sugar
1 c. sifted flour
1 1/2 t. cream of tartar
1 t. vanilla
1 c. sugar

Preheat oven to 350°F. In a very large mixer bowl, bring egg whites to room temperature. Meanwhile, sift powdered sugar and flour together 3 times. Set flour mixture aside.

Add cream of tartar and vanilla to egg whites and beat with an electric mixer on medium to high speed till soft peaks form (tips curl). Gradually add sugar, about 2 T. at a time, beating on medium to high speed until stiff peaks form (tips stand straight up). Sift 1/4 of the flour mixture over beaten egg whites; fold in gently. Repeat, folding in remaining flour mixture, using 1/4 of the flour mixture each time. Gently pour into ungreased 10-inch tube pan. Gently cut through the batter with a knife. Bake on the lowest rack for 40 to 45 minutes or until top springs back when lightly touched. Immediately invert cake in pan and cool thoroughly.

Buttermilk-Lemon Pudding Cake

Okay, all you die-hard foodies: If you like tang, you got it! When you mix buttermilk and lemon in any recipe, you are going to have tang, and this cake will be right up your alley.

1 1/2 c. buttermilk
Juice and grated zest of one lemon
1/2 c. lime juice
4 egg yolks
1/4 c. flour
1 c. sugar, divided
1/2 stick (4 T.) butter or margarine, softened
Pinch salt
4 egg whites
Sauce, *recipe below*

Preheat oven to 350°F. Butter or oil an 8 × 8 × 2-inch square baking pan. In a bowl, whisk together the buttermilk, egg yolks, lemon juice and grated zest, lime juice, salt, sugar, butter, and flour until smooth.

With an electric mixer, beat the egg whites until soft peaks form. Continue beating while adding the sugar until stiff peaks form. Gradually fold the liquid mixture into the egg whites in stages. Pour batter into the baking pan and place pan into a larger baking pan. Add enough hot tap water to the larger pan to a level half way up the sides of the cake pan. Bake 45 to 50 minutes or until the top is browned and the cake is springy but moves slightly when jiggled. Remove the cake pan from the water bath and cool on a rack; refrigerate until well chilled. Make the sauce.

Sauce:
1 c. jam or preserves, such as raspberry or blueberry
1 T. dark rum

Bring fruit preserves and rum to a boil, spoon cake onto plates and pour fruit sauce around the edge of the plates. This desert can be made a day ahead, making it ideal for entertaining.

Hot Fudge Pudding Cake

Talk about decadent! Once you try this dessert cake, you will not be able to stop at a mere one serving. Served with Chantilly Cream, I can't think of a more fulfilling chocolate dish, period!

1 1/2 c. sugar	1/2 c. butter or margarine, melted
1 c. flour	1 t. vanilla
8 T. cocoa	1/2 c. dark brown sugar
2 1/2 t. baking powder	1 1/2 c. hot water
2 pinches salt	Whipped or Chantilly Cream
1/2 c. milk	1 can fruit cocktail (optional)

Preheat oven to 350°F. In a large bowl, combine and mix 1 c. sugar, flour, 4 T. cocoa, baking powder, and salt. Stir in milk, butter, and vanilla; beat until smooth. Pour batter into an 8- or 9-inch square baking pan, ungreased. Stir together remaining sugar, brown sugar, and remaining cocoa; sprinkle mixture evenly over the batter. Pour water over the top but do not stir! Bake for 35 to 40 minutes or until center is just about set and barely moving when baking pan is jiggled. Cool for 10 to 15 minutes and spoon into dessert bowls. Spoon sauce from the bottom of the pan over the top of the cake to give it the fudge effect. Serve warm with whipped cream or Chantilly Cream or strain fruit from fruit cocktail and add to bowls.

Chantilly Cream:
For every cup of whipped cream, whisk in 1/4 t. almond extract.

To Make Plum Cake. Mix one pound of currants, one drachm nutmeg, mace, and cinnamon each, a little fat, one pound citron, orange peel candied, and almonds bleach'd, six pounds of flour (well dry'd) beat twenty one eggs, and add with one quart new ale yeast, half pint of wine, three half pints of cream and raisins.

–*American Cookery*, 1796

Individual Chocolate Sauce Cakes

What could be better than a rich chocolate cake filled with flowing thick chocolate sauce when your fork breaks into it? I can't think of anything. So try this delectable dessert and receive "warm" raves from friends and family alike as they demand to know how the chocolate got inside the center of the cake.

4 squares semisweet chocolate
1/2 c. butter or margarine
1 c. powdered sugar
3 eggs
3 egg yolks
7 T. flour
Whipped cream

Preheat oven to 425°F. Liberally spray muffin tins with nonstick cooking spray. Place on baking sheet. Microwave chocolate and 1/2 c. butter in large microwaveable bowl on high for 1 minute or until butter is melted. Stir with wire whisk until chocolate is completely melted. Stir in sugar until well blended. Whisk in eggs and egg yolks and stir in flour. Divide batter between muffin cups. Bake 12 to 14 minutes or until the outside edges are firm but the center is soft. The middle will not feel like it is done cooking but that is exactly the secret behind this dessert. Carefully loosen the edges of cakes and serve immediately with whipped cream.

Although we are in love with chocolate products, many people are switching to carob as a healthier alternative. Here are some comparisons:

CHOCOLATE	VS.	CAROB
real chocolate taste		chocolate flavor
has caffeine		no caffeine
low in fiber		twice the fiber
low in calcium		twice as high in calcium
high in calories		1/3 the calories
high in fat		1/16 the fat

Chocolate is, however, 3x higher in protein, 5x higher in potassium, 8x higher in phosphorous, and 10x higher in iron

Snow Fort Cake

This festive cake resembles the snow forts you built when you were a child. The covering of coconut transforms this cake into a pristine dome of delight. Hope you enjoy!

1 Recipe for Poke Cake
3 to 4 c. flaked coconut
2 c. cold milk
2 pkg. (4 serving size) white chocolate or vanilla pudding mix
1/2 c. powdered sugar
Whipped topping

Preheat oven to 350°F. Prepare Poke Cake recipe (minus the gelatin mixture) with 1 c. coconut. Bake according to directions for Poke Cake. Cool completely on wire racks.

Pour milk into medium bowl and add dry pudding mix and powdered sugar. Beat with wire whisk for 3 minutes or until well blended; mixture will be thick. Stir in 8 oz. whipped topping and cool 30 minutes.

Place 1 of the cake layers on serving plate; spread top with 1 1/2 c. of the topping. Sprinkle with 1/2 c. coconut and cover with second layer of cake. Spread remaining pudding mix on sides and top of cake; press remaining coconut onto sides and top of cake. Garnish with candied cherry or fruit slices heaped in center of cake for color appeal.

How would you like to use the recipe below to clean up with?

Grammy Martha's Lye Soap:

Get a barrel and bore a small hole in the bottom and put a tub underneath to get the lye. Put straw on inside of barrel first. With 5 bushels of unslacked lime, pour one layer of ashes then lime and add water. Ashes should be dry. Continue in this manner until all ashes and lime are used. Let sit for awhile, when lye is ready in tub, an egg will barely float in it. If not strong enough, pour it back through the ashes and add more water if need be.

Honeyed Zucchini Spice Cake

We all love and remember zucchini bread from year to year, but I wanted something zippier. Combining zucchini with spices and a fruited topping and transforming this well-known bread into a cake seemed sensible to me. I, therefore, eloped with my imagination and vôila! Here is a cake I think you will truly enjoy during the brisk New England fall season, or wherever you are, when zucchinis can be found at many roadside vegetable stands for pennies a pound.

3 c. peeled, grated zucchini
1 1/2 c. flaked coconut
5 eggs
1 c. vegetable oil
2 T. vanilla
1 1/2 c. sugar
1 c. honey
3 1/2 c. flour
3 t. cinnamon
2 t. nutmeg
1 t. ginger
1 t. baking soda
2 t. baking powder
1 t. salt
Pineapple Cream Cheese Frosting

Preheat oven to 350°F. Grease and flour 2 cake pans (10-inch). Combine zucchini and coconut; set aside. Beat together eggs, oil, and vanilla in large bowl until well blended. Beat in sugar and honey and gradually add all other dry ingredients until well incorporated. Stir in zucchini mixture. Pour into both cake pans and bake 35 to 40 or until done. Remove from oven; let set for 10 minutes and loosen with knife around edges. Remove to wire rack and cool completely. Frost with Pineapple Cream Cheese Frosting.

Pineapple Cream Cheese Frosting:

Beat together 1 package (8 oz.) softened cream cheese with 1/2 c. softened margarine until creamy. Add 1 can (8 oz.) crushed pineapple, drained. Gradually add 1 lb. (4 1/2 c.) powdered sugar, beating until smooth and creamy.

In the early days of American colonization, right up until the nineteenth century, whistling was not allowed in a Yankee kitchen. It is said to keep bread from rising, sour milk, and spoil apple cider!

Sally Lunn's house in Bath, Somerset, England

Civil War Sally Lunn Cake

This "coffee cake" (known as Popdoodle Cake many centuries ago) is named after a lady from Bath, Somerset, England, named Sally Lunn who made these at her pastry shop during the eighteenth century. It wouldn't be for another 100 years before they became popular in the North during the Civil War.

1/2 c. sugar
1 c. milk, scalded
2 t. salt
1/2 c. butter or margarine, melted
1/2 c. warm water
1 pkg. dry yeast
3 eggs, slightly beaten
5 c. sifted flour
1 t. nutmeg
3 pt. fresh strawberries
Whipped cream

Preheat oven to 400°F. Grease and sugar (not flour) a 10-inch tube pan or bundt cake pan. Combine the milk, 1/4 c. sugar, salt and butter in a bowl and cool to lukewarm. Combine the water and yeast in a large mixing bowl and stir until yeast is dissolved. Add the milk mixture and eggs and mix well. Beat in the flour gradually until smooth. Cover and let rise in warm place for 1 hour or until just about doubled in bulk. Stir down and turn into cake pan. Cover and let rise for about 30 minutes or until almost doubled in bulk once again. Mix remaining sugar and nutmeg, sprinkle over the top of the cake; bake for 40 minutes or until done. Remove from oven and cool for 5 minutes. Remove from pan onto a serving platter and mound strawberries in the center. Serve with whipped cream.

Yeast is the earliest known leavening agent. Ancient Egyptians used it in their beer making about 2000 B.C. and then discovered its ability to produce leavened bread. They also saw that a piece of dough from one batch of bread could be added to the next loaf in order to rise. This method of bread making remained virtually unchanged for 3800 years, until the 1800s, when yeast could be purchased in stores.

Pear Cake with Dutch Hard Sauce

This whole food pear cake is delicious without the Dutch Hard Sauce, but for those of you who wish for even more sweetening and a creamy sauce to envelope every bite, indulge!

Cake:
3/4 c. butter or margarine
1 c. honey
3 eggs
2 c. flour mixed with 1 t. cornstarch
2 t. baking powder
Grated rind of 1/2 lemon

Topping:
1/4 c. butter or margarine
2 T. honey
1 c. chopped walnuts
1 t. cinnamon
1 T. pear liqueur (optional)
8 ripe pears

Preheat oven to 350°F. Beat the butter and honey until creamy; gradually add the eggs, sifted flour/cornstarch, baking powder and lemon rind. Put mixture into a greased 9-inch cake pan. Peel, quarter and core the pears; cut them into thin strips lengthwise and arrange in a ring on top of the cake mixture.

For the topping, melt the butter and honey for 2 minutes in the microwave. Stir in the walnuts, cinnamon, and pear liqueur. Spread the honey and nut mixture over them and bake for 40 to 45 minutes or until a toothpick inserted in the center comes out clean. Remove from oven and leave in pan for 10 minutes before removing to a serving plate.

Dutch Hard Sauce:
1/4 c. butter or margarine
1 c. powdered sugar
2 T. sour cream
1/2 t. vanilla
1/4 t. nutmeg

Cream butter and powdered sugar until fluffy. Add remaining 1/2 c. powdered sugar alternately with sour cream. Add vanilla and nutmeg and whip until smooth. Serve with Pear Cake.

Good Ol' Scripture Cake

This is a cake made entirely of ingredients found in the Bible. You will be able to follow this recipe with ease and hopefully enjoy this Puritan cake with gusto (but don't enjoy it too much, our pilgrim fathers have a reputation you know!) Please allow this cake to rest overnight before serving.

    1/2 c. Judges 5:25
    3/4 c. Jeremiah 6:20
    2 1/2 c. I Kings 4:22
    1 t. Amos 4:5
    Dash Leviticus 2:13
    II Chronicles 9:9
    3 Jeremiah 17:11
    1/2 c. Judges 4:19
    1/2 c. I Samuel 14:25
    1 c. I Samuel 30:12
    1 C. Nahum 3:12
    1/2 c. Numbers 17:8

Preheat oven to 325°F. In a large mixing bowl cream Judges 5:25 (butter or margarine); blend in Jeremiah 6:20 (molasses). Sift together I Kings 4:22 (flour); Amos 4:5 (baking powder); Leviticus 2:13 (salt); and II Chronicles 9:9 (1/2 t. cinnamon, 1/4 t. ground cloves, 1/8 t. ground ginger). Combine Jeremiah 17:11(beaten eggs); Judges 4:19 (sour milk or buttermilk [you may use whole milk here]); and I Samuel (honey); stir to combine.

Add the egg mixture and the sifted dry ingredients alternately to creamed mixture. Mix well and stir in I Samuel 30:12 (raisins); Nahum 3:12 (chopped figs); and Numbers 17:8 (chopped almonds). Turn mixture into greased and lightly floured 9 × 5 × 3-inch loaf pan. Bake for 75 to 85 minutes. Let cool in pan for 10 minutes and then turn onto a serving platter. When cooled completely, wrap tightly and store overnight before serving.

All-American Chocolate Chip Cookies

You know! The cookie almost every cook can't find the right recipe for? Well here it is.

    2 1/2 c. flour
    1 t. baking soda
    1/2 t. salt
    1 c. (2 sticks) butter or margarine, softened
    1 c. brown sugar
    3/4 c. granulated sugar
    3 t. vanilla
    2 eggs
    12 oz. chocolate chips

In a mixing bowl, blend together the flour, soda, and salt. In a separate bowl, with an electric mixer, beat the butter until smooth and fluffy. Add the sugars and vanilla, continue beating until well incorporated. Slowly, and with the mixer on low, incorporate the flour mixture a little at a time until dough is blended well. Add the eggs, continue mixing on low, and lastly add the chocolate chips. When all blended well, cover the bowl

Oatmeal Cookies

with plastic wrap and refrigerate for at least 30 minutes.

Either line a baking sheet with parchment paper or spray with nonstick cooking spray. Scoop out the cookie dough and place on baking sheet, leaving at least 2 inches in between each mound. Use any size scoop you want; I prefer a 1/4-cup measure. Chill once again for 15 minutes. Preheat oven to 350°F. Place in oven and bake for 10 to 12 minutes, or until golden. Remove, let cool for 2 minutes if using nonstick spray, then transfer to platter or rack. If using parchment, you can transfer immediately.

Massachusetts and Pennsylvania have one thing in common: Their official state cookie is the chocolate chip cookie. And did you know that over half of all baked goods made at home is...the chocolate chip cookie?

These soft, cake like cookies have no equal when the raisins plump up during baking—a childhood favorite. If you would like, boil the raisins for 5 minutes, drain, and add to the cookie recipe. The raisins will be twice the size without loss of flavor.

3/4 c. flour
1 1/2 c. old-fashioned rolled oats
1 t. baking powder
1 1/2 t. cinnamon
1/4 t. salt
1/2 c. (1 stick) butter or margarine, softened
1 c. sugar
1 egg, beaten
2 t. vanilla
1/2 c. raisins (optional)
1/2 c. chopped walnuts (optional)

Preheat oven to 350°F. Line a baking sheet with parchment or spray with nonstick cooking spray. In a large bowl, combine flour, oats, baking powder, cinnamon, and salt; set aside. Using a mixer, in a separate bowl, beat butter until fluffy. Add brown sugar and continue beating. Add the egg and vanilla and beat until smooth. Slowly, and on low, beat in the flour mixture until well incorporated. Drop the batter by the rounded tablespoonful onto the prepared baking sheet. Leave 2 inches between each mound. Bake 12 to 13 minutes or until set. Remove to rack if using one, if not, let cool on sheet for 10 minutes, and then remove to platter.

Stir in the raisins and nuts after beating in the flour if you would like.

In Hamamatsu, Japan, eel cookies are a favorite. Made with butter, garlic, and crushed eel bones, the taste is topped off with eel extract.

Peanut Butter Cookies

Let the kids help roll these cookies in sugar before placing on cookie sheet. These children's favorites stay soft for a long time if baked according to recipe.

- 1 c. flour
- 1 t. baking soda
- 1/4 t. salt
- 3/4 c. butter or margarine, softened
- 1 1/4 c. peanut butter
- 3/4 c. sugar plus extra for coating
- 1 c. brown sugar
- 2 eggs, lightly beaten
- 2 t. vanilla
- 1 c. chopped, salted peanuts (optional)

Preheat oven to 350°F. Line a cookie sheet with parchment paper or grease with nonstick cooking spray. In a bowl, mix together flour, baking soda, and salt; set aside. Using a separate bowl and a beater, beat the butter until fluffy. Beat in the peanut butter until smooth. Add the sugars and blend until smooth. Add the eggs and vanilla, blending well. Stir in the flour mixture, on low, until well combined. Stir in the peanuts.

Shape the dough into tablespoon-size balls, roll in sugar and place on the cookie sheet, leaving 2 inches between each ball. With a fork, press the dough balls slightly to flatten and make a criss-cross pattern on top of each. Bake for 10 to 12 minutes, or until the cookies are golden brown and set in the middle. Remove to a wire rack if using parchment. Let cool for 10 minutes if using spray, then transfer to rack or platter.

Peanut Butter and Jelly Cookies

Nothing wrong with sandwiching two of these cookies together just as you would a peanut butter and jelly sandwich. For the crunchy peanut butter fanatic, substitute crunchy peanut butter for smooth.

- 1 c. (2 sticks) butter or margarine
- 1 c. peanut butter
- 2 t. vanilla
- 2/3 c. brown sugar
- 1/2 c. sugar
- 2 eggs
- 2 c. flour
- 1 c. your favorite preserves or jelly (whisk jelly until smooth)

Preheat oven to 350°F. In a large bowl, beat butter, peanut butter, and vanilla with mixer until smooth. Add the sugars and continue beating until well blended. Add the eggs and mix only until just blended. Add the flour slowly, beating on low until a dough ball is formed. Do not over mix. Pinch off rounded teaspoon-sized pieces, roll into balls and place on an ungreased cookie sheet 2 inches apart. Press your fingers in each ball to create a well. Fill each well with a half teaspoon of the preserves or jelly. Bake for 10 minutes or until lightly browned and firm. Remove from oven and let cool on pan for 5 minutes before transferring to rack or platter to cool completely.

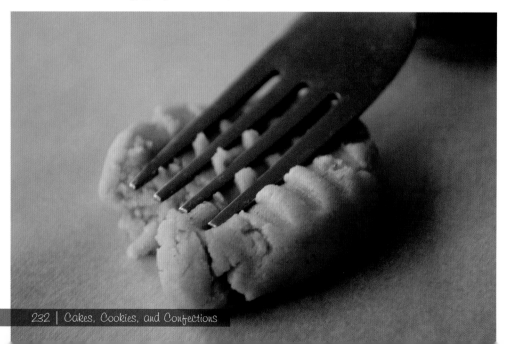

The children were lined up in the cafeteria of a Catholic elementary school for lunch. At the head of the table was a large pile of apples. The nun made a note, and posted it on the apple tray: "Take only one. God is watching."

Moving further along the lunch line, at the other end of the table was a large pile of chocolate chip cookies. A child had written a note, "Take as many as you want. God is watching the apples."

Old-Fashioned Soft Molasses Cookies

Sugar Cookies

These cookies are very versatile but able to stand by themselves. Try dipping half in melted dark chocolate and the other half in melted white chocolate. They're great for piping designs or frosting. Let the kids help.

1/2 c. (1 stick) butter or margarine, softened
1/2 c. powdered sugar
1/2 c. granulated sugar
1 egg
1/2 c. vegetable oil
2 t. vanilla
2 3/4 c. flour
1/2 t. baking soda
1/2 t. cream of tartar
1/2 t. nutmeg
Pinch salt
3/4 c. granulated sugar

In a large mixing bowl, beat the butter until fluffy with a mixer. Add the sugars and mix until smooth. In a separate bowl, mix the egg, oil, and vanilla well, blend into the butter mixture and beat until incorporated well. Cover and chill for at least an hour.

Preheat oven to 350°F. Line a baking sheet with parchment paper or spray with nonstick cooking spray. In another bowl, combine flour, baking soda, cream of tartar, nutmeg, and salt. Mix the flour mixture with the butter mixture until blended very well. Place the 3/4 c. sugar into a bowl. Pinch off 1/4-cup-sized pieces of dough and form into a ball. Roll in the bowl of sugar until well coated. Flatten each ball to about 1/4 inch thick and roll in sugar again. Place on prepared sheet pans, with 2-inches separating each cookie. Bake 10 to 12 minutes or until golden and set well. Remove to rack if using parchment. If using spray, let cool for 10 minutes and place on rack or platter to cool.

No cookie says "the taste of home" quite like soft molasses cookies. I think it's the waft of cloves while baking that truly brings back memories. To make this recipe *Spiced* Molasses Cookies, simply add 1 t. allspice.

2 t. baking soda
1 c. hot water, not boiling
1 c. molasses
1 c. sugar
1 egg
4 1/2 c. flour
1 t. salt
1 t. cinnamon
1 t. ginger
Pinch cloves

Stir baking soda into hot water until dissolved; add molasses. In a separate bowl, cream shortening with sugar until light, beat in egg. Stir together flour, salt, and spices in another bowl. Add half of the dry ingredients to the molasses mixture and blend well. Add the remaining flour mixture and stir until combined. Chill for 1 hour. Roll out and cut into shapes on a lightly floured board, using cutters dipped in flour or cocoa to prevent sticking. Transfer to greased cookie sheets and bake in a preheated 350°F oven for 10 to 15 minutes (depends upon size of cookies), or until done. Cool on wire racks.

Ginger Snaps

Now I have to add gingersnaps to this book because of their timeless place in our childhood. Thin and crispy, these gems really do harken back to the olden days.

    3/4 c. shortening
    1 c. brown sugar, firmly packed
    1 egg
    1/4 t. salt
    4 T. molasses
    2 1/4 c. flour
    2 t. baking soda
    1/2 t. cloves
    1 t. cinnamon
    1 t. ginger

Preheat oven to 350°F. Cream together shortening and brown sugar until well mixed, light, and fluffy. Beat together well the egg, salt, and molasses and then mix these into the above. Sift together flour, baking soda, ground cloves, cinnamon, and ginger. Add dry ingredients to first wet mixture and combine well. Chill in the refrigerator a few hours or overnight. After chilled, shape dough into walnut-sized balls and place on a greased cookie sheet, allowing room for expansion. Flatten balls with a fork until they are roughly 2 1/2 inches in diameter. Bake in 350°F oven 12 to 15 minutes. Do not let get too brown.

Royal Icing on Ginger Snaps pairs well. The sweetness of the icing and the spice of the cookie create a great multi-level treat. This Royal Icing dries to a smooth, hard finish. One word of caution however. If you have any left over, it is next to impossible to use it again. Re-beating the icing breaks it down so it is virtually unusable.

    1 egg white, room temperature
    Lg. pinch of cream of tartar
    2 c. sifted powdered sugar
    2 to 4 T. water

Combine all ingredients in mixing bowl. With an electric mixer, beat on medium speed until very smooth. Start with 2 T. water and if it is too firm, add a tablespoon of water at a time until the consistency is right for the cookies to be frosted with. Simply use a tablespoon to pour over the tops of the cookies to be frosted. Royal Icing is also used for decorating cakes by piping as well. Its gloss and smoothness makes a great base for coloring as well. Just add a drop or two, or three, at the end of beating, mixing in very well.

Snickerdoodles

With crispy edges and chewy centers, these cinnamon dusted cookies have been a long-time favorite up and down the East Coast for generations.

    1/2 c. (1 stick) butter or margarine
    1 c. sugar, divided
    1 egg
    1 t. vanilla
    1 1/2 c. flour
    Pinch salt
    1/2 t. baking soda
    1 t. cream of tartar
    3 t. cinnamon

Preheat oven to 350°F. Line a cookie sheet with parchment or spray with nonstick cooking spray. With a mixer, beat the butter until fluffy. Add 3/4 c. sugar and mix until smooth. Add the egg and vanilla; mix well. In a separate bowl, blend the flour, salt, baking soda, and cream of tartar. Add to the butter mixture and beat until combined well.

Mix together 1/4 c. sugar with the cinnamon in a bowl.

Break off 1/4 c. pieces of dough and roll into balls. Roll these balls in the cinnamon sugar mixture until well coated. Place on cookie sheet with 2 inches separating each ball. Bake 8 to 10 minutes or until they are set and cracks start appearing on top. Remove to rack or if using spray, let cool 10 minutes then remove to rack or platter.

Coconut Macaroons

So easy to make. Press a cherry in the center of each before baking or squeeze a small piece of chocolate in the center of each directly after baking for that little extra touch.

14 oz. sweetened shredded coconut
14 oz. sweetened condensed milk
1 t. vanilla
2 eggs, room temperature
1/4 t. salt
Melted chocolate (optional)

Preheat oven to 325°F. Spray a cookies sheet with nonstick cooking spray or use parchment paper to line with. Combine the coconut, condensed milk, and vanilla in a large bowl. Whip the egg whites and salt on high with beaters or whisk until they are little more than soft peaks. Carefully fold the whites into the coconut mixture. Drop the batter onto the prepared sheet pans by the tablespoon. Bake for 25 to 30 minutes or until golden brown on top. Remove and cool. Dip in melted chocolate if desired.

Yankee Hermits

With the addition of molasses to these cookies, they have been transformed from a great New York cookie to an even better New England flavored treat.

2 c. flour
1 t. baking soda
Pinch salt
1 1/2 sticks butter or margarine, softened
1 c. brown sugar
2 t. cinnamon
2 t. dried ginger
1/2 t ground cloves
1/4 t. nutmeg
3 t. espresso powder
1 egg
1/3 c. molasses
1 c. raisins
1 c. walnuts, chopped (optional)

Preheat oven to 350°F. Line a baking sheet with parchment or spray with nonstick cooking spray. Stir together flour, baking soda, and salt until blended. In a separate mixing bowl, beat the butter until fluffy and add the brown sugar; mix well. Stir in the cinnamon, ginger, cloves, nutmeg, and espresso powder until mixed very well.

In a separate bowl, stir the egg and molasses together and add to the butter mixture. Blend in well and add the dry ingredients slowly, beating until well incorporated. Fold in the raisins and walnuts.

Scoop out by the 1/4-cup measure and mound on the prepared pan, leaving 2 inches between each mound. Bake for 12 to 14 minutes or until they are golden brown and set. Remove and transfer to cooling racks if using parchment. If using spray, let cool 5 minutes before removing to racks or platter.

Butter Cookies

I think these are the only cookies that just plain don't need any flavor added, other than what is listed. They have a profile that is second to none.

1 c. flour
1/2 c. cornstarch
1/2 c. powdered sugar
3/4 c. (1 1/2 sticks) butter, room temperature
1/2 c. finely chopped walnuts (optional)

Preheat oven to 300°F. In a large bowl, blend together flour, cornstarch, and powdered sugar until well combined. Add butter and thoroughly blend with mixer. Stir in the walnuts. Drop by the tablespoonful onto ungreased baking sheet, leaving an inch space between each mound. Bake 20 to 22 minutes or until lightly browned.

Dilemma: Some cookies are done before others on the same pan.
Correction: Make sure all cookies are the same thickness if rolling. If mounding, make sure the mounds are all the same size before cooking. You can also rotate the cookie sheet halfway through cooking in case your oven cooks unevenly.

Dilemma: The cookies are too dry and brittle when transferring to rack or plate.
Correction: Make sure you put the correct amount of egg in the recipe. Egg is a binder for most cookies. Also if your cookie has a rather high amount of fat, it will be susceptible to falling apart, just handle them with care and ease. Allow them to cool on the baking sheet until room temperature before attempting to remove them to a plate or rack.

Dilemma: The cookies spread out too much when cooking.
Correction: Too much grease on cookie sheet. The cookie batter was too warm or thin when placed on cookie sheet. The batter was too thin (not enough flour) when mixing. If you are making more than one batch of cookies and using the same pan, make sure the pan is cool before adding more cookie dough. Also, too much leavening (baking powder or soda) may have been used.

Dilemma: The cookies are too dark on bottom or too crisp around the edges.
Correction: Your cookie pan is a dark color; the oven was too hot; you were baking on the bottom rack; or the sheet pan was too thin (a very common problem).

Dilemma: Cookies still stick to pan, or mold, after baking.
Correction: Either you didn't correctly grease the pan or the cookies were left to cool too long on the prepared pan after baking. In molds, try sprinkling and coating the molds with flour after spraying or greasing. Tilting the molds so that flour evenly coats all sides and bottom usually prevents sticking.

Mexican Wedding Cakes

This is the only food item that changed its name solely for political reasons. Initially known as Russian Tea Cakes, the people of the United States, during the Cold War era, decided that since these cakes were often made for weddings and we disliked the Soviet Union, why not change the name to Mexican Wedding Cakes? These cakes can be drowned in a snowfall of powdered sugar to be authentic.

1 c. (2 sticks) butter or margarine, softened
2 c. powdered sugar
3 t. vanilla
2 1/2 c. flour
1/4 t. salt
1 c. finely chopped pecans

Preheat oven to 350°F. Line a cookie sheet with parchment or spray with nonstick cooking spray. With a mixer, beat butter until fluffy. Add 1/2 c. powdered sugar and vanilla and blend until smooth. Stir the flour, salt, and pecans together in a separate bowl and add the butter mixture. Beat on low until well incorporated. Break off 1/4-cup sized pieces and roll in your palms into ball shape. Place on cookie sheet and separate 2 inches apart. Bake 20 to 25 minutes or until golden brown and set well. Remove from oven and let cool 5 minutes.

Gently remove cookies to a plate, sprinkle half of the remainder of the powdered sugar onto cookie sheet and place the cookies on top of the powdered sugar. Sprinkle the remainder of the powdered sugar on top of the cookies, cool and roll them in the sugar.

Chocolate Biscotti

Biscotti is one of those recipes that was lost for many centuries, only to be rediscovered in the nineteenth century. Actually, to be grammatically correct, biscotti is the plural of biscotto. You should have a beverage handy and dunk these cookies before eating. Italians usually serve biscotti with Vin Santo, a dessert wine.

1/2 c. (1 stick) butter or margarine, melted
1/2 c. flour
1/2 c. cocoa
2 t. baking soda
Pinch salt
1 c. sugar
2 eggs
2 t. vanilla
3/4 t. almond extract
4 oz. chocolate chips
1 1/2 c. sliced almonds

Preheat oven to 350°F. Line a baking sheet with parchment or spray with nonstick cooking spray. In a large bowl, blend together flour, cocoa, baking soda, and salt. Add the sugar and stir to combine. In a separate bowl, whisk the eggs with vanilla and almond extract. Add the dry ingredients along with the melted butter. With a mixer, beat the mixture on low until combined. Blend in the chocolate chips and almonds. Divide the dough in half. Shape each in a log about 7 inches long, 3 inches wide, and 1 inch high. Place both in the center of the prepared sheet pan, at least 2 inches apart.

Bake for 20 to 22 minutes or until set. Remove from oven, leave on pan and lower oven temperature to 325°F. Transfer logs to a cutting board and cut on the diagonal into 1/2-inch-thick slices. Place these slices on their sides back onto the baking sheet and continue baking for 15 to 17 minutes, or until firm. Remove and transfer to racks to cool.

Anise Biscotti

Even though an Italian baker is credited with first baking these twice-baked cookies and serving them with wine, many countries have adopted their own version of these hard cookies. The English have their rusks, the French have their *biscotte* and *croquets de carcassonne*, the Germans with *zwiebacks,* while the Greeks bake *paxemadia*.

2 c. flour
2 t. baking powder
1/4 t. salt
3/4 c. sugar
2 eggs, lightly beaten
1/2 c. (1 stick) butter or margarine, melted
1 t. anise extract
1/3 c. anise seed

Preheat oven to 350°F. Line a cookie sheet with parchment or spray with nonstick cooking spray. Blend together flour, baking powder, salt, and sugar. Add the eggs, melted butter, and anise extract, mix very well. Add the anise seeds and mix until well blended. Follow the directions given in the Chocolate Biscotti preparation for rolling, cutting, and baking.

Madelines

There are many versions of the origin of Madelines, but the most credible is that they were first made, and named after, the convent in the French town of Commercy. The nuns at St. Mary Magdalene (St. Madeleine) made and sold the cookies to support themselves and their school. After the French revolution, the monasteries were closed, and the nuns sold the recipe to the bakers of the town for a large amount of money.

    4 eggs
    Pinch salt
    1/2 c. sugar
    2 t. vanilla
    1 c. flour
    1/2 c. (1 stick) butter or margarine,
       melted and chilled
    1 t. grated lemon zest

Preheat oven to 375°F. Spray Madeline pans with nonstick cooking spray. In a large bowl, beat the eggs and salt until foamy with electric mixer. Slowly add the sugar and continue beating until mixture is pale and is ribbon like when beaters are held over the mixture, about 5 minutes. Add vanilla and blend in. Fold in the flour, butter, and lemon zest.

Start filling the Madeline cups 3/4-full with the batter. Bake for 10 minutes or until they are golden brown and spring back when touched in the middle. Remove and quickly invert onto baking sheet. Cool completely.

Chocolate Madelines

Want to add even more flavor? Add 1 T. grated orange rind to this recipe. These cake like cookies are known the world over and I think you will find the reason why when you bite into one.

    3 oz. chocolate chips
    1/2 c. butter or margarine, in pats
    2 eggs
    1/2 c. sugar
    Pinch salt
    1/2 c. flour
    1 t. vanilla

Preheat oven to 350°F. Spray a 12-cup Madeline pan with nonstick cooking spray. Melt the chocolate and butter together in the microwave at 30 second intervals until melted. Stir to combine. In a separate bowl, beat eggs and sugar with a mixer until very thick and ribbon like when beater is lifted from the bowl, about 5 minutes.

In another bowl, blend the salt and flour, add eggs; mix well. Add the chocolate mixture and vanilla, blend very well. Pour into Madeline cups 3/4 full and bake for 12 to 14 minutes or until bouncy in the middle and set. Remove from oven and immediately invert onto baking sheet to cool completely.

Chocolate Fudge Brownies

The origin of the brownie is shrouded in mystery. It is widely believed that a housewife in Bangor, Maine, while making chocolate cake, forgot to add baking powder to her recipe. When the cake didn't rise, and because of our ingrained frugality, she cut the unleavened treat into squares and served them anyway. It is true that Fanny Farmer published a chocolate brownie recipe in 1906, but the Bangor story was said to have occurred years before it was mentioned in a 1912 cookbook published in Bangor.

    4 oz. chocolate chips
    1/2 c. (1 stick) butter or margarine
    1 1/2 c. sugar
    1 T. instant espresso powder
       dissolved in 1 T. warm water
    3 t. vanilla
    2 eggs
    3/4 c. flour
    1 c. chopped walnuts (optional)

Preheat oven to 350°F. Spray and flour the inside of an 8-inch square baking pan. Scatter flour into the pan and tilt to coat all sides and bottom. Melt the chocolate and butter in the microwave in 30 second intervals until completely melted; stir together and set aside. In a separate bowl, blend in the melted chocolate mixture, sugar, espresso, and vanilla, beat very well. Stir in the eggs, continue beating until fully incorporated. Add the flour, beating on low power until thoroughly combined. Stir in the walnuts.

Pour the batter in the prepared baking pan and bake for 30 minutes, or until a toothpick inserted about 2 inches from the edge has just a little moist cake clinging to it. The center may not seem done but it is done enough. Remove from oven and cool completely.

Homemade Baby Ruth® Candy Brownies

I love the taste of Baby Ruth candy bars, so I created this brownie getting as close to the candy bar as I could. I added oatmeal to give it more substance, but it doesn't take away from that great flavor that has been around so long.

2/3 c. butter or margarine
1 c. brown sugar
1/4 c. corn syrup
1/4 c. peanut butter
1 t. vanilla
1 c. rolled oats

Preheat oven to 375°F. Grease and flour a 13 × 9-inch square pan. Combine butter, sugar, and corn syrup in a saucepan. Over low heat, stir and cook until butter melts and the sugar dissolves. Add the peanut butter and vanilla. In a bowl with the oatmeal in it, pour the butter mixture over the oatmeal and mix very well. Press mixture into prepared pan evenly. Bake for 12 minutes and remove from oven.

Place chocolate and butterscotch chips in a microwave safe bowl and melt in 30 second intervals, stopping to stir each time you add 30 seconds. When melted, add the peanut butter and peanuts, blend well. Pour over the baked mixture and cool before cutting.

Topping:
12 oz. package chocolate chips
6 oz. butterscotch chips
2/3 c. peanut butter
1 c. peanuts

Peanut Butter Chip Brownies

It's almost as if peanut butter and chocolate just have to be together. I don't know if it's the old commercial but these brownies won't have you complaining about "you got your chocolate in my peanut butter" again.

1/2 c. (1 stick) butter or margarine
4 oz. semi-sweet chocolate
1/2 c. sugar
2 eggs
2 t. vanilla
1/2 c. flour
12 oz. peanut butter chips
8 oz. chocolate chips

Preheat oven to 375°F. Grease or spray, with nonstick cooking spray, an 8-inch square baking pan, then flour. Melt butter and semisweet chocolate in a small saucepan over low heat, stirring until the chocolate just melts. Remove from heat and cool. Beat sugar and eggs in a large bowl until light and fluffy. Blend in the vanilla and chocolate mixture. Stir in the flour until well mixed, and then fold in the peanut butter chips.

Spread the batter evenly in the prepared pan and bake 25 to 30 minutes or until firm and dry in the middle. Remove from oven and sprinkle chocolate chips over the top evenly. Set aside to cool. When the chocolate chips have melted, spread them over the brownies and refrigerate until the topping has hardened. Cut to serve.

Raspberry and Fudge Brownies

If you like raspberry truffles, you'll love this brownie. The bittersweet chocolate really allows the raspberry preserves to stand out.

1/2 c. (1 stick) butter or margarine
3 oz. bittersweet chocolate
2 eggs
1 c. sugar
2 t. vanilla
3/4 c. flour
1/4 t. baking powder
Pinch salt
1/2 c. sliced almonds (optional)
3/4 c. raspberry preserves
6 oz. chocolate chips

Preheat oven to 350°F. Grease and flour an 8-inch square baking pan. Melt butter and bittersweet chocolate in a small saucepan over low heat. Remove from heat and cool. In a separate bowl, with a mixer, beat eggs, sugar, and vanilla until fluffy. Beat in the chocolate mixture. In another bowl, mix flour, baking powder, and salt well. Add to egg/sugar mixture, beating slowly until just incorporated.

Spread 3/4 of the batter into the prepared pan, sprinkling the almonds

evenly over the top. Bake 10 minutes and remove from oven. Gently spread the preserves over the almonds. You may need to microwave the preserves to have spreadable consistency. Smooth the top and continue baking for 25 to 30 minutes or until the top feels firm. Remove from oven and sprinkle the chocolate chips over the top. Let rest for 5 to 7 minutes until the chocolate has melted. Spread the melted chips over the brownie evenly. Cool completely before cutting into squares.

Rocky Road Brownies

Chewy, chocolaty with a bit of crunch—they'll remind you of the old-fashioned Rocky Road Ice Cream.

1/2 c. butter or margarine
1/2 c. cocoa
1 c. sugar
1 egg
1/2 c. flour
1/4 c. milk
2 t. vanilla
1 1/2 c. mini marshmallows
1 1/2 c. chopped walnuts (optional)
6 oz. chocolate chips

Preheat oven to 350°F. Grease and flour an 8-inch square baking pan. Combine butter and cocoa in a saucepan over low heat, stirring constantly, until smooth. Remove from heat and stir in the sugar, egg, flour, milk, and vanilla. Mix until smooth.

Spread batter evenly in the prepared pan and bake for 25 to 28 minutes, or until the center feels firm. Remove from the oven; sprinkle the marshmallows, walnuts, and chocolate chips over the top. Return to the oven for 3 to 5 minutes, or until the topping is warm enough to melt together. Remove and cool completely before cutting.

Lemon Squares

Lemon on lemon. The refreshing and clean taste of this fruit pops in your mouth when you bite into this confection.

2 c. flour	4 eggs
1/2 c. powdered sugar	1 3/4 c. sugar
1/4 t. salt	1/4 c. flour
1 c. (2 sticks) butter or margarine, softened	1/2 t. baking powder
Grated zest of 1 lemon	1/2 c. lemon juice
1 t. vanilla	Grated zest of 1 lemon
Lemon Topping:	1/2 c. powdered sugar for dusting

Preheat oven to 350°F. Spray a 9 × 13-inch square baking pan with nonstick cooking spray. Dust with flour, tilting the pan to evenly coat the sides and bottom. For the crust, mix the flour, powdered sugar, and salt until blended. In a separate bowl, beat the butter until fluffy, add the zest and vanilla and continue beating until mixed well and a ball is formed. Remove and press firmly into the prepared pan for the crust. Bake 20 minutes; remove pan and cool.

For the topping, with an electric beater, beat the eggs until fluffy. Slowly add the sugar and continue to beat, on high, until it is thick and ribbon-like, about 5 minutes. In a separate bowl, combine the flour and baking powder well. Add the lemon juice and zest; blend well. Add the flour mixture to the butter mixture and beat well. Pour this topping onto the crust and bake for 23 to 25 minutes, or until topping is set in the middle. Remove and cool. Dust the top heavily with powdered sugar.

Tollhouse Squares

I don't think I have ever known anyone not to like tollhouse squares or cookies. I have omitted any nuts in this recipe for those of you who simply can't eat nuts. I hope you enjoy. These chewy, dense squares can be made with 1/2 c. chopped walnuts if you desire.

2 c. flour	2 eggs
1 t. baking soda	2 t. vanilla
1 t. salt	1 c. (2 sticks) butter or margarine, melted
1 c. sugar	12 oz. chocolate chips
1/2 c. brown sugar	

Preheat oven to 350°F. Grease a shallow half sheet pan or large cookie pan. In a large bowl, blend the flour, baking soda, salt, sugar, and brown sugar. Add the remaining ingredients and mix very well. The batter will be very stiff. Pour into the prepared pan and smooth the top. Bake for 20 to 25 minutes or until the center is firm and the sides have slightly pulled away from the pan.

Haystacks

There are so many variations of this recipe that use everything from chow mein noodles to potato chips. I find bran flakes to be crispy and neutral in taste, and it doesn't hurt to add a little goodness to something already so addictive.

1/4 c. butter or margarine
1/2 c. peanut butter
2 c. butterscotch chips
6 c. bran flakes
6 oz. chocolate chips

Combine butter, peanut butter, and butterscotch chips in a saucepan over low heat. Cook, stirring frequently, until melted and mixed thoroughly. Remove from heat. In a large bowl, place the bran flakes. Pour the melted butterscotch mixture over. Stir with a spoon until all the flakes are coated evenly. Stir in the chocolate chips. Spoon 1/4-cup measures onto baking sheet and refrigerate until firm.

CHAPTER 13

Desserts

Blueberry Fritters

Ever feel like finding something to snuggle up with to relax and enjoy your surroundings? Well look no further than your…bowl of Blueberry Fritters.

A warm kiss of stickiness—only a child's sticky kiss is better.

Vegetable oil for frying
1 c. flour
2 t. baking powder
4 t. powdered sugar
1/4 t. salt
1 Tsp. cinnamon
1 t. vanilla
1/3 c. milk
1 egg
1/2 c. fresh or frozen blueberries
Maple syrup

Heat 3 inches of vegetable oil in sturdy pot to 360°F or fire up your deep fat fryer according to manufacturer's instructions. Mix all dry ingredients. Add milk and vanilla to egg and beat well, slowly stir into dry ingredients. When batter is smooth, fold in blueberries until mixed evenly. Drop 2-oz. scoops slowly into vegetable oil, and cook until golden brown, about 3 to 4 minutes. Remove fritters onto rack or paper towel-lined platter. Serve with a generous portion of warm maple syrup.

Blueberry Warble with Custard Sauce

This is my take on a fun, delicious, and vibrantly tasty dessert that the kids will love. I call it Warble because it shimmies and shakes like a gelatin dessert should, but has more of a grown-up characteristic that everyone will enjoy.

One package (3 oz.)
   raspberry flavored gelatin
1 3/4 c. water
1 1/2 cups frozen blueberries
1 egg plus one egg yolk
1/2 c. milk
2 T. sugar
1 t. vanilla

Warble: Prepare gelatin with 1 3/4 c. of water (1 cup boiling water to dissolve gelatin, followed by 3/4 cup cold water). Pour gelatin about 1 inch high in custard or any decorative mold that holds 6 to 8 ounces. Add 2 tablespoons of frozen blueberries to each one. Chill in refrigerator. Add remainder of gelatin and berries. Berries will float, forming layers. Let cool again, chill for several hours or overnight.

Custard Sauce: Mix eggs, milk, and sugar in top of double boiler over high heat or use saucepan. If using saucepan, whisk frequently to prevent scorching and reduce heat to medium-low. Stir until it begins to thicken, about 5 minutes. Do not boil. The mixture should coat a spoon. Remove from heat and add vanilla. Cover and chill in refrigerator.

To Serve: Dip molds for 10 to 15 seconds in hot water and carefully loosen edge of gelatin-berry mixture from mold with a knife. Turn onto a chilled plate. Spoon custard sauce around Blueberry Warble.

New England Blueberry Grunt

Referred to as Grunt in Massachusetts and Slump in the rest of New England, this tasty, pastry-topped dessert resembles cobbler in many ways. With Grunt, however, you cut in the baked topping after the dish has cooked so that the top and bottom of this sweet treat is mixed together.

6 c. fresh blueberries
3/4 c. sugar
4 T. cornstarch
3/4 c. water
2 c. flour
3 t. baking powder
1/4 t. salt
1/4 c. sugar
3 T. butter or margarine, softened
3/4 c. milk
Dash cinnamon (optional)

Preheat oven to 350°F. Combine blueberries with 3/4 c. sugar and 1/2 c. water in a large saucepan and bring to a boil. In a small bowl, whisk together 1/4 c. water with cornstarch until lump-free. Reduce heat to low and continue cooking until the berries are soft, about 6 minutes. Add the cornstarch mixture and stir well until thickened and smooth. Pour into an ungreased casserole dish or 8 × 8 × 2-inch baking pan.

Meanwhile, mix flour, baking powder, sugar, and salt together in a large bowl. Cut in the butter and gradually stir in enough milk to make a very soft dough. Drop by the tablespoon on top of blueberry sauce and bake for 18 to 20 minutes, or until the top is browned and a toothpick inserted in the topping comes out clean. Remove from oven and, with 2 knives, cut the biscuit topping into the blueberries. Serve with ice cream, whipped cream, or by itself. Best served directly from the oven.

Strawberry Fritters

Did you know that strawberries are the only fruit that have their seeds on the outside? Rich chocolate or caramel sauce should adorn these light and airy mini-beignets.

1 qt. strawberries
2 eggs
3/4 c. milk
1 T. plus 1 t. butter or margarine, softened
2 t. vanilla
1 c. flour
3 T. powdered sugar
1/4 t. salt
1 1/2 t. baking powder
Vegetable oil for frying

Heat oil in deep, flat-bottomed, large stock pot to 350°F. Hull and quarter strawberries. Whisk eggs, milk, butter, and vanilla together in large bowl. In separate bowl, blend together flour, powdered sugar, salt, and baking powder. Join wet ingredients with dry and blend until almost all lumps have disappeared. Add strawberries and blend until all berries are coated.

Dip heaping tablespoonfuls of batter into the oil and fry a few at a time for 1 1/2 to 2 minutes, or until browned. Remove with slotted spoon and continue with remainder of batter. Cool slightly and enjoy within 30 minutes, before they get soggy.

True Strawberry Shortcake

So many of us take the easy way out when it comes to Strawberry Shortcake. You can find sponge cakes already made in stores so all you have to do is add strawberries and whipped cream. Take a few and make this classic the way it was meant to be made, it's just sweet enough to have you begging for seconds.

4 c. sifted flour
6 t. baking powder
1/2 t. salt
3 T. sugar
3/4 c. shortening
1 1/4 c. milk
2 eggs, beaten
2 T. melted butter or margarine
2 t. powdered sugar
1 c. heavy cream,
   whipped to stiff peaks
1 t. vanilla
1 qt. fresh strawberries
1/2 c. sugar

Preheat oven to 350°F. Sift together flour, baking powder, salt, and sugar. Cut in shortening with your fingers or two forks until small pea-sized balls of shortening are seen. Add milk and eggs; mix well. Knead on floured surface and roll out until it is 1 1/2 inches thick. Cut out with cookie cutter or rim of glass that has been dipped in flour to prevent sticking. Cut out to whatever size you prefer. Place on ungreased cookie sheet, top each with a little melted butter and sprinkle sugar over the top. Bake for 30 to 35 minutes or until top is golden brown and the bottom is lightly browned.

Remove from oven and let cool. Meanwhile, fold powdered sugar into whipped cream and add vanilla. Reserve about 12 whole strawberries and set aside. Crush remaining berries that have been hulled and combine with sugar. Let set for at least 1/2 hour to help extract juice from the strawberries.

To serve, halve each biscuit and fill with a little whipped cream and crushed strawberries. Put top on and ladle more crushed strawberries, followed by more whipped cream and add sliced fresh strawberries.

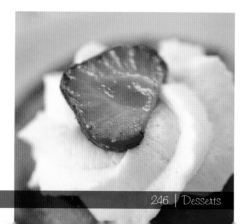

No-Fail Sandwich Cookie Cheesecake

There was only one way I could get my kids to eat cheesecake and that was by using these cream filled cookies in it somehow. They'd eat spinach if I put these cookies on top.

1 pkg. (18 oz.) sandwich cookies
1/4 c. melted butter or margarine
4 pkgs. (8 oz. ea.) cream cheese,
   softened
1 c. sugar
1 t. vanilla
1 c. plain yogurt
4 eggs

Preheat oven to 325°F. Place 30 cookies in food processor, cover, and process until finely ground. Add to large bowl and add butter; mix well. Press firmly onto bottom of 13 × 9-inch baking pan.

Beat cream cheese, sugar, and vanilla in large bowl with electric mixer until well blended. Add yogurt and mix well. Add eggs, 1 at a time, beating just until blended after each egg. Chop remaining cookies and gently stir in 1 1/2 c. of the chopped cookies into cream cheese mixture. Pour over crush; sprinkle with remaining chopped cookies. Bake 45 minutes or until the center is almost completely set. Remove from oven and refrigerate at least 4 hours.

Do try these at home.

Eating yogurt everyday isn't just a great way to meet your calcium needs. If you're prone to frequent yeast infections, it can help reduce the recurrences. "It's the *lactobacillus acidophilus* cultures in yogurt that help create a more normal bacterial environment," says Dr. Bunnell in the *Annals of Internal Medicine*. Other home remedies include:

Try a little bit of pineapple when you are feeling overstuffed from eating. It is loaded with enzymes that help you digest food.

Used tea bags contain tannic acid, which helps reduce inflammation associated with sunburns.

A small spoonful of sugar, swallowed quickly before the crystals have time to dissolve, may be a cure for hiccups. Some say that sugar stimulates the diaphragm's phrenic nerve, which stops spasms.

Do not drink milk for heartburn, its protein will only stimulate acid production.

Coffee acts as a mild bronchodilator, and when the bronchial tubes are open, you can breathe easier if you are an asthmatic.

Raspberry Cheesecake

Since ancient times, cheesecakes have been served at various Greek and Roman festivals. In America, George Washington's mother included her own recipe for cheesecake in her cookbook. A spring form pan is best suited for this type of "cake". The sides can be unhinged to allow easier cutting.

2 c. graham cracker crumbs
3/4 c. butter or margarine, melted
3 pkgs. (8 oz. ea.) cream cheese, softened
3/4 c. sugar
3 t. vanilla
3 eggs
1 c. fresh raspberries

Preheat oven to 350°F. In a small mixing bowl stir together crumbs and butter until well combined. Press into the bottom and about 2 inches up the sides of a 9-inch spring form pan. Set aside.

In a large mixing bowl beat cream cheese, sugar, and vanilla with an electric mixer on medium speed until light and fluffy. Add eggs and beat on medium speed just until combined. Pour half of cheese mixture into crust, sprinkle with raspberries and pour remaining cheese mixture on top. Bake for 40 to 45 minutes or until center is almost set. Cool in refrigerator for at least 3 hours.

Creme de Menthe Cheesecake

In Australia, there is a popular drink called Minted Peas. It's a beverage that mixes Crème de Menthe with cola. I think I will stick with this.

1 c. chocolate cookie crumbs
3 T. sugar
4 T. butter or margarine, melted
4 pkg. (8 oz. ea.) cream cheese softened
1 1/4 c. sugar
4 eggs
3 t. vanilla
1 pkg. creme de menthe chocolate thins, chopped
1 pkg. creme de menthe chocolate thins, unchopped
3 T. heavy cream

Preheat oven to 350°F. Mix crumbs and 3 T. sugar in a small bowl; add butter and mix well. Press onto bottom of 9-inch spring form pan. Beat cream cheese and 1 c. sugar in large bowl with electric mixer at medium speed until well blended. Add eggs and vanilla; mix on medium speed just until well combined. Stir in 1 pkg. chopped creme de menthe thins and pour into crust. Bake for 60 minutes or until center is almost set; remove from oven and cool at room temperature. Run knife around inside edge until loosened.

Set aside 10 to 12 thins out of other package. Place remaining thins and heavy cream in microwaveable bowl; microwave on high 30 to 40 seconds until candies are melted and mixture, when stirred, is smooth. Pour over cheesecake, spreading over top to cover surface and drizzle down the sides. Place rest of thins with one corner tucked into cheesecake on top as if the candies are melting into the pool of chocolate sauce on top.

Mint has had a variety of uses besides flavorings for many thousands of years. Ancient Romans, Greeks, and Hebrews perfumed their temples with leaves of this herb. They also took baths perfumed with mint for nerves and muscles.

To relieve the pain of insect and animal bites, the oil from these leaves was close at hand. Mint tea was rumored to whiten teeth and cure headaches and indigestion.

Turtle Cheesecake

Pecans, caramel, and chocolate combined with a decadent cheesecake batter. What could be more pleasing?

2 c. crushed chocolate wafers
1/4 c. butter or margarine, melted
1 c. chopped pecans
3 pkg. (8 oz. ea.) cream cheese, softened
1 1/4 c. sugar
2 T. flour
1/2 t. salt
2 t. vanilla
4 eggs
2 T. whipping cream
Caramel Topping, *recipe below*

Preheat oven to 350°F. Combine chocolate wafers and butter; press on bottom of 9-inch spring form pan. Sprinkle the pecans over the crust evenly. Beat cream cheese in large bowl until creamy. Add sugar, flour, salt, and vanilla and mix well. Add eggs, one at a time, beating well after each addition. Blend in cream and pour over crust. Bake for 50 to 60 minutes or until center is almost set. Remove from pan, loosen sides and let cool before removing from spring form pan. Drizzle with Caramel Topping and then Chocolate Topping; refrigerate. Sprinkle with pecans before serving.

Caramel Topping:
1/2 a 14-oz. bag caramels
1/3 c. whipping cream

Combine caramels and whipping cream in small saucepan; stir over low heat until melted and smooth.

Chocolate Topping:
1 package (4 oz.)
  German sweet chocolate
1 t. butter or margarine
2 T. whipping cream
1 c. chopped pecans

Combine German sweet chocolate (or use chocolate chips), butter, and 2 T. whipping cream in small saucepan; stir over low heat until smooth

---

To make your own caramels; melt 1 c. butter or margarine in a large pot. Add 1 lb. brown sugar and 1 c. light corn syrup and mix very well. Cook and stir over medium heat to firm ball stage (245°F), about 12 to 15 minutes. Remove from heat; stir in 2 t. vanilla and pour into buttered 9 × 9 × 2-inch pan. Cool and cut candy into little squares.

Orange Cappuccino Cheesecake

There are so many no-bake cheesecake recipes out there, but none of them truly compare to the effort and creaminess you get from a classically baked cheesecake. The taste of orange and coffee truly burst from this cheesecake.

2 c. finely chopped nuts
1 c. plus 2 T. sugar
4 T. butter or margarine, melted
4 pkg. (8 oz. ea.) cream cheese, softened
3 T. flour
5 eggs
1 c. sour cream

2 T. instant coffee
1/2 t. cinnamon
1/4 c. orange juice
2 t. grated orange peel
Whipped cream
Cinnamon sugar (optional)
Orange rind, zested (optional)

Preheat oven to 350°F. Combine nuts, 2 T. of the sugar, and the butter; press onto bottom of 9-inch spring form pan. Beat together cream cheese, the remaining sugar, and the flour in large bowl until well blended. Add eggs, one at a time, beating well after each addition. Blend in sour cream, coffee, cinnamon (mixed with the orange juice), grated orange peel and stir until all is dissolved. Pour into crust and bake for 50 to 60 minutes or until center is almost set. Remove from oven, loosen around the inside edges, and let cool before removing spring form pan. Sprinkle top of cheesecake with whipped cream, cinnamon sugar, and orange curls if desired. Serve.

Cappuccino is made with 1 shot of espresso, hot steamed milk, and topped with a frothy head of milk. Dust with cinnamon or cocoa.
Other coffees are:
Coffee Mocha: 1 shot espresso topped with the froth from hot chocolate.
Coffee Latte: 1 shot of espresso with a good amount of steamed milk. Some are served with a slightly higher amount of milk than cappuccino. Topped with a large amount of foam.
Macchiato Latte: Served in a large glass, it is mostly steamed milk with a small amount of espresso on top.

Sugarplum Ring

The Sugarplum Ring is a coffee cake that utilizes yeast as a leavening agent. While there are other coffee cakes that use this method, most New England coffee cakes use baking powder or baking soda as a leavening agent, but I find that yeast gives it a special lightness that is needed during the holiday season. You can further adorn this Sugarplum Ring with a long festive candle, small pinecones, a tip or two of cedar, and pine and holly berries.

Have you ever heard of a Sugar Plum Tree?
'Tis a marvel of great renown!
It blooms on the shore of the Lollipop Sea
In the garden of Shut-Eye Town.
                          –Eugene Field

1 pkg. dry yeast	3/4 c. sugar
4 c. sifted flour	1/4 c. butter or margarine, melted
3/4 c. milk	2 t. cinnamon
1/2 c. sugar	1/2 c. red cherries, candied
1/2 c. shortening	1/2 c. whole almonds
1 t. salt	1/2 c. dark corn syrup
2 eggs, beaten well	

Preheat oven to 350°F. In a large mixing bowl, combine yeast and 2 c. flour. Heat milk, the 1/2 c. sugar, shortening, and salt until just warm, stirring occasionally to melt shortening. Add to dry mixture in mixing bowl; add eggs. Beat at low speed with electric mixer for 30 seconds, constantly scraping sides of bowl. Beat 3 minutes at high speed. By hand, add remaining flour and mix until soft dough is formed. Mix thoroughly and place in a greased bowl, and then flip over so that greased side is up; cover with towel and let rise until almost double in bulk. Punch down and let rest 10 minutes.

Divide dough into 4 equal parts; cut each part into 10 pieces and shape into balls. Dip balls in the melted butter, then in the sugar that is blended with the cinnamon. Arrange 1/3 of the balls in well-greased, 10-inch tube or bundt cake pan, sprinkle with some of the almonds and cherries. Repeat with two more layers. Mix corn syrup with butter left from dipping balls; drizzle over the top. Cover and let rise in warm place until it almost doubles in volume once again. Bake for 35 to 40 minutes, remove from oven and let cool 10 minutes before loosening the sides and inverting onto a serving dish. Decorate whichever way you choose.

Deacon Porter's Hat

Deacon Porter, an early trustee of Mount Holyoke College, wore a stovepipe hat, style 1837. When students at the college were served a steamed pudding made of suet, molasses, currants, and raisins, they wittingly called it Deacon Porter's Summer Hat, which has since been shortened to Deacon Porter's Hat. The recipe below has been updated for today's palate, unless you want suet in your pudding.

3/4 c. molasses
1/2 c. safflower oil
3/4 c. milk
1 1/2 c. flour
1 t. baking powder
3/4 t. cinnamon
Pinch salt
1/2 t. ground cloves
1/4 t. nutmeg
1/8 t. ginger
3/4 c. chopped walnuts
1 c. raisins
Hard Sauce, *recipe below*

Stir together the molasses, oil, and milk. Combine flour, baking powder, cinnamon, salt, ground cloves, nutmeg, and ginger in bowl. Incorporate wet ingredients and dry together and mix well. Fold in walnuts and raisins. Pour into an empty coffee can or equivalent mold with one end open.

Silhouette of a man with a stove pipe hat

Place a large stock pot on top of stove with a small wire rack inside to rest coffee can onto. Pour boiling water to bring it halfway up side of can, cover, and turn heat to medium-high. Steam for 2 hours or until pudding has set. Remove pudding from stove carefully, let sit for 10 minutes and invert onto serving platter. Serve Hard Sauce separately.

Hard Sauce:
5 T. unsalted butter, softened
1 c. powdered sugar
1 T. heavy cream
2 t. vanilla

Whip butter until light. Add powdered sugar, slowly beating continuously until fluffy. Stir cream and vanilla into butter mixture until smooth.

Mass-Mont Baked Apples

This recipe is aptly named after the two states which contributed to its flavor, Massachusetts for its cranberry sauce and Vermont for its maple syrup and Cheddar cheese. You will be hard pressed to find a better tasting baked apple dish in all of Mass-Mont!

6 medium tart apples
1/2 c. chunky cranberry sauce
1/2 c. chopped walnuts
1/2 t. cinnamon
1/4 t. ground cloves
2 T. butter
1/2 c. maple syrup
1/2 c. shredded,
    very sharp Cheddar cheese

Core apples within 1/2 inch from bottom. Preheat oven to 350°F. Place apples in baking dish. Stuff each apple with cranberry sauce, then walnuts. Sprinkle cinnamon and cloves onto each. Top with 1 t. butter, maple syrup, and grated cheese. Bake for 25 to 30 minutes, or until apples are soft but not mushy.

Fruit Ambrosia

What a great change from the usual fruit salad. Use fat-free topping or even half sour cream or yogurt with the whipped topping.

1 container (8 oz.) frozen whipped topping, thawed
2 1/2 c. shredded coconut
1 can (8 oz.) fruit cocktail, drained
1 can(8 oz.) pineapple chunks, drained
1 can (11 oz.) mandarin oranges, drained
3 c. miniature marshmallows
1 jar (10 oz.) Maraschino cherries, drained
1 t. nutmeg
1 t. cinnamon

In a large bowl, combine all ingredients, cover, and refrigerate for at least 1 hour.

The great cranberry crop of New England

Apple Brown Betty

Though not as old as Apple Pandowdy, Brown Betty is a spin off from that dish, originally using buttered bread crumbs in place of a biscuit crust. I have altered this recipe slightly to today's tastes. If true Brown Betty is wanted, then use bread crumbs, sugar, and a little melted butter to cover the seasoned apples before baking.

6 medium apples, peeled,
   cored, and sliced
1/2 c. flour
1/2 c. brown sugar
1/4 c. butter or margarine, softened
3/4 t. cinnamon
1 c. granola

Preheat oven to 350°F. Place sliced apples into greased, 2-qt. casserole dish or baking pan. In a bowl, mix flour, brown sugar, margarine, cinnamon, and granola. Thoroughly blend and spread over top of apples. Bake for 35 to 40 minutes or until apples are tender but not mushy.

Traditional Bread Pudding

Although this multi-national dessert holds its own (well maybe with a dab of real or whipped cream), try it with one of the dessert sauces located in this cookbook.

2 1/2 c. milk
2 T. butter or margarine
1 1/2 c. bread cubes
1/2 t. cinnamon
1/2 c. raisins (optional)
1/2 t. lemon juice
Grated rind of 1/2 lemon
3 eggs
1/8 t. nutmeg
3 T. sugar
Topping

Preheat oven to 325°F. Heat the milk with the butter over medium heat, stirring until the butter melts. Remove from the heat and add the bread cubes, cinnamon, and raisins. Blend in the lemon juice and grated lemon rind. Separate the eggs, and beat the yolks into the milk mixture along with the sugar slowly, constantly whisking. Beat the egg whites until soft peaks; fold them into pudding mixture gently and slowly. Pour into shallow baking dish, sprinkle with nutmeg and sugar. Bake for 1 hour, remove from oven and let cool. Serve with topping.

Topping:
2 T. sugar
1 c. heavy cream

Whip heavy cream until soft peaks form. Add the sugar slowly while continuing to beat. Stop when stiff peaks form.

Apple Pandowdy (1855)

Fill a heavy pot heapin full of pleasant apples, sliced. Add 1 c. molasses, 1 c. sugar, 1 c. water, 1 t. cloves, 1 t. cinnamon, cover with your favorite biscuit mix and slope it over the sides. Bake overnight in slow oven or away from fire. In the morning cut hard crust into the apple, easily mixing and serve with yellow cream.

–The Yankee Chef Archives

Chocolate Bread Pudding:

Stir in 1/2 c. cocoa into milk before heating. Dot the top of the bread pudding with broken pieces of milk or dark chocolate before baking.

Apple-Maple Bread Pudding:

Peel, core, and dice 3 apples and mix with bread cubes along with 1/2 c. maple syrup. Top with apple pie filling before baking.

To make A Whitpot, cut half a loaf of bread in slices, pour thereon two quarts milk, six eggs, rose-water, nutmeg, and half a pound sugar; put into a dish and cover with paste. Bake slow one hour.

–New American Cookery, 1805

Chocolate Caramel Bread Pudding

For all of you that just like bread pudding, this is for you. Once you've tasted this chocolate infused recipe, you will be transformed into a bread pudding lover.

6 oz. bittersweet chocolate,
   chopped
2 c. heavy cream
1 1/2 c. milk
3 T. cocoa
2 t. vanilla
7 c. challah bread,
   cut into 1-inch cubes
6 oz. semisweet chocolate chips
4 oz. caramel candy chews, halved
1/2 c. sugar
1 egg
5 egg yolks
1/4 t. salt

Preheat oven to 350°F. Place the bittersweet chocolate in a large bowl and set aside. Place the cream, milk, cocoa, and vanilla in a medium pot and bring to a simmer over medium heat. Remove from heat and pour into bowl of chocolate. Gently stir to combine and set aside.

In a large bowl, whisk together sugar, egg, yolks, and salt. Pour the cream mixture into the egg mixture in a slow, steady stream, whisking continuously until combined. Place the challah in a large bowl; pour the egg-cream mixture over the bread, and let sit, tossing occasionally, until the bread absorbs the liquid, about 30 minutes. Gently mix

chocolate chips and the soaked bread together. Spoon half of the pudding into a deep, 1-quart baking pan, sprinkle with half of the caramel candies and top with the remaining pudding and caramel. Tightly cover the pie with aluminum foil, bake for 40 minutes, uncover, and continue to bake until the liquid has set and the caramel is melted, about 20 more minutes.

Unsweetened chocolate, also called bitter chocolate, is used in baking where a sweetener is needed.

Semi-sweet chocolate is just right for nibbling and is a little less sweet than sweet chocolate. Used mostly for dipping.

Sweet chocolate is unsweetened chocolate with sugar and additional cocoa butter added. Great for all desserts.

Milk chocolate is the same as sweet chocolate but with the addition of chocolate liquor and milk or cream.

Rhubarb Maple Toasted Bread Pudding

Yankee Chef Jack Bailey and I were sitting down one day and I tested his kitchen prowess by asking him what he could do with three ingredients. I told him rhubarb, bread, and maple syrup. Within five to ten minutes, he had written down this recipe. I went to work the next day and made it. Absolutely fantastic! Not only the flavor but the simplicity.

4 slices white bread
1 c. milk
4 T. butter or margarine
2 eggs
1/2 c. maple syrup
1/4 c. plus 1 T. sugar
1 c. chopped rhubarb
Maple Flavored Whipped Cream, *recipe below*

Preheat oven to 350°F. Toast bread and tear into small pieces. Place in large bowl. Heat milk with 2 T. butter until butter melts. Pour over bread. Use remainder of butter to grease 2-qt. casserole dish. After 10 minutes of soaking, beat eggs with maple syrup and 1/4 c. sugar. Add rhubarb and mix with bread mixture. Pour all onto casserole dish, sprinkling remaining sugar on top. Bake for 45 minutes or until set. Serve warm with Maple Flavored Whipped Cream.

Stereoscopic picture of children enjoying a New England sleigh ride

Maple Flavored Whipped Cream:
1 1/2 c. heavy cream
3 T. sugar
1/2 c. maple syrup

With a hand-held electric mixer on high, whip cream until stiff peaks form. Add sugar and maple syrup and continue beating until well combined.

Traditional Indian Pudding

This is only one version of this true New England dish. Maple syrup and honey can be substituted for molasses but it just wouldn't be the same. This pudding was enjoyed with savory dishes as well as eaten for dessert in many Yankee homes of old.

5 c. milk, divided
4 T. yellow cornmeal
1/2 c. molasses
3 T. sugar
2 T. butter or margarine
1 1/2 t. cinnamon
Whipped topping
Real vanilla bean ice cream

Heat milk in medium-sized saucepan over medium-high heat. Bring 3 c. milk to scalding and add cornmeal in small stream, constantly stirring. Reduce heat to medium and cook for 20 to 25 minutes, stirring frequently. Remove from heat when thickened. Add molasses, sugar, butter, and cinnamon. Transfer to 1 1/2-qt., buttered casserole dish and pour 2 c. cold milk over the top. Do not stir! Bake for 2 1/2 hours. Serve with whipped cream or ice cream, but don't you dare put that cheap vanilla ice cream on it. Some people like the taste of nutmeg and ground cloves in their Indian pudding as well. What the hey, give it a shot.

Marmalade Indian Pudding:
Add 1 c. your favorite marmalade to the 3 cups of milk being scalded.

Home of Robert Frost

American poet Robert Frost loved blueberries so much he wrote a poem about them. You guessed it; the poem was called "Blueberries," and here are the beginning lines

You ought to have seen what I saw on my way
To the village, through Mortenson's
    pasture to-day:
Blueberries as big as the end of your thumb,
Real sky-blue, and heavy, and ready to drum
In the cavernous pail of the first one to come!

Baked New England Rice Pudding

This, my friends, is the standby favorite of our heritage. I don't remember reading about any Thanksgiving or Christmas gathering from generations gone by that didn't have this Rice Pudding adorning the table. But don't wait for the holidays; any cold winter night can only be warmed up with the smell of New England's favorite comfort dessert.

1 qt. milk
3/4 c. sugar
4 eggs, beaten
1 t. vanilla
2 c. cooked white rice
3/4 t. cinnamon
1/2 t. nutmeg
1/4 t. salt
1 c. raisins
Light cream (optional)

Preheat oven to 350°F. Grease a 2-qt. baking dish. In a medium saucepan over medium heat, scald milk. Set aside to cool. In a separate bowl, beat sugar, eggs, and vanilla until well blended. Stir rice and spices into cooled milk. Stir egg mixture into rice mixture. Stir in raisins. Pour batter into prepared baking dish and place in a large, shallow pan. Pour in water to a depth of one inch. Bake for 1 hour, uncovered. Gently stir contents well and continue baking an additional 30 minutes or until toothpick inserted in middle comes out clean. Remove and let sit for 10 minutes before serving with light cream. You can also stay true to Yankee fashion by serving with cinnamon and butter or cold with whipped cream.

Stovetop Coconut Rice Pudding

This rice pudding is so flavorful and thick, you will make it again during the Holidays, guaranteed!

1 c. white rice
1/2 c. sugar
1/2 t. salt
3 c. water
1 can (14 to 15 oz.)
    unsweetened coconut milk
1 mango, peeled and sliced
1/2 c. sweetened, flaked coconut,
    toasted

In 3-qt. saucepan, heat rice, sugar, salt, and water to boiling over high heat. Reduce heat to low; cover and simmer for 20 minutes. Increase heat to medium; stir in coconut milk and cook, uncovered, stirring occasionally, until rice is tender, about 10 minutes.

Transfer rice pudding to serving bowl; cover and refrigerate at least 2 hours or overnight to serve cold. Top with mango slices and toasted coconut before serving.

Here are some types of corn puddings from years gone by:

Hasty Pudding: A quickly cooked gruel of cornmeal boiled in almost equal parts with milk or water. Hasty pudding was also called "loblolly."
Indian pudding: A slightly more liquid version of hasty pudding but was boiled in a bag containing various spices.
Suppawn: A thick mixture of cornmeal and milk, eaten either hot or cold from the pot, or allowed to cool. Then it could be also sliced and fried in fat.
Mush: A watery type of suppawn eaten with sweetened fruit or molasses.
Samp Porridge: An Indian goulash featuring cornmeal cooked for a minimum of three days with meats and vegetables. After the prolonged simmering, this mixture becomes so thick that it could be removed from the pot in one solid chunk.

Macadamia Strawberries Foster

I took the idea of Bananas Foster and kicked it up a notch with nuts and berries. I think you'll agree that you won't taste another dessert quite like this.

2 T. butter or margarine
1 c. brown sugar
1/2 c. dry roasted Macadamia nuts, chopped
1 t. cinnamon
1/2 t. nutmeg
2 pints strawberries, hulled
1/2 c. strawberry liqueur
1/2 c. dark rum
Vanilla ice cream

In large skillet, melt butter over medium heat. Add brown sugar and stir until smooth. Add Macadamia nuts, cinnamon, and nutmeg. Cook until smooth and bubbly. Add strawberries and cook until just tender, about 10 to 12 minutes. Remove from heat and add strawberry liqueur and rum. Carefully ignite with long handled match and continue cooking until the flame has extinguished, stirring almost constantly with a very long handled spoon. Serve over ice cream.

Baked Orange-Almond Rice Pudding

What a great way to use up leftover white rice. The addition of a couple teaspoons of dark rum just might have you sharing this recipe.

1 1/2 c. sliced almonds	1 t. orange extract
1 qt. milk	1/4 t. salt
6 eggs, beaten	3 1/2 c. white rice, cooked
1 1/2 c. brown sugar	Whipped topping
1 T. grated orange peel	

Preheat oven to 325°F. In food processor, grind half the almonds. Stir together milk, eggs, brown sugar, orange peel, orange extract, salt, and ground almonds until well combined. Stir in rice. Turn mixture into greased 13 × 9-inch square baking pan. Bake, uncovered, for 40 to 50 minutes, or until golden browned—a toothpick inserted in the middle will come out clean. Serve cooled with whipped topping and slivered almonds over the top.

Blueberry Bavarian Cream

Bavarian cream donuts were traditionally filled with cream sweetened with sugar and thickened with gelatin, hence the name. But I added this, reduced that, and came up with this exceptional dessert.

1 c. boiling water
6 oz. raspberry-flavored gelatin
3/4 c. plus 2 T. cold water
5 c. fresh blueberries, divided
1/4 c. sugar
1 1/2 c. whipping cream

In a large bowl, combine gelatin and boiling water; stir until dissolved. Stir in cold water until well-combined. Chill until set, about 1 hour.

In a medium saucepan, combine 1 1/2 c. blueberries, sugar, and 2 T. water. Bring mixture to a boil over medium-high heat. Cook until the berries burst, about 3 minutes. Cool. Fold 1 1/2 c. uncooked blueberries into the sauce. Place remaining blueberries in a blender; pulse until a chunky puree forms. Add dissolved gelatin; pulse just to combine. Pour mixture into a large bowl. In another bowl, beat cream until soft peaks form. Fold 1/4 of the cream into the blueberry mixture; fold in remaining cream. Spoon half of the blueberry sauce into 8-ounce glasses, distributing evenly. Top with half the blueberry-cream mixture and repeat.

Grilled Bananas with Orange Cream

The Louisiana-born Bananas Foster doesn't even compare to this Yankee dish. I call it Yankee because the first Yankee Chef created this dish and it is a superb dessert.

1 1/2 c. heavy cream
2 T. orange juice
2 T. powdered sugar
1 t. vanilla extract

2 bananas
4 strawberries, cut in half
1 T. canola oil

Combine cream, orange juice, sugar, and vanilla. Whip until stiff. Slice bananas once lengthwise and once sideways. Sear or grill bananas and strawberries with oil over high heat until they are dark brown. Serve warm with cream mixture topping the fruit.

The Hasty Pudding Club Theater

Although many of us have heard of Hasty Pudding in prose and song, do we really know what it is? Simply and briefly put, it is a mixture of cornmeal and liquid boiled down to a mush. Many of us have only heard of Hasty Pudding because of the Hasty Pudding Club, which is a social club for Harvard students. It was founded in 1770 by Nymphus Hatch, a junior at Harvard. The club is named for the traditional American dish (based on a British dish) that the founding members ate at their first meeting. The Hasty Pudding Club was originally established in Concordia Discors to bring together undergraduates in friendship, conversation, and camaraderie. It is the oldest collegiate social club in America.

The Pudding is currently the only club on campus that is coed and has members from all four years. Membership to the social club is gained through a series of lunches, cocktail parties, and other gatherings, which are referred to as the "punch process." In the past, membership in the Pudding was obligatory to joining waiting clubs and, eventually, final clubs. This tradition is no longer upheld. The Pudding holds its social activities in a clubhouse near Harvard Square. These include weekly "Members' Nights," dinner and cocktail parties, as well as its elaborate theme parties, such as "Leather and Lace."

The club counts five U.S. Presidents (John Adams, John Quincy Adams, Theodore Roosevelt, Franklin Delano Roosevelt, and John F. Kennedy) among its noteworthy members.

The Hasty Pudding Theatricals, the Radcliffe Pitches, and the Harvard Krokodiloes were founded at the Hasty Pudding Club. All of these groups are part of the Institute of 1770 and share clubhouse space as well as retain various social affiliations with the Pudding; their activities are focused on the performing arts, and they select members through open auditions.

Hot Coconut-Banana Nuggets with Blueberry Sauce

6 T. raspberry jelly
2 1/2 c. frozen blueberries
2 T. sugar
2 T. cornstarch
1 T. water
1 t. lemon juice
4 firm bananas
1/4 c. flour
1 egg
1 1/2 c. sweetened
  shredded coconut
Oil for deep frying

Put raspberry jelly and blueberries in a saucepan and stir over medium heat until berries start to soften, about 5 minutes. Add sugar. Stir until dissolved. Mix cornstarch in water until smooth. Add to blueberry mixture and cook for 4 to 5 minutes until sauce is clear and thickened. Stir in lemon juice and let cool slightly.

Peel bananas and cut in pieces about 1 1/2 inches long. Place in flour to dust. Whisk egg in small bowl. Turn banana pieces in egg and roll in shredded coconut to coat well.

Heat oil in fryer or saucepan and fry banana nuggets until they are golden brown, about 3 minutes. Drain on paper towel and serve with blueberry sauce.

Bananas, of course, are full of potassium, which is good for your heart, nerves, kidneys, and bones. Bananas are also known to have a calming effect on the brain and help to create a stable mood. They are also full of vitamin B6, which helps your body make hemoglobin, a crucial ingredient in your blood. One banana a day can also provide you with 16% of the daily recommended fiber intake. The best part about bananas? They are extremely affordable at about 35 to 40 cents per pound.

Yankee Blueberry Crisp

What a wonderful thing. To live in New England and have the worlds' best blueberries. The succulently blue color of this crisp can only be topped by the warmth it brings sharing it with someone special.

5 c. fresh blueberries
1/4 c. sugar
1/2 t. grated lemon rind
1 c. diced peeled apples
1/2 c. brown sugar
2 t. cinnamon

1 t. nutmeg
1/2 c. flour
1/2 c. chopped pecans (optional)
1/2 c. rolled oats
3 T. butter or margarine, softened
1/8 t. salt

Preheat oven to 325°F. In a small bowl, combine the blueberries, sugar, lemon rind, and apples. Mix well and place in a well-buttered, 8 × 8 × 2-inch pan.

In a medium bowl, combine brown sugar, cinnamon, nutmeg, flour, pecans, oats, and salt; rub in the butter with your fingers until it resembles coarse crumbs. Spread evenly over the blueberry filling. Bake 45 minutes or until the crust is brown.

Apple-Cranberry Crisp

It's hard to believe that it wasn't until the early quarter of the 1900s that apple crisp was mentioned in any text. By the smell and taste, you'd think our ancestors would have enjoyed this as we do.

3/4 t. orange peel, grated
1/3 c. orange juice
8 apples, peeled, cored,
   and sliced 1/2 inch thick
2 c. frozen cranberries
1/2 c. raisins
1 1/2 t. cinnamon
1/2 t. salt
1/2 t. nutmeg
1/3 c. plus 1/4 c. brown sugar
1/3 c. plus 2 T. flour
1/2 c. rolled oats
4 T. butter or margarine

Preheat oven to 350°F. In 2-quart baking dish, toss grated orange peel, orange juice, apple slices, cranberries, raisins, cinnamon, salt, nutmeg, 1/3 c. brown sugar, and 2 T. flour.

In small bowl, mix oats, remaining 1/3 c. flour, and remaining 1/4 c. brown sugar. Cut in margarine until mixture resembles coarse crumbs. Sprinkle over apple mixture. Bake uncovered 35 to 40 minutes, or until apples are tender and top is browned.

Fuji apples are a cross between a Red Delicious with an antique Ralls Janet apple. Japan's most popular apple, Fujis are firm, crunchy, and juicy apples with a low-acid sweetness.

Granny Smith apples are from Australia and hold up well in baking and sautéing. They are light green and have a sweet tart flavor.

Braeburn apples hail from New Zealand and are a descendant of the Granny Smith. They are green-yellow with an orange-red blush and are crisp and juicy. Braeburns hold up well when baked as well.

Rome Beauty apples are named for the Ohio Township in which they were discovered. This deep-red apple is firm with a slightly juicy flesh and a tough skin. Excellent for cooking and baking, this apple holds its shape very well.

McIntosh is Canadian born and does not hold its shape well, although it is one of the best eating apples around and is indispensable for making cider and pies.

Stayman apples are closely related to the Winesap. They have a semi-firm texture with a wine-like flavor.

York Imperials have a lopsided shape but are firm, tart, and juicy. They are both red and green in color

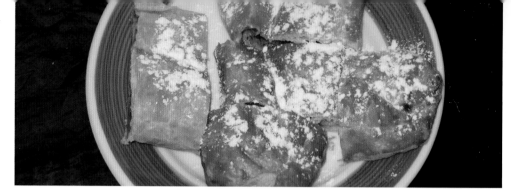

Caramel Apple Dessert

You will be caramelizing in this recipe, so you can see just how easy it is to do what very high paid chefs do. Remember, the darker the color of the caramel, the less sweet it is. This recipe will remind you of caramel apples on a stick, but much easier to eat.

10 apples
1 c. sugar
1/2 c. unsalted butter, or
    you may use salted butter
    or margarine if desired
1 t. vanilla
1/2 c. chopped nuts

Peel, core, and wedge each apple into eighths. In large skillet over medium heat, melt sugar until golden brown, stirring constantly. Add butter and blend. Add apples and stir to coat. Cover and reduce heat to medium-low. Continue cooking for 10 minutes or until apples are cooked. Remove lid and add vanilla; stir. Serve warm over ice cream with chopped nuts over the top.

Apple Strudel

In true Viennese fashion, this Austrian national dish should be enjoyed with absolutely nothing on it or with it, save a napkin.

3 apples, peeled, cored, and thinly sliced
1/2 c. sugar
1/2 c. raisins
1/2 c. walnuts, chopped
1/2 t. cinnamon
1/2 t. nutmeg
1/4 t. salt
1 c. dried bread crumbs
1/2 pkg. (16 oz.) phyllo dough, thawed
1/2 c. butter or margarine, melted
Powdered sugar

Preheat oven to 350°F. Grease large cookie sheet. In large bowl, toss apples, sugar, raisins, walnuts, cinnamon, nutmeg, salt, and 1/4 c. bread crumbs. Cut two 24-inch lengths of waxed paper; overlap 2 long sides about 2 inches. Fasten with cellophane tape.

On waxed paper, arrange 1 sheet of phyllo (about 12-by-16 inches); brush with some melted margarine and sprinkle with a tablespoon of bread crumbs. Continue layering phyllo, brushing each sheet with melted margarine and sprinkling every other sheet with crumbs.

Starting with the long side of the phyllo, spoon apple mixture to within about 1/2 inch from edges to cover about half of phyllo rectangle. From apple-mixture side, roll phyllo, jelly-roll fashion. Place roll, seam side down, on cookie sheet and brush with remaining melted margarine. Bake until golden brown, about 35 to 40 minutes. Sprinkle with powdered sugar and cut to serve.

Apples best for eating raw: Gala, Golden Delicious, Red Delicious, MacIntosh
Apples best for cooking: Gravenstein, Rhode Island Greening, York Imperial, MacIntosh
Apples best for baking: Cortland, Northern Spy, Winesap, York Imperial.
Apples for all-purpose: Crispin, Criterion, Empire, Jonagold, Jonathan, Lady Apple, Macoun, Newtown Pippin, Winesap, and Stayman.

Plum Cobbler

In order to achieve a true cobbler, arrange biscuit dough in a fashion that resembles the cobblestone streets of old, hence the name Cobbler.

2 1/2 lbs. red or purple plums, pitted and cut into bite-sized pieces
1/2 c. sugar
2 T. flour
2 c. dry, prepared biscuit mix (or make your own, see my recipe)
1/4 c. yellow cornmeal
3/4 c. water

Preheat oven to 350°F. In large bowl, toss plums with sugar and flour. Spoon plum mixture into shallow 2-quart glass baking dish. Cover loosely with foil and bake until plums are very tender, 35 to 40 minutes.

Remove baking dish from oven. In medium bowl, stir biscuit mix, cornmeal, and water just until combined. Drop by the spoonful on top of cooked plums. Bake cobbler, uncovered, and until biscuits are browned and plum mixture is bubbly, 20 to 25 minutes longer. Serve warm.

To make Peach Pickles. Stick 2 or 3 cloves into each peach in a 9 lb. batch. Put in a large pot with a few sticks of cinnamon and cook until tender. Take them out on a platter to cool. When cold put into jars. Pour the cold syrup over them. Let stand overnight then seal up.

–The Yankee Chef Archives

Blueberry-Strawberry Buckle

I could wake up to this every morning for breakfast. The taste of both berries complement each other well. It's also a perfect celebratory dessert for the Fourth of July, with its red, white, and blue theme.

1/2 c. butter or margarine, softened
1 c. sugar
1 egg
1 t. vanilla
1 1/2 c. flour
1 t. baking powder
1 t. salt
1/2 c. milk
1 c. fresh blueberries
1 c. sliced, fresh strawberries
3/4 t. cinnamon
1/2 t. nutmeg
Vanilla ice cream or whipped cream

Preheat oven to 350°F. Grease a 9-inch square baking pan. In a small bowl, cream 1/4 c. butter and 1/2 c. of the sugar. Blend in egg and vanilla. In a separate small mixing bowl, stir together 1 c. of the flour, baking powder, and salt. Add dry ingredients to creamed mixture alternately with milk; stir until well blended. Pour batter into prepared baking pan. Arrange fruit over batter. In a small bowl, combine remaining sugar, remaining flour, cinnamon, and nutmeg. Cut in remaining 1/4 c. butter until mixture resembles coarse crumbs. Sprinkle crumb mixture evenly over fruit. Bake for 30 to 35 minutes until top is browned and bubbly. Serve with ice cream or whipped cream.

Floating Island

This recipe usually has meringue "clouds" floating on top but I tweaked it and the outcome is fantastic. The rich Honey Meringue Sauce is much tastier than the classic and complements the custard beautifully.

1 qt. milk
3 egg yolks, well beaten
2 T. cornstarch
2 T. milk
1/2 c. sugar
1/4 t. salt
1 t. vanilla

Scald milk in top of double boiler or equivalent. Stir in egg yolks slowly and whisk. In small bowl combine cornstarch with 2 T. milk and mix until smooth. Add to milk mixture. Add sugar and salt. Continue cooking, whisking almost constantly until thickened. Remove from heat and cool for 30 minutes. Stir in vanilla. Chill and serve with Honey Meringue Sauce.

Honey Meringue Sauce:
2 egg whites
2 c. honey

Combine the honey and egg whites and beat vigorously or use electric mixer until the sauce forms a light fluffy sauce.

Ol' Gooseberry Fool

Never heard of or seen gooseberries in the supermarket? Well I assure you they are easier to find than you think. Canned gooseberries are more universal though. If using canned gooseberries, simply ignore the cooking part of this recipe and go straight to the straining segment.

1 qt. ripe gooseberries
2 c. water
4 egg yolks
1 T. butter or margarine
1 c. sugar
Pinch salt
1 c. whipping cream
2 T. powdered sugar

Top and stem the gooseberries, stew in water, just enough to cover, over medium heat in large saucepan until tender, about 15 to 20 minutes. Remove from stove and press through a colander, leaving the skins behind, into a large bowl. In a small bowl, beat egg yolks until light and creamy. Add butter, sugar, salt, and beaten egg yolks to gooseberry juice. Stir to combine. In separate bowl, beat the whipping cream with an electric mixer until stiff, add powdered sugar and beat an additional 5 seconds.
To assemble, ladle gooseberry puree into individual serving dishes and top with whipped topping.

Chocolate Crunch Bark

For a different taste, or for those who "like their coffee strong enough to float a spoon," use very dark chocolate; the bitterer, the betterer.

1 pkg. (8 squares)
   semisweet chocolate
1 pkg. (6 squares)
   white baking chocolate
3 T. peanut butter
8 vanilla-flavored wafers
1/4 c. dried cranberries, minced

Place semisweet chocolate and white chocolate in separate microwave-safe bowls. Microwave each, separately, until melted, follow package directions for microwave melting. Add peanut butter to white chocolate and stir to blend. Crumble wafers in separate bowl and evenly distribute over both bowls of chocolate.
Onto waxed paper, pour dark chocolate. By the spoonful, dot dark chocolate with the melted white chocolate. With 2 butter knives, in scissor fashion, cut into chocolates to marble. Immediately sprinkle chopped cranberries over the top and refrigerate until firm, about 1 hour. Coarsely break into various sized pieces.

Peanut Brittle

Think you can buy peanut brittle or most of these confections cheaper than you can make them? Guess again. It just takes a little time and patience, something I have noticed we are starting to lack these days.

1 c. sugar
1/2 c. corn syrup
1 T. butter or margarine
2 c. cocktail or dry-roasted peanuts
1 t. baking soda
1 t. vanilla

Spray large baking sheet with cooking spray; set aside. Mix sugar and corn syrup in large microwaveable bowl and microwave on high 5 minutes. Stir in butter and peanuts. Microwave an additional 3 to 4 minutes, or until light golden in color. Add baking soda and vanilla, stir until foaming stops. Immediately spread peanut mixture on prepared baking sheet and cool completely. Break into pieces.

Two-Layer Fudge

There's so much you can do with this recipe such as adding 1 cup of dried cranberries or even swapping the peanut butter chips for butterscotch. Either way, this makes a great offering during the holidays.

1 c. peanut butter chips
1 c. semisweet chocolate chips
2 1/4 c. sugar
1 jar (7 oz.) marshmallow creme
3/4 c. evaporated milk
1/4 c. butter or margarine
1 t. vanilla or almond extract

Line an 8-inch square pan with foil, extending the foil over the edges. In a medium bowl, place peanut butter chips. In a second medium bowl, place chocolate chips. In heavy 3-quart saucepan, combine sugar, marshmallow creme, evaporated milk, and butter. Cook over medium heat, stirring constantly, until mixture comes to a boil; boil 5 minutes, stirring constantly. Remove from heat; stir in vanilla. Immediately stir half of the hot mixture until chocolate chips are completely melted. Quickly spread over top of peanut butter layer. Cool to room temperature; refrigerate until firm.

Creamy Fudge

This is a no-fail recipe that needs no candy thermometer or waiting for the right time to take off the heat. So chocolaty and smooth, you won't go back to any other recipe.

1 can (14 oz.) sweetened condensed milk
1 lb. semisweet chocolate, chopped
1 oz. unsweetened chocolate, chopped
2 t. vanilla
1/8 t. salt

In 2-quart saucepan, combine condensed milk and chocolates. Cook over medium-low heat 5 minutes or until chocolates melt and mixture is smooth, stirring constantly. Remove saucepan from heat; stir in vanilla and salt. Pour chocolate mixture into an 8 × 8-inch square pan; spreading evenly. Refrigerate until firm.

Peanut Butter and Jelly Bars

My prediction? After making a pan of these, cutting them, and setting them out for the kids when school lets out, you'll be thinking of every excuse as to why there is only half a plate left by the time they get home.

1 1/2 c. flour
1/2 c. sugar
3/4 t. baking powder
1 egg, beaten
1/2 c. butter or margarine
3/4 c. grape jelly
1 2/3 c. (10-oz. pkg.)
    peanut butter chips, divided

Preheat oven to 350°F. Grease a 9-inch square baking pan. Stir together flour, sugar, and baking powder. Cut in butter until it resembles coarse crumbs. Add egg; blend well. Reserve half of mixture; press remaining mixture onto bottom of prepared pan. Spread jelly over crust. Sprinkle 1 c. peanut butter chips over jelly. Stir together reserved crumb mixture with remaining 2/3 c. chips; sprinkle over top. Bake 25 to 30 minutes or until lightly browned. Cool completely before cutting into squares.

Many generations ago, gelatin was known by various names such as "glue" and used for far different recipes than we do today, as shown below:

To Make Glue Broth: Take a leg of beef, veal, venison or any other young meat, because old meat will not so easily jelly. Pare off all the fat, in which there is no nutriment, and of the lean. Make a very strong broth after the usual manner, by boiling the meat to rags until all the goodness be out. After skimming off what fat remains, pour the broth into a wide stew pan, well tinned, and let it simmer over a gentle, even fire until it comes to a thick jelly. Then take it off and set it over boiling water, which is an evener heat and not so apt to burn the broth to the vessel. Over that let it evaporate, stirring it very often until it be reduced, when cold, into a solid substance like glue. Then cut it into small pieces, laying them single in the cold, that they may dry the sooner. When the pieces are perfectly dry, put them into a canister, and they will be good, if kept dry, a whole East India voyage.

    –The Yankee Chef Archives

You will see a number of Whoopie Pie recipes here. I have included so many because so many of us here in New England enjoy these delicious and rich pastries and there isn't a cookbook out there (that I can find) that has more than two or three recipes for them. With the dozens of varieties you can create, I thought it only acceptable to open your eyes to some of those varieties and see why Maine made this hearty sweet its official snack cake.

Old-fashioned Whoopie Pie

2 c. flour
1 1/4 t. baking soda
2 t. baking powder
1 t. salt
1/2 c. cocoa
1 t. vanilla
1 c. milk
1/2 c (1 stick) butter or margarine
1 c. brown sugar
1 egg
Filling, *recipe below*

Preheat your oven to 350°F. In a bowl, whisk together the flour, baking soda, baking powder, salt, and cocoa until well mixed. In another small bowl, mix the vanilla and milk. Using an electric mixer at medium-high setting, beat together the butter and brown sugar until fluffy and pale. Next, add an egg and mix until it's mixed in evenly. Lower the speed on your electric mixer and alternate between adding in a bit of the flour mixture and a bit of milk until it is all mixed. On two large, greased baking sheets, place 1/4 c. mounds of batter roughly two inches apart. Place in the upper portion of your oven. Bake about 11 to 13 minutes or until springy to the touch. Remove from oven and cool on a rack or let stand for 5 minutes and remove to platter to cool thoroughly. Scoop filling onto one half of the Whoopie pie cake and close with the other half.

Filling:
1 1/4 c. confectioners sugar
1/2 c. (1 stick) butter or margarine, softened
1 t. vanilla
2 c. marshmallow cream

In a bowl, beat together your confectioners sugar, butter, vanilla, and marshmallow using an electric mixer on the medium setting. You should mix until the filling is nice and smooth.

Pumpkin Whoopie Pies

1 c. shortening
2 c. packed brown sugar
2 eggs
1 t. vanilla extract
3 1/2 c. flour
1 1/2 t. baking powder
1 1/2 t. baking soda
1 t. salt
1 t. ground cinnamon
1 t. ground ginger
1/2 c. canned pumpkin
Filling, *recipe below*

Preheat oven to 350°F. In a large bowl, cream shortening and brown sugar until light and fluffy. Add eggs, one at a time, beating well after each addition. Beat in vanilla. Combine the flour, baking powder, baking soda, salt, cinnamon, and ginger; add to creamed mixture alternately with pumpkin. Drop by rounded tablespoonfuls 2 inches apart

onto greased baking pans; flatten slightly with the back of a spoon. Bake for 12 to 14 minutes or until springy to the touch. Remove from oven and cool on a rack or let stand for 5 minutes and remove to platter to cool thoroughly. Scoop filling onto one half of the Whoopie Pie cake and close with the other half.

Filling:
1 1/4 c. powdered sugar
1/2 c. (1 stick) butter or margarine, softened
2 c. marshmallow creme
1 t. vanilla

In a bowl, beat together your confectioners sugar, butter, vanilla, and marshmallow using an electric mixer on the medium setting. You should mix until the filling is nice and smooth.

Chocolate Mint Whoopie Pies

2 c. flour
1/2 c. cocoa
1 1/4 t. baking soda
2 t. baking powder
1 t. salt
1 c. milk
1 t. vanilla
1 stick (1/2 c.) butter or margarine, softened
1 c. brown sugar
1 egg
Filling, *recipe below*

Preheat your oven to 350°F. In a bowl, whisk together the flour, baking soda, baking powder, salt, and cocoa until well mixed. In another small bowl, mix together the vanilla and milk. Using an electric mixer at medium-high setting, beat together the butter and brown sugar until fluffy and pale. Next, add an egg and mix until it's mixed in evenly. Lower the speed on your electric mixer and alternate between adding in a bit of the flour mixture and a bit of milk until it is all mixed. On two large, greased baking sheets, place 1/4 c. mounds of batter roughly two inches apart. Place in the upper portion of your oven. Bake about 11 to 13 minutes or until springy to the touch. Remove from oven and cool on a rack or let stand for 5 minutes and remove to platter to cool thoroughly. Scoop filling onto one half of the Whoopie Pie cake and close with the other half.

Filling:
2 T. butter or margarine, softened
1 1/3 c. confectioners' sugar
1/8 t. mint extract
4 drops green food coloring (optional)
4 t. milk

In a small bowl, combine butter and confectioners' sugar until crumbly. Beat in extract, food coloring (if desired), and milk. Spread on the bottoms of half of the cakes; top with remaining cakes.

Lemon Whoopie Pies

1 1/2 c. flour
1/2 t. baking powder
1/4 t. baking soda
1/4 t. salt
6 T. butter or margarine, room temperature
1 c. sugar
1 t. finely grated lemon zest
1 egg
1 T. lemon juice
1 t. vanilla
1/2 c. milk
Lemon Cream Cheese Filling, *recipe below*

Position a rack in the middle of the oven. Preheat the oven to 350°F. Line 2 baking sheets with parchment paper and butter the paper. To prepare the cookies, sift the flour, baking powder, baking soda, and salt into a medium bowl and set aside. In a large bowl, using an electric mixer on medium speed, beat the butter, sugar, and lemon zest until smoothly blended, about 1 minute. Stop the mixer and scrape down the sides of the bowl as needed during mixing. Add the egg, lemon juice, and vanilla, mixing until blended, about 1 minute. The batter may look curdled. On low speed, add half the flour mixture, mixing just to incorporate it. Mix in the milk, then the remaining flour just until it is incorporated and the batter looks smooth again. Drop heaping tablespoons on the prepared baking sheet, spacing them about 3 inches apart. Bake the cookies one sheet at a time until a toothpick inserted near the center comes out clean and the tops feel firm, about 12 minutes. With the exception of a thin line at the edges, the tops of the cookies should not brown. Remove from oven and cool on a rack or let stand for 5 minutes and remove to platter to cool thoroughly. Scoop filling onto one half of the Whoopie Pie cake and close with the other half.

Lemon Cream Cheese Filling:

6 t. butter or margarine, room
   temperature
6 oz. cream cheese, room
   temperature
1 t. vanilla
1 t. grated lemon zest
2 T. lemon juice
2 3/4 c. powdered sugar

In a large bowl, using an electric mixer on low speed, beat the butter, cream cheese, vanilla, lemon zest, and lemon juice until thoroughly blended and smooth, about 1 minute. Add the powdered sugar and mix until smooth. If your filling is too soft to hold its shape, refrigerate until it is firmer, about 30 minutes. Turn half of the cookies bottom side up leaving 1/4-inch plain edge, use a thin metal spatula to spread each with almost 1/4 cup of filling. Gently press the bottoms of the remaining cookies onto the filling.

Lemony Gingerbread Whoopie Pies

These spiced-just-right Whoopie Pies combine two popular flavors in one fun treat. The moist cookies are rolled in sugar before baking for a bit of crunch

3/4 c. butter or margarine, softened	1 t. cinnamon
3/4 c. packed brown sugar	1 t. baking soda
1/2 c. molasses	2 t. baking powder
1 egg	1/4 t. salt
3 c. flour	1/2 c. sugar
2 t. ginger	Filling, *recipe below*

In a large bowl, cream butter and brown sugar until light and fluffy. Beat in molasses and egg. Combine the flour, ginger, cinnamon, baking soda, baking powder, and salt; gradually add to creamed mixture and mix well. Cover and refrigerate for at least 3 hours. Shape into 1-in. balls; roll in sugar. Place 3 inches apart on greased baking sheets. Flatten to 1/2 inch thick with a glass dipped in sugar. Bake at 350°F for 11 to 13 minutes or until set. Remove from oven and cool on a rack or let stand for 5 minutes and remove to platter to cool thoroughly. Scoop filling onto one half of the Whoopie Pie cake and close with the other half.

Filling:

3/4 c. butter or margarine, softened	1 1/2 c. powdered sugar
3/4 c. marshmallow creme	3/4 t. lemon extract

In a small bowl, beat butter and marshmallow creme until light and fluffy. Gradually beat in confectioners' sugar and extract. Spread filling on the bottoms of half of the cookies, about 1 tablespoon on each; top with remaining cookies.

Banana Whoopie Pies

1/2 c. butter or margarine, softened	1/2 c. milk
3/4 c. sugar	2 c. flour
1/4 c. packed brown sugar	1/2 t. salt
1 egg	2 t. baking powder
1 t. vanilla	1/2 t. baking soda
1/2 c. mashed ripe banana	Filling, *recipe below*

Preheat oven to 350°F. In a large bowl, cream butter and sugars until light and fluffy. Beat in egg and vanilla. In a small bowl, combine banana and milk. Combine the flour, salt, baking powder, and baking soda; gradually add to creamed mixture alternately with banana mixture. Drop tablespoonfuls 2 in. apart onto greased baking sheets. Bake for 12 to 15 minutes or until springy to the touch. Remove from oven and cool on a rack or let stand for 5 minutes and remove to platter to cool thoroughly. Scoop filling onto one half of the Whoopie Pie cake and close with the other half.

Filling:

1 pkg. (8 oz.) cream cheese, softened	1 c. confectioners' sugar
1 c. creamy peanut butter	1 t. vanilla extract
3 T. butter or margarine, softened	Additional confectioners' sugar

For filling, in a large bowl, beat the cream cheese, peanut butter, and butter until fluffy. Beat in confectioners' sugar and vanilla until smooth. Spread filling on the bottoms of half of the cookies, about 1 T. on each; top with remaining cookies. Dust with additional confectioners' sugar. Store in the refrigerator.

Red Velvet Whoopie Pies

2 oz. semisweet chocolate, chopped
3/4 c. butter or margarine, softened
1 c. sugar
2 eggs
1/2 c. sour cream
1 T. red food coloring
1 1/2 t. white vinegar
1 t. clear vanilla extract
2 1/4 c. flour
1/4 c. baking cocoa
2 t. baking powder
1/2 t. salt
1/4 t. baking soda
Filling, *recipe below*

Preheat oven to 350°F. In a microwave, melt chocolate; stir until smooth. Set aside. In a large bowl, cream butter and sugar until light and fluffy. Beat in the eggs, sour cream, food coloring, vinegar, and vanilla. Combine the flour, cocoa, baking powder, salt, and baking soda; gradually add to creamed mixture and mix well. Stir in melted chocolate. Drop tablespoonfuls 2 in. apart onto greased baking sheets. Bake for 11 to 13 minutes or until edges are set and springy to the touch. Remove from oven and cool on a rack or let stand for 5 minutes and remove to platter to cool thoroughly. Scoop filling onto one half of the Whoopie Pie cake and close with the other half.

Orange Almond Cream Whoopie Pies

2 c. flour	1/3 c. vegetable oil
1 t. baking soda	Zest of 1 to 2 oranges (depending on size)
2 t. baking powder	1 c. sugar
1/4 t. salt	3/4 c. milk
1 egg	Filling, *recipe below*

Preheat your oven to 350°F and line a baking sheet with parchment paper. In a bowl, mix the flour, baking soda, baking powder, and salt; set aside. In another bowl, mix the egg, oil, orange zest, and sugar. Add the dry ingredients to the wet, alternating with the milk, until all the ingredients are well combined. Drop the dough, a teaspoonful at a time, onto the prepared baking sheet, taking care to leave enough space between the cookies as they expand a little while baking, but not too much. Also try to keep the shape as round and even as possible, it makes it easier to match the cookies after they are baked. Bake the cookies about 10 to 12 minutes, until they are slightly golden around the edges, but do not over bake them, you want them to be tender, not hard. Remove from oven and cool on a rack or let stand for 5 minutes and remove to platter to cool thoroughly. Scoop filling onto one half of the Whoopie Pie cake and close with the other half.

Filling:

1 pkg. (8 oz.) cream cheese, softened	3 1/2 c. sifted powdered sugar
5 T. butter or margarine, room temperature	1/2 to 3/4 t. almond extract

In the bowl of your mixer, preferably fitted with a paddle attachment, mix the cream cheese and the butter until light and well blended. Add the sifted powdered sugar, in batches, until the filling is perfectly smooth. Add the almond extract, mix well.

Filling:

- 1 pkg. (8 oz.) cream cheese, softened
- 1/2 c. butter or margarine, softened
- 2 1/2 c. powdered sugar
- 2 t. vanilla

In a large bowl, beat cream cheese and butter until fluffy. Beat in confectioners' sugar and vanilla until smooth. Spread filling on the bottoms of half of the cookies, about 1 T. on each. Top with remaining cookies. Drizzle with melted baking chips and chocolate; sprinkle with nuts. Store in the refrigerator.

Strawberry Whoopies

2 1/4 c. flour
1 1/2 t. baking powder
1/2 t. salt
4 T. butter or margarine, room temperature
4 T. shortening
1/2 c. packed, brown sugar
3/4 c. granulated sugar

2 eggs
1/ 2 c. milk plus 2 T. milk
1 t. baking soda
2 t. baking soda
1/2 t. vinegar
1 t. vanilla
Filling, *recipe below*

Position a rack in the center of the oven and preheat it to 350°F. Line two baking sheets with parchment paper. Sift together the flour, baking soda, baking powder, and salt into a bowl. In a separate bowl beat the butter, shortening, and both sugars until light and creamy, about 3 minutes. Add the eggs and 1/2 c. milk and beat until combined. In a measuring cup, combine 2 T. milk, baking soda, and vinegar. Add the milk mixture to the batter along with the flour mixture and beat on low until just combined. Add the vanilla and beat on medium for about 2 minutes until completely combined. Using an ice cream scoop, drop batter onto the prepared baking sheets about 2 inches apart. Bake one sheet at a time for about 11 to 13 minutes each, or until the cakes begin to brown. Remove from oven and cool on a rack or let stand for 5 minutes and remove to platter to cool thoroughly. Scoop filling onto one half of the Whoopie Pie cake and close with the other half.

Filling:

1/2 cup (1 stick) butter
  or margarine, softened
1 1/4 to 2 c. confectioner's sugar
3 c. Marshmallow Fluff

1 t. vanilla
1/2 c. fresh strawberries,
  chopped, strained

What I like to do is chop the strawberries and allow them to macerate in sugar overnight, use a mesh strainer and press chopped strawberries into the mesh to release as much juice as you can. Done this way, you'll probably need to gradually add more confectioners' sugar than the recipe calls for in order to stiffen up the mixture.

Beat together butter, confectioners' sugar, marshmallow, vanilla and strawberries in a bowl with electric mixer at medium speed until smooth, about 3 minutes. Refrigerate for 15 to 20 minutes. Using the same cookie scoop you used to measure the cake batter, scoop up some filling and place it on the flat side of one cake. Place another cake, flat-side down, on top of the filling and gently squish down. Serve immediately, at room temperature. These can be covered and sit in the refrigerator over night though!

Spiced Whoopie Pies with Maple Cream Filling

2 c. flour
1 t. cinnamon
1/2 t. ginger
1/2 t. baking soda
2 t. baking powder
1/4 t. nutmeg
1/4 t. salt
1/8 t. ground cloves
3/4 c. butter or margarine, softened
1 c. brown sugar
1 egg
2 T. molasses
1/2 c. sour cream
Filling, *recipe below*

Preheat oven to 350°F. In medium bowl, mix flour, cinnamon, ginger, baking soda, baking powder, nutmeg, salt, and cloves. In a large bowl, using your stand mixer or hand mixer on medium, beat butter until smooth. Add brown sugar and beat 3 to 4 minutes or until creamy. Add egg and molasses, and beat until well blended. With mixer on low speed, beat in flour mix alternately with sour cream, beginning and ending with flour mix until just blended. Spoon batter by heaping tablespoons onto greased cookie sheets 2 1/2 inches apart. (You should get about 30 cakes.) Bake cakes one sheet at a time 11 to 13 minutes or until cakes spring back when pressed lightly. Remove from oven and cool on a rack or let stand for 5 minutes and remove to platter to cool thoroughly. Scoop filling onto one half of the Whoopie Pie cake and close with the other half.

Filling:
3 c. powdered sugar
8 oz. cream cheese, at room
   temperature
4 oz. (1/2 cup) butter or margarine,
   room temperature
3 T. maple syrup
1 t. vanilla

Beat all ingredients together for 5 to 7 minutes at medium to high speed until fluffy.

Blueberry Whoopie Pies

Use the same cake recipe and instructions as with Spiced Whoopie Pies, but instead of Maple Cream Frosting, use the filling recipe below.

Filling:
1 pkg. (8 oz.) cream cheese,
   softened
1 jar (7 1/2 ounce)
   marshmallow creme
2 c. blueberries
   (fresh or frozen. If frozen, thaw)

In a large bowl, using your hand mixer on medium speed, beat cream cheese until smooth. Reduce speed to low, add marshmallow creme, and beat until just blended. Fold in blueberries.

Amish Oatmeal Whoopie Pie Cookies

3/4 c. butter or margarine, softened
2 c. brown sugar
2 eggs
2 c. flour
1/2 t. salt
2 t. baking powder
1 t. cinnamon
2 c. quick-cooking oatmeal, not instant
2 t. baking soda
3 T. boiling water
Filling, *recipe below*

Preheat oven to 325°F. Cream butter, sugar, and eggs. Sift together flour, salt, and baking powder and add to creamed mixture. Add cinnamon and oatmeal. Mix well. Add soda to hot water and add to batter; mix well. Drop by tablespoon onto greased cookie sheet and bake 15 to 17 minutes or until springy in the middle. Remove from oven and cool on a rack or let stand for 5 minutes and remove to platter to cool thoroughly. Scoop filling onto one half of the Whoopie Pie cake and close with the other half.

Filling:
1 egg white
1 T. vanilla
2 T. milk
2 c. powdered sugar
1/4 c. vegetable shortening

Combine egg white, vanilla, milk, and 1 c. of powdered sugar. Cream well. Beat in mixing bowl about 10 minutes. Add remainder of sugar and vegetable shortening. Beat an additional 2 to 3 minutes.

Reverse Whoopie Pies

3/4 c. (1 1/2 sticks) butter or
   margarine, room temperature
1 1/4 c. sugar
3 eggs
2 t. vanilla
3 3/4 c. flour
1 t. baking soda
2 t. baking powder
1/2 t. salt
1 c. milk
Filling, *recipe below*

In large mixing bowl with mixer set to medium speed, mix butter and sugar until well blended, about 3 minutes. Add eggs one at a time, mixing until smooth after each. Mix in vanilla. In another bowl, stir together flour, baking soda, baking powder, and salt. Add half the flour mixture to butter mixture and mix on medium speed until combined. Add 1/2 c. milk beat on medium speed until smooth and slightly fluffy in texture. Repeat with the remaining flour and then the remainder of the milk, batter will be thick and slightly springy. Line 2 baking sheets with parchment paper and butter the paper. Drop 2 tablespoons of batter onto the baking sheets. Leave 2 inches between to allow for spreading. Bake in a preheated 350°F oven for 11 to 13 minutes or until they are puffed and set but still soft when touched lightly with fingertips. Remove from oven and cool on a rack or let stand for 5 minutes and remove to platter to cool thoroughly. Scoop filling onto one half of the Whoopie Pie cake and close with the other half.

Filling:
2/3 c. unsweetened cocoa powder
2 1/3 c. powdered sugar
1/2 c. (1 stick) plus 2 T. butter or margarine, room temperature
2 c. marshmallow creme
3 T. milk
1/2 t. vanilla
Pinch salt

Combine cocoa, sugar, butter, and marshmallow creme and beat on high until light and fluffy. Add the milk and vanilla and continue beating until smooth throughout.

Coffee Cake Whoopie Pies

1 1/2 c. flour
3/4 c. sugar
2 1/2 t. baking powder
1/2 t. salt
1 egg, beaten
1/3 c. butter or margarine, melted
1/2 c. milk
1 t. vanilla
Topping
Filling, *recipe below*

Preheat the oven to 350°F. In a large bowl, combine all dry ingredients for the cake together. In a separate bowl, combine all wet ingredients. Slowly, incorporate wet with dry and beat until almost lump free. Drop by the 1/4-cup measure onto a cookie sheet with parchment paper and sprinkle with topping evenly. Bake 13 to 15 minutes or until done. Remove from oven and cool on a rack or let stand for 5 minutes and remove to platter to cool thoroughly. Scoop filling onto one half of the Whoopie Pie cake and close with the other half.

Pineapple Whoopie Pies

Topping:
1/2 c. brown sugar
1/4 c. flour
1/4 c. butter or margarine, melted
1 t. cinnamon
1 c. finely chopped walnuts

Combine all ingredients in a bowl well.

Filling:
1 lb. cream cheese
1/2 c. (1 stick) butter or margarine, softened
2 c. powdered sugar
2 t. vanilla

Combine all ingredients in bowl and whip or beat until smooth.

1 1/2 c. flour
1/2 c. brown sugar
2 t. baking powder
1/2 t. cinnamon
1/2 t. salt
1/2 t. baking soda
1 can (8 oz.) pineapple, crushed, and undrained
4 egg whites
1/4 c. applesauce
Topping: 2 T. sugar mixed with 1/2 t. cinnamon
Filling, *recipe below*

Preheat oven to 350°F. Line 2 baking sheets with parchment paper and butter the paper. Mix dry ingredients for cake together. Mix remaining cake ingredients together in a separate bowl; stir into dry ingredients until just moistened. Drop by the 1/4-cup onto baking sheet and top with cinnamon-sugar topping mixture. Bake 11 to 13 minutes. Remove from oven and cool on a rack or let stand for 5 minutes and remove to platter to cool thoroughly. Scoop filling onto one half of the Whoopie Pie cake and close with the other half.

Filling:
1/2 c. (1 stick) butter or margarine, softened
1 1/4 c. confectioners sugar
2 c. marshmallow cream
1 c. pineapple tidbits, squeezed very dry

Cream butter and sugar until well blended. Add the marshmallow cream and continue beating until smooth. Add the pineapple and blend together until well incorporated. Fill your Whoopies.

Althaea officinallis, the marshmallow plant, has been used since antiquity by the Egyptians. The root was cooked in a honey sweetened confection and used for medicinal purposes. Hence this seventeenth-century cure by a Boston physician: "Marshmallows are mainly hot, of a digestion softening nature, eases pains, help bloody fluxes, the sonte and gravell; being bruised and well boiled in milk, and the milk drunk is a gallant remedy for the gripings of the belly and the bloddy flux."

Chocolate Mousse

Some say mousse is a hard dessert to make. Nothing could be more far-fetched. Whenever you use gelatin, just make sure you soften it in cold water first, then mix it with whatever you want to gel. Keep in mind, 1 teaspoon of gelatin is enough to gel 1 c. of liquid.

I t. unflavored gelatin
I T. cold water
2 T. boiling water
1/2 c. sugar
1/4 c. dark cocoa powder
I c. cold whipping cream
I t. vanilla

In small cup, sprinkle gelatin over cold water and let stand 2 minutes to soften. Add boiling water; stir until gelatin is completely dissolved and mixture is clear. Cool slightly. In small mixing bowl, stir together sugar and cocoa. Add whipping cream and vanilla; beat on medium speed of electric mixer until stiff. Add gelatin mixture; beat until well blended. Spoon evenly into serving dishes and refrigerate about 30 minutes.

Easy Chocolate Pudding

Now, I know it's so much easier to make instant pudding, but please, try this deep chocolate tasting pudding. You'll be making it again before this one cools.

2 bars (I oz. each) unsweetened
   baking chocolate, broken
2 1/2 c. milk, divided
I c. sugar
1/4 c. cornstarch
1/2 t. salt
3 egg yolks, slightly beaten
I T. butter
I t. vanilla
Whipped topping

In medium saucepan, combine chocolate with 1 1/2 c. milk; cook over low heat, stirring constantly with whisk, until chocolate is melted and mixture is smooth. In medium bowl, stir together sugar, cornstarch, and salt; blend in remaining 1 c. milk and egg yolks. Gradually stir into chocolate mixture. Cook over medium heat, stirring constantly. Remove from heat; stir in butter and vanilla. Pour into bowl; press plastic wrap directly onto surface. Refrigerate 2 to 3 hours or until cold.

Butterscotch Pudding

When was the last time you saw anyone make Butterscotch Pudding. It's a shame it has been so neglected in the past few decades. Triple this recipe for pie.

I T. butter or margarine
I c. brown sugar
I 3/4 c. scalded milk
3 T. cornstarch
1/4 t. salt
1/4 c. cold milk
I t. vanilla
2 egg whites, beaten stiffly

Melt butter in medium saucepan over medium heat. Add brown sugar and stir frequently until sugar melts. Add hot milk slowly and heat until smooth, stirring constantly. Mix cornstarch and salt with cold milk and add to hot mixture. Cook, stirring constantly until mixture thickens. Cook 5 minutes longer. Cool slightly, fold in flavoring and egg whites, turn into serving dishes and chill.

Those of you who enjoy butterscotch should enjoy toffee; they are almost the same thing. To make butterscotch, sugar is only boiled to the soft crack stage while with toffee, the sugar is boiled to the hard crack point.

Chocolate Marshmallow Pudding

How much easier can it get? You won't find this pudding in an instant mix box!

10 large marshmallows
1/4 c. milk

4 oz. (1 large bar) milk or dark chocolate
Whipped topping

In the top of a double boiler, heat marshmallows and milk over lightly boiling water until marshmallows are melted. Add chocolate and stir until melted and smooth. Transfer to a metal bowl and chill about 30 minutes or until cooled. Serve with whipped topping.

Vermont Maple Pudding

A dessert like no other you have tasted. The amalgamation of sweet and salty nudges it's way into today's palate.

1 c. flour
1/2 t. salt
1 1/2 t. baking powder
1/4 c. brown sugar
1/2 c. milk
1 t. vanilla
1/4 c. butter or margarine, melted
1 c. raisins (optional)
1/2 c. chopped walnuts (optional)
3/4 c. real maple syrup
1/3 c. water
Light cream or whipped topping

Preheat oven to 350°F. Mix the dry ingredients together until well blended. Add the milk, vanilla, and butter; mix until combined. Place batter in 1-qt. casserole. Sprinkle with raisins or chopped nuts. In a saucepan, bring maple syrup and water to a boil. Pour over the batter and bake for 35 to 40 minutes. Serve warm with light cream or whipped topping.

Strawberry Pretzel Squares

There are so many uses for flavored gelatin and this is no exception. Again, using salty and sweet together results in a whirlwind of distinctions.

2 c. finely crushed pretzels
1/2 c. sugar, divided
2/3 c. butter or margarine, melted
12 oz. cream cheese, softened
2 T. milk
1 c. whipped topping
2 c. boiling water
1 pkg. (8-serving size) strawberry flavored gelatin
1 1/2 c. cold water
4 c. fresh, sliced strawberries

Preheat oven to 350°F. Mix pretzels, 1/4 c. of the sugar and the butter. Press firmly onto bottom of 13 × 9-inch baking pan. Bake for 10 minutes; remove. Beat cream cheese, remaining 1/4 c. sugar and milk until well blended. Gently stir in whipped topping. Spread over crust and keep in refrigerator until ready to use.

Stir boiling water into gelatin in large bowl at least 2 minutes or until completely dissolved. Stir in cold water. Refrigerate 1 1/2 hours or until thickened. Stir in strawberries and spoon over cream cheese layer. Refrigerate at least 3 hours or until completely set.

On January 15, 1919, the Purity Distilling Company, located on Commercial Street in Boston, had a little cleanup to do. One of their 2-million-gallon holding tanks let loose a wave of molasses that nearby residents said sounded like a train going by beneath their feet. *The Boston Globe* reported that people "were picked up by a rush of air and hurled many feet." Others had debris hurled at them from the rush of sweet-smelling air. A truck was picked up and hurled into Boston Harbor by a 35 mph and 8-foot wave of molasses. Approximately 150 were injured; 21 people and several horses were killed—some were crushed and drowned by the molasses.

To make Almond Custard. Take a pint of cream, blanch and beat a quarter of a pound of almonds fine, with two spoonfuls of rose-water. Sweeten it to your palate. Beat up the yolks of four eggs, stir all together one way over the fire, till it is thick; then pour it out into cups.

—The Frugal Housewife, 1772

Baked Custard

The creamy texture of this soft-set custard is pleasantly enhanced with vanilla and nutmeg.

3 eggs, slightly beaten
1/4 t. salt
1/4 c. sugar
3 c. scalded milk
1 t. vanilla
Nutmeg

Preheat oven to 350°F. Combine eggs, salt, and sugar. Add milk slowly, stirring constantly. Add vanilla and pour into custard cups. Sprinkle with nutmeg and place in pan with 1/4-inch hot water. Bake 30 to 35 minutes or until a toothpick inserted in middle comes out clean and it has set. Or you may pour into a 9-inch square baking pan and bake as directed above.

Fresh Peaches with Maple Yogurt

Why spend the money on artificially flavored peach yogurt when you can have this recipe? It's more filling and much more flavorful.

1 pint plain yogurt
1 c. maple syrup
8 peaches, wedged

In small bowl, combine yogurt and maple syrup until well combined. Serve on the side with the wedged peaches. Or try these peaches, or other fresh fruit with homemade Crème Fraîche (*see page 279*). Don't be afraid of making Crème Fraîche, it is very easy and quite a complement to fresh fruit.

Plum Duff

The original Plum Duff was a stiff flour pudding with raisins or currants, boiled in a bag. You'll find this Duff easier to prepare and ready to be handed down in your family.

1/2 c. brown sugar
1/4 c. melted butter or margarine
1 egg, beaten
1 c. seeded, cooked prunes
1/2 c. flour
1/4 t. baking soda
1/4 t. baking powder
1/4 t. salt
1 T. milk

Preheat oven to 350°F. Grease muffin tin. Add sugar to melted butter in large bowl. Cool slightly and stir in the egg. Cut prunes into bite sized pieces. Place in food processor or blender and puree only until mashed. Mix all dry ingredients together in separate bowl. Add fruit pulp to sugar mixture, stir well. Add flour mixture and continue to stir until well incorporated. Add milk and blend. Fill each muffin cup until it is 2/3 full and bake for about 25 minutes or until toothpick inserted in middle comes out clean. Serve warm with any fruited dessert sauce.

DESSERT SAUCES

Hard Sauce

1/3 c. butter or margarine
1 c. powdered sugar
1/4 c. your favorite wine
Nutmeg

Cream the butter and add the sugar slowly, constantly beating. Add wine and nutmeg very slowly while whisking. Completely blend and serve. This age-old sauce goes great with many of the dense, sweet cakes such as pound cake, bread puddings, and pumpkin pies.

Strawberry Hard Sauce

1/4 c. butter, softened
1 1/4 c. powdered sugar
1/2 c. fresh, sliced strawberries

Cream butter and add sugar gradually. Continue creaming until well blended. Add strawberries and beat until light and evenly colored. Serve with lemon pound cake, coffee cakes, or other cakes.

Fresh Cranberry Sauce

1 1/2 c. boiling water
2 c. sugar
4 c. fresh cranberries

Whisk together the water and sugar until sugar is dissolved. Add cranberries and cover. Cook over medium-high heat until popping stops, about 20 minutes. Remove from heat, pour into bowl and chill. Mix before serving. Yes, you can use this on ice cream and sundaes, as well as a side dish for savory dishes.

Spiced Cranberry Sauce

I qt. whole, fresh cranberries	2 whole cinnamon sticks
I I/2 c. orange marmalade	2 c. sugar

Rinse cranberries and place in medium sized saucepan. Cover with water and a lid; cook over medium heat until cranberries stop popping. Remove from heat. With potato masher, mash the softened cranberries; removing any skin that floats to the surface of the mash water. Add marmalade, cinnamon sticks and sugar. Keep cooking until it thickens without the lid, about 20 minutes. Remove from heat and let sit on stove top until it reaches room temperature. Remove cinnamon sticks. Use with the same desserts and savory dishes as you would Fresh Cranberry Sauce.

Raisin Sauce

I I/2 c. apple juice or cider	I c. raisins
4 T. lemon juice	4 T. cornstarch
I/4 c. cider vinegar	4 T. water
I c. brown sugar	I T. butter or margarine

Over medium-high heat, add apple juice, lemon juice, vinegar, and brown sugar to a medium sized saucepan. Bring to a boil and add raisins. Continue cooking until raisins have plumped up. In small bowl, combine cornstarch with water and mix until smooth. Add to raisin sauce and continue stirring constantly until mixture has thickened. Remove from heat and serve hot. Just as delicious on ham as sweet breads and ice cream, by the way.

Apricot Sauce

I I/2 c. apricot jam	2 T. sugar
I/2 c. water	I T. apricot brandy (optional)

Heat apricot jam in a small saucepan over medium heat. Stir in the water and sugar and heat to boiling, increasing heat to medium-high. Reduce heat to low and continue cooking 5 to 10 minutes, stirring constantly. Stir in apricot brandy and serve either hot or cold. Again, great on ice cream and even your breakfast muffins.

Hot Apple Topping

I/2 lb. butter or margarine,
   cut into pats
3 c. peeled, cored, and diced apples
I c. brown sugar
I c. golden raisins
2 T. cinnamon
I c. apple juice or cider

Place pats of butter in bottom of oven-safe casserole dish. Pre heat oven to 350°F. Arrange diced apples in layer and sprinkle with sugar, raisins, and cinnamon evenly over apples. Add juice and place in oven for 20 to 25 minutes, frequently stirring until apples are soft but not mushy. Add more water if necessary to prevent scorching and burning. Remove and place in bowl to use as sauce. Need I tell you that sundaes are the perfect vehicle for this topping?

Blueberry Sauce

This delectable sauce just screams to be loaded on top of ice cream.

I/2 c. sugar
I I/2 T. cornstarch
4 T. water
I T. lemon juice
2 c. fresh blueberries

Mix sugar, cornstarch, water, and lemon juice in non-aluminum saucepan. Bring to a boil over medium-high heat. Add blueberries and boil about 4 to 5 minutes or until thickened, constantly stirring and mashing with your whisk.

Soft Caramel Sauce

1 c. sugar
1/4 c. water
1 T. corn syrup

1/4 c. butter or margarine
1 c. heavy cream
1/8 t. salt

Combine sugar, 1/4 c. water, and corn syrup in heavy saucepan over high heat. Bring to a boil, stirring with wooden spoon. Dip a brush in water to get sugar crystals off side of pan. Reduce heat to medium high and do not stir! Continue until golden brown (not dark brown), about 6 minutes. Remove from heat and gently swirl by tilting pan, twice. Add 1/4 c. butter and slowly stir until melted. Add cream and stir again. If it seizes, place back on medium heat and stir for 1 minute, until smooth. Add 1/8 t. salt. Pour into glass containers. This will thicken upon standing. Ice cream screams for this!

Hot Fudge Sauce

Duh.... What can't you use with this? I would put it on steak if my kids didn't lose their appetite at the thought.

1 can (14 oz.) sweetened condensed milk
6 T. butter or margarine, cut into pats
1/4 c. heavy cream
1/8 t. salt

1 T. vanilla
1 oz. bitter chocolate, chopped
5 oz. semisweet baking chocolate
Glass jars with lids

Combine sweetened condensed milk, butter, heavy cream, salt, and vanilla in medium saucepan. Heat on medium and cook until tiny bubbles form around the edge, stirring with wooden spoon. Remove, add bitter chocolate and semisweet chocolate and stir until smooth. Pour into jars and cool without lids. When cooled, place lids on top and refrigerate.

Crème Fraîche

This high butterfat soured cream is much less pungent than ordinary sour cream and is delightful as a dipping compliment to fresh fruit. It is also used extensively in finishing sauces because of its ability to withstand high heat without curdling.

2 T. sour cream or buttermilk
1 c. heavy cream

Combine and beat until very smooth. Let sit at room temperature at least 12 hours, uncovered. Cover and refrigerate. Use on top of fresh fruit or savories, such as a complement on top of soup or even a smoked salmon accompaniment.

CHAPTER 14

Pies

Single Flaky Pie Crust

When I say flaky, I mean it. If made properly, you can see the layers when cutting into this gorgeous crust.

1 egg, beaten
5 T. cold water
1 t. vinegar or lemon juice
1 t. salt
1 c. shortening, cold
3 c. flour

Combine egg, water, vinegar and salt in medium bowl; set aside. Cut shortening into flour in a separate large bowl until mixture resembles coarse crumbs. Add egg mixture; mix with a fork or you hands to form a dough that just barely holds together. If using your hands, do this step rather quickly. Press together to form ball. Quickly roll out on lightly floured surface to a circle 1 inch larger than an inverted pie pan. Press into pie pan, trim excess dough from around rim of pan and flute edges if desired. Promptly refrigerate until needed.

Double Flaky Pie Crust

Double the recipe and roll out second crust the same size as first. Lay between 2 sheets of waxed paper and keep refrigerated until needed.

Graham Cracker Crust

Many chefs use cinnamon in their graham cracker crust but I am not one of them. I think it detracts from the pie itself, but by all means, add 1/2 t. for a little extra flavor.

2 c. graham cracker crumbs
3 t. sugar
6 T. butter or margarine, melted

Mix all ingredients and press in bottom of 9-inch pie pan. Place in refrigerator for a half hour to firm. You may season this Graham Cracker Crust with a 1/2 teaspoon of cinnamon and 1/2 teaspoon of nutmeg if desired.

Vanilla Wafer Crust

3 c. crushed vanilla wafers
1/2 c. butter or margarine, melted

Combine crushed vanilla wafers and butter in small bowl. Press firmly in bottom of 9-inch pie pan. Refrigerate for a 1/2 hour until firmed.

Chocolate Wafer Crust

Use same amount of chocolate wafers in place of vanilla wafers.

Chocolate-Pecan Crust

Add 3/4 c. chopped pecans to crust mix.

Vanilla-Nut Wafer Crust

Follow Vanilla Wafer Crust recipe but add 1/2 c. finely crushed pecans to mixture.

Single Lemon-Flavored Flaky Pie Crust

1 c. flour
1/4 c. sugar
1 T. grated lemon peel
1/2 c. butter or margarine, melted
1 egg yolk, slightly beaten
1/2 t. vanilla
1 t. lemon juice

Combine flour, 1/4 c. sugar, and 1 T. lemon peel in medium bowl. Mix in butter until mixture resembles coarse crumbs. Stir in egg yolk, vanilla, and 1 t. lemon juice. Press evenly in 9-inch pie pan; trim and flute edge if desired.

Master Cream Pie Filling Recipe

Use this base for any cream pie filling and use your imagination. By substituting the same amount of brown sugar for the white, you have yourself an authentic butterscotch pie.

3 c. milk
4 egg yolks
1 1/2 c. sugar
1/2 t. salt
4 heaping (I mean heaping!) T. cornstarch
1 t. vanilla

In top of double boiler, over medium-high heat, scald milk. Add egg yolks and whip thoroughly. In separate bowl, thoroughly combine sugar, salt, and cornstarch and add to hot milk mixture. Continue whisking and cooking until cream has thickened and is smooth, about 6 to 7 minutes. Add vanilla and whisk to combine.

Silky Chocolate Cream Pie

If it's chocolate you're craving, here's the answer. Finely dice some fresh strawberries and sprinkle them over the whipped cream for a beautiful dessert.

Single Flaky Pie Crust, uncooked
Master Cream Pie Filling
9 T. cocoa
3 T. butter or margarine, melted

Preheat oven to 375°F. Prick pie shell with tines of fork around the bottom and sides. Bake for 5 minutes or until golden brown. Remove from oven. In small bowl, whisk together cocoa and melted butter until smooth. Add to milk mixture before thickening with sugar/cornstarch mixture. Beat well. Pour chocolate cream into baked pie shell. Cover snugly with plastic wrap and refrigerate for 3 hours or until set and cold.

Banana Cream Pie

If you decide to decorate this pie with fresh sliced bananas, be sure only to slice what you need. As you know, bananas take no time at all to brown.

1 Single Flaky Pie Crust, uncooked
Master Cream Pie filling
2 ripe bananas, mashed
3 t. banana extract

Preheat oven to 375°F. Prick pie shell with tines of fork around the bottom and sides. Bake for 5 minutes or until golden brown. Remove from oven. Make Master Cream Pie Filling and add mashed bananas and banana extract to thickened cream filling. Whisk well and pour into baked shell. Cover tightly with plastic wrap and refrigerate at least 3 hours or until firm.

Black-Bottomed Banana Cream Pie

Follow Banana Cream pie recipe but before pouring cream mixture into baked crust melt 4 squares semisweet baking chocolate with 2 T. butter or margarine in microwave-safe bowl, on high, for 1 minute, or until butter is melted. Stir until chocolate has completely melted (you may have to microwave an additional 15 seconds). Drizzle into bottom of pie crust. Top with sliced bananas and then pour cream mixture into pie.

Bananas consistently are the number one complaint of grocery shoppers. Most people complain when bananas are overripe or even freckled. In fact, spotted bananas are sweeter, with a sugar content of more than 20%, compared with 3% in a green banana.

Coconut Cream Pie

Many people don't use coconut extract in their pie, but I find the addition to be a must if you really crave that island taste.

Single Flaky Pie Crust, uncooked
1 c. flaked coconut
1 t. coconut extract
  (or more if desired)
Master Cream Pie Filling

Preheat oven to 375°F. Prick bottom and sides of pie crust with tines of fork. Bake for 5 minutes or until golden brown. Remove. Add flaked coconut and coconut extract to thickened cream filling before pouring; mixing well. Wrap tightly with plastic wrap and refrigerate for at least 3 hours or until set and cold.

Chocolate Candy Bar Pie

This is like a mousse with the taste of s'mores.

20 large marshmallows
6 dark chocolate bars
1/2 c. milk
1 c. whipped topping
Graham Cracker Crust

Combine marshmallow, chocolate bars, and milk in top of double boiler. Heat until chocolate and marshmallows melt. Cool and then fold in whipped topping. Pour mixture into pie crust; sprinkle a few graham cracker crumbs over top and refrigerate at least 3 hours or until set.

Baby Ruth was first made in 1920 and originally called a Kandy Kake by the Curtis Candy Company of Chicago.

Bit-O-Honey® was first made in 1924, originally by the Schutter-Johnson Co., of Chicago.

Charleston Chews® originated in 1922 by Fox-Cross Candy Co. of Emeryville, California.

Chiclets® mid 1930s named after the founder's "chunky" little daughter.

5th Avenue® was first produced by William H. Luden of Reading, Pennsylvania, in 1923.

The Heath Bar® was introduced as Heath's English Toffee in 1928, often referred to as "H &H's" bar, because the Hs were capitalized, becoming the present name in 1932.

Junior Mints® were first made in 1949 after a play on Broadway called Junior Miss.

Hershey's Kisses® were introduced in 1907.

M&M's® were first available in 1941 and peanut M&M's in 1954.

Mary Jane® was first made in 1914.

Milk Duds® were introduced in 1926 and first made by the Holloway Company of Chicago.

Milky Way® bars were first available in 1923, **Mr. Goodbar®** in 1925, **Mounds®** in 1922, **Almond Joy®** in 1948, **Reeses Cups®** in 1923, **Sky Bars®** in 1937, and **Snickers®** in 1930.

3 Musketeers® were first made in 1932 and was named after the 1844 novel by A. Dumas

Tootsie Rolls® were introduced in New York City in 1896 and named after creator Leo Hirschfield's daughter, whose nickname was Tootsie.

Yankee Pumpkin Pie

Enjoyed for centuries now, this pumpkin pie is spot on when it comes to the spices. Some real cream would be just what's needed, if you really want to go back in time.

Single Flaky Pie Crust, uncooked	1/2 t. nutmeg
2 eggs	1 3/4 c. canned or cooked pumpkin
1/2 c. sugar	3 T. molasses
1 t. cinnamon	3/4 c. evaporated milk
1/2 t. salt	Whipped topping
1/2 t ginger	

Preheat oven to 425°F. In a mixing bowl, beat eggs, sugar, cinnamon, salt, ginger, and nutmeg. Beat in the pumpkin, and molasses; gradually add the milk. Pour into the crust and cover the edges loosely with tin foil. Bake for 10 minutes, remove foil, reduce heat to 350°F and bake an additional 28 to 30 minutes or until knife inserted in the middle comes out clean. Cool for at least 2 hours and serve with whipped topping.

Since time immemorial, including even today, adulteration of various foods and beverages is and was rampant. In colonial times, it was punished severely. Two men found guilty of adulterating wine were buried alive in England. Literature of this period here in New England tells of adding brick dust to ginger, "unhealthy" stuff in pepper, and storing dried spices in damp cellars to increase weight.

Grasshopper Pie

I agree that frugality and cost play a factor in this pie, but at least make it on occasion. "It is a crowd pleaser," as the old advertisement goes.

25 large marshmallows
1 c. heavy cream
4 T. green creme de menthe
4 T. white creme de cacao
1 c. whipping cream,
    whipped to stiff peaks
Chocolate Wafer Crust

Combine marshmallows and heavy cream in top of double boiler over medium high heat. Cook until marshmallows have melted; cool. Fold in liqueurs and whipped cream and pour into chilled crust. Sprinkle some graham cracker crumbs over the top. Freeze until firm.

Pecan Pie

I have found that taking 2 cups of apple cider and boiling it over medium-high heat until it reduces to 1 1/4 cup and using it instead of corn syrup gives this pie a sweet, apple taste that surpasses that of corn syrup.

3 eggs, lightly beaten
1 1/4 c. corn syrup
1/2 c. brown sugar
2 T. butter or margarine
1 t. vanilla
1 1/2 c. pecan halves
Single Flaky Pie Crust, uncooked

Preheat oven to 350°F. In a mixing bowl, combine eggs, corn syrup, sugar, margarine, and vanilla. Stir in pecans.

Place the pastry crust on a sheet pan on a rack in the oven. Pour the pecan mixture into the pie crust and bake for 40 to 45 minutes or until a toothpick inserted in the middle comes out clean.

Many chefs still believe in lard as the base for that perfect pie crust. Lard is rendered, clarified pork fat, with 98 to 100% fat content—it is high in saturated fat. In pastry-making, lard forms large, grainy crystals that in turn produce superior flakiness. Many bakers use a combination of lard and butter.

MINCEMEAT 101

First called Christmas Pie; it came about at the time when the Crusaders were returning from the Holy Land during the eleventh century. They brought with them many different types of oriental spices, including the all-important cinnamon, cloves, and nutmeg. These three spices were intended as the three gifts given to the Christ child by the Magi. To further honor the Christ Child, the mincemeat pie was first made in an oblong casing that was cradle shaped, with a place for the Christ Child to be placed on top. It was also considered lucky to eat one mincemeat pie on each of the twelve days of Christmas, ending with the Epiphany, which was on January 6. As the decades and centuries passed, so did the form and content of this pie, slowly being made in a round pan with suet, spices, and dried fruit.

A Proper Newe Booke of Cokerye, declarynge what maner of meates be beste in season, for al times in the yere, and how they ought to be dressed, and serued at the table, bothe for fleshe days, and fyshe dayes. Believe it or not, that was the name of a cookbook that had the very first reference and recipe for a mincemeat pie:

To make Pies—Pies of mutton of beef must be fine minced and seasoned with pepper and salt, and a little saffron to colure it, suet or marrow a good quantity, a little vinegar, prunes, greater raisins and dates, take the fattest of the broathe of powdred beyfe, and yf you wyll have paestroyall, take buhyter and yolkes of egges and so tempre the flower to make the paeste.

Oliver Cromwell (1599–1658), the self-proclaimed Lord Protector of England for almost 10 years, hated Christmas. He thought of it as a pagan holiday because it was not sanctioned by the Bible and it promoted drunkenness and gluttony. His council abolished Christmas on December 22, 1657. He ordered soldiers to take to the streets and remove, by force if necessary, all food being prepared in any household that was for the purpose of the holiday.

This was the beginning of all mincemeat pies being banned. It wasn't until King Charles II's ascension to the throne in 1660 that Christmas was restored along with all the glorious tidbits of food that promoted this holiday.

During the seventeenth and eighteenth centuries, mincemeat pies, also known as Shred or Secret Pies, were being made in various shapes. Was it because mince pies were known throughout England by their shape during its ban, so families began making them in odd shapes to hide them from the searching soldiers, and the tradition just continued?

Here's a song called "The World Turned Upside Down," by Thomason Tracts, written in 1646 that describes the ban on Christmas and the Shred (mincemeat) pie;

To conclude. I'le tell you news that's right,
Christmas was kil'd at Naseby fight:
Charity was slain at that same time,
Jack Tell troth too, a friend of mine,
Likewise then did die,
Rost beef and shred pie,
Pig, Goose and Capon no quarter found.

Final Chorus:
Yet let's be content and the times lament,
you see the world is quite turned round.

Believe it or not, this ban on Christmas and its food was brought over here to New England during the mid-1600s. Many towns in New England banned mincemeat pies at Christmastime. Christmas itself was banned in Boston from 1659 to 1681.

In a book entitled **Swan Among Indians; Life of James G. Swan, 1818-1900**, by Lucile Saunders McDonald, his diaries and journals were put together for the first time in print. He makes mention of a different type of mincemeat pie enjoyed during Christmas dinner; whale mincemeat! It was Christmas, 1861, when three Boston men sat down in a trading post to eat. James Swan had prepared this feast, which consisted of roast goose and duck stew along with all the trimmings. For dessert, mincemeat pie was made out of the whale.

A few months previous, the local Indians had brought James some whale meat, which he often ate in the absence of red meat. He boiled it, minced it fine, and added some chopped apples from the nearest tree, wild cranberries, raisins, currants, salt, nutmeg, cloves, allspice, cinnamon, and of course some molasses and sugar. When he packed it in a large stone jug, he poured over it some New England rum and sealed it up. All he had to do was scoop some out and put it in a pastry, which he did, and bake it. Once out of the fireplace oven, he set it on the table to cool while they ate dinner. When dinner was over, the smell of this pie must have whetted their sweet tooth because all 4 men ate that pie and wanted more.

Homemade Mincemeat Pie

2 apples, peeled, cored, and minced
1 c. golden raisins
1/2 c. dark raisins
3/4 c. currants
1/2 c. brown sugar
2 oz. beef suet*
1/4 c. brandy (optional)
2 T. lemon juice
2 t. grated lemon zest

2 t. grated orange zest
1/2 t. allspice
1/2 t. nutmeg
Double Flaky Pie Crust, unbaked
1 egg, beaten
2 t. sugar
Whipped topping
Ice cream

Stir together all ingredients except whipped cream and ice cream. Let sit in the refrigerator overnight. Preheat oven to 350°F. Put a baking sheet in the middle of the oven. Stir the mincemeat well and spoon it into the pie shell. Top with the second shell and crimp edges. Cut off excess and decoratively flute. In a small bowl, combine egg and sugar; mix well. Brush the egg mixture over the top and vent. Bake 50 to 55 minutes, or until nicely browned on top and thick juices start bubbling through the vent holes or slits. Cool and serve with whipped topping or ice cream.

Beef suet is simply the fat found around the kidneys. Used in steak and kidney pudding also, it is a necessary food item for Arctic explorers and those who traverse the colder regions of earth, because of the high food energy requirements.

Apple Pie with Cider Sauce

Dad would never have thought of serving apple pie (at any of his restaurants) without a slab of Cheddar cheese either beside it or on top of it, melted so that every bite had a slight, salty kick. That is the Yankee way!

3 lbs. apples, peeled, cored,
   and sliced thin
1 t. lemon juice
2/3 c. sugar
3/4 t. cinnamon
3 T. cornstarch
Double Flaky Pie Crust, uncooked
1 egg, beaten
1 T. milk

Preheat oven to 350°F. In large bowl, combine apples and lemon juice; toss to coat. In separate bowl combine sugar, cinnamon, and cornstarch and blend well. Pour over prepared apples and toss with your hands until evenly coated. Pour into uncooked pie crust and spread evenly and press gently to make firm. Cover with pie crust dough, gently pushing to condense apples and crimp around edges. Remove excess dough and flute.

Cut steam vents in top and brush with 1 beaten egg combined with 1 T. milk. Bake 50 to 60 minutes or until crust is golden brown and filling is bubbly. Remove and serve with Cider Sauce, warmed and poured over the top.

Cider Sauce:
2 c. apple cider
6-inch stick of cinnamon
2 T. butter or margarine
3 T. honey
2 T. cornstarch

In a medium saucepan combine the apple cider and stick cinnamon. Bring to boiling over high; reduce heat to medium-low and simmer, uncovered, about 20 minutes. When cider has reduced to about 1 cup, remove cinnamon stick.

In another saucepan, melt butter; whisk in honey and cornstarch until smooth. Stir in the cider mixture and cook over medium heat until thickened and bubbly. Cook and stir 2 more minutes.

Boiled Cider Apple Sauce

Some families used to make this sauce by the barrel many generations ago, keeping it in the cellar to freeze, chopping off bits throughout the winter to thaw and eat as is.

3 lbs. sweet apples, peeled and cored
1 qt. sweet cider, reduced in half by boiling

Put apples in a kettle, add cider, and simmer 3 to 4 hours, stirring to break up the apples. When tender and mushy remove and can in a mason jar. Now that's old-fashioned!

Apple Crumb Pie

Many people give you recipes for Deep-dish Apple Pie. I think every apple pie should be deep dish, especially Apple Crumb. Load just as many apple slices as you can shove in between the crusts. There, it's deep dish.

3 lbs. apples, peeled, cored, sliced thin
2/3 c. sugar
1/2 c. raisins
3 T. cornstarch
3/4 t. cinnamon
1 container (8 oz.) sour cream
1 1/2 t. vanilla
Single Flaky Pie Crust, uncooked
Crumb Topping, *recipe below*

Preheat oven to 350°F. In large bowl, toss apples, sugar, raisins, cornstarch, and cinnamon until well combined. Set aside. Add sour cream and vanilla to apple mixture and toss well to coat evenly. Spoon apple mixture into chilled pie crust. Sprinkle top of apples evenly with Crumb Topping. Place sheet of foil underneath pie plate; crimp foil edges to form a rim to catch any overflow during baking. Bake pie loosely with foil to prevent over browning if necessary during last 20 minutes of baking. Remove and cool.

Crumb Topping:
1 c. flour
1/2 c. brown sugar
1/2 t. cinnamon
5 T. butter or margarine, melted

In medium bowl, add flour, brown sugar, cinnamon, and melted butter or margarine. Mix until well combined.

Vermont Cheddar Apple Crumb Pie

Follow Apple Crumb Pie recipe but when making crumb topping, add 3/4 c. Vermont Cheddar cheese, shredded.

Key Lime Pie

You will find dozens of variations of Key Lime Pie out there, each alluding to its authenticity. This recipe, if you use true Key limes, is the real deal. If you can't find Key limes, using normal limes will easily be acceptable, without any difference in taste.

1 c. vanilla wafer crumbs
1/4 c. plain granola
5 T. butter or margarine, melted
Filling, *recipe below*

Preheat oven to 350°F. In a mixing bowl, combine dry ingredients. Pour melted butter over mixture. Using a wooden spoon, gently mix ingredients until wet. Lightly spray non-stick coating inside a 9-inch pie pan. Pour crust mixture into pan and press mixture along the sides of the pan using a fork. Then press remaining mixture evenly on the bottom of the pan to form a crust. Bake for 5 minutes and set aside to cool.

Filling:
3 egg yolks
1 t. Key lime zest
1 can (14 oz.) sweetened
  condensed milk
1/2 c. Key lime juice (fresh if
  possible)

Using an electric mixer at full speed, beat egg yolks and zest for 5 minutes or until mixture has a shiny luster. Slowly pour condensed milk into the mixture and beat for another 3 minutes or until thickened. Reduce mixture to low and add juice, just enough to combine. Pour the filling into the cooled pie crust and bake for 12 minutes or until the filling is completely set.

Marlborough Pie

You don't know how I hated to put this recipe in here because of the length of it. Being a Yankee, I abhor long, drawn out recipes. I have numbered the steps involved because it will be easier for you to follow, depending on the items used in this recipe.

Juice and peel of 1 lemon
  (omit if using applesauce)
2 large fresh apples
  or 1 c. applesauce
1 c. sugar (use only 1/3 c.
  if applesauce is used)
3 eggs
1/2 c. butter
1/2 recipe for Puff Pastry (*below*) for
  bottom shell, or favorite
  one-crust pastry recipe

If fresh apples are used, follow Step 1. If using applesauce, begin with Step 2.

1. Squeeze lemon and grate peel into large bowl. Grate apples and lemon juice and toss to coat apples (to prevent darkening).
2. Pour sugar over fruit and mix well.
3. Prepare Puff Pastry. Line deep, 8-inch pie plate, with pastry.
4. Beat eggs until light.
5. Cream butter until soft and add eggs, blending well.
6. Stir butter and egg mixture into sweetened fruit and spoon into pie pastry.
7. Bake 15 minutes at 400°F. Reduce heat to 350°F and bake 45 minutes more or until knife inserted into center comes out clean. Cool before serving.

Puff Pastry:
2 c. butter
3 1/2 c. whole-wheat flour,
  measured after sifting
1/2 c. cold water

Blend 2/3 c. butter and 2 c. of flour. Add 1/2 c. cold water, stirring gradually. Roll out on a floured board. Dot with half the remaining butter, sprinkle with 3/4 c. of remaining flour, dusting some on rolling pin, and roll up like a jelly roll. Roll this out and repeat, to use up the flour and butter.

Cherry Pie

Although almond extract is expensive, there are so many desserts and toppings you can use it in, with this recipe being at the top. With just a hint of lemon juice, this is one pie best served with whipped cream.

2 cans (14.5 oz. ea.) cherries in
   water, drained, liquid reserved
1/4 c. cornstarch
2/3 c. sugar
1/2 t. almond extract
2 t. lemon juice
3 to 4 drops food coloring
Double Flaky Pie Crust, uncooked
1 T. milk
1 egg

Preheat oven to 350°F. Pour reserved cherry juice into medium saucepan. Mix cornstarch and sugar together in small bowl. Pour in saucepan and stir well. Add almond extract and lemon juice. Stir and cook over medium heat for 4 to 5 minutes, or until thickened. Remove from heat and add red food coloring; mix. Place drained cherries in medium bowl and pour liquid over cherries and gently fold with spatula; mix without crushing fruit. Set aside.

Place filling in crust and place other pie crust dough over the top. Seal and crimp edges. In small bowl, combine egg and milk and whisk; brush over top of pie. Vent and bake for 50 to 60 minutes, or until crust is golden and filling is bubbly and syrupy.

Or if you have the patience, use a criss-cross pattern (called lattice) with dough strips cut from the top layer of rolled out dough.

Chocolate Cherry Cheese Pie

Pucker up for a pie that'll get your mouth watering before you even try it. Cherries go so well with cream cheese and this is no exception.

2 oz. unsweetened baking
   chocolate, broken
4 pkgs. (3 oz. ea.)
   cream cheese, softened
1 1/4 c. sugar
3 eggs
1/2 t. vanilla
Graham Cracker Crust
Sour Cream Topping, *recipe below*
1 can (21 oz.) cherry pie filling

Preheat oven to 350°F. In a small microwaveable bowl, place chocolate and microwave on high for 1 to 1 1/2 minutes, or until chocolate is melted and smooth when stirred. Cool. In small mixer bowl on medium speed of electric mixer, beat cream cheese and sugar until smooth. Add eggs; beat well. Stir in vanilla and melted chocolate until completely blended. Pour into crust and bake for 20 minutes or until almost set in the center.

Remove from oven and prepare Sour Cream Topping; spread over pie. Continue baking 10 minutes or just until set. Cool completely until firm. Just before serving, spread cherry pie filling over top of pie.

Sour Cream Topping:
1 c. sour cream
1/3 c. sugar
1/2 t. vanilla

In a small bowl, combine all ingredients and blend until smooth.

Maple Custard Pie

Vermont, look out! This Yankee Chef has the perfect marriage of your maple syrup and the old standby, egg custard. Sprinkle the top of this pie with a touch of nutmeg.

4 eggs
2 c. milk
3/4 c. real maple syrup
Single Flaky Pie Crust, uncooked
Maple Whipped Cream,
  recipe below

Preheat oven to 350°F. In medium bowl, beat eggs; add remaining ingredients except Maple Whipped Cream. Beat well. Pour into crust and bake 45 minutes or until toothpick inserted in middle comes out clean. Cool. Serve either warm or chilled with Maple Whipped Cream.

Maple Whipped Cream:
1 c. whipping cream
1/4 c. real maple syrup

In mixing bowl, combine both ingredients and beat on high until stiff.

Bird's Nest Pudding, 1901

Served at my great grandfather and great grandmother's wedding:

Pare and core without quartering enough quick-cooking tart apples to fill a pudding-pan; make a custard of one quart milk and the yolks of six eggs; sweeten, spice, pour over apples, and bake; when done, use the whites of eggs beaten very well with six tablespoons white sugar; spread on the custard, brown lightly, and serve either hot or cold. If necessary, apples may be baked a short time before adding custard.

Eggnog Custard Pie

What can go better with custard pie than eggnog? The rum extract really does a splendid job converting an ordinary pie into something even more desirable.

4 eggs
1/3 c. sugar
1 t. rum extract (optional)
1/2 t. vanilla
1/4 t. salt
3 c. eggnog
Single Flaky Pie Crust, uncooked
Grated nutmeg

Preheat oven to 350°F. Beat eggs, sugar, rum extract, vanilla, and salt. Add eggnog and pour into pie crust. Sprinkle liberally with nutmeg and bake for 45 to 50 minutes, or until a knife inserted comes out clean. Cool and refrigerate.

Orange Meringue Pie

I came up with this pie many years ago when Dad and I were just sitting doing nothing. It has a deliciously fresh flavor that just might convert you from the classic lemon.

Single Flaky Pie Crust, unbaked
1 1/4 c. sugar, divided
6 T. cornstarch
1/2 t. salt, divided
1 1/2 c. warm water
3 egg yolks, beaten
1 T grated orange rind
1/4 t. grated lime rind
1/2 c. orange juice
2 T butter or margarine
3 egg whites, room temperature

In France and Canada, eggnog is called *Lait de Poule*, which translates to "milk of chicken." Why "milk of chicken"? No one seems to know.

Preheat oven to 375°F. With tines of fork, prick bottom and sides of pie shell. Bake for 5 minutes or until lightly browned. Set aside. Mix 1 c. sugar, cornstarch, and 1/4 t. salt in a heavy saucepan and stir in warm water. Bring to a boil over low heat, stirring constantly, then cook, stirring constantly, for 8 to 10 minutes or until clear and thick. Remove from heat. Stir several spoons of hot mixture into beaten egg yolks and mix well. Pour back into saucepan, stirring, and bring to a boil. Add the grated rind of both the orange and the lime, cook over low heat for 5 to 6 minutes. Remove from heat and stir in orange juice and butter. Cool and pour into pie shell. Chill.

Place egg whites and remaining salt in a medium bowl and beat until soft peaks form. Add remaining sugar, 1 T. at a time, beating well after each addition, and beat until stiff peaks form. Spread over filling, securing meringue to edge of pie and bake for 4 minutes or until meringue is golden brown all over. Remove and immediately chill.

Old Fashioned Pear Pie

Never had Pear Pie? You are in for a treat. Mace accents this very fragrant baked goodie without overpowering the cinnamon and pears.

1/2 c. sugar
2 T. cornstarch
1/4 t. ground mace
1/2 t. cinnamon
10 to 12 Bartlett pears, peeled and sliced or chunked
Double Flaky Pie Crust, unbaked
1 T. butter or margarine, melted
1 egg white
1 T. sugar

Preheat oven to 350°F. In a medium bowl, combine sugar, cornstarch, mace, and cinnamon. Add pears; toss lightly. Turn pears into bottom crust and dot with butter. Cover pears with top crust and seal edges. Trim and flute edge. Mix together butter, egg white, and sugar in small bowl. Brush crust with the egg white mixture. Cut slits in top to let steam escape. Bake 40 to 45 minutes or until browned and bubbly.

To Make an Apple or Pear Pie: Make a good puff paste crust, lay some round the side of the dish. Pare and quarter your apples and take out the cores, lay a row of apples thick. Throw in half the sugar you design for your pie, mince a little lemon peel fine, throw over and squeeze a little lemon over them, then a few cloves, here and there one, then the rest of your apples and the rest of your sugar. You must sweeten to your palate, and squeeze a little more lemon. Boil the peeling of the apples and cores in fair water, with a blade of mace, until it is very good. Strain it and boil the syrup with a little sugar, till there is but very little and good. Pour it into your pie, put on the upper crust and bake it. You may put in a little quince or marmalade, if you please.

-The Frugal Housewife, 1772

Chocolate Mint Mousse Pie

Airy, light, decadent, chocolaty…it just goes on and on with this pie.

Single Flaky Pie Crust, unbaked
1 t. unflavored gelatin
1 T. cold water
2 T. boiling water
1/2 c. sugar

1/3 c. dark cocoa
1 c. cold whipping cream
1 t. vanilla
Mint Cream Topping, *recipe below*

Preheat oven to 375°F. Prick bottom and sides of crust with tines of fork. Bake 5 minutes or until golden brown. Cool completely.

In small cup, sprinkle gelatin over cold water; let stand 2 minutes to soften. Add boiling water; stir until gelatin is completely dissolved and mixture is clear. Cool slightly, about 5 minutes. Meanwhile, in small mixing bowl, stir together sugar and cocoa; add whipping cream and vanilla. Beat with electric mixer on medium speed until stiff, scraping bottom of bowl occasionally. Add gelatin mixture; beat just until blended and pour into prepared crust. Prepare Mint Cream Topping; spread over filling and refrigerate about 2 hours.

Mint Cream Topping:
1 c. cold whipping cream
2 T. powdered sugar

1/2 t. peppermint extract
Green food coloring

In small mixing bowl on medium speed of electric mixer, beat whipping cream, powdered sugar, peppermint extract, and several drops green food color until stiff.

Peanut-Peanut Butter Pie

This is not your ordinary cream-style Peanut Butter Pie. It reminds me of Pecan Pie but without the taste of pecans. Great, pronounced peanut butter flavor and not as filling as the cream-based variety.

4 eggs
1 1/4 c. dark corn syrup
3/4 c. sugar
3/4 c. creamy peanut butter
3/4 t. vanilla

1 1/2 c. salted or dry roasted
Single Flaky Pie Crust, unbaked
Whipped cream
Peanuts

Preheat oven to 350°F. In large bowl, with mixer on medium speed, beat eggs, corn syrup, sugar, peanut butter, and vanilla until smooth; stir in peanuts. Bake 55 to 60 minutes or until toothpick inserted 1-inch from the pie edge comes out clean.

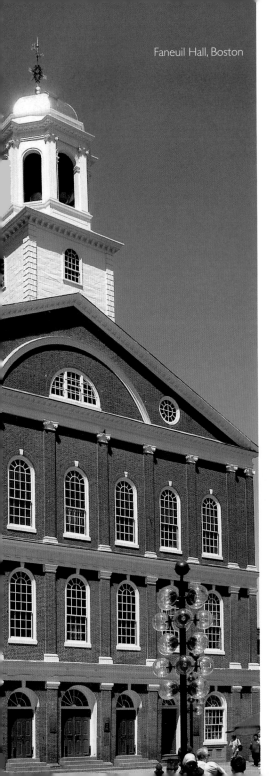

Faneuil Hall, Boston

Boston Cream Pie

Now, this recipe looks long and drawn out, and it very well is, but don't let that stop you from taking a little time to create this time-honored Yankee classic.

1/2 c. butter or margarine, softened	1 1/2 t baking powder
1 c. sugar	1/4 t. salt
2 eggs, plus 2 yolks	1/2 c. milk
1 t. vanilla	1 recipe Vanilla Bean Pudding, *recipe below*
1 1/4 c. flour	Chocolate Glaze, *recipe below*

Preheat oven to 350°F. Oil and flour bottom of an 8-inch cake pan. Beat the butter and sugar together at medium-high speed until fluffy. Beat in the eggs and yolks, one at a time, and add the vanilla. Stir the flour, baking powder, and salt together using a whisk. Reduce mixer speed to low and beat the flour mixture into the butter-egg mixture, adding it in thirds and alternating with the milk. Beat until the batter is smooth. Transfer to prepared pan and bake about 35 to 40 minutes or until toothpick inserted in the middle comes out clean. Cool completely.

To assemble, split the cake using a long serrated knife. Spread pudding over the bottom half of the cake and place the top layer over the pudding. Pour Chocolate Glaze over the cake, allowing it to drip down the sides of the cake.

Vanilla Bean Pudding:

3/4 c. milk	1/2 c. sugar
1 c. heavy cream	1/4 t. salt
1 vanilla bean (or 2 t. of vanilla)	1 1/2 t. butter or margarine
2 T. cornstarch	1/2 t. vanilla
2 egg yolks	

Heat the milk, cream, and vanilla bean (slitting the bean lengthwise and scraping the seeds into the milk) until just simmering in a heavy-bottomed medium pot over medium heat. Whisk the yolks, cornstarch, sugar, and salt together and stream the hot milk mixture, while whisking continuously, into the egg mixture. Return to the pan and cook, while whisking until the mixture thickens and just begins to boil. Immediately transfer to a clean bowl. Pick out and discard vanilla bean. Stir in the vanilla extract and the butter. Press plastic wrap against the surface to cover and chill.

Chocolate Glaze:

1/2 c. heavy cream	1 T. butter or margarine
4 oz. dark chocolate	3 T. corn syrup

Heat heavy cream to a boil and pour into a medium-sized heatproof bowl filled with chocolate, butter, and corn syrup. Let sit for 1 minute and stir until smooth. Let cool to thicken slightly.

Maine Blueberry Pie

Now, I know I have named many recipes in this book with the name "Maine" in them, but this one is different. Maine blueberries are one of a kind. They are known the world over and the flavor is unequaled anywhere.

1 qt. Maine fresh blueberries
1/2 c. sugar
1/2 t. cinnamon
2 t. lemon juice
3 T. cornstarch
Double Lemon Flavored Flaky
  Pie Crust, unbaked
1 T. milk
1 egg

Preheat oven to 350°F. In large bowl, combine blueberries, sugar, cinnamon, lemon juice, and cornstarch until thoroughly combined. Pour blueberry mixture into bottom pie crust. Place second pie dough, rolled out, over top of blueberries. Press gently to compact blueberries and seal around edges. Cut off excess dough and flute. In small bowl, whisk egg and milk and brush top of pie. Slit and bake for 45 to 50 minutes, or until crust is browned and filling is bubbly and syrupy.

Raspberry Pie

Use the same ingredients and cooking time as Maine Blueberry Pie, just substitute the same amount of raspberries for blueberries.

Open-Faced Maine Blueberry Pie
(ha, I added Maine again!)

This recipe is uncontested as my all-time favorite pie. Absolutely nothing says New England as Blueberry Pie does. No whipped cream is needed, no spices in the filling itself (with the exception of sugar), and no one to share it with as well (a little Yankee humor here).

30 gingersnaps
1/2 c. plus 2 t. sugar
1/2 c. butter or margarine, melted
2 T. cornstarch
3 t. cold water
3 pints fresh blueberries

Preheat oven to 350°F. In food processor, blend gingersnaps and 2 T. sugar until fine. Pour into large bowl and add melted butter until evenly moistened. Press into 9-inch pie pan. Bake 7 minutes; remove. In 2-quart saucepan, blend cornstarch and cold water until smooth. Add half the blueberries and remaining sugar to cornstarch mixture; heat over medium-high to boiling. Cook 3 minutes, crushing blueberries with fork or potato masher. Remove from heat and stir in remaining blueberries. Pour blueberry into crust and chill until firm, about 4 to 5 hours or overnight.

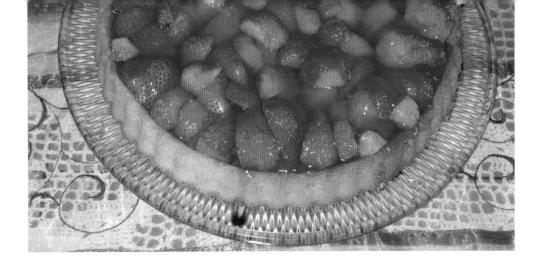

Oak Pond Strawberry Glaze Pie

This recipe belongs to my dad, who made it every Sunday at the Oak Pond Restaurant. Senator Margaret Chase Smith enjoyed this pie on her monthly visit to Dad's restaurant after she ate the lasagna.

Lemon Flavored Flaky Pie Crust
1 c. water
1 1/2 qts. fresh strawberries,
   hulled and sliced
1 c. sugar
3 heaping T. cornstarch
Red food coloring

Preheat oven to 375°F. Prick sides and bottom of pie crust with tines of fork. Bake for 8 to 9 minutes or until lightly browned.

Prepare filling. In food processor or blender, combine water and 1/2 qt. strawberries and puree. Strain through fine sieve into medium-sized saucepan. Over medium-high heat, combine strawberry juice, sugar, cornstarch, and 3 to 4 drops red food coloring. Whisk until smooth and cook until thickened, about 8 to 10 minutes. Remove from heat.

Place half of the remaining strawberries in pie crust and spoon half the thickened juice over evenly. Repeat. Stir gently with fork to evenly coat each slice of strawberry and refrigerate until set and cooled, about 4 to 5 hours.

Yankee Food Quiz

Match the traditional Yankee food names in column one with the more common names in column two. Answers at the end of the chapter.

1.	Sinker	A.	Apple pie
2.	Collision mat	B.	Pig's feet
3.	Machine oil	C.	Syrup
4.	Cluck and grunt	D.	Egg
5.	Hen fruit	E.	Ice cubes
6.	Sea dust	F.	Glass of water
7.	Goober grease	G.	Beans and franks
8.	Army chicken	H.	Ketchup
9.	Cincinnati oysters	I.	Bananas
10.	Boston strawberries	J.	Eggs and ham
11.	Army strawberries	K.	Salt
12.	Red paint	L.	Prunes
13.	Eve with a lid on	M.	Donut
14.	One from the country	N.	Beef stew
15.	Bossy in a bowl	O.	Root beer float
16.	Black cow	P.	Beans and ham
17.	Stars and stripes	Q.	Waffle
18.	One from the city	R.	Peanut Butter
19.	Clinks	S.	Glass of buttermilk

Strawberry-Rhubarb Pie

While in Florida one year I looked and looked for a Strawberry-Rhubarb Pie and couldn't find one anywhere. Thank goodness I am back in New England and can enjoy one of my favorite sweet and tangy delights.

1 1/4 c. sugar
3 T. cornstarch
1/2 t. vanilla
1/4 t. salt
Double Flaky Pie Crust, unbaked
2 pints strawberries, hulled and
   halved
1 lb. rhubarb, cut into 1/2 -inch
   pieces
1 egg
1 t. milk

Preheat oven to 350°F. In large bowl, gently toss strawberries, rhubarb, sugar, cornstarch, vanilla, and salt until well mixed. Spoon mixture into uncooked pie crust and top with remaining pie crust. Seal around edges and flue or crimp. In small bowl, whisk together egg and milk and brush top of pie until moistened completely. Vent and bake about 45 to 50 minutes, or until crust is browned and filling is bubbly and thickened.

> To Make A Pye With Pippins: Pare you pippins and cut out the cores, then make you coffin of crust. Take a good handful of quinces sliced and lay at the bottom, then lay your pippins on top, and fill the holes where the core was taken out with syrup of quinces, put into every pippin a piece of orangado, then pour on top the syrup of quinces, then put in sugar, and so close it up, let it be very well baked, for it will ask much soaking, especially the quinces.
>
> *–The Compleat Cook's Guide*, 1683

Wild Blueberry Mascarpone Semifreddo

Semifreddo is Italian for "half-cold." It is a class of semi-frozen desserts, typically ice-cream cakes, semi-frozen custards, and certain fruit tarts. It has the texture of frozen mousse because it is usually produced by uniting two equal parts of ice cream and whipped cream. Such a dessert's Spanish counterpart is called *semifrion*. In Italian cuisine, the semifreddo is commonly made with gelato as a primary ingredient. It is typical of the Italian region of Emilia-Romagna.

1 vanilla bean
1/2 c. milk
3 egg yolks
5 t. sugar
2 1/2 c. blueberries
   plus extra for garnish

1 c. mascarpone cheese
1 oz. bittersweet chocolate, finely chopped
2 t. chopped pistachios
Fresh mint leaves

Cut vanilla bean in half lengthwise and scrape out seeds. Place milk in small saucepan and add vanilla seeds. Heat milk over medium heat until almost boiling.

In bowl, whisk egg yolks and sugar until creamy. Pour milk gradually into egg mixture, whisking constantly until thickened. Let cool.

Meanwhile, puree 1 cup of the blueberries in a blender; set aside.

Using an electric mixer, slowly beat mascarpone until creamy and smooth. Slowly beat in egg mixture until combined and lightened. Fold in blueberry puree, remaining blueberries, and chocolate. Pour into small loaf pan lined with plastic wrap and freeze for about 4 hours or until firm.

Turn loaf out onto serving platter and remove plastic wrap. Cut into 1-inch slices and garnish with pistachios, blueberries, and mint.

Frozen Sundae Pie

This recipe is for the kids in the kitchen. Let them take the lead and you follow.

20 sandwich cookies, crushed
5 T. butter or margarine, melted
1 tub (8 oz.) whipped topping, thawed
1 c. cold milk
1 pkg. (4 oz. serving size) instant vanilla pudding mix
1/2 c. chocolate chips, melted
1/3 c. sweetened, condensed milk
Chopped nuts
Cherries

Mix the crushed cookies with butter and press into a 9-inch pie pan; refrigerate. Set aside 1/2 c. whipped topping. Pour milk and pudding mix into a large bowl and whisk for 2 minutes. Stir in the remainder of the whipped topping and spoon into the crust; smooth the top. Mix the melted chocolate with the sweetened, condensed milk until combined, and spoon over the pie. With a butter knife, have your child create designs into the pie filling, swirling to create a marble effect. Freeze at least 4 hours. Dollop some of the reserved whipped topping on top when serving and add some of the nuts and a cherry.

Ginger Peach Ice Cream Pie

Crystallized ginger is so bold that I only put a half cup in here. Try it first, then you can add as much as your taste buds can handle. I load it on, especially with an ice cream pie.

12 graham crackers, 2 squares each
5 T. butter or margarine, softened
1/2 c. chopped, crystallized ginger
1 3/4 c. peach spreadable fruit
1 qt. peach ice cream (or French vanilla)
1 firm, ripe peach

Pulse graham crackers in a food processor or blender until fine crumbs. Add the butter and 2 T. ginger, pulse again until crumbs are moist. Press firmly on the bottom and up the sides of pie tin. Freeze 30 minutes until firm. Meanwhile, stir spreadable fruit and remaining crystallized ginger together and spread half of it over the top; cover and refrigerate the rest. Freeze pie for 1 hour or until firm. Top with scoops of remaining ice cream and freeze for 3 hours or until hard.

Peel, pit, and thinly slice the peach. Stir into reserved ginger-peach mixture. Cover and refrigerate until serving time. About 20 minutes before serving, transfer pie to refrigerator and spoon on the remainder of the ginger-peach mixture.

Grasshopper Ice Cream Pie

This version of a Grasshopper Pie is very easy. Grab a child to help, but share the spoons.

2 c. finely crushed chocolate cookies
5 T. butter or margarine, melted
1 qt. green mint chocolate chip ice cream
1 qt. chocolate ice cream
1 c. heavy cream
1 T. powdered sugar
12 chocolate mint wafers

Combine crushed cookie crumbs and the butter together in a medium bowl until the cookie crumbs are moistened. Press into a 9-inch pie pan, bringing up the sides slightly. Refrigerate 30 minutes or until set. In the meantime, take out the mint chocolate chip ice cream to soften for about 15 minutes. Scoop the softened ice cream into a bowl and stir until smooth. Spread over the cookie crust evenly and cover with plastic wrap; freeze for 1 hour or until firm. Follow the same step with the chocolate ice cream and spread evenly over the mint ice cream; freeze 1 hour or till hard.

When ready to serve, whip the heavy cream into stiff peaks with powdered sugar. Make chocolate mint wafer curls by microwaving 1 mint for 2 to 3 seconds, hold with paper towel and with vegetable peeler, gently shave off curls from the long edge. Repeat until you have the desired amount of curls to garnish. Refrigerate for a few minutes to handle before sprinkling them onto pie. Top each slice of pie with whipped cream and curls.

Peach Melba Ice Cream Pie

I don't know what it is about the name Melba that just doesn't appeal to men. Just grab a slab and run with this very flavorful treat.

1/4 c. butterscotch or caramel ice
    cream topping
2 T. butter or margarine
30 vanilla wafers, crushed in blender
    or food processor
1 c. peach preserves
1 qt. vanilla ice cream
3/4 c. raspberry spreadable fruit
1 c. raspberries
2 peaches, sliced
1/2 c. spreadable fruit*

Coat a 9-inch pie plate with nonstick cooking spray. Leave ice cream out at room temperature to soften slightly, about 20 minutes. Meanwhile, heat topping and butter in a saucepan over low heat until butter melts. Add cookie crumbs to topping mixture and blend well. Press onto the bottom and up the sides of pie pan slightly. Stir preserves well into the ice cream in a large bowl. Spread half into the crust. Put pie and bowl of ice cream into the freezer for 1 hour or until firmed well. Remove bowl 20 minutes before starting next step.

Spread pie with pourable fruit and cover with remaining ice cream mixture in bowl. Freeze 4 hours or until solid; remove 20 minutes before serving. Top with berries, peaches, and spreadable fruit.

You can make fruit spreadable by microwaving for 30 seconds and stirring.

Frozen Peanut Butter Cream Pie

Extra smooth and rich for hungry ice cream lovers.

40 vanilla wafers, crushed
1/2 c. butter or margarine, melted
1/2 t. cinnamon
12 oz. pkg. peanut butter morsels
4 egg yolks, beaten
1 1/2 c. sugar
1 c. milk
1 c. light cream or half and half
1 t. vanilla
2 c. heavy cream

In a large bowl, combine the wafers, butter, and cinnamon until well mixed. Press into a 13 × 9 × 2-inch pan; freeze while making recipe. Finely chop morsels; set aside. In saucepan, combine egg yolks, sugar, milk, and light cream and cook over medium heat until thickened and bubbly, stirring almost constantly, about 10 to 12 minutes. Place pan in cold water bath and continue to stir until cooled. Stir in the morsels and vanilla. Whip heavy cream until soft peaks form and slowly fold into the morsel mixture. Turn out into the prepared 13 × 9 × 2-inch pan, carefully spreading evenly. Cover with film wrap and freeze 4 hours or until firm.

Answers to Mix and Match on page 297:

1) M
2) Q
3) C
4) J
5) D
6) K
7) R
8) G
9) B
10) I
11) L
12) H
13) A
14) S
15) N
16) O
17) P
18) F
19) E

APPENDIX

Here are some of the most common substitutions and conversions for kitchen measurements:

1 t. baking powder	1/4 t. baking soda plus 1/2 t. cream of tartar
1 c. cake flour	1 c. minus 2 T. all-purpose flour or 7/8 c. all-purpose flour plus 2 T. cornstarch
1 square unsweetened chocolate	3 T. unsweetened baking cocoa plus 1 T. butter, margarine, or shortening
1 oz. semisweet baking or bittersweet chocolate	1 oz. baking chocolate plus 1 T. sugar
1 c. semisweet chips	6 oz. baking chocolate, chopped
1/4 c. cocoa	1 oz. (square) chocolate, decrease fat called for in recipe by 1/2 T.
1 T. cornstarch	2 T. flour or 2 T. tapioca or 1 1/2 T. arrowroot
1 c. light corn syrup	mix 1 c. sugar with 1/2 c. liquid used in recipe or 1 c. honey
1 c. dark corn syrup	3/4 c. light corn syrup plus 1/2 c. molasses or same amount of maple syrup
1 c. pastry flour	1 c. all-purpose flour minus 1 T.

1 c. self-rising flour	1 c. all-purpose flour plus 1 1/2 t. baking powder and 1/2 t. salt
1 jar of marshmallow creme	melt 16 oz. marshmallows and 3 1/2 T. corn syrup in double boiler
2 1/2 c. marzipan	2 c. almond paste, 1 c. powdered sugar, and 2 T. corn syrup
1 c. brown sugar	1 c. granulated sugar plus 1 T. molasses or dark corn syrup
1 c. dark brown sugar	1 c. granulated sugar plus 2 T. molasses
1 c. powdered sugar	1 c. granulated sugar plus 1 t. cornstarch finely ground in blender
2 t. granulated sugar	1 packet Equal® brand
One 2-inch vanilla bean	1 t. pure vanilla extract
1 cake compressed yeast	1 package or 2 t. active dry yeast
1 c. buttermilk or sour milk	mix 1 T. white vinegar or lemon juice with 1 c. milk, let stand 5 minutes; 1 c. whole milk with 1 3/4 t. cream of tartar; 3/4 c. plain yogurt and 1/4 c. milk

Mascarpone cheese	cream cheese
1 c. sharp Cheddar cheese	1 c. milk Cheddar, 1/8 t. dry mustard, and 1/4 t. Worcestershire sauce
1 c. half and half cream	7/8 c. whole milk plus 1/2 T. butter or 3/4 c. whole milk plus 1/4 c. heavy cream
1 c. light cream	1/2 c. heavy cream plus 1/2 c. whole milk
1 c. light cream (for cooking)	7/8 c. whole milk plus 3 T. butter
1 c. Crème Fraîche	1/2 c. sour cream plus 1/2 c. heavy cream
1 c. sweetened condensed milk	1 c. evaporated milk plus 1 1/4 c. sugar, cooked over low heat until sugar is dissolved
1 can (12 oz.) evaporated milk	12 oz. cream
1 c. whole or low-fat milk	1/2 c. evaporated milk plus 1/2 c. water
1 c. sweet milk	1/2 c. evaporated milk plus 1/2 c. water
1 c. sour cream	1 c. plain yogurt plus 3 T. melted butter
1 c. sour cream for baking	1 c. plain yogurt plus 1 t. baking soda
1 c. sour cream for dips	1 c. cottage cheese plus 1/4 c. plain yogurt and blend in processor
1 egg substitute	2 egg whites plus 1 to 3 t. vegetable oil for each yolk omitted
1/4 t. chili oil	1/4 t. salad oil plus pinch of cayenne
1 T. sesame oil	1 1/2 t. sesame seeds sautéed in 1/2 t. vegetable oil

4 T. red wine vinegar for salad dressing	3 T. cider vinegar plus 1 T. red wine
1 t. allspice	1/2 t. cinnamon and 1/2 t. ground cloves
1 t. apple pie spice	1/2 t. cinnamon plus 1/4 t. nutmeg and 1/8 t. cardamom
1 t. arrowroot	1 T. flour or 1 1/2 t. cornstarch
1 t. baking powder	1/4 t. baking soda plus 5/8 t. cream of tartar
1/3 c. dry bread crumbs	1 slice of bread
3/4 c. soft bread crumbs	1 slice of bread
1 c. ketchup	1 c. tomato sauce plus 1/2 c. sugar and 2 T. vinegar
1 c. chili sauce	1 c. tomato sauce, 1/4 c. brown sugar, 2 T. vinegar, 1/4 t. cinnamon and a dash each of ground cloves and allspice
1/2 t. cream of tartar	1 1/2 t. lemon juice or vinegar
1 small clove garlic	1/8 t. garlic powder or 1/4 t. instant, minced garlic
3/4 t. garlic salt	1 clove or 1/2 t. minced fresh garlic plus 1/8 t. salt
1/8 t. powdered ginger	1 T. fresh ginger, grated
1 t. dried herbs	1 T. fresh herbs
1 c. honey	1 1/4 c. sugar plus 1/4 c. liquid (use the liquid called for in the recipe)
1 c. mini marshmallows	10 large marshmallows
1 c. buttermilk	1 c. plain yogurt
1 t. pumpkin pie spice	1/2 t. cinnamon, 1/4 t. ginger, 1/8 t. allspice, and 1/8 t. nutmeg
1 c. uncooked rice	3 c. cooked
15 oz. tomato sauce	6 oz. tomato paste plus 1 c. water

Equivalents

1/2 oz. butter or margarine	1/8 stick or 1 T.
1 oz.	1/4 stick or 2 T.
16 oz.	4 sticks or 2 c.

12 oz. bag of chocolate morsels	1 c. melted or 2 c. unmelted
1 c. heavy cream	2 c. whipped
8 to 10 egg whites	1 c.
12 to 14 egg yolks	1 c.
1 lb. flour	4 c.
1 medium lemon	3 T. juice and 1 T. grated rind
1 medium orange	1/3 to 1/2 c. juice and 2 T. grated rind
1 lb. apples	3 medium or 3 c. sliced
4 1/2 oz. chopped nuts	1 c.
1/4 c. popcorn kernels	8 c. popped
1 lb. brown sugar	2 1/4 c.
1 lb. powdered sugar	4 1/2 c.

1 dash		6 drops	
24 drops		1/4 t.	
3 t.	1 T.	15 ml	1/2 oz.
1 oz.		1/8 c.	
1/3 c.		2.6 oz.	
4 T.	1/4 c.	2 oz.	
5 T. plus 1 t.		1/3 c.	
3/4 c.		6 oz.	
16 T.	1 c.	8 oz.	
2 c.		1 pint	
2 pints		1 qt.	

EPILOGUE

I am constantly seeking information on New England because of my love for our country and its beginnings and because Dad always told me to never stop learning. "No matter how much you think you know, two things will always happen," he preached, "you will always make mistakes, no matter how good you think you are and you can never know everything!"

I miss Dad, even writing of him fleetingly brings my sadness to the forefront, but alternately it brings my best right up alongside it as well. It is with his guidance, both in the past, written and oral, that I will continue this series of cookbooks of his favorites, as well as Yankee favorites that I will persevere in this endeavor.

As I wrote in his obituary, "Although but a glimpse in their lives, we will see him live on forever in his grandchildren." His grandchildren, in part my children, have also pressed me for knowledge. I have always told them to use their imagination when drawing, writing, coloring, and something as simple as walking...strolling down a path or sidewalk looking around at your surroundings. Think about what it would be like to be so small you are rafting through the air on that beautiful autumn leaf that just fell from that oak, or being a miniature river driver on the huge piece of grass, hanging on with your spiked boots, all the while balancing on that "log" so as not to fall into the raging river flowing along side the sidewalk. Your imagination and openness is key in the kitchen as well, so don't be afraid to try something new. If you don't like it...now you know, don't you?

We love you, Grampy Jack.

INDEX